West Orange Public Library
46 Mt. Pleasant Avenue
West Orange, NJ 07052

LOYALTY BETRAYED:

JEWISH CHAPLAINS IN THE GERMAN ARMY
DURING THE FIRST WORLD WAR

The publication of this book was made possible by grants from Uri Tänzer in honour of his grandfather Rabbi Aron Tänzer, and the Ruth Ivor Foundation in honour of her father Rabbi Bruno Italiener.

WEST ORANGE PUBLIC LIBRARY

Gerald Gurland Holocaust Collection

Loyalty Betrayed:
Jewish Chaplains in the German Army During the First World War

Peter C. Appelbaum

VALLENTINE MITCHELL
LONDON • PORTLAND, OR

First published in 2014 by Vallentine Mitchell

Middlesex House, 920 NE 58th Avenue, Suite 300
29/45 High Street, Edgware, Portland, Oregon,
Middlesex HA8 7UU, UK 97213-3786 USA

www.vmbooks.com

Copyright © 2014 Peter C. Appelbaum

British Library Cataloguing in Publication Data:
An entry can be found on request

ISBN 978 0 85303 847 4 (Cloth)
ISBN 978 0 85303 837 5 (Ebook)

Library of Congress Cataloging in Publication Data
An entry can be found on request

All rights reserved. No part of this publication may be reproduced in any form or by any means, electronic, mechanical, photocopying, reading or otherwise, without the prior permission of Vallentine Mitchell & Co. Ltd.

Printed by CMP (UK) Ltd, Poole, Dorset

This book is dedicated to the German rabbis who served, alongside their assistants, as chaplains during the First World War, some of whom gave their lives during the war for *Volk* and Fatherland, and some of whom were murdered during the Holocaust by the nation they had once served with such pride and devotion.

זכור

Zachor

Contents

List of Plates	ix
Preface and Acknowledgements	xi
Foreword by Rabbi Jonathan Wittenberg	xv
Historical Introduction by Michael A. Meyer	1
1. The Torch of War is Lit! 1813–1871	15
2. Georg Salzberger: Compassion and Courage	25
3. Martin Salomonski: Zola in Chaplain's Uniform	83
4. Bruno Italiener: Hope, Patriotism and Kindness	121
5. Leo Baeck: Chaplain and Neo-Kantian Philosopher	145
6. Aron (Arnold) Tänzer: Mover, Shaker and Creator of Soup Kitchens	175
7. *Sabbathgedanken* (Sabbath Thoughts)	239
8. Reinhold Lewin: The War as a Jewish Experience	271
9. A Greeting from the Field Chaplains for the 1915 Autumn Holiday Season; Miscellaneous Memoirs	281
10. Chaplain Conferences	299
11. Epilogue – Betrayal	307
Appendix A: Biographical Table of Rabbis	317

Appendix B: Biographical Table of Rabbinical Assistants and Rabbis Serving as Soldiers	327
Appendix C: German First World War Military Ranks	331
Appendix D: Hebrew and Jewish Religious Terms	333
Appendix E: Place Names Then and Now	337
Appendix F: German-Jewish Associations	341
Bibliography	343
Index	347

Plates

1. Jewish Chaplains Conference of the West, St Quentin, 5 August 1915. Copyright: Jewish Museum, Frankfurt.
2. Jewish Chaplains Conference of the East, Riga, February 1918. Copyright: Jewish Museum, Frankfurt.
3. Jewish chaplains of the West. Copyright: Jim Herzog.
4. Jewish Chaplains in front of the B'nei Brith Lodge hospital train. Copyright: Jewish Museum, Frankfurt.
5. Rabbi Martin Salomonski with his brother Moritz (left) and cousin Hans (right), both physicians. Copyright: Jim Herzog.
6. Rabbi Leo Baeck flanked by Catholic and Evangelical chaplains. Copyright: Marianne Dreyfus (private collection).
7. Rabbi Leo Baeck with soldiers. Copyright: Marianne Dreyfus (private collection).
8. Rabbi Aron Tänzer in uniform with medals. Copyright: Leo Baeck Institute, NYC.
9. Rabbi Aron Tänzer at a Seder in Pinsk. Copyright: Leo Baeck Institute, NYC.
10. Rabbi Aron Tänzer with soup kitchen board members. Copyright: Leo Baeck Institute, NYC.
11. Rabbi Aron Tänzer flanked by his sons Friederich (Fritz) on the left and Paul on the right. Copyright: Uri Tänzer (private collection).
12. Burial site of Rabbi Aron Tänzer. Copyright: Uri Tänzer (private collection).
13. Rabbi Leopold Rosenak. Private collection: courtesy Rachel Aber Schlesinger.
14. Letter from 'Reich Potato Department' (Reichskartoffelstelle) permitting Rabbi Rosenak to travel to neutral Netherlands to obtain potatoes. Copyright: Leo Baeck Institute Archives, Jerusalem.
15. Rabbi Leo Baerwald with horse, cart and young assistant in France, c. 1916. Copyright: Staatsarchiv München and Jane Vogel-Kohai.

16. Rabbi Jacob Sonderling distributes gifts to Jewish children in Poland. Copyright: Jewish Museum, Frankfurt.
17. Rabbi Alexander Winter, flanked by Protestant (left) and Catholic (right) chaplains. Copyright: Naftali Winter (private collection).
18. Rabbi Alexander Winter with Reb Chaim Halevi Soloveitchik, also known as the Brisker Rebbe (1853–1918). Copyright: Naftali Winter (private collection).
19. Siegfried Alexander during the war. Copyright: Hannah Goldwyn (private collection).
20. Rabbi Paul Lazarus. Copyright: Alte Synagoge Essen, Archiv, AR.4004.
21. Invitation signed by Paul Lazarus for Pesach celebration in Macedonia, 1917. Copyright: Center for Jewish History, Jerusalem.
22. Chanukah programme in Kovno, 1916. Copyright: Centrum Judaicum Berlin, CJA 1, 75, Ve 1, Nr. 397, #13020, Bl. 221.
23. Yom Kippur service in Brussels, 1915 apparently organized by Offizierstellvertreter Baum. Copyright: Leo Baeck Institute, NYC.
24. Chanukah 1916 on the Eastern Front. Copyright: Jewish Museum, Frankfurt.
25. Seder in Riga, 1918. Copyright: Jewish Museum, Frankfurt.
26. Rosh Hashanah in Brussels with 1,600 Jewish soldiers. Copyright: Jim Herzog.
27. Seder on Western Front, 6–7 April 1917. Copyright: Jim Herzog.
28. Hand-written menu for both Seder evenings in St Quentin, 1915. Copyright: Centrum Judaicum Berlin: CJA 1, 75, C Ve 1, Nr. 380, Bl. 127.
29. Jewish burial on the Western Front. Copyright: Jim Herzog.
30. Jewish headstone on the Western Front. Copyright: Jim Herzog.
31. Pulpit, Ner Tamid and Aron Kodesh, France. Copyright: Jim Herzog.
32. Burial site of Rabbi Saly (Sali) Levi at Berlin Weissensee (author's collection).
33. Rabbi Siegfried Alexander at a memorial service in Berlin Weissensee cemetery in 1936 commemorating the 12,500 Jews who died for Germany during the First World War (after propagation of the Nürnberg racial laws). Copyright: Bildarchiv Pisarek / akg-images.

Preface and Acknowledgements

The path that brought me to this book is strange indeed. I was born in South Africa to South African-born parents and grandparents, all four of whom had emigrated from Lithuania looking for a better life in the goldfields of the Transvaal. My education was English-style with emphasis on the then two official languages (English and Afrikaans) and Latin, and I studied Hebrew privately. School led directly to medical school without, as is the case in the United States, interposition of a college education in the liberal arts.

My first exposure to the German language came at the beginning of my houseman year with a six-week language primer at the hands of my Karlsruhe-born Hebrew teacher, and there the language lay until the start of my microbiology residency in the early 1970s. For reasons which I still cannot explain, I felt the irresistible urge to learn the German language properly. Could it have been because of my developing love for the music of Wagner and my upcoming trip to the Bayreuth festival, or the Hoffmansthal *Jedermann* which I was about to see in Salzburg? Who can say? I acquired an excellent school teacher and weekly lessons for a period of three years gave me the foundations on which to build a thorough knowledge of the German language.

I completed my residency in 1974 and emigrated to the US in 1978. My academic career (1975–2011) consisted of running clinical microbiology laboratories and performing research into microbiology, bacterial drug resistance and antibacterial activity. A great deal of seminal research – which changed the face of the profession – followed from my work; however, the last few years of my academic career witnessed a decrease in funding and in the perceived importance of antibacterial research which I intuited to be irreversible in the short run. Rather than fight a losing battle, I elected to retire: but what to do for someone with a still active intellect who, like Tennyson's Ulysses, was searching for 'some work of noble note' yet to be done?

A wise man told me: 'you have written hundreds of scientific papers and prepared hundreds of presentations, so you can write and collate literature. Find something that interests you, and write.' I followed his advice, and this is the result.

This book could not have been written without the aid of a great many people. Without the teaching skills of Siegbert Silbermann and Ingrid Kidder my German would not be what it is today. I thank Alex Vgontzas, Barton Browning and Israel Schwierz for initial advice, wise counsel and encouragement. The Leo Baeck Institute in New York City, with its wonderful cataloguing system and digitization, helped me immensely in my literature search: I thank them for permission to use the material from Rabbi Tänzer. Frank Mecklenburg was one of the first to have faith in a fumbling amateur: also Tracey Beck, Michael Simonson, Marlene Myers, Laura Paustian, Rivka Schiller, and David Rosenberg, who put up with my initial clumsiness and ineptitude. Professor Marc Saperstein had enough faith in me to become, literally and figuratively, my Rabbi. This book contains the solid imprint of his scholarship and learning. I thank Professor Michael Meyer for the honour of his Historical Introduction, and Felicity Rash (Queen Mary's College, London) for her assistance in checking my amateur translations and making the necessary corrections. Rabbi Jonathan Wittenberg gave me encouragement and spiritual support during a difficult time and gave me my first opportunity to talk in public on this subject. I thank him also for his personal contribution. Martin Sugarmann went out on a limb for me, bringing my work to the attention of the publishers, and Harold Pollins also gave advice. I thank Pierre Purseigle and the many members of the First World War Society for their advice and assistance: you are all a unique resource. Hans Hubert Gerards and Beate Knoblach opened their home to me, besides assisting with acquisition of second-hand material and arranging trips to archives. Leona Charles, Kathleen Krisza and Esther Dell of the Hershey Medical Center library did yeoman service in obtaining references which were not in their current purview of expertise. Sabine Hank and Hermann Simon of the Centrum Judaicum Berlin are acknowledged for their 2010 'Feldrabbinersonderausstellung' [Jewish chaplain special exhibition] in Schnaitach, Franconia. Ann Sherwin transcribed the hand-written *Sütterlin* diaries of Rabbi Aron Tänzer which I could otherwise not have deciphered, and Hadassah Assouline (Centre for the History of the Jewish People, Jerusalem) provided useful archival assistance. Nadine Garling helped with advice on the former Lübeck Jewish community which led to additional information on the Carlebach-Rosenak family and Rabbi Alexander Winter. Hanneke Takken provided valuable information on German Protestant chaplains. Klaudia Kosowska-Shick helped with software and insertion of photographs and Barbara Lipchin assisted with contacts in Israel. Thanks also to Heather Marchant for her prompt and careful editing, and to Ashley Stahle for assistance with proofreading.

I am grateful to the following for provision of copyright permission for the use of archival texts and/or photographs: Michael Simonson and Tracey Beck (Leo Baeck Institute, New York City); Anja Siegemund (Leo Baeck Institute, Jerusalem); Hadassah Assouline (Central Archives for the History of the Jewish People, Jerusalem); Sabine Hank and Hermann Simon (Centrum Judaicum Berlin); Michael Lenarz (Jewish Museum, Frankfurt); Andreas Heusler (Bavarian State Archives, Munich); Anna Siebert (AKG Images, London); Martina Strehlen (Old Synagogue, Essen); Uri Tänzer, James Herzog, Jane Vogel-Kohai, Hannah Goldwyn, Naftali Winter and Rachel Aber Schlesinger for sharing photographs from their private collections. Naftali Winter kindly shared and permitted translation of the edited Hebrew translations of his father's war memoirs with me. Marianne Dreyfus granted copyright approval for both photographs and the material in Chapter 5 which was originally digitized on the Deutsche National-Bibliothek website but has since been removed. I thank Isca Wittenberg for permission to cite and translate the diaries of her father Georg Salzberger; James Herzog gave approval to translate and cite the diaries of his grandfather Martin Salomonski; and Hannah Finburgh gave permission to translate and cite her father Bruno Italiener's sermons. Approval for the use of some Italiener material was also obtained from Alan Fell (Ruth Ivor Foundation). Excerpts from the *Biographisches Handbuch der Rabbiner* are cited and translated in Chapter 9 courtesy of Walter de Gruyter.

The first will come last and the last first: my steadfast, loving and above all tolerant wife Addie (a true *Eishet Chayil*) for her patience, forbearance and assistance during the long travail and birth of this, my first, book, and my daughter Madeleine (my *naches*-machine) for the love and support that only a daughter can give to her Dad.

Any translating errors or misleading statements which appear in this book are mine alone: no-one else can be blamed.

Foreword

RABBI JONATHAN WITTENBERG

'Comrades!' Thus the dead hail us: 'You hardly knew us, but we know you. You cannot see us, but we can see you with the clear sight of the spirit, and our ears can hear your every word. Remain loyal ... Remain united, German comrades.'

The occasion was the dedication of the military cemetery at La Mourière in September 1917, and my grandfather, Rabbi Dr Georg Salzberger, who spoke these words, was, like virtually all German Jews irrespective of their religious denomination, a dedicated patriot. He was stationed on the Western Front near Verdun for the duration of the Great War, one of a number of Jewish chaplains to serve in the German Army. Their role at that time has understandably been overshadowed by the terrible fate which overtook them and virtually the entire Jewish community of continental Europe scarcely more than two decades later. Nevertheless it forms a significant part of the history of German Jewry in relation both to its ideals and to its nemesis.

I am therefore very grateful to Peter Appelbaum, who has written a timely book which will make an important and challenging contribution as Europe prepares to mark the centenary of the commencement of the First World War. In particular, he has brought to light documents which have long been all but forgotten, among them the war diaries of my grandfather together with those of several of his colleagues. They will not only add an unusual perspective to our knowledge of the war itself, but also increase our understanding of Jewish identity in early twentieth-century Germany, prior to the broad embrace of Zionism on the one hand and the rise of Nazism on the other. With their deep and proud patriotism, which it is impossible to absorb other than with a painful awareness of the irony of history, these diaries will no doubt engender complex reactions and invite reflection on the ongoing question of how minorities negotiate their multiple identities and loyalties.

Without ever forgetting the terrible suffering he had witnessed, my grandfather nevertheless often spoke warmly of his years as a chaplain. I remember how he would recall what he saw as the generally positive relations with his Catholic and Protestant colleagues and how, on one particular occasion when they each had to give an address, they pushed him forward saying, 'The Old Testament came first'. He talked of the often supportive attitude of the High Command, notwithstanding which he would sometimes have to intercede on behalf of Jewish soldiers who had encountered anti-Semitism. He spoke with appreciation of the occasion when one of the generals attended a service he led and refused to countenance any deference to his rank, explaining that 'Here before God we are all equal'. He recounted meeting the Kaiser's son, who, if I'm not mistaken, he described as always preceded by two large dogs. He talked of how he and his Catholic and Protestant colleagues on the Western Front at Verdun could often be seen in animated, but friendly, debate. He told of how he visited the many field hospitals in the sectors of the front where he was stationed, bringing small gifts of cigarettes and food to the wounded soldiers irrespective of whether they were Christians or Jews, and helping them to write letters home. He and his fellow rabbis would return time and again in their writings to the fate of the wounded and their efforts to assist them, which they saw as perhaps the most significant part of their activity as chaplains.

But my grandfather also never forgot how, on his journey to the front in 1914, when his companions in the staff car asked him whether he was Catholic or Protestant and he answered that he was Jewish, the ten-hour ride took place in total silence.

My grandfather would note with deep sadness that when he returned to Frankfurt after the war almost all of his most talented students were dead. He was obviously pained by the defeat of Germany, which was to have consequences which would determine his destiny in ways he could never in his worst nightmares have conceived. Yet even after his experience of the Nazi years, including his internment in Dachau and his eventual flight with his immediate family to London, he still, to a degree, harboured warm feelings about the Germany of those and the subsequent Weimar years, despite their growing perils.

Most of all he would tell us how he and his fiancée wrote to each other every single day, always believing that the war would swiftly be over, as the Kaiser had promised at its outset, and that they would soon be reunited and free to wed happily in the great peace

FOREWORD   xvii

which would follow a German victory. Eventually, in the late spring of 1917, he took a furlough from the army and he and his beloved Natalie Charlotte were finally united in marriage. The only material possessions of which I ever heard my grandfather lament the loss when the family fled Nazi Germany in April 1939 were those letters.

So it was with a sense of gratitude to the author for offering this opportunity to recover his voice and those of his colleagues that I turned to these pages. The different diaries quoted certainly reflect the horrors of war. They tell of the comfort Jewish soldiers found in the very fact that they had ministers of their own faith, and in the services arranged by them with so much care and effort often only just behind the front lines. They show the great importance the rabbis attached to their visits to the many field hospitals across their, often huge, sector of the war zone. They also testify to the sustained support of the home communities in not only paying their salaries, but also providing their chaplains with substantial supplies of prayer books, food and gifts with which to boost the morale of the soldiers, especially the wounded.

Yet the experience of studying these materials is complex. While on the one hand they are deeply engaging and draw the reader into the terrible environments they so vividly describe, they also present attitudes which it is hard for contemporary readers to understand, especially perhaps those brought up like myself on the poetry of Wilfred Owen, Siegfried Sassoon and Isaac Rosenberg, and on Erich Maria Remarque's *All Quiet on the Western Front*. It isn't that the horror of war is absent from the writings of the chaplains. Particularly haunting is my grandfather's imaginative identification with a wounded soldier stranded on the battlefield:

> Will I be found while there's still time? Oh, how my wounds burn! Will I be captured by the enemy? This night without end! Would that it were already morning! Comrade, pick me up and take me with you! Comrade, comrade, water, just a sip of water! I'm dying of thirst. Mother![1]

Those of us who were not there cannot possible imagine the terrible battlefields of the Great War.

There is tenderness and compassion too. There is deep pity for the plight of the wounded, and for their families back home waiting for news, anxious lest critical details of their loved one's condition may have been concealed from them and often turning to the rabbis in the hope of receiving further information. There is deep fellow feeling for the soldiers to whom they minister, together with a profound and humble awareness of the responsibility to find the right words with which to help them maintain their strength of spirit as they return to their perilous duties. There is also at times a haunting sense of beauty. Several writers draw attention to the paradox of the unimaginably appalling scenes of battle set amidst the glory of nature, noting the clear night skies, the crescent moon, an orchard full of trees with ripe fruit.

But the predominant tone is often that of a fierce German patriotism, with its firm emphasis on order, duty and sacrifice. Such nationalism strikes an often distasteful note to today's reader. Thus it is hard to comprehend Rabbi Dr Salomonski's evident pride that:

> The German soldier has shown his superiority, and what was interpreted as error has on the contrary proven to be the secret of his success ... The ever-mocked German thoroughness, milked like a cow in different comic papers, overflows in patriotism and has preserved itself! ... The German spirit has not remained static: from tiny beginnings great creations have unfolded, the U-boat, weapons in aeroplanes, gas.[2]

The irony is immeasurable, and tragic, especially when one learns that Rabbi Salomonski perished in Auschwitz in 1944. But might it not have been apparent to a man of the spirit, even at the time, that the effects of the 'great creations' referred to were considerably less than laudable? Or does such a retrospective judgment indicate a failure to appreciate what it must have been like to be caught up in the midst of the horrors of a long and terrible war, desperate for one's own country to win? If so, how is it that others were able to form less partial judgments?

'I saw him go, wordless and without hesitation', wrote my grandfather in a New Year's meditation about Abraham leading his son Isaac to be sacrificed, the Scriptural portion read on the second day of the festival, 'And I saw a thousand fathers following in his footsteps'. I would have liked to be able to ask my grandfather how the vision of such sacrifice left him feeling. I couldn't help but contrast his words with Wilfred Owen's famous 'Parable of the Old Man and the Young', in which, even when the angel calls down from heaven to Abraham and tells him not to slaughter his child, the obstinate old man, obeying pride instead,

> ... would not so, but slew his son,
> And half the seed of Europe, one by one.³

Brought up on Owen's poetry, which depicts the heart-rending futility of war and the utter waste of so many millions of young lives, it is hard to read the words of those who believed not only in a German victory, at least until 1916 by when it had become clear that the conflict had developed into a tragic stalemate, but in the meaning and justice of such a victory.

I have sometimes asked myself whether my grandfather's patriotism was less a reflection of his actual convictions than of what he felt bound to say as a chaplain in the front lines. There were, after all, well-documented pressures on Jews to show their patriotic fervour. Long before the ill-advised Jews' census of 1916, the German War Ministry was subject to a barrage of letters complaining that Jews were shirkers who avoided service in the front lines in favour of safer jobs at the rear, and that they were profiteering from the war. In an important rabbinic letter to an orthodox questioner who asked what was to be done because service in the army would inevitably entail breaking the Sabbath laws, the leading Berlin rabbi Dr David Zvi Hoffmann replied that failure to enlist would bring the entire community into disrepute and profane the name of Heaven. It was thus not only a civic but a religious requirement that one do one's duty by the Fatherland.⁴ There is ample evidence attesting to widespread support for this view, if such encouragement was even necessary given the spirit of patriotism which swept through the Jewish community at the start of the war, filling the synagogues to overflowing on 5 August 1914, the day of prayer mandated by the Kaiser.

But on consideration I doubt if it was really the case that my grandfather's sentiments and those of the overwhelming majority of his colleagues were simply to be attributed to duress. What then is to be made of them? In the first instance it has to be acknowledged that one cannot judge from the sidelines the feelings which may have flowed through the hearts of the combatants in one of the most prolonged, wretched and bloody conflicts in history. Maybe it was necessary for most soldiers to feel an intense patriotism, not because when all things were considered impartially that was the right thing to do and say, but because emotionally and spiritually it was the only way to manage the encounter with so much injury, death and devastation.

No less importantly in the context of this book, it would be wrong to pass judgement over the patriotism of the vast majority of the Jewish community without considering what it may have meant to be Jews in Germany at that time. The war was seen by many both as the ultimate test of equality between Christian and Jew and as furnishing its final proof. My grandfather was convinced that the Jewish contribution to the war would never be forgotten; that those who had witnessed Jews fighting, suffering and dying together with Christians as Germans for the sake of Germany would never be able to return to the old anti-Semitism of the pre-war era. A new age was being born in the trenches, a new awareness that all were brothers together, a new kind of peace, if not between Frenchmen and Germans, then at least between German Christians and German Jews. This belief would be shaken to the roots by the *Judenzählung*, the pernicious Jews' census, in the autumn of 1916.

To my grandfather and many thousands like him, 'Jewish' and 'German' did not merely describe two conflicting cultures, or even two separate facets of their identity which sat sometimes more and sometimes less easily side by side. The twin ideals of *Bildung* and *Kultur*, of an education and culture which were at once moral and aesthetic and which developed the innermost sensitivities and qualities of character, were understood both as profoundly Jewish and as quintessentially German. What animated such patriotism among so many Jews was not therefore a desperate desire to shed their pariah status, which had in fact largely been left behind by most of them at least a generation earlier, but a heartfelt conviction that German and Jew belonged together, that in essence they represented the same moral principles and the same intellectual and spiritual ideals. This was probably nowhere more clearly expressed than in the tract published by the philosopher Hermann Cohen in 1915, *Deutschtum und Judentum*. Besides hoping for a German victory to liberate his Russian coreligionists in particular from the oppressive regime under which they were suffering, and to achieve complete equality between Jews and Christians for the sake of their common advancement of monotheism, he declares that:

> We are living amid the high emotions of German patriotism, the conviction that the unity between Germanness and Jewishness,

for which the entire history of German Jewry has paved the way, will finally shine as a *cultural historical truth* in German politics and in the life of the German people, and even in the *spirit* of the German people.[5]

A further reason for the special bond between them emerges in the diaries of my grandfather: Jew and German are both felt to be maligned for similar reasons. Despised for their thrift, their success and their alleged love of wealth and power, German and Jew are not only allies in ideology but also companions in the misfortune of the prejudices they attract. By contrast, the French and the British, but especially the former, emerge as ill-disciplined and lacking in honour in the manner in which they conduct the war. Attention is drawn to the purported benefits of German occupation, which include fairness, good governance and consideration towards the local population. I have no doubt that, for his part, my grandfather's aversion to things French was based on the Dreyfus affair, which he experienced as a schoolboy when, in response to a letter in which he explained that he was Jewish, his French penfriend wrote back denouncing Judaism and urging him to embrace Christianity at once, for the sake of his eternal soul. He understood such French anti-Semitism as a betrayal of the vaunted values of *égalité* and *fraternité*, ideals which his experience of the front line suggested to him that the Germans truly upheld. (Not surprisingly, French Jews, including their rabbis, often felt every bit as patriotic as their German counterparts.)

The *Judenzählung* had a profound impact on all the Jews serving in the Kaiser's armies. Referring to it with great sadness as a terrible disappointment, my grandfather noted that it had at least drawn Jews of all opinions and denominations together. Now they all experienced and understood themselves as Jews and would go home after the end of the war determined to practise their faith and affirm their Jewish identity more fully. No doubt it was impossible for anyone at the time to envisage quite how deep the gulf between German and Jew would soon become. Struggling to be optimistic and alluding to his beloved Goethe, he described anti-Semitism as that force which always intends to do what is evil but ultimately ends up bringing about at least some degree of good. No doubt he was trying to encourage his coreligionists to make the best of a bitter blow. But it must already have been hard to maintain such optimism.

His younger contemporary and later friend Ernst Simon was to reflect on the *Judenzählung* as the beginning of his rediscovery of his true identity, an inner journey which led him to Zionism:

> The dream of commonality was over. The deep abyss, which had never entirely disappeared, opened up once more with terrible force. It could not be bridged by common suffering and bleeding, not by common language and work, not even by common civilisation and manners ... We were now ready to experience Judaism as something positive ... With open hearts we revelled in the good fortune of being able to live together with Jewish comrades.[6]

Looking back on these sentiments and convictions with the so-called benefit of hindsight, it feels like an understatement to talk about the irony of history. It is probably true to say that never has any stance been so thoroughly and violently discredited by subsequent events as that of the patriotic German Jew towards his idealised homeland. At the close of his book Appelbaum documents the subsequent fate of the chaplains who gave years of selfless service and risked their lives for their *Vaterland*. Leo Baeck, the official leader of German Jewry in the terrible years of the 1930s and early 1940s, survived Theresienstadt and found a new home in London and America after the war. Some, including my grandfather and his immediate family, were fortunate in managing to flee Germany just in time. Yet others, or their descendants, perished in the gas chambers. With these unthinkable experiences the former hopes and ideals of German Jewry perished forever.

Or did they? I was brought up in the 1960s and 1970s at my grandparents' Sabbath table around which almost every adult was a refugee from either Germany or Austria. All things German were by no means despised. On the contrary, I was always taught to distinguish between the criminal horrors of Nazism on the one hand and high German culture on the other. In the bookcase were beautiful editions of Goethe, Schiller, Lessing and Heine. Above all, Lessing's Nathan remained the paragon of wisdom and the spokesman of German culture at its best, with his vision of true equality between the bearers of the three great monotheistic faiths. The ideals for which my grandfather had seen himself as fighting in the Great War were by no means dead.

Was that division between Nazism on the one hand, and German culture on the other, simply a way of accommodating oneself to so complex and painful a past without having to make a total, radical break with the hopes and experiences of an earlier part of one's life? Was it no more than one possible way of making sense of the complexity of one's own story? That is no doubt partly the case. Yet I think that there is more to it than this. However deeply misapplied hindsight was to show it to have been in that particular context, the vision of a culture to which all can truly belong despite differences of faith is not something to be despised. That the German Jewish dream was fatally flawed is not now in dispute. Yet not only at the time, but even in retrospect, it felt to many of the Jewish protagonists of the First World War era like something for which it was worth risking life and limb, an ideal for which it was worthy to have fought.

On receiving an award in his late 80s for his work in inter-faith relations, my grandfather spoke about his three-fold loyalties: to Britain for saving his life and the lives of his family, to Germany as the country and culture he had loved for much of his life, and, most profoundly of all, to his Jewish faith.

NOTES

1. G. Salzberger, *Aus meinem Kriegstagebuch. Von dem Feldgeistlichen bei der 5 Armee.* (Frankfurt am Main: Sonderabdruck aus der Monatschrift *Liberales Judentum*, 1916).
2. M. Salomonski, *Ein Jahr an der Somme* (Frankfurt an der Oder: Verlag der königlichen Hofbuchdruckerei Trowitzsch & Sohn, 1917).
3. 'The Parable of the Old Man and the Young', in *The Collected Poems of Wilfred Owen*, edited with an Introduction and notes by C. Day Lewis and with a Memoir by Edmund Blunden (London: Chatto and Windus, 1974), p.42.
4. David Zvi Hoffmann, *Melamed Leho'il* (Frankfurt: 1926), Responsum 42 (my translation).
5. Hermann Cohen, *Deutschtum und Judentum*, Werke (Hildesheim: 1978–97, 16 vols), Vol.16, pp.528–30 (trans. on website of *Germanhistorydocs*; italics in the original).
6. Ernst Simon, *Unser Kriegerlebnis* (1919), quoted in Michael A. Meyer (ed.), *German Jewish History in Modern Times*, vol.4 (New York: Columbia University Press, 1998), p.14.

Historical Introduction

MICHAEL A. MEYER

At the time that Jews in modern Europe began to integrate into non-Jewish society they had neither experience as soldiers nor desire to join the military. When in 1764 Maria Theresa of Austria demanded the recruitment of fifty-six Jewish men, the community protested vigorously and eventually succeeded in gaining acceptance of a payment instead. Army service was not only dangerous but meant the inability to observe Jewish ritual in encampments far from Jewish institutions. Attempts to recruit Jews were regarded as a *gezerah*, an evil decree. Yet whereas medieval states allowed them to substitute tax payments for military service, the new nation states were reluctant to grant that exemption. Thus, when a quarter of a century later Maria Theresa's successor, the enlightened Joseph II, issued a similar order, no choice was given but to obey. The distinguished rabbi of Prague, Ezekiel Landau, travelled to the army camp and, in the presence of non-Jewish soldiers, offered the Jewish recruits words of consolation. He urged them to accept their lot without grumbling, to recite their prayers without embarrassment, and to avoid ritually forbidden foods as long as possible. These admonitions were to be expected. But Landau also added a new political note when he spoke of 'what fame and what love you will then carry away among all honest persons as well as among your coreligionists!'[1] According to Landau, military service was not an unmitigated evil; it could bring honour and greater acceptance for Jews within the non-Jewish societies in which they lived.

A similar, more positive, attitude to military service was expressed by French Jewry caught up in the public enthusiasm for Napoleon Bonaparte. When Jewish notables from the French domains gathered in Paris for a grand state-instituted conclave and were asked by French officials whether or not Judaism required its adherents to defend France, they arose and shouted: 'Jusqu'à la mort!' In their eyes service in the Napoleonic army was a sacred and honourable obligation.[2] Their patriotic enthusiasm came into play despite the fact that Jews in one army were now fighting fellow Jews in another.

Similar fervour was expressed by Jews in Prussia during the 1813–14 Wars of Liberation against Napoleon. The law of 11 March 1812 had just given Prussian Jews a large measure of equality and they were eager to prove themselves worthy of their new status. As two young Jewish men put it, on the battle field 'the barriers of prejudice will come tumbling down ... Your fellow soldiers ... will not deny you the name of brother, for you will have *earned* it' [emphasis in original].[3] In fact, Jews joined the army disproportionately, with 561 volunteers; fifty-five Jewish officers fell at the battle of Waterloo and seventy-two Jews were awarded the iron cross.

We do not know of any rabbinical contact with these Jewish soldiers. At the beginning of the nineteenth century the rabbinical role was still what it had been in the Middle Ages: rabbis served as teachers and administrators of Jewish law. Pastoral functions devolved upon the community as a whole. Nor, following the Wars of Liberation, were there many Jewish soldiers to be given religious support in German armies. The tightly knit Prussian officer corps was highly prejudiced against outsiders; the Jewishly active Meno Burg, who managed to achieve staff officer status, provided the lone exception. Only Jews who had converted to Christianity had a slightly better chance of rising in the ranks. The Bavarian army, by contrast, did appoint some Jewish officers, especially physicians and supply officers.[4]

Yet at times of war Jews eagerly served Germany's cause. They participated in the Franco-German War of 1870–71, once more attempting to show that the emancipation process, which was then reaching its culmination in all of Germany, was not without justification. Some 10,000 Jews volunteered for service. Meanwhile, a new generation of rabbis had appeared, whose roles were more analogous to those of Christian clergy. Thus it is at this point that we find the first effort to bring an organized religious service to Jewish soldiers who were fighting for Germany. Austria had preceded Germany in this regard. There Jewish military chaplains had served Jewish soldiers in wartime since 1859. In Germany, by contrast, the Prussian position, still expressed in 1866, was that 'on account of the relatively small number and [wide] distribution of Jewish soldiers across the whole army, the employment of Jewish military chaplains is neither possible nor necessary'.[5] Yet the question necessarily had to arise as to whether, in the wake of civil emancipation, Jews should nevertheless be allowed to have their own chaplains, at least in wartime. The Mannheim Jewish community took the initiative by supporting a rabbinical student, Dr Isaac Blumenstein, in his endeavour to take on the role of chaplain in the German army. Blumenstein did gain permission to do so, as did three other students at the Breslau rabbinical seminary thereafter. As we know from his reports in the Jewish press, he was also granted travel at army expense and treated respectfully by the commander of the First Army Corps, General Manteuffel, although, unlike his Christian counterparts, he received no salary and was supported instead by the Mannheim Jewish community.

The services for Yom Kippur, the Jewish Day of Atonement, that Blumenstein conducted at Sainte Barbe, the German army camp outside Metz, were depicted on a widely circulated tapestry as an outdoor gathering on a massive scale. In truth, they were a much more modest affair, held in two small rooms, one assigned to Blumenstein and another to his neighbour, a Königsberg physician. Still, however modest, this Jewish commemoration of the most sacred Jewish holy day in a military setting was memorable for the few dozen who attended. Blumenstein reports that when, basing himself on a biblical text, he spoke of 'return to one's own home in peace', he was interrupted by the weeping and sobbing of his listeners and had to pause for several minutes before continuing. But he also notes that there was a small number of soldiers who were reluctant to affirm their Jewishness either on account of indifference to the Jewish religion or because they sought to hide their identity. An additional Day of Atonement service for Jews in the German army was held at the Rothschild palace at Ferrières outside Paris.[6]

In other countries the appointment of Jewish military chaplains had likewise been a slow process. During the American Civil War, President Abraham Lincoln signed a bill making it possible for a few rabbis to serve as chaplains for the Union forces, principally to visit the Jewish wounded in the hospitals. None, however, served in the Confederate army. Thereafter, American Jewish chaplains did not reappear until the First World War when, after a special Act of Congress, they were appointed for service with the fighting forces. Six rabbis initially served, their number later swelling to thirty, most of them graduates of Hebrew Union College, the Reform seminary. They were given the rank of first lieutenant and one was wounded in action. Since they needed to travel widely, the American Jewish Welfare Board purchased Ford automobiles for each of them, thereby making them the envy of their Christian colleagues.[7] The British army employed nine Jewish chaplains in the First World War, one for each army headquarters, with their senior rabbi achieving the rank of major. By contrast, the French army had no official chaplains of any religion since France abided by a strict separation of Church and State that had been inaugurated in 1905. However, French rabbis did serve informally, one of whom, Abraham Bloch, was killed as he sought to extend a crucifix to a wounded Christian soldier.[8]

With the outbreak of the war, German Jews joined the vast majority of non-Jewish Germans in believing that their cause was just. Germany had not sought war; war had been forced upon it. As far away as the United States, Jews of German origin shared that feeling, holding it publicly until America entered the conflict. Not only German Jewish liberals – who had been fervent patriots for generations – shared the enthusiasm. So did almost all of the Zionists, who had been far more moderate in their affirmation of German political objectives but who were no less deeply German by culture than were their opponents within the Jewish communities. Opposition came almost exclusively from Jews on the far political Left.

As in 1813 and in 1870, likewise in 1914, Jewish hopes for complete acceptance in Germany had very recently been raised. A resurgence of anti-Semitism, this time with racial justification, had occurred in the 1880s, a backlash effect following the constitutional enshrinement of equality a decade earlier and the consequent greater penetration of Jews into significant areas of the German economy and culture. Not only had anti-Semitic literature been circulated and anti-Jewish attitudes penetrated the intellectual establishment, but anti-Semitic parties had gained significant representation in the German parliament. However, the Reichstag election of 1912 produced a turnaround. From sixteen seats in the election of 1907 the numbers of the anti-Semites fell to three. Representation of right-wing parties generally was reduced while Social Democrats more than doubled their numbers. It is therefore not surprising that on the eve of the war German Jews were hopeful about their future in Germany. Like their fellow Germans, they declared the war a defensive one. Judging by the widespread silence on the issue, they did not – at least publicly – pay much attention to the fact that, if they joined the German army, they would be fighting against fellow Jews. Some of them, seeking a Jewish justification for the war, looked only to the Eastern Front, enabling them to declare it a battle against a blatantly anti-Semitic Tsarist Russia. After all, the Russian government had been directly and indirectly involved in recurrent pogroms ever since 1881, the most notorious of which had occurred in Kishinev in 1903. Biblically oriented German Jews also identified Russia with Amalek, the archenemy of the ancient Israelites.[9]

At the outset of the war ten thousand Jews volunteered for service, certain that the Kaiser's call for unity among all political and religious factions would include them as well. Ultimately, about a hundred thousand would serve. Jews could now become officers in the German army.[10] Two thousand achieved officer status, though they were almost invariably limited to the lower ranks and their presence raised complaints in certain circles. Germany's ally, Austria-Hungary, was more generous. Its army not only included more than two thousand Jewish officers – a remarkable proportion of nearly one to five – but raised two Jews to the high rank of field marshal and six to that of general.[11]

By the First World War the notion that Jewish soldiers in the German army should receive the services of Jewish clergy had become obvious to even the highest officials. In accordance with the wishes of the emperor an army order was issued that was to be strictly carried out on 30 September, the date of the Day of Atonement in 1914. It specified that all Jewish soldiers, to the extent that they were not in the line of fire and hence indispensable, were, under the leadership of Jewish reserve officers and officer replacements at the brigade level, to be present at a particular place on the morning of Yom Kippur. Thereupon they would search for an occupied city behind the front lines in order to conduct religious services. Since in Northern France there were no synagogues at hand, it was foreseen that soldiers in the various army corps would pray instead in Catholic churches. On the Eastern Front, by contrast, these services in 1914 were conducted in synagogues along with local coreligionists.[12]

Initially six Jewish military chaplains served in the German army. Later their numbers grew to about thirty. Unlike the Christian chaplains, they drew their pay entirely from the communities they had served in peacetime. On the community rolls they were regarded as having obtained an extensive paid vacation from their normal duties. The military gave them nothing more than free train passage, a wagon with two horses and a two-seater carriage. It was noted that the initial group of six was also capable of riding a horse if necessary.[13] Beginning in August 1915, their financial situation improved somewhat in that they were henceforth entitled to a reimbursement of expenses. But they continued to receive no salary and the payment of expenses was granted only out of a sense of fairness since the Prussian Ministry of War held to the view that Jewish military chaplains possessed no legal right to such reimbursements. An order of 1916 defined their relationship to the army as merely 'contractual' and in at least one instance the road to gaining official status was strewn with complications.[14]

The Jewish chaplains' dress was similar to that of the Christian chaplains, which basically resembled the uniform worn by officers. However, no rank was indicated. Like their Christian counterparts, they wore a white arm band on which a red cross stood out brightly. In some cases the rabbis' armbands also displayed a violet-coloured Star of David, in others the Jewish chaplains wore a Star of David around their necks to set them apart from their colleagues who dangled a cross.[15] Rabbi Aron Tänzer also received a revolver which, on one occasion, he used to scatter an unfriendly crowd.[16]

The Jewish chaplains were assisted by the Verband der deutschen Juden, the association of German Jews created in 1904 for the purpose of conducting relations with state authorities. As an umbrella organization that transcended factions within the Jewish community it was best able to deal with the various matters pertaining to Jewish military chaplaincy. These included negotiations with the War Ministry and the supply of prayer books as well as other religious goods, including a military edition of the Hebrew Bible. The very thin prayer books, which could easily be stuffed into the pocket of a uniform, consisted of twenty-nine pages of German text and twenty-six of Hebrew. Although they constituted an extreme abbreviation of the usual service and added some German folk songs, the Hebrew text did not contain any variations from liturgical tradition. Their anonymous compiler, Rabbi Leo Baeck, clearly intended them for private, rather than public devotion and that they be broadly acceptable.[17] From time to time, as circumstances permitted, the chaplains would come together for conferences where items of mutual concern were placed on the agenda. His colleagues chose Rabbi Baeck, then newly installed in Berlin, to chair these sessions.

That the work of the Jewish chaplains met with appreciation not only from those who received their attention is attested both by the Jewish communities who supported them and were eager to learn of their work and by non-Jewish authorities. By the end of the war, various chaplains could boast of the medals they had received for their work. These included the iron cross second class, the Hamburg Hanseatic cross, an Austrian medal, and in at least one instance even a Turkish decoration.

Their multifaceted work was based on the model offered by Christian chaplains, who possessed experience that the rabbis lacked.[18]

An area of activity that was of considerable consequence to the Jewish soldiers was the ability of their chaplains, whenever necessary, to intercede on their behalf with the military authorities. At least some of the soldiers felt they could trust the rabbis more than they could their immediate military superiors. When they encountered anti-Semitism in the army, they could ask the Jewish chaplain to pass their complaint on to a higher military authority.[19] When they required special permission to attend services, the rabbi could speak on their behalf.[20] For their part, the military authorities sometimes called on the Jewish chaplains when they required information regarding policy toward local Jews in occupied territory. And when it was decided to establish special military libraries for the soldiers, Rabbi Leopold Rosenak was invited, along with non-Jews, to join the commission carrying out the project.[21]

Perhaps the activity that was most appreciated by the Jewish soldiers was the attention their chaplains paid to the wounded. Lying alone in field hospitals far from home among men with whom they may have had little in common except for their war experience, these unfortunates were grateful for rabbinical visits. Exercising their pastoral role as did their Christian colleagues, rabbis sought to comfort and to give hope. They brought little gifts, usually otherwise unobtainable food items generally known as *Liebesgaben*, 'gifts of love', that came from Jewish communities at home. Sometimes they would write letters for the wounded soldiers, to parents or to other loved ones. When the occasion presented itself the Jewish chaplains did the same for Jewish prisoners of war.

In Germany, unlike in the United States, the pastoral role had been peripheral to their work, consisting mainly of preaching, teaching religion in schools, and, if they were so inclined, contributing to Jewish scholarship. Under military conditions, concern for the individual Jew – the soldier – became central.

In regard to the healthy Jewish warriors the rabbis had to ask themselves whether they bore any responsibility for their sexual morality. Whereas extensive use of tobacco and alcohol was understandable in war, lack of self-control in sexual conduct was another matter. At the conference of Jewish chaplains in Lille on 26 May 1915 it was decided that they should discuss sexual problems with the men following the religious services. They would stress that there was a special measure of bravery in maintaining self-control. Moreover, as Jews, both religion and patriotism obligated them to such discipline.[22]

The rabbis on the Eastern Front had an additional task that consumed much of their time: aside from serving the Jewish soldiers they also bore responsibilities vis-à-vis the local Jewish population. By order of the commanding officer on the Eastern Front, Rabbi Rosenak was called upon for advice regarding religious practice, education and related matters in regard to the Jewish population in the entire area under his control. In February 1916 he was asked to collect 20,000 marks from a Jewish charity to create workshops that would employ the local population in Vilna and thereby remove them from the streets. In some instances Jews in the East, along with others, were required to perform *Arbeitsdienst*, work service for the German army. Serving their religious needs, it was felt, would improve morale. On one occasion Rosenak composed a notice in Hebrew warning local Jews that there was danger of the spread of various communicable diseases, especially cholera. Local rabbis were to sign and post the notice and everyone aware of an outbreak of these diseases was immediately to notify both a physician and the local commandant of the German army. The poverty of the Jewish population in the East, worsened by the war, created a moral burden for the German chaplains serving there. Rosenak writes to his wife that on the holiday of Simchat Torah poor Jewish women with their children and infants in tow pressed into the synagogue where he was conducting services and screamed for bread. He reports that he ascended the pulpit and asked for order and then, in front of the open Holy Ark, promised immediate steps to relieve their distress.[23] For the German chaplains serving in the East, the encounter with their Eastern European coreligionists was at best ambiguous. While they could admire their devotion to Judaism, their lack of European culture and mores set a barrier between them and the local Jews.

The performance of their duties brought the Jewish chaplains into much closer contact with Christian clergy than they had been accustomed to before the war. From time to time it required them to minister to non-Jewish soldiers when there was no chaplain of their own faith available. That Christian chaplains and soldiers were generally accepting of their Jewish colleagues was seen as an encouraging development that helped to give the war experience a special character for the rabbis.[24]

The unprecedented ecumenism took various forms. On at least one occasion Rabbi Rosenak led a nondenominational service together with an Evangelical colleague.[25] When there were no rabbis available, Jewish soldiers sometimes attended services in the field led by Catholics or Protestants. After one such occasion, led by a priest, a Jewish soldier recalled: 'I must say I have rarely experienced a more uplifting celebration.'[26] Another wrote that a similar service had been devoid of Christian dogma and that he preferred the attractive music and sermon to sitting alone in his musty quarters on a Sunday morning.[27] Christian soldiers would also occasionally attend Jewish worship. For the closing Yom Kippur service in 1917, for example, the Tenth Army's commander, General Hermann von Eichhorn, and some members of his staff were in attendance.[28] On a different occasion a young Christian officer was completely carried away by his experience of Jewish worship.[29] Yet another, following his attendance at a Jewish service, told the rabbi: 'Between blood and iron – a precious hour.'[30] Rabbi Georg Salzberger hoped that this closer acquaintance with Judaism gained by non-Jewish visitors would have a lasting beneficial effect on their relationship to the minority faith.[31]

Especially in Northern France, where synagogues were not located near the army camps, Jewish worship was conducted in a local church – an unprecedented and somewhat eerie experience. In medieval times Jews had been forced into churches to hear conversionary sermons. Now, as one participant in a Yom Kippur service in 1914 recalled, the Jewish military chaplain, Rabbi Wilde from Magdeburg, was giving a Jewish sermon in a Christian sacred space that also served as a field hospital and military dormitory. Rabbi Wilde was so overcome by the occasion that after a few words his voice faltered, he could not go on and began to weep.[32]

The Jewish chaplains had no choice but to adapt to whatever facilities were available to them. On one occasion Rabbi Leo Baeck was forced to conduct services in a cave. In the absence of candlesticks for the required blessing, one of the Jewish military chaplains simply used two wine bottles instead, wittily proclaiming: 'C'est la guerre!'[33]

The sermons that the rabbis delivered in the army context differed from those of their Christian counterparts and also from the style they had employed at home. Although their words were not free of patriotic verbiage, they were less militant than those of non-Jewish colleagues. Liberal Judaism, in particular, had stressed that the universalism which followed from strict monotheism was essential to the Jewish faith and that it was that message which gave Judaism its ongoing mission in the modern world. Even at a time of war it remained a central notion that could not be abandoned. It appears especially in the sermons delivered by Rabbi Leo Baeck. Yet some rabbis also drew on canonical texts for the purpose of strengthening military morale. Psalm 27 especially lent itself to this purpose. It could be read as a *Kriegspsalm*, a war psalm, especially when stressing such verses as the third: 'Should an army besiege me, my heart would have no fear; should war beset me, still would I be confident.'[34] Frequent reference was made, of course, to the military prowess of the ancient Maccabees. Compared to the sermons they delivered to their congregations at home, the chaplains' sermons to soldiers sacrificed elegance of expression for spontaneity and relevance. The rabbis did not so much preach as speak directly to the men's spiritual and emotional concerns.

The religious services as such likewise differed from the pattern set in the impressive, high vaulted synagogues the military chaplains had served in peacetime. Rabbi Reinhold Lewin notes that they were considerably shorter and less polished. Instead of a choir the ad-hoc congregation itself did the singing. Unlike the usual Liberal service, there was no organ. And since there was also no cantor, the service was conducted entirely by the chaplain unless he had delegated a portion of it to one of the attending soldiers.[35] The distance, both physical and spiritual, between rabbi and congregant, which was typical of the German synagogue, melted away under these conditions. Instead of standing above the worshippers on a raised pulpit, the military chaplain spoke from within their midst. Formality gave way to informality; congregation became community. This was true especially during the celebration of holidays, among which the communal Seder service on Passover eve brought special pleasure. Photos taken of the chaplains frequently showed them together with their soldier congregants.

There were, of course, Jewish soldiers who kept away from anything explicitly Jewish and there must have been others who were unmoved by the services. However, there are enough positive reports to conclude that the worship conducted by the Jewish military chaplains deeply affected many. Coming in from the field, often dirty and unshaven, the soldiers entered a very different sort of atmosphere from that of the camp. For a few minutes they were not soldiers but worshipful Jews. Among their coreligionists, listening to familiar words and melodies, they could feel a sense of at-homeness that was absent in the camp. Numerous letters home from Jewish soldiers in the field attest that they had never participated in devotions that were as stirring as those they experienced in France on Yom Kippur in the year 1914.[36] One soldier from Heilbronn wrote to a friend about a service he had attended that November conducted by Chaplain Jacob Sonderling: 'The manner in which he spoke to us was so straightforward, so pertinent and gripping that our otherwise hardened soldier-heart became as soft as butter – but that may have been necessary, and afterwards all of us surely felt lighter around the heart than before.'[37] Some Jews, unaccustomed to prayer, learned to pray for the first time, even if they had to spend Yom Kippur in the trenches; others found God.[38]

For the Jewish military chaplains their war experience was both special and memorable. Unlike a few of their Christian colleagues, no Jewish chaplains serving in the German army were mortally wounded; they seem to have been little exposed to gunfire. Their experience was more one of deeply felt empathy for their coreligionists who did suffer danger, injury and death. They believed fervently in the German cause, justified the conflict, but did not sanctify war as an end in itself. Rabbi Leo Baeck, their chosen leader, was without question a German patriot, but that patriotism was based more on the humanistic strand in German culture than on the nation state. To a greater degree than among his colleagues, his conscience was deeply troubled by war with its spiritual and physical injuries and its cruel death. He could justify it only if its goal transcended narrow national interest and had a moral purpose. The burden on conscience would be relieved only by faith that the outcome would benefit humanity.[39]

However, as the war dragged on, the hope for a German victory and its idealized consequences melted away. The unprecedented brutality of the war crushed the earlier idealism. Enthusiasm ebbed; fatalism gained ground. Rabbi Lewin noted that the religious fervour had given way to doubt about God's presence in their midst. He was driven to ask: 'Why does the Deity not have mercy upon us and tear open the bonds in which we are ensnared?'[40] For Baeck the war experience may well have been a factor in his later theological move from a broad and optimistic rationalism to a greater appreciation of a more personalized and experiential religion.[41]

The crisis of faith spawned by the lengthening and increasingly futile war was accompanied by the need to explain the likely possibility of a German defeat. Following numerous complaints that Jews were allegedly failing to meet their frontline responsibilities in adequate numbers, the War Ministry ordered a census of Jews serving in the German army, thereby singling them out as likely lacking in a proper willingness to sacrifice for the fatherland. The Jewish community was eventually able to bring about cancellation of the census, but the damage had been done.[42] Instead of serving the cause of Jewish equality, the war in its later stages had raised up anew the spectre of anti-Semitic exclusion. The Jewish war experience did therefore point toward the future. But it was not the future that Baeck had imagined. It was not a broader vision of humanity that would gain power in little more than a decade, but an unprecedented racist regime.[43] When war broke out again a generation later, the Jewish chaplains still alive who had served in the German army were to be found on the other side of the conflict.

NOTES

1. Ruth Kestenberg-Gladstein, *Neuere Geschichte der Juden in den böhmischen Ländern*. Erster Teil: *Das Zeitalter der Aufklärung, 1780–1830* (Tübingen: Mohr, 1969), pp.69–72 (p.71).
2. Diogene Tama (ed.), *Transactions of the Parisian Sanhedrim [sic]; or, Acts of the Assembly of Israelitish Deputies of France and Italy, Convoked at Paris by an Imperial and Royal Decree Dated May 30, 1806*, trans. F.D. Kirwan (London, 1807), pp.134–5, 181.
3. Michael A. Meyer, *The Origins of the Modern Jew: Jewish Identity and European Culture in Germany, 1749–1824* (Detroit, MI: Wayne State University Press, 1967), p.139; Rolf Vogel, *Ein Stück von uns. Deutsche Juden in deutschen Armeen 1813–1976: eine Dokumentation* (Mainz: von Hase & Koehler Verlag, 1977), pp.27–8, 31.
4. Jacob Rosenthal, *Episodah shel 'rish'ut'? 'Sefirat ha-yehudim' bemilhemet ha-olam ha-rishonah* (Jerusalem: Ha-kibbutz hame'uhad and Leo Baeck Institute, 2005), pp.23–7.
5. *Jüdisches Lexikon* (Berlin: Jüdischer Verlag, 1927), 4/1, p.184.
6. *Allgemeine Zeitung des Judentums* 42 (1870), pp.823–4, 857–61, 873–4.
7. For the history of the Jewish chaplaincy in the United States see Louis Barish (ed.), *Rabbis in Uniform: The Story of the American Jewish Military Chaplain* (New York: Jonathan David, 1962), and Albert Isaac Slomovitz, *The Fighting Rabbis: Jewish Military Chaplains and American History* (New York: New York University Press, 1999).
8. *Jüdisches Lexikon* 4/1, p.183.
9. Rosenthal, *Episodah shel 'rish'ut'?*, pp.30–6.
10. For the German-Jewish war experience and especially its later commemoration see Tim Grady, *The German-Jewish Soldiers of the First World War in History and Memory* (Liverpool: Liverpool University Press, 2011).
11. Ibid., p.189; Michael Berger, *Eisernes Kreuz und Davidstern. Die Geschichte jüdischer Soldaten in deutschen Armeen* (Berlin: Trafoverlag, 2006), pp.127, 142.
12. *Im deutschen Reich*, October 1914, pp.397–8.
13. Ibid., p.397.
14. *Jüdisches Lexikon* 4/1, p.184. Rabbi Jakob Sonderling told one of the Jewish soldiers how much difficulty he had had in gaining his appointment and then in having himself invested as a chaplain. Eugen Tannenbaum (ed.), *Kriegsbriefe deutscher und österreichischer Juden* (Berlin: Neuer Verlag, 1915), p.136. Conditions did vary somewhat according to local circumstances and in the course of the war. A slightly different account is therefore given by Rabbi Aaron Tänzer (below, pp.175-7).
15. Tannenbaum (ed.), *Kriegsbriefe deutscher und österreichischer Juden*, p.145; Berger, *Eisernes Kreuz und Davidstern*, p.143, and see plate 18, a photo of a Jewish, Catholic, and Protestant chaplain.

16. See below, p.187.
17. *Feldgebetbuch für die jüdischen Mannschaften des Heeres* (Berlin: H. Itzkowski, 1914).
18. Arnold Vogt, *Religion im Militär. Seelsorge zwischen Kriegsverherrlichung und Humanität. Eine militärgeschichtliche Studie* (Frankfurt am Main: Peter Lang, 1984), pp.582–3. Vogt gives a detailed account of various issues relating to the chaplaincy that were argued between Jewish communal authorities and the governments of German states as well as within the Jewish communities, pp.579–614.
19. Ulrich Sieg, *Jüdische Intellektuelle im Ersten Weltkrieg. Kriegserfahrungen, weltanschauliche Debatten und kulturelle Neuentwürfe* (Berlin: Akademie Verlag, 2001), pp.113–14.
20. Tannenbaum, *Kriegsbriefe deutscher und österreichischer Juden*, p.183.
21. Hoppe, Felddivisionsgeistlicher beim Stab des Oberbefehlshaber Ost to Armee-Rabbiner Dr Rosenak, 24 August 1916, Leopold Rosenak Collection, Leo Baeck Institute Jerusalem.
22. Sieg, *Jüdische Intellektuelle im Ersten Weltkrieg*, p.126.
23. Undated letter to 'Geliebter Schatz', Rosenak Collection.
24. However, in occupied France German Catholic soldiers gravitated to local Catholic priests in preference to German Protestant or Jewish clergy. See Patrick J. Houlihan, 'Local Catholicism as Transnational War Experience: Everyday Religious Practice in Occupied Northern France, 1914–1918', *Central European History* 45, no.2 (2012), pp.233–67 (p.240).
25. 'Bericht über meine Tätigkeit v. 27. August bis 24. Sept. 1915', Rosenak Collection.
26. Tannenbaum, *Kriegsbriefe deutscher und österreichischer Juden*, p.89.
27. Reichsbund Jüdischer Frontsoldaten (ed.), *Kriegsbriefe gefallener Deutscher Juden* (Berlin: Vortrupp Verlag, 1935), p.12.
28. David J. Fine, *Jewish Integration in the German Army in the First World War* (Berlin and Boston, MA: de Gruyter, 2012), p.36.
29. Reichsbund Jüdischer Frontsoldaten (ed.), *Kriegsbriefe gefallener Deutscher Juden*, p.28.
30. 'Bericht über meine Tätigkeit'.
31. See below, pp.30, 67–8, 76–8, 139.
32. Tannenbaum, *Kriegsbriefe deutscher und österreichischer Juden*, p.68.
33. Ibid., p.145.
34. *Feldbriefe der Posener Rabbiner an die jüdischen Soldaten der Provinz Posen*, 2nd series (Frankfurt am Main: M. Lehrberger & Co., 1916). These rabbis were not military chaplains but felt spiritual responsibility for Jewish men from their communities.
35. See below, pp.47–54, 64–5, 159–60, 194, 277.
36. *Im deutschen Reich*, p.398.
37. Tannenbaum, *Kriegsbriefe deutscher und österreichischer Juden*, pp.135–6.
38. Sabine Hank and Hermann Simon (eds), *Feldpostbriefe Jüdischer Soldaten, 1914–1918* (Teetz: Hentrich & Hentrich, 2002), Vol.1, p.313; Reichsbund Jüdischer Frontsoldaten (ed.), *Kriegsbriefe gefallener Deutscher Juden*, p.29.
39. Michael A. Meyer (ed.), *Leo Baeck Werke*. Vol. 6: Briefe, Reden, Aufsätze (Gütersloh: Gütersloher Verlagshaus, 2003), p.123.
40. See below, p.257.
41. See below, chapter 10, p.305.
42. Rosenthal, *Episodah shel 'rish'ut'?*, pp.58, 85; Werner T. Angress, 'The German Army's "Judenzählung" of 1916 – Genesis – Consequences – Significance', *Leo Baeck Institute Year Book* 23 (1978), pp.117–37.
43. When after the war Rabbi Rosenak, who had received a letter of commendation from General Ludendorff for his work in the East and also established a relationship with General Hindenburg, wrote to the latter regarding the resurgence of anti-Semitism, he received a reply implying that anti-Semitism was justified on account of 'bad Jewish elements' that were operative especially in the economic and political spheres. Hindenburg to Rosenak, 23 February 1921, Rosenak Collection.

CHAPTER ONE

The Torch of War is Lit! 1813–1871

The association of Germany's rabbis with Jews fighting for the Fatherland has a long history. Immediately after the Jews of Prussia were permitted to serve in the Wars of Liberation against Napoleon, Prussia's civilian rabbis assisted the national effort. Although they were not permitted to serve as chaplains they preached enthusiastic patriotism to departing soldiers.

On 11 March 1813, the 70-year-old chief rabbi of Silesia, Aaron Karfunkel, gave the Jewish volunteers from his area advice, later reported as follows:

> Go forth to battle for King and Fatherland! The moment that you enter military service you must think only of King and Fatherland, and your religious duties cease! You may enjoy what is offered to you. You need not put on phylacteries when you are unable to do so. Take them with you, but you do not need to use them. Also you need not pray formally but think of God as often as you can and pray the *She'ma* in your hearts only. God will accept your service for King and Fatherland as a prayer, and will send you back to your family adorned with honours.[1]

The following excerpts from the sermon 'Hoffnung und Vertrauen' [Hope and Confidence] preached by Vice-Ober-Landesrabbiner Meyer Simon Weyl in the Great Synagogue in Berlin on 28 March 1813 at the departure of the Prussian army and in presence of several Jewish volunteers demonstrates how ardently German Jews wished to be accepted into their country as full partners, and vehemently denies the charge laid at the Jews' door that they are not by nature fighters, but cowards who shirk military duty:

> My second purpose is to make you, young protectors of the Fatherland, aware of your incipient duties; to commend you to trust in God and to be loyal to our king, who has allowed you to serve as volunteers; and to assure you of God's protection. Plead my cause, O LORD, with them that strive with me: fight against

them that fight against me. Take hold of buckler and shield, and rise up for my help. Draw out also the spear, and stop the way against them that persecute me: say to my soul, I am your salvation (Psalm 35: 1–4).

The word 'peace' has struck us with deep wounds ... Not every rest refreshes or brings peace. This 'peace' is an exhaustion, by which we lose rather than gain strength and is not a peace that we can love.² Much more, we must desire a war that will give us a real, beneficial and refreshing peace. King Solomon has written (Ecclesiastes 3: 8): 'There is a time for war, and a time for peace' ... in other words there is a time to hate peace, and a time to love war. If this is so, we must not shun war. A war like the one which our beloved king undertakes cannot be harmful to mankind! May this war help us to strengthen his hand! May we take comfort in that we suffer not only for the sake of righteousness but also for our dear king.

O Eternal God, let the time not be distant when we may see our beloved ones, surrounded by their children, crowned with the palm of peace, and delighting in congratulations and joyful thanks of Your subjects. Hear, O Eternal, the words of my mouth and the thoughts of my heart: increase and double his years! Satisfy him with long life and show him Your eternal salvation! Long live our good King Frederick William III! And let the whole congregation say: Amen.³

A subsequent sermon, preached by Rabbi Levin Joseph Saalschütz on 19 April 1815 at the opening of the Synagogue in Königsberg and also dedicated to the volunteers of the Königsberg Jewish community who went out to fight Napoleon a second time, also reflects the patriotism and warlike spirit of the times:

The torch of war has again been lit! The borders of Germany are threatened a second time. All the German people raise their voices to you with one voice, one will, and one feeling. Prussia, old in strength but newly arisen, proves itself anew. From all over Prussia men and boys come, crowding around the flag, around their justly beloved king and queen, burning with righteousness for king and Fatherland. The sword is unsheathed for the second time: who can withstand this heroes' throng, each man humble and brave, fighting for right? You too, high-souled young men, are seized by a powerful force, to join our brave fighting men. Not conscripted but of your free will, you have decided to dedicate your arm, your strength, to king and country. God will bless you, God will be with you, and His all-powerful hand will protect and defend you and will crown you with victory and fame.

(To departing recruits) Parting from you is deeply moving, but it is emotion and love born of good deeds. Go, brothers and friends. You deserve our respect, our devotion. Wherever you are, you are always near to our hearts and remain in our midst. And when (as we are sure you will) you return victorious, you will be rewarded by the warm thanks of your king, your Fatherland, each man with humble mien and humble heart. How strongly your hearts will beat after you have achieved peace. Then great and small, young and old, will bless you and say: 'These are the men who with their blood fought for peace and tranquillity. Hail to them and thanks!' Hail the king, Hail our Fatherland, hail brave sons of our Fatherland![4]

Immediately after Jews were allowed to serve in the army, Emmanuel Loewe from Landsburg an der Warthe requested the War Ministry to install Jewish chaplains, but his request was denied and Jewish soldiers were sworn in by civilian rabbis.[5] Jews also served during the Schleswig-Holstein War of 1864, the war between Prussia and the Austrian Confederation of 1866, and the Franco-Prussian War, also without their own chaplains.[6]

The first official Jewish holiday celebrated in the German army was Yom Kippur on 4–5 October 1870, before the besieged city of Metz, at the start of the Franco-Prussian War. The service is depicted idealistically in textile and poetry forms by Berthold Oppenheim and Gustav Philippson, respectively,[7] but is described with greater accuracy and detail in two articles in the *Allgemeine Zeitung des Judentums*. Excerpts from the report of a soldier who was present follow:

Please allow me, as a Jewish soldier stationed in front of Metz to take up a small part of your newspaper with a report from the current theatre of war which may be of some interest to your readers. This is not a report of battle, for this would go against the well-known policy of your newspaper, but rather one of the recent Yom Kippur day; it is probably the first ever official celebration of a Jewish festival day in the Prussian army.

Since Rosh Hashanah passed without any kind of consideration taken for Jewish soldiers who wanted to celebrate the festival, we were all the more pleasantly surprised when, two days before Yom Kippur, by Corps Command of Excellency von Manteuffel,[8] regiments and battalions were directed to free all soldiers of the Mosaic faith from their duties from 5.00 p.m. and throughout the following day so that they could celebrate Yom Kippur, and to give them leave to go to St Barbe, the current location of Army Headquarters: this, on condition that units in question were not called to battle on these days. Luckily this did not happen and so we Jewish soldiers of the First Army Corps had the great joy of being able to see a deeply, heart-felt wish satisfied, and experience in communal devotion a traditional Yom Kippur service, in the manner of our ancestors.

None of us until this time has prayed with more ardent devotion in beautiful temples back home than we did in this small, low room with broken door, windows without panes, and walls pock-marked by shells. From time to time, not far from us, our cannons thundered near Metz and we felt the transience of our existence and need to make our peace with our God – because all too soon it could be too late – in the innermost depths of our hearts in a way that we had not anticipated. Many, to whom the inner meaning of Yom Kippur had up to now been foreign, will now understand it with unforgettable clarity.

Out of seventy-one Jewish men serving in the Army Corps about sixty [ordinary] soldiers turned out, together with several staff physicians and a few clerks from military administration: all were joyful to be able to celebrate Yom Kippur. One could tell that most of the Jewish soldiers were intelligent from the fact that most consisted of non-commissioned officers, conscripted soldiers and a few volunteers, and that an air of gentility and good education predominated such as is seldom seen in an assembly of so many soldiers. The place set aside for prayer consisted of two small rooms; two lights placed in bottles burned on the *Misrachtisch*, and a few rifles stood to the side of the table. The community itself consisted of all kinds of soldier ranks in full battle dress, because they awaited the alarm signal which could be given any minute.

A non-commissioned officer acted as prayer leader. He recited the prayers simply but with deep understanding, and Dr

Blumenstein spoke profoundly moving words which suited the occasion and made many present weep. We parted from one another in an elevated mood and deeply moved in our hearts, with the promise to meet each other again the next day. Unfortunately twenty comrades were not permitted to do so, because their regiments, located in the *avant-garde* of forward outposts, were engaged in battle and they could not obtain leave. But most of us, who were in Reserve, spent the day in fervent prayer, with hearts filled with thanks to God who had, sometimes quite miraculously, protected us from the close threat of death and injury. When sun set and evening approached, and the thunder of guns echoed in our ears in place of the sounds of 'The Lord He is God',[9] we parted with solemn comfort in our hearts and in firm hope that God, who has protected us thus far, would also allow us a safe return to our longed-for Fatherland.[10]

The following passage is an excerpt from the report by the Chaplain involved, Rabbi Isaak Blumenstein:

The choice of location was a not insignificant problem. It is worth mentioning that I was offered use of the Catholic church, although it would have to be cleared of the large number of soldiers living there at the time! However because a physician from Königsberg, my immediate neighbour, was prepared to vacate the room next to mine, services took place in these two rooms. Almost all Jewish soldiers from regiments one, five, forty-three and forty-four appeared for services on Tuesday evening, Yom Kippur eve. They came from Thorn, Culm, Danzig and Tilsit and many had been proposed for distinction with the Iron Cross. I started services a little before 6.00 p.m. A non-commissioned officer recited the prayers most adequately. Before the concluding *Aleinu* I gave a sermon based upon Jeremiah 31: 15–16,[11] 'This is what the Lord says: Refrain your voice from weeping, and your eyes from tears: for your work shall be rewarded, declares the Lord; and they will return from the land of the enemy. So there is hope for your descendants, says the Lord, and your children will return to their own land.'

I urged my soldiers to take heart, to trust and hope in God, and told them that each should, on this holy day, praise God with their ancestor Jacob and pray with a full heart: 'If God will be with me and will watch over me on this dangerous journey I am taking and so that I return safely to my father's household after achieving a glorious peace, then the Lord will be my God.'[12] An inner voice would then announce the words of the Eternal, He who hears all sincere prayers. Your self-sacrificing, fearless devotion will not be in vain because 'there will be a reward for your deeds', and you will return crowned with fame from the land of your enemy. Out of the mighty deeds which the sons of the Fatherland are accomplishing with God-given courage and strength, God's promise of a great future for the Fatherland sounds loud and clear. And the children who have been estranged for nearly two centuries will again return to their mother's bosom.[13]

I then developed the significance of *Yom Kippur* under prevailing military conditions and concluded with a prayer for the king, our protector, his allies, the German army, the German race and for Israel. The entire service was marked with truly uplifting devotion; prayers had seldom been as profound and moving as they were that evening. When I spoke of the prayers of our Patriarch (Jacob) about 'returning to my own home in peace', I had to stop for several minutes because I was interrupted by the sobbing and weeping of my audience. With the exception of the few soldiers who were on duty in the field hospital, all the remaining soldiers returned to their quarters after the service; many had to travel for three hours.

The next morning the soldiers appeared at the appointed time. The prayer leader from the previous day led the *Shacharit* and *Mussaph* prayers and, in the absence of a Torah scroll, I explained the content of the daily portion[14] and the *Haftarah* from Isaiah (57: 14 to 58: 14). In connection with the verse concerning the death of the sons of Aaron, I explained the nature of their empty ardour which had led to their downfall, because it was without morality and faith and consisted only of 'strange fire' out of which search for vain greatness and false glory develops; by contrast real, genuine devotion flows out of striving for righteousness, truth and love, which lead to victory. Because there were many in the community mourning soldiers who had fallen in battle, I spoke of the deep, exemplary but silent mourning of Aaron over the death of his beloved sons.[15] As is the custom, *Yizkor* was recited after *Shacharit* and I intoned a special prayer for our fallen warriors. After the end of *Mussaph* a few soldiers remained behind occupied with objects of devotion. At 3.00 p.m. the devout crowd returned, with the exception of the few who had to hold themselves ready for the next day's outpost duty. Another non-commissioned officer asked to lead the *Minchah* and *Ne'ilah* prayers, which we prayed together.

After services ended at sundown I directed a few more words of recognition to those present for their devoted participation in the services, which I will remember for the rest of my life. When I finished, Sergeant First Class Hirschberg from Culm who, as I heard, is about to promoted to Lieutenant, thanked me most sincerely in the name of his comrades. I was asked to deliver the thanks of all present to the Grand Ducal City Rabbinate who made these services possible. I was told that soldiers had been longing to pour out their burdened hearts in an hour of communal worship; this desire had now been satisfied and they would go out to face the future in happy mood and with quiet consciences.

I ask the Grand Ducal City Rabbinate to kindly allow me to make a few concluding remarks: No-one who has come to know, from personal experience, the frame of mind of our Jewish soldiers could deny urgency for appointment of Jewish chaplains. While some are indifferent about their religion or shy about acknowledging it openly, this is only the case for a tiny minority. The great majority of Jewish soldiers are filled with longing for religious involvement. They possess prayer books, *tzitzit* and *tefillin*, and those who do not have these express an ardent desire to do so. There is deep religious feeling and need for proper leadership. The undeniable difficulty stemming from the fact that Jewish soldiers are scattered throughout the regiments – does not mean that it is impossible, but rather demonstrates the great urgency for fixed appointments of Jewish chaplains. The need and possibility of spiritual activity for Jews in our army is reflected in the fact that General von Manteuffel has accepted my mission and allowed me to perform it, even if only for a portion of the (Jewish) soldiers.

Respectfully yours, Dr I. Blumenstein[16]

After the High Holidays of 1870, following extensive correspondence with the Prussian War Ministry and correspondence in the *Allgemeine*

Zeitung des Judentums and *der Israelit* (official newspaper of orthodox German Jewry), the Prussian War Ministry finally agreed to appoint three rabbis (Isaak Blumenstein from Mannheim; Adolf Lewin and Benjamin Rippner, both from Posen) as chaplains and to provide them with free transportation, food and quarters in enemy territory, although it refused to give them military rank or remuneration.[17] After the war the government again ignored the Jewish community in conducting official thanksgiving services.[18] The chaplains returned home and were not replaced. Because Jewish one-year volunteers could not become Reserve-officers or enter the Prussian Officer's Corps, there was no perceived need for Jewish chaplains during peacetime and conditions remained the same until after the start of the First World War.

When the First World War began, the Prussian War Ministry still limited admission of Jewish chaplains to volunteers, employed under the same circumstances as before. This, despite the request from the Verband der deutschen Juden on 6 August 1914 that chaplains for Jewish soldiers be appointed, as was the case for Catholics and Protestants. The request was understandable because at war's onset approximately 10,000 Jews volunteered for military service. Although the Verband was prepared to shoulder the costs, the first six Jewish chaplains could not take up office before 6 September 1914,[19] and further chaplain appointments were delayed.[20] One year after the war began, the War Ministry decided to provide a monthly expense allowance to Jewish chaplains. This occurred, as was explained, 'in consideration of fairness' and it was emphasized that no right to remuneration was thereby admitted. A second decree in 1916 designated a Jewish chaplain as being in a 'contractual relationship'.

Several of these Jewish chaplains have left us records of their thoughts, sermons and diaries, some in book(let) form, others as handwritten notes. Because time has dimmed and in some cases erased their memory, their written words are offered here, translated into English by myself, in the hope that their long-stilled voices and the messages that they brought may be heard once more in our own time.

Despite discrimination and anti-Semitism, German Jews felt secure in a much-loved Fatherland and a *Kultur* which they had uniquely made their own, and to which they were contributing greatly. So what would be more natural than for Jews to fight, and rabbis to serve as chaplains, when the Fatherland was threatened? The sermons and memoirs in this book are not mere dusty archival remnants. Principles and values do not change, neither does what is good and honourable in the German character. These rabbis represent a cross-section of the *Bildungbürgertum*, the educated (often highly educated) German middle class, and what they said and wrote is worthy of close study. National characteristics are easy to caricature and subtlety was not part of German foreign policy during the Wilhelmine era. Nevertheless, a great flowering of knowledge occurred during this period, no more so than with Germany's Jews represented by their clergy. Not only were these men learned in Jewish matters, but they were also steeped in the literature, philosophy and thought of their country of birth.

According to the Marburg neo-Kantian Hermann Cohen (whose closest disciple after his death was Leo Baeck), Jewishness complemented Protestantism, producing a symbiotic whole.[21] Many Jews vigorously supported this point of view, which was unfortunately not generally shared in the Christian population. Because Germany had become unified only in 1871, it might be said that Jews were the Germans with a true *Volksgefühl* (national identity) whose primary loyalty was to their newly unified nation, and not their individual German state. Despite discrimination which never entirely disappeared, especially in the army, patriotism was at the root of German-Jewish identity.

NOTES

1. Cited by Theodor Zlocisti, 'Die Einsegnung der jüdischen Soldaten in Breslau, 1813', *Im Deutschen Reich*, September 1900, pp.443–5. Also cited in: E. Lindner, *Patriotismus deutscher Juden von der napoleonischen Ära bis zum Kaiserreich* (Frankfurt am Main: Peter Lang GmbH, 1997), p.61. This injunction is based upon a text published in 1842, based on the memory of a witness to the occasion.
2. The second Treaty of Tilsit signed on 9 July 1807 ceded about one-half of Prussia's pre-war territories to Napoleon.
3. M. Stern, *Aus der Zeit der deutschen Befreiungskriegen 1813–1815* (Berlin: Verlag Hausfreund, 1918). This sermon appears as a separate booklet at the end of the pamphlet: M.S. Weyl, *Hoffnung und Vertrauen. Predigt wegen des Ausmarsches des väterlandischen Heeres gehalten in Gegenwart mehrerer freiwilligen Jäger jüdischen Glaubens in der große Synagoge zu Berlin* (A.W. Schade), pp.1–16.
4. Stern, *Aus der Zeit der deutschen Befreiungskriegen*. This sermon appears as a second separate booklet: *Rede und Gebet zur Einweihungsfeier der Synagoge und zur Einsegnung der freiwilligen Krieger der israelitischen Gemeinde zu Königsberg* (Haberlandschen Buchdruckerey, 1815), pp.1–13. See also Lindner, *Patriotismus deutscher Juden*, pp.68–9.
5. A. Vogt, *Religion im Militär. Seelsorge zwischen Kriegsverherrlichung und Humanität. Eine militärgeschichtliche Studie* (Frankfurt am Main: Peter Lang, 1984), p.110.
6. M. Berger, *Eisernes Kreuz und Davidstern: Die Geschichte jüdischer Soldaten in deutschen Armeen* (Berlin: Trafoverlag, 2006), pp.32–106; Vogt, *Religion Im Militär*, pp.110–13.

7. A. Elon, *The Pity of it All: A Portrait of the German-Jewish Epoch 1743–1933* (New York: Henry Holt and Company, 2002), pp.203–5.
8. Edwin Freiherr von Manteuffel (1809–1885), a German Field Marshall noted for his successes in all three Bismarckian wars.
9. Formula from 1 Kings 18: 39 repeated seven times at the end of Yom Kippur concluding service.
10. L. Hirschberg, 'Ein Yom-Kippur im Kriegslager', *Allgemeine Zeitung des Judentums* (18 October 1870).
11. In some versions, the verses are numbers 16–17.
12. Genesis 28: 20–1, with some changes and additions.
13. Alsace and Lorraine.
14. Leviticus 16: 1–34.
15. Leviticus 10: 1–6.
16. I. Blumenstein, 'Der jüdischer Gottesdienst im Felde', *Allgemeine Zeitung des Judentums* (1 November 1870).
17. Berger, *Eisernes Kreuz und Judenstern*, p.142; see also Vogt, *Religion im Militär*, p.113.
18. I. Schorsch, *Jewish Reactions to German Anti-Semitism, 1870–1914* (New York: Columbia University Press, 1972), p.27.
19. Vogt, *Religion Im Militär*, p.586.
20. U. Sieg, 'Empathie und Pflichterfüllung. Leo Baeck als Feldrabbiner im ersten Weltkrieg', in *Leo Baeck 1873–1956. Aus dem Stamme von Rabbinern, 2001*, ed. G. Heuberger and F. Backhaus (Frankfurt am Main: Jüdischer Verlag im Suhrkampf Verlag, 2001), pp.44–5.
21. P. Mendes-Flohr, 'Neue Richtingungen im jüdischen Denken', in *Deutsch-jüdische Geschichte in der Neuzeit. Band III. Umstrittene Integration 1871–1918*, ed. S.M. Lowenstein, P. Mendes-Flohr, P. Pulzer and M. Richarz (Munich: C.H. Beck, 2000), pp.350–5.

CHAPTER TWO

Georg Salzberger: Compassion and Courage

Georg Salzberger (see Plates 1, 3 and 4) volunteered for duty as Jewish chaplain immediately after war was declared and served from September 1914 to the autumn of 1918. An English translation of his published memoirs of his early duty, including service at Verdun in 1916,[1] follows:

Jewish Holidays in the Field[2]

Proverbial Jewish holiday weather appeared after some hesitation during the first New Year of the war. For too long our brave soldiers have had to suffer not only from the enemy, but under a cold rain which caused more suffering than enemy fire. From early morning I sat in the car with an officer of Supreme Command who was coincidentally travelling the same way as me. We crossed Verdun, travelled through Mars-La-Tour of proud memory[3] and, with difficulty winding through ever thicker columns of ammunition and baggage carts, made a stop that afternoon in front of the General Command of the — Corps in W.

The sun sank blood-red in the west. That morning battle was still raging in this not unpleasant village at the foot of the Lorraine mountains. In the churchyard, which looked out over the vineyards of the broad valley, one clearly still saw traces of bitter French resistance. And now our soldiers had occupied the dirty houses and clean French country roads, as if it had happened weeks ago. The Division Commander received me with welcome friendliness. He was pleased that Jewish comrades also had their chaplain: they had repeatedly asked about me. It would not be easy to bring my community together, because tactics of the time worked against the gathering of large troop formations out in the open. Additionally, only soldiers who were free of duty could take part in religious services. I remarked that I was there in the first place for spiritual assistance, and wished to comfort and console the wounded; also that in this regard loving-kindness neither made nor could make distinction between Christians and Jews. And in any case the usual religious separations fell away, leaving only the soldier who was doing his duty against the enemy. With visible joy, His Excellency agreed with me.

I had to hold the second day festival service for myself alone. How the trusted age-old prayers of my childhood again became new and alive! *Avinu Malkeinu*: 'Our Father Our King, frustrate the design of our enemies!' 'Our Father Our King, cause salvation speedily to spring forth for us.' *Zochreinu*: 'Remember us for life, Oh King, who delights in life.' How I was struck by the truth of the poetic words: 'Man is like a flower that fades and a shadow that passes, like a fleeting dream.'[4] No, life cannot be the highest good. The heroic figure of our original ancestor appeared before me from the Torah scroll which rolled open before me, and I heard God's word to him: 'Take now your son, your only son, whom you love and offer him as a sacrifice before me.'[5] I saw him go, wordless and without hesitation, to offer up the dearest thing that God's mercy had given him and that was now demanded back. And I saw a thousand fathers following in his footsteps. Only mothers cannot hide their tears; it is a piece of themselves from whom they must part for ever and they feel as if their hearts would bleed to death. 'Rachel weeping for her children and refusing to be comforted, because they are no more.' But look! A glimmer of heavenly light breaks through her tears. 'Restrain your voice from weeping and your eyes from tears, for your work will be rewarded', declares the Lord. 'They will return from the land of the enemy, so there is hope for your descendants, and your children will return to their own land.'[6] – return to a praiseworthy bravely fought peace – that is the beginning and the end of our New Year's prayers. My service was quiet but it seemed as if countless others prayed with me.

Only when the festival had concluded could I assemble a few Jewish comrades around me there. I addressed a few heartfelt words at the conclusion of the prayers to my devout audience. A New Year – it had not begun for us because in the field one loses the concept of time. But it had been a 'Day of Remembrance' for us, of our parents' house, of our synagogue, in which they prayed fervently for us, a warning of the 'Day of Judgment' that God will cause to pass over nations and kingdoms. And if the shofar sound, Israel's ancient war signal, was not heard on 'The day of the Blowing of the Shofar',[7] instead cannons roared across the mountains and one could hear windows shattering. A strange contrast! Here peace, and outside war. But I was happy to be able to give my co-religionists this hour of inner peace on enemy territory. From the wall a picture of Christ looked gently down at us.

Had he not been a pious rabbi, and had he not preached peace in the middle of a world bristling with weapons?

During the Ten Days of Penitence both my community and with it my 'synagogue', which one had to enter by slipping through a stable, grew. The roomy quarters of two Jewish reserve officers witnessed a very strange sight on *Kol Nidrei* eve. On the table in front of the bed, between two burning candles, stood a German rabbi, grey field hat on his head and *talit* around his long field uniform. This rabbi intoned, quite badly though with great fervour, the tune that has carried the soul of our people, our entire history, with its deep melancholy and complete confidence, through from sadness to loud and joyful confidence. I cannot think of any more effective transition from this beautiful melody to the evening service proper, than when *Venislach* is read: a prayer for forgiveness of the entire Jewish people, including the stranger who dwells in their midst, because the entire people sins in error. These words speak of deep understanding of the human soul: it is as if the breath of the Lord's Atonement breathes onto us from them. Following this, I read all the important prayers: the *Tefilah*, the Confession of Sins,[8] *Avinu Malkenu*, but I was sorry that with them I couldn't bring my brothers nearer to God because most understood no Hebrew. An *ex tempore* German translation of the words lacks the proper meaning and the field prayer books are far from satisfactory for the High Holy Days.

Division Command had announced a service for the Jewish soldiers in the morning. As a result I found twenty-five congregants, some of them physicians, some from neighbouring towns – a tiny number compared to the large number of Jews in the field, to whom no chaplain can come and who must, even if free of duty on this most holy day, do without any services at all.

We Jews have no group singing or chorales. We certainly do not lack a sense of music, but everyone sings the synagogue tunes as he wishes – perhaps a result of Jewish individualism. Therefore, when there is no trained choir, and the congregants cannot follow the service themselves, they are dependent on the Prayer Leader (myself). All the same, I tried to make them acquainted with the essential meaning and nature of the Yom Kippur morning and main services. I also read and translated from the Torah scrolls, which were kept in a closet probably used for other purposes. The Torah portion dealt with the nobility and holiness of this Sabbath of Sabbaths.[9] And then I read the powerful passage from the Prophets about the worth of a true fast.[10]

During *Mussaph* I also read the moving *Avodah* service: the three fold sanctification of the King of Kings must have looked strange enough, with us all praying in the presence of noisy enemy weapons.

Yom Kippur! With what sublime feelings I awaited this day in normal times! It always seemed to me that I put ordinary people aside along with my everyday clothes and, fervently seeking peace, stood before my God. And now? And here? Can we be confident of God's love, we who are filled with hate? Can we beg for mercy when we practice none, for atonement when entire nations cut each other in two in bloody battle? Our religion proclaims a kingdom of eternal peace through this day of peace with God, a time when all people will be bound together, to do God's will wholeheartedly. Is our dream not a delusion? How otherwise could a world war break out in our century of high civilization, a war so powerful and terrible the like of which has never been seen before in the history of mankind? But we are not as unreconciled as we appear. We see our nation's political parties reconciled, when a short time ago they argued bitterly. Class and creed are also reconciled. All have merged into one confederation for our Fatherland.[11] We have finally thoroughly learnt to put something great, the common good, above all that is particular and separates us, sacrificing property and blood for the same ideal. Why should the time not come when nations who pray to the same Father recognize each other as brothers, children of the same Father? We shall not see it ourselves but we shall fight brave and pure, so that our grandchildren can experience it – the Great Day of Atonement for all Mankind.

That was more or less my train of thought, which I shared with my friends praying with me. And at the end we begged God's mercy for our beloved Kaiser, our brave army, and our dear Fatherland. We parted with warm handshakes with the firm purpose of arranging another service at another time. For *Ne'ilah* we were once more only a few; the remainder had to perform their duties or couldn't travel in a second time from the surrounding areas. But nobody could stop me crying out my profession of God's unity[12] with all my heart and soul into the starry night.

Arrangement of Sabbath services is usually not allowed here. Religious service and military service are not easily united. I therefore used Sunday, the Festival of Succot, to teach my congregation the weekly Torah reading – the swan song of (Moses) our great prophet[13] and how he prepared himself for his last voyage – and the meaning of

Succot, the festival of tabernacles. Never had it touched me so deeply as a festival of harvest of wine and fruit. Boundless fields with ripe grapes that no-one harvests, trees heavy with plums and pears that have to rot on the boughs across the entire valley. But the harvest symbol, the celebratory garland, is lacking. The path to the churchyard is sown with shining horse chestnuts, out of which we made chains for the succah when we were children. There is no succah here but many of us live happily in the shot-up houses. Medical units build huts in the forest and decorate them with branches; not as a sign of trust in the protection of God, who was with our fathers in the wilderness, but as protection against cold autumn nights. When after the service ended I looked out of the window, a column of wagons carrying green branches went past. The wagoners wanted out of charitable human love to bring help to the battlefield victims although they themselves were in danger from the deadly fire in the process. I looked at them for a long time and the words of the prayer struck me: 'Oh God, spread out over us the tabernacle of Your peace.'

Spiritual Care in the Field[14]

My staff officers didn't know at first how to behave with me: A rabbi, who certainly came from another world or, at the very least, another century. But literary, philosophical and religious discussions opened their eyes to the fact that a rabbi is also a human being, standing with both feet on this well-grounded earth in the middle of the present, part of the current powerful upheavals. Since that time our relations have become friendly.

For services I have been given a large prayer-room. Previously it may have been a stable. But why, at a time when churches become horse stalls, should God's house not be made out of a stable? Both of my Christian colleagues conduct their devotions there, because the church is filled up with wounded. During good weather they mostly hold their services in God's open air and the chorales, sung by a thousand male voices accompanied by the regimental band, echo solemnly across the wide plain. Before I became chaplain Jewish soldiers took part in church services and listened attentively to the pastor's sermons – a sign of how greatly they need religion. Representatives of the other two faiths treated their Jewish attendees with the greatest consideration. There could be no talk of polemics where there was only one war, against the enemies of the Fatherland. But especially because of that, the pastors greeted the arrival of a Jewish chaplain with no less joy than did the soldiers themselves.

It does not need to be said that the same unanimity which exists amongst shepherds also exists amongst their flock. If here and there a thoughtless word may fall from lips of Christian officers or men, no harm is meant, it is just a reminiscence of bygone days. In war, as expected from the start, a spirit of comradeship without differences reigns. Every man depends on his comrade and must, for good or ill, get on with him. Living in such close proximity allows people to get to know one another very well: each man is who he is, and we Jews can only rejoice in this. When one gets to know us, one will also understand and respect us. The old observation that *Judenhaß* [hatred of Jews], insofar as it isn't a family tradition, grows out of personal experience and can also be uprooted by personal experience, is confirmed here daily.

I have already met more than 120 Jewish comrades: one-tenth have already been promoted after battle, and a further tenth have been awarded the Iron Cross. I have found that, where strict honesty, conscientiousness and intelligence are required, Jews are treated preferentially. I know from officers' statements that many Jewish soldiers volunteer for dangerous patrols and show courage and no fear of death, thereby giving the lie to the old fables of Jewish cowardice. What is most gratifying of all is that not a single soldier makes a secret of his faith. The very opposite: each one knows how to gently deflect anti-Semitic behaviour. With proud ambition to show our Jewish love of Fatherland, even though this love is not always requited, God be thanked that we can bury the past: military promotion is no more opposed by insoluble religious limitations. I must admit to have been heartsore in the past at the sight of so many educated and militarily excellent co-religionists who have been able to be promoted only to non-commissioned officer, or at best vice-sergeant major. This will now remove the quiet resignation that was previously behind all the efforts of our warriors, and will give fulfilment of their duty a boost of unclouded joy.

Whatever the future holds, the generation which has experienced this war cannot fall back into old anti-Jewish prejudices. And if the living should forget the unanimity of faithfulness to Fatherland, then the dead will speak for them. One of the striking events that I experienced in this war was when a Protestant, a Catholic and a Jew all fell together in the same artillery attack. On that occasion, the Protestant pastor was entrusted with the graveside prayer by the Division Chief, but I didn't want to be deprived of showing my last respects to my fellow-Jew. I harnessed my little landau and my young assistant drove my colleague and myself over the wooded hills to D. below. It was already getting dark when we arrived at the military cemetery behind the town. Brigadier-General von W. received us with his staff, and around the shovelled-out graves the fallen men's comrades stood close together in a wide arch. Solemn stillness reigned when the pastor, beginning with a Psalm, spoke of the fate of heroes that had been fulfilled here once again. After that I directed a few words to those assembled, in which I pointed out the coincidence that had united all three faiths here in death that we should take as a symbol and as a warning in life: We all acknowledge one Father and one Fatherland. All heads were bared when the pastor recited the Lord's Prayer. The biers sank into the grave and chaplains, officers and men drew near to each throw three handfuls of earth on the brave departed ones. It was a deeply moving funeral in the dusk of evening that I will never forget. We drove back in silence, past holes without number which enemy shells had dug into the mountain road. The sickle new moon stood silvery clear in the heavens and the eternal stars shone in the pure air. If only they could speak! What have they not seen here below of pain and misery, but also of beauty and happiness, crazed delusion and sacrificial enthusiasm, during the past millennia!

Good Germans and good Jews: this was always our watchword, and it has become a battle cry in the field. Now we experience more strongly than ever before how inseparably both are linked in us. Without being a chauvinist, one can say that Judaism and Germanness must look for and find each other, because their beings are related. Whatever one can say about French spiritual flexibility and English business sense, the decisive factor is that the Jewish heart corresponds with German nature. Because in moral sensitivity and thinking and the resultant unswerving faith and readiness to sacrifice for an ideal, only a people of real *Kultur* [culture] can stand firm against an entire world of enemies and keep intact the surge of national zeal.

This war shows that Germans and Jews are both unloved if not hated by others because they are misunderstood. Germans have been the people of poets and thinkers, as Jews have been the people of prophets and psalmists. But between then and now a chasm yawns; people say that both we Jews and we Germans have become rich and striven for more and more possessions, becoming in the process spiritually and morally degenerate. Our diligence is famous, as is our energy and thoroughness; but we cannot be forgiven for the fact that we have been successful – we Germans and we Jews. We are cursed as barbarians and mocked as unworldly, incorrigible dreamers. Perhaps our time will learn from this partially malicious and mendacious, partially foolish and short-sighted distortion of the truth by Germany's enemies, and also allow us Jews to experience justice.

It is an extremely rewarding task for a chaplain to bring the religious content of our Torah in its eternal truth to those who hear it. The essential portions of *Shacharit*, so well compiled in the field prayer book, contribute to this. They tell of the Lord of the Universe, who created the human soul pure; they admonish us to keep our soul pure through truthfulness and permeate it with devoted love of God; they beg for true possessions of life, the last and highest of which is peace. Then follows taking out of the Torah scroll and reading aloud of the weekly portion, to which three to five comrades are called up. Following the reading I give a short talk in which I remind everyone of faithfulness to the king and also to the King of Kings, and I end with a prayer for the victory of our good German cause. After returning the Torah to the Ark, I read aloud Psalm 145, *Kaddish* for those who mourn, and end with *Aleinu*. On occasions I add a Psalm in German, and also translate some of our Hebrew prayers for the many who do not know our Holy language. The entire service doesn't last more than an hour.

Because very few soldiers can be excused duty on the Sabbath, I have felt compelled to reschedule religious services for Sunday; but I always leave a second service during the week for those who have been under fire that Sunday. In the beginning the number of participants was small because the divisional order was not sufficiently timely or widely announced. But lately I count thirty, forty, even fifty people who come to pray. They come from nearby or from surrounding areas on foot or horse, often an hour's journey from here. They are physicians and soldiers, from private to deputy officer, all branches of the armed forces, academics, merchants and craftsmen, orthodox, liberal and 'freethinkers', Zionists and 'assimilationists' from all corners of our Fatherland. We usually meet centrally, but I have repeatedly travelled to far-away villages. I remember clearly the journey on a foggy and dark October morning and the tiny community assembled on the mountain slope who prayed with me, while dew moistened the leaves of our prayer books.

Contact with Jewish comrades naturally does not limit itself to religious services. I meet daily with many who are quartered at the same place as I was just to chat. Others look me up in my little room. We sit together comfortably and I listen to tales of the deprivation-filled life in the trenches or to the account of a bitter fight in the forest. Alternately we sketch out battle plans or tell dream-like stories of home and peace! Quickly the entire and often oppressive burdens of army life are forgotten in the joy of being able to talk, man to man, once more. When a volunteer enters, our hearts are gladdened by his rejoicing on seeing a long-missed bed, a stove, his moving thanks for a few cigars, a glass of cognac. Spiritual assistance in such instances becomes physical care. These youths, many of whom were very spoiled at home in peacetime, surely never ate or drank with such appetite. And this is a healthy school for our sons, because they learn how much a man can bear and do without, when he has no alternative.

I am loathe to take leave of the volunteers. We say '*Auf Wiedersehen*' and I am secretly afraid that one or the other might not return. But they stride away with firm tread, looking around with pure eyes. How quickly have they ceased to be ghetto slaves and gain new youth as Maccabees! I look forward to Chanukah as I did in the days of my childhood with inner excitement. It will not bring peace, but perhaps daily a better promise of victory.

In the Field Hospital[15]

One evening my comrades took me to observe a night battle. The strange thing about modern battles is that during the day they can only be heard while spectators see, far and wide, no people and no shooting. Only night, which had previously veiled everything, exposes its terrible secret to the eye. We walked in the dark down the country road: every light could become a dangerous traitor. Only lanterns of the pairs of guards whom we had to pass lit up our faces briefly. The battle could be just a few thousand metres away; hardly had we reached a hill on the road when we heard clearly firing and exploding of shells, alternating with rapid fire of infantry and clattering of machine-gun fire. Now an artillery salvo roared over the field; did it come from the German or the French side? A little further and we saw flashes of light, now here now there, and straight after followed a roaring bang. Suddenly all became still and a great sparkling star rose vertically from the plain, stopped for a few seconds, and extinguished itself. But then there were explosions from all sides, as if hell itself had opened up. Burning towns flamed like giant torches on the horizon, and the ghostly light of a floodlight darted over the night sky.

We spoke little on the way back. Each had his own thoughts, probably the same in all of us. How gruesome must close quarter fighting be at night, when apart from the fighting itself one is prey to a hundred unseen fears! Someone trips over a tree-root and falls into a hole, someone falls over the body of a comrade, a third gets entangled in barbed wire and cannot get loose despite superhuman efforts. And all the while bullets whiz by the entangled soldier and fall very near him, and entire rows of attacking soldiers are mowed down by machine gun fire. A shell explodes and in the surrounding area blows human bodies to bloody shreds. One man who seemed invulnerable to fire is shot in the heart and sinks silently to the ground. One amongst many, but a world of strength and lust for life and its possibilities is extinguished with him, just like a happily burning candle that one blows out – pah! But happy is he who enters Valhalla without pain or bitterness. Others who have been badly wounded remain alive lying, perhaps between two lines of fire, perhaps in the midst of their own soldiers, who heedlessly storm by him, over him – such suffering cannot be described in words. Will fighting last much longer? Will I be found while there is still time? Oh, how my wounds burn! Will I be captured by the enemy? This night without end! Would that it were already morning. Comrade, pick me up and take me with you! Comrade, comrade, water, just a sip of water. I'm dying of thirst – Mother!

Comrade! Comrade! I will never forget the sound of this word as long as I live. I didn't hear it on the battlefield, but I heard it untold times in field hospitals. God be thanked that only a few remain lying helpless outside, suffering the most painful death. Many drag themselves, alone or supported by comrades, behind the Front and are bandaged and sent back to the rear with whatever transport is available. Many are picked up by medical orderlies and carried away from the line of fire. For while the bullets are still raining down, a widely spread and great organization becomes active – those who remove death's sacrifice from him, ease war's wounds, and where possible heal them.

In every large battle the Medical Corps marches out. About 800 metres behind the line is a troop first-aid unit, and another 1,000 metres back the main first-aid centre is situated. Ambulances with wounded, marked with a white flag and the Geneva Red Cross, stop between the two stations. The assistant medical orderlies, three to a stretcher, lay it down where the ambulance has stopped. As soon as the company leader gives the command, they swarm out (often exposing themselves to terrible danger) and bring wounded out of the line of fire to the troop first-aid unit, where physicians apply the first dressing. The wounded are then laid upon stretchers that have been readied and lifted up into transports which then travel to the nearest field hospital. The main unit serves as relief for the troop unit. In the field hospital dressings are examined and renewed. Urgent cases remain there for daily treatment; some are, when necessary, taken to the operating room. Those fit for further transportation are sent to a larger hospital which lies outside the operational area, or else further away to a garrison hospital or a hospital near home. The further from the Front, the more complete the medical facilities. The sick, especially those suffering from infectious diseases, who require special care for a longer time, are mostly treated in the larger military hospitals. The spread of typhus/typhoid[16] and diarrhoea is, unfortunately, a feature of war. More depressing than visiting the wounded is a walk through the infectious disease hospital: seemingly endless barrack room corridors in which lie emaciated, febrile figures.[17]

The positional warfare which has existed for the past four months has luckily led to a diminution of new wounded almost everywhere. Both main dressing stations have not been in use recently. I have visited almost daily the field hospitals of the division to which I until recently belonged. The church, pastor's home, school and also apartment buildings have been turned into hospitals. In the beginning the wounded lay only on straw mats or long wooden cribs; many mats were later replaced by iron bedsteads and bolsters, pillows, linen and sheets.

The first visit I made to the rather large 'church' in S., which had been made into a field hospital, led me into a never-imagined world of pain. To the right and the left of the nave, where previously pews had stood, lay, the one next to the other in rows of three and four, unfortunate victims of this bloody war. On pulpit steps and around the altar, where a few weeks before the pastor had sounded words of brotherly love, brothers united by wounds inflicted by the enemy's hatred were writhing, convulsed by pain. A nauseous stench of blood, sweat and carbolic acid numbs me. I clench my teeth and walk through the rows. A man with wide-open eyes and a ghostly look raises his gaunt hand and whispers: 'Quickly, quickly!' I want to calm him but the words die in my throat. It suddenly seems to me as if they are all standing up from their sick-beds and pushing their way out: and that outside they are joined by others and yet others – an endless column of gasping, hobbling cripples pouring over the streets, squares, towns and nations. What do they want? They raise their arms, their stumps and call the initiators of this homicide to account. See, this is your work! I think that I see and hear them myself, and flee terrified from that place of horror.

But I return the next morning with field postcards in my pocket. First I think to check whether there are any Jews amongst the wounded. But the stereotypical question of each man's religion seems to me to be so painful for the poor souls and so unsuitable for the acts of lovingkindness which I want to initiate, that I decide to talk to each of them. In my pursuit I forget my terrible surroundings and overcome the horror. 'Who wants to write home?' All want to. I hand out postcards. I let each man who can sit up in bed and hold a pencil write himself – an unfamiliar hand might frighten next of kin. For others I write, let them dictate, or when speaking is too exhausting, I myself write a short note to the given address. How many tears I have seen shed when a soldier wrote to his father, mother, fiancée or the wife that he had brought home shortly before the war: 'I must unfortunately tell you …' If the man has left it to me to give unhappy news, he usually asks me to play down its seriousness: 'Please don't make it sound too bad, Rabbi'. But I don't need to be asked. I merely faithfully relate the facts, of when, where and how the soldier was wounded – Nothing is more unsettling to those far away than uncertainty; but I clothe facts in their mildest form and always leave room for hope. How moving is the sensitivity of brave men who in their pain still enquire concernedly whether their loved ones at home are in good health, or don't forget to congratulate on birthdays or wedding days! And then there are other letters: someone wants to dictate to me: 'This is my last letter to you.' I protest energetically. Another tells me that, when he was wounded, he had asked a comrade to tell his wife that he was dead. I hasten to revive the poor woman's hope. How much pain and joy can be contained in a piece of paper! Tragicomedy also occurs. One letter begins with the words: 'Dear wife, I must tell you that on … I fell in battle.' 'But comrade', I interrupt him, 'you are still alive'. It takes a while before he understands the mistake. As thanks he offers me ten pfennig which he looks for with difficulty in his bloody uniform.

I am always pleased to forward money to next of kin. It is almost impossible even for men immediately behind the front to send money home, and for the wounded this is a further unnecessary burden. During the past months, the mail has sent millions of marks from the field to the *Reich*, thereby strengthening its finances anew. But for my patients I bring the small gifts which they cannot buy: chocolate, peppermint, biscuits, candy, fruit and, especially desired, newspapers and cigarettes. Thanks to tireless kindness from good friends back home I have been able to store up a warehouse of such gifts in my little room. To many I daren't give anything to eat or drink, however insistently they beg for water, because they have been shot in the abdomen. I can only, often without believing in their recovery, console them that I will give them these things at a later time. One knows how receptive a helpless man is to weakly-based encouragement, and also what his spiritual condition means for the course of his healing. In the same way as a physician sometimes tends to spiritual needs, so the chaplain really becomes a physician as well.

Do material and spiritual things not merge into one? I experienced this most acutely one evening when, after an attack by our troops, we had nearly 1,000 wounded in the town. All rooms were filled to overflowing. I climb the hazardous steps to a garret, where dozens of men lie on straw, completely exhausted. Horror waits to seize me, but I know the antidote: keep myself busy, to help them. Words alone are of no assistance. The poor souls crave a refreshing drink. I quickly bring soup, tea and bread. We ladle soup and tea from our bottomless buckets into the greedily emptied cups. How good it tastes! Do I have any cigarettes? Luckily I have a few; and I can't bring myself to refuse the wounded these comforts in their need. I know that a stray spark could set fire to the straw and so endanger the lives of everyone in the poor little room much more than danger in the field from which they have escaped. What can I say but: 'Be careful, comrades! Good night!'

With time I get close to some individual men, and gain the inner freedom and serenity which transfers itself to the patient and can only then bring him spiritual relief. Most not only live with physical pain, but also longing for the love of his loved ones. It is my job to give them a ray of sunshine, some of the peace of home. I read a young man's postcard to be forwarded: 'Dear Martha! As you write, I should report for duty at home but it isn't so easy. Because when I am healthy again I will take up rifle in hand and return to fight the enemy. I do not think of returning home. You must remember that we have sworn to the Fatherland to conquer or to die. These are also my thoughts: to triumph or to die. Until we meet again, your Anton.' And on the side he wrote: 'We will be happy when we see each other again.' When asked to reply on their conscience and honour, most men would admit that they wish the war would end. When would they return home at last? That is the ever-recurring question. One thing can be said confidently: there is no bitterness in the hearts of these men who often seal their loyalty to the Fatherland with the greatest of all sacrifices. They are all permeated with the feeling that this war was necessary and that we must hold fast until we are victorious. No-one doubts that we will triumph. Not least because of this belief they have an astonishing power of perseverance. They might sometimes groan, but they are not sorry for themselves: some are even able to draw upon the good and trusty German sense of humour of our men in the field. One soldier who participated in exhausting marches at the beginning of the campaign, opines, pointing to his amputated leg: 'First they marched too much, now they don't march enough.'

By contrast, French patients complain and scream. Clearly they feel like prisoners and their officers may have caused them to be afraid of Germans, who 'shoot' all prisoners of war. To me, it seems that their lack of self-control may have other reasons: their more lively temperament, weaker nerves caused by inferior conditions in the French trenches, and the revolting enjoyment of absinthe which does nothing to increase resistance and stamina. It goes without saying that the French, together with all their exotic compatriots[18] in the field hospital, receive the same loving and careful attention and nursing care as all who have done their duty for their Fatherland. Even I, German barbarian that I am, do not pass by them without giving them their indispensable cigarettes and candy.

Whatever can be done to cheer up the wounded or deflect their worries is done. They are preferentially recommended for distinction with the Iron Cross and it is a solemn moment for all when an officer enters and with warm words of praise presents this best of all awards to the brave patients. One time, during a service, I heard the organ being played in the church. As gentle as angels of peace the sounds hovered in the room, uplifting the heart, and for a moment all troubles were cast off and disappeared. When the pastor began with the words of the Psalmist: 'I will lift up mine eyes unto the hills', moaning could still be heard here and there. But very soon it became still … 'He who watches over you neither slumbers nor sleeps.' All hands were folded and silence reigned everywhere. 'The Lord will keep you from all harm. He will watch over your going out and your coming in both now and forevermore ...'[19] A heartfelt 'Amen' was heard from the entire attentive congregation. A real religious faith, which only glowed weakly in some soldiers, is kindled into a fire in future hours, days and weeks of this life and death struggle, which plays out here silently. 'God has helped until now, he will help in the future.' 'God does not abandon His people.' I heard many say this. Many ask for the Eucharist and for the Last Rites at their hour of death.

When all carry the same burden, all religious and social barriers which were previously carefully built up and maintained fall away of their own accord. My glance falls upon a patient's card. He writes to his sister that every day a Protestant, Catholic and 'even' a Jewish chaplain visited, to help them pass the time. Yes, that is in fact quite important, to pass the time, which seems endless. Everyone wants to know how goes our war in France and Russia. There's been another victory! How their eyes shine. Many want (surely not for the first time) to tell stories of the battle in which they were wounded, how a man nearby was killed, how a friend was miraculously saved and how he himself sank to the ground wounded. How he will pay back the red breeches![20] Not all here have been wounded by the enemy's fire. One threw his hand-grenade too late, another shot himself accidentally with his own rifle, a third was wounded by a horse's hoof. (Anyone who has encountered horse and wagon colonnades in narrow roads is astonished that comparatively few accidents occur.) Each soldier wants to hear, talk, laugh, just not to think. This makes spiritual treatment of an educated man more difficult: he thinks and broods. If indeed a difference (apart from their characters) between the wounded is possible, it is the one that our sages described as the comparison between a man of education and an '*Am-ha'aretz*'.[21] When I meet a sixth-former, a student, a teacher – one recognizes them at once by their hands and the way they speak – we have an intuitive understanding from eye to eye and they shake my hand more firmly.

Of course we must also speak of the future – the young physician who has lost his right arm, the teacher whose limbs are paralyzed for life are not easily convinced that they have not lost all of their self-worth and that their lives merely require a new content. But the adaptability of youth, as well as splendid medical care, with all its possibilities, for all who have been crippled by the war, are no empty consolation. I know that, even though they shake their heads tiredly now when one speaks to them of the future, they will resign themselves ever more patiently to their fate.

Patience is the medicine which more than anything else assists in the natural healing process. The healthy person only learns to appreciate and practice this properly here, in the field hospital. Some severely wounded who at first glance one gives up for lost, even those with lung and head injuries, sometimes gradually heal; the patients leave their bed and sometimes one meets them, walking with difficulty step by step, but laughing happily. There is nothing that gladdens the heart more than seeing such a patient getting better. And most do get better, thanks to excellent medical care. Amputations are performed as seldom as possible, and bullets removed only in the most or least serious cases. Shrapnel wounds are sometimes felt under the wounded man's skin and then it is not long until he holds the metal in his hands. He will preserve these to show his children when he sits with them on a winter's evening in a warm sitting-room: by the familiar light of the table lamp he will tell his children again and again about the Great War.

Much worse is the devastation wrought on the human body by dumdum bullets and satanic shrapnel splinters. In these cases hope of saving the wounded is too often disappointed. One evening a young soldier was brought in, completely covered with splinter wounds. I was astonished to see him laughing and praised his bravery. His neighbour opined: 'Wait, comrade, tomorrow you will feel the pain.' 'I will stifle it', replied the brave young man. The next morning he was my first visit. The sheets were pulled over his head. 'Is he sleeping?' I asked his neighbour. 'Yes, the eternal sleep', was his answer. He had died during the night. Then there was a volunteer who had been shot in the lung and breathed with difficulty. He had only a few more hours left to live, the doctor told me. He grasped my hand; I had to sit next to his bed and read from the newspaper which I had brought along. I read with subdued monotonous voice, so that he could fall asleep. When I thought him to be asleep, I paused. 'Very interesting', he said, without having understood a word. 'Read further!' And I read further. Eventually he fell asleep and did not awake again. A stocky Bavarian lay in bed for weeks. Both his legs had been amputated but it looked as if by this his life had been saved. Suddenly his condition worsened and the onset of tetanus made us fear the worst. As I saw him lying there, bloody froth coming out of his mouth and with eyes staring up at the ceiling, I didn't want to address him and thereby increase his suffering. 'Don't you know me any more, Herr *Pfarrer?*' he gasped. 'But of course I know you, dear comrade.' He gave me to understand that I should write to his wife. I had repeatedly written to her, telling her of his progressive improvement. But what should I say now? He dictated: 'Dear wife, I am doing well', but could go no further. Naturally I wrote differently, to prepare the poor woman for the painful news. The day after, when the brave soldier was buried, I received a letter from his wife; she had a foreboding of bad news and wanted to see her husband one last time. I attempted to comfort her, as one always tries to in such cases, by telling her that her husband had died a hero and that she will want to bear this act of God no less bravely than he had.

It is somewhat of a comfort that those who die in the field hospital are usually spared their death agony, because of the numerous morphine injections that they receive to dull their pain. By the dozen the dead are buried in the churchyard, some in their uniforms, others wrapped in white linen. Led by an officer, a column of soldiers gives their dead comrades the final escort. After a short speech by a chaplain, the burial mound is stacked up while the soldiers pray. Most times small pine trees and wreaths are used as decoration and a wooden cross, on which at least the number of the dead man is inscribed, is always erected. But this war drags even the dead out of their repose. The shells that come hissing from hidden artillery jaws on the other side of the mountain churn up even the graves. Shells are only meant for opponents who are fighting but in reality do not ask about white flags, church or school. Many times they explode in the ground near our field hospital, driving the helpless wounded to tears. One time the entire field hospital had to be relocated to a more protected town in the neighbourhood. Hardly had the school building been cleared when a 20 centimetre shell destroyed all the window-panes. There is no such thing as safety in the field in this war. Death lurks everywhere. Enemy planes that, high up and hardly audible, hover over us, can blow us to unrecognizable pieces with one bomb; with one of their sharp steel darts they can pierce through us like a piece of wood. In the long run, looking death in the eye calms one. One learns to appreciate how powerless is man against fate, how frail is life and how negligible the existence of one human being. But at the same time one learns to understand that only faithful discharge of duty to one's community gives worth and permanence to our apportioned days and hours on this earth. In the service of a *Volksgemeinschaft* [people's community][22] like our German one, the consciousness of being able to work as hard as we can during this great time lifts us above all suffering.

I have during the course of three months seen thousands of wounded, from all districts of our Fatherland. They show in their patience a heroism no less great than that on the battlefield itself: their love of Fatherland, trust in the victory of German arms and faith in a just God is even more genuine when under the pressure of human suffering the frenzy dies down and their innermost soul is exposed. How can I convey the efforts of the doctors and their assistants to alleviate the suffering of these patient, promising young men, their compatriots, the nation and army? This is a glorious chapter of German science just as is our oft-scorned military spirit, and we Jews can be proud to be able to show that we belong in the legions who accomplish deeds of compassion, from the lowly medical orderly to the senior surgeon. We Jews represent a disproportionately high number of those who serve in the Medical Corps. The confidence that I could provide a drop of balsam in the wounds of at least some of the wounded, even just with a word, reconciles me to all the horror that I have seen.

A few men are always among the unlucky ones, to whom not even this comfort can be given. Their spirit is deranged. They speak feverishly of the battle and scream in terror. Then they become quiet and whisper tenderly 'mother'. The Hebrew for God's mercy [*Rachamim*] is taken from the word for womb [*Rechem*]. Hate cannot triumph in the end, because we were all born of a mother.

In Enemy Territory[23]

What I first heard about the modern Gallic people was in bitter earnest. It was the time when the Dreyfus affair[24] made not only France, but the entire civilized world, hold its breath. The wild hatred of Jews which this battle unleashed did not win me over to the French. But nevertheless, when one day our language teacher asked us which pupils would like to correspond with a French boy of the same age, I reported immediately and obtained the address of my unknown French partner. I wrote him letters in French, and he letters to me in German. The effort at rapprochement between German and French was in full swing when in one of my letters I came to speak to M. Alphonse about the topic of religion: I told him that I was a Jew. The reply arrived in French and included only a few lines, written in the greatest passion: '*A bas Dreyfus! A bas les Juifs! Ils sont tous traîtres à la patrie!*' [Down with Dreyfus! Down with the Jews! They are all traitors to our Fatherland!] And then followed the advice that, if I didn't wish to be damned to hell, I should become a Catholic.

I didn't follow that advice, but thought about all this for a long time afterward. What kind of nation could they be, in which even the youth were so poisoned by religious and political fanaticism, that even their (to us) famed politeness is disregarded? Not to speak of ideals of liberty, equality, fraternity?

It is to be hoped that the population of France, who have been living for weeks and months together with German soldiers, judge '*les boches*' more fairly than the French masses, incited by their government and newspaper mouthpieces. Clearly entire towns of this beautiful, blooming land have been reduced to ashes by German as well as French fire, but they are proportionally not many. In the other towns and in occupied towns large and small, inhabitants are treated harshly. They obviously carry the burden of billeting the troops, and must put up with having to collect foodstuffs and other things necessary to our war effort. But rapidly organized strict order ensures that for every material service the citizens receive a stamped voucher to be redeemed at the end of the war, or alternatively settled by the War Distribution Department. The population has, building upon their good experiences in 1870, rapidly accepted this form of payment. Families, understandably consisting only of women, children and old men, can, as much as they are in the position to, obtain what they require for nourishment from the military canteen; otherwise, they are fed by the German authorities. In many places, such as in the towns and cities, some can continue to keep their stores open. The traffic between the inhabitants and their uninvited guests is managed in a friendly, even cordial manner.[25]

One can now travel from Sedan, along the river Maas, in comfortable Belgian corridor coaches not only to Z— but also a significant distance further southwards. One can easily see what the admirable extension of the enemy's railways means for the transport of our wounded, and of troops and equipment to the Front, even if the great victories in the East were not proof of this. A French rail connection between Metz and Verdun already existed but had been destroyed. But time passes and it will be rebuilt.

Z— is a friendly little town that outwardly has hardly been affected by the war. Only the sturdy stone bridge over the Maas which one passes on the way from the station has, like so many other surrounding bridges, been blown up by the French and replaced by our engineers with a wooden bridge. A burned-out house stands on the same road. Two or three houses near the hospital have been completely destroyed – the work of German aerial bombardment at the beginning of the campaign. Even in peacetime, Z— housed many soldiers, and its military hospital did not need to change its purpose when the Germans arrived. With long artillery and infantry barracks, now used as infectious disease wards or for lightly wounded soldiers, it functions now as a field hospital. School rooms have been arranged as work rooms for the High Command. Hundreds of electric wires, and even more invisible mental threads, come together. From here, again, the thoughts and will of some of the great mass of dutiful officials are transmitted by radio or telephone to the giant apparatus of an army on the march: the trenches west of the Argonnes, mountains of Lorraine, east to the plain of the Woëvre, even to the already conquered forts south of Verdun. Verdun, with its tough defenders, is becoming narrower and more surrounded by our troops as time passes.

On one occasion, a procession of more than 600 recently captured French soldiers were brought past the church in the presence of the Kaiser. He bowed, and greeted them in a courtly manner. This greeting also applied to the French officers who marched at the head of the column. There was no parade on the Kaiser's birthday:[26] but French bells tolled and German flags waved, and doors and windows of soldiers' quarters were resplendent with the greenery of pine branches. At night the town was lit up. The shining illumination of our *Reich* capital did not move me as much as the dull little lights in the windows of these alleyways. I brought out my Chanukah lamp that had, six weeks earlier, shed its light into the hearts of our young Maccabees, and which I certainly didn't think I would use in the field myself. And again the eight little lights shone into the night as they had done in Jerusalem 2,000 years ago.

On a Journey through the Army[27]

Only in the rear echelon of occupied territories is it as easy as buying a ticket, getting on to a train according to its schedule, and travelling to the desired destination. In operational areas there are many more means of transport, but they are less comfortable. The soft cushions of a private car, racing the wind as though there were no obstacles in time and space, are of course the perfect way to journey through army positions.

Between villages wide meadows and fields extend, some of them perhaps fertilized by human blood. A lonely wooden cross stands on a slope. In autumn and winter everything looked like a giant grave. But in spring meadows were resplendent in their fresh green, and red poppies shone in between, as if soaked with the most precious juice. The harvest season now nears: the abundant grass has already been cut and heaped into piles of hay which is loaded onto wagons and taken back to the homeland. The unusually heavy traffic together with continuous rain had caused numerous holes in the road. Now, with the aid of Russian and also sometimes French prisoners they are being overlaid with rough gravel and smoothed with a steamroller (which is much more reliable than the frequently talked-of Russian 'bulldozer').[28].

It is not easy for the Jewish chaplain to arrange services in the field. One cannot depend on the experience of potential predecessors and there is no means of transportation that one can use for rapid travel to the desired destination. The chaplain must, alone and independently, plan his duties inside a widely extended army, always prepared to revise his plans in the interests of military necessity. Along with this go visits to army and field hospitals, soldiers' cemeteries, prisoner of war camps, enquiries about the missing, and the large amount of correspondence attached to all of these charitable services. But good will and practice eventually overcome all difficulties, and consciousness of having done one's duty as well as the moving gratitude of comrades and their next of kin are the greatest reward.

When an automobile is at my disposal, I stop with it at every field hospital that we pass by and enquire in the orderly room about the Jewish ill or wounded. If one is admitted, I look him up, talk to him, give him reading material, ask if he has any specific wishes, and write to his loved ones about his condition. If I don't find any, I travel further. Unfortunately time does not suffice for a bed-to-bed visit, as I formerly did on a daily basis as 'Division Chaplain'. In urgent cases I am notified by telephone and told immediately about each fatality. Fallen comrades are usually buried in the zone of enemy fire. The burial of a young Jewish medical student is deeply imprinted in my memory. He had served for a time as a field hospital orderly, but his desire for action gave him no rest until he reported to the Front as an infantryman. Here he became a victim of his foolhardy courage. He was buried in the military cemetery a few hundred paces behind the trenches in front of which he fell. I delivered his eulogy in the presence of the comrades he had led, and several officers. A lieutenant spoke after me of the rare military and human virtues with which he had gained the esteem and love of all who knew him. Wreaths were laid and everyone came forward to throw the three spadefuls of earth onto his coffin. How many times have these battle-tested men already stood at a comrade's open grave! These men have surely become hardened by war but are by no means blunted: This is demonstrated by the loving care with which they invest and enclose these military cemeteries.

Each mound is covered with plants and many have a memorial of wood or stone, decorated with amazing artistic taste. When it is in my power, I see to it that a Jewish grave is provided with a memorial tablet instead of the usual birch cross. When I am told about a specific Jewish grave I always try to look it up and say a quiet prayer before it. Often the man I seek lies in a 'mass grave': these two words may sound terrible to those at home. But this is not the case, for these graves too are beautifully cared for. I believe that if parents and spouses saw how the dead are honoured here, they would no longer request that the dead be disturbed and exhumed, so that they can be transported home, however understandable it is that those who are dearest to them should rest near to home. Enquiries for those missing in battle are arduous and almost always unsuccessful. I have looked for hours and days in our cemeteries and on our battlefields, whether it be for soldiers or officers, Jews or Christians, French or Germans. How gladly would I give painful certainty to those who fret in uncertainty! But because the unfortunate souls have usually been missing since the previous autumn, we can discover only in exceptional cases what conscientious official enquiries could not ascertain.

Sometimes I have also visited a Russian prisoner of war camp. Once the camp physician told me in conversation of an intelligent Russian, who because of his knowledge of German had been 'appointed' as interpreter. 'A Jew?' I asked. 'Yes, the only Russian Jew.' I allowed myself to be led through the long airy barracks where the stocky blond sons of the Tsar's empire with their blunt, wide faces sat around a long table. They were busy carving rare and exotic birds out of wood and ate a great deal: no matter how much bread over and above their ration they were slipped, they were never satisfied.

'Wildmann!' calls the doctor and, as soon as the man reports to us, takes us into his room. W., stocky and blond like his compatriots but with a much more intelligent facial expression, tells me in not-quite-flawless German about his experiences of war and suffering. 'And how are you doing now?' 'Better than good', he adds beaming. When I finally ask him if he needed anything specific, he mentions only one thing: He wants a Jewish calendar so that he can find out the dates of the High Holidays. If only I could fulfil all the wishes of our brothers in the East so easily!

But all these visits were only a sideline. The main purpose of my journey through the army was to conduct services.

Our Services in the Field[29]

In mobile war, services in the field depend on chance. Immediately before or after the battle perhaps a chaplain may be able to collect the troops for a shorter but more impressive service. Otherwise he must limit his spiritual care to the wounded and perform loving service for the dead and dying. By contrast, static warfare provides rest and routine not only to military but also to religious life. According to a schedule that is subject to only a few variations, chaplains in the West have been able, for at least a year, to provide for their 'flock' almost as during peacetime. To be sure, this only applies to the Christian chaplain, who as Division Pastor works in a spatially narrow area which he generally shares with two other assistant chaplains. By contrast, the Jewish chaplain is the only 'spiritual head' of an entire army; and if, as in my case, this constitutes a double army, the strict implementation of orderly religious services, even in a long static war, is next to impossible.

To get through at all, I must hold services either behind the lines or even at Division level. I arrange each service, by place and time, about a week beforehand by telephone or else personally with the responsible division adjutant or corps commander. Then the latter, assuming that the military situation allows for conducting of a religious service, includes the corresponding command in his order of the day. Services in the more circumscribed Fifth Army usually allow me to be back at my garrison again by evening. I then set aside one or two days for field hospital visits and to make new arrangements. By contrast if I make the rounds through the neighbouring Army Division von Strantz, I find myself at a new division every day. It is clear from this that I may not fix a Friday evening or Sabbath morning service under these circumstances. Apart from night, there is no time that cannot be used for religious purposes. In this way all Jewish soldiers in the army have the opportunity (apart from festivals) to attend a Jewish religious service every six to eight weeks. But the number of men who have not taken part in any services, despite them being in the field since the beginning of the war, is probably not small. The fault usually does not lie with the men: it can be found more in the fact that Division Command, due to coincidence or carelessness, has not circulated the message widely enough or in time. The same complaint is heard from Jewish chaplains in all armies, indeed from chaplains of all faiths. There can be no talk about lack of accommodation by upper military echelons.

Soldiers are generally not 'commanded' to take part in services, they are allowed to choose whether or not to do so. Therefore it is important that Command places clear and explicit value on religious activity. Regimental Commanders and Division Adjutants have attended our services repeatedly in order, as they explained later, to show their respect for each kind of true religion. Individual divisions have voluntarily authorized a Jewish chaplain's assistant to hold services to allow the Jewish soldiers to have a service every fourteen days, as is the case for their Christian comrades. And it certainly speaks for active participation that a Division General once congratulated me because I could report an unusual number of 200 participants for a normal service.

It is not easy to specify where we hold our services. They take place everywhere, but generally not in the trenches. Out of curiosity, I once descended into this world-famous domicile of real war heroes; but trenches are not suitable for assembly of the widely-dispersed Jewish soldiers. We come together at as central a location as possible behind the Front. If we are fortunate a town hall, schoolhouse or soldiers' home provides a hall which we use as a prayer room. Less pleasant are the usually low and narrow soldiers' quarters, a 'bombproof' dugout, or a cellar, where heads crowd together by the light of a candle. A garage, barn or tavern must also on occasion serve as a 'synagogue'. If a tent has not been erected for religious services, I far prefer a church or chapel. Only religious narrow-mindedness could object to a Jewish service in a Christian house of God. I rather believe that we should acknowledge with thanks the broadmindedness with which the Catholic Church allows us entry. Was it not one of our Prophets who taught the noble words: 'Have we not all one Father, has not God created us all?'[30]

One could argue that, in the absence of an appropriate closed room, services should most suitably be held in the open. And indeed, like the Christian communities in the field, we have in many areas found a place to assemble outside, in the shade of trees during the midday heat and under the starry sky in a lovely cool autumnal evening breeze. Once in early morning we were so near behind the enemy's position that only a small grove hid us from them and we were not able to sing, so as not to direct their fire onto us. But as full of atmosphere as such a service sometimes is, it is exposed to many disruptions that disturb one's composure. Furthermore, in many places large open-air gatherings are forbidden because of danger of air attack. What about synagogues? Naturally, where one exists and is large enough, we use it with joy! I think of a Friday evening service which I held in the smart synagogue in Sedan, after three months of harsh life in villages or in the field. In our army's domain on French soil I have up to now discovered only three *temples israélites*. One was a real synagogue with traces of the war damage in the portal, in the badly shelled town of St Mihiel; on the pulpit, where otherwise the Rabbi of Verdun stood many times a year, I stood on a Friday evening and preached to a German community in field-grey. The other two synagogues were customized large living rooms in apartment buildings, one in Longwy at the foot of the obsolete fortress, the other in Thiaucourt. In the latter I recently found the floor covered with sandbags as protection against aerial bombardment. It hardly needs to be said that our military authorities have made provision that nobody enters these rooms unbidden. I was quite moved when I saw the Torah scrolls in their peaceful shrine, rolled to the place where the French prayer leader had read the words out to his community at the end of August or beginning of September, already under the thunder of cannon-fire.

I have been in the field for a year and during this time have met over 2,000 Jewish comrades from all parts of our Fatherland. Specific field communities, grouped around a central brigade, have evolved and I know in advance with a certain amount of confidence which faces I will see here and there. Sometimes one of my faithful is missing: he is wounded or has been killed. But new members always join us. The number of participants fluctuates. I have sometimes held services without 'ten adult males',[31] but on average there are thirty–forty present. Naturally all branches of the military and all ranks are represented. There are noticeably large numbers of non-commissioned officers and sergeant majors, on occasion an acting officer or an officer, and almost always a physician or administrative official. Often soldiers come from far-away trenches, rifle slung over shoulder and cartridge case in their belts, and straight after services return to their positions.

During services I give a talk – to call it a sermon would be too much. I do not stand on a pulpit and wear no cassock. Dressed in the same field grey as my audience, service cap on head and *talit* around my shoulders, I speak as a comrade to my comrades. Thought through before but not developed, modest and unadorned in the manner of speech and simple in delivery, such a 'field sermon' is nothing less than a work of art. The shorter and pithier, the better. These are real men to whom I speak. The war has taught them both to act and to be silent. The more they have experienced of this time of iron, the less they are inclined to talk about it; and those who talk the most have experienced the least. I myself am sometimes afraid to 'take up the word', when here in the field there are only deeds. Will the word grasp my audience as well? The war has hardened the mens' hearts against the horrors of death. And yet they are so receptive and so thankful for every word – more than ever before! All want to hear it: something more uplifting, more beautiful, than the usual eternal monotony that they hear: something that carries them away from the oppressive closeness for a few hours, that stimulates their thinking, frees their spirit, strengthens their will. Nothing philosophical or apologetic, but something really human, something of goodness and joy, that breathes the air of home and hope for peace. But also something that does not lack either a warlike or a specifically Jewish tone. The preacher best counters the danger of repeating himself (which is especially great during wartime when everything depends on one issue) by, as in peacetime, keeping to the Holy Writings.

At the end of the service I hand out Jewish newspapers and periodicals which I have brought with me, several copies of whose latest issues editorial staff and associations kindly send to us, as chaplains, on a regular basis. For a few seconds, there is a questioning and pushing that weakens the otherwise strict military discipline. Liberal, conservative, Zionist, revisionist periodicals: all are grabbed up in a flash. Not uncommonly, one copy must suffice for the entire division. Not a single copy was left of the special commemoration publications that the Verband der deutschen Juden handed over via the Jewish chaplain to their Jewish comrades on Chanukah, Pesach, Shavuot, and Rosh Hashanah. This is not just due to the rage for reading to kill boredom, the worst enemy in static warfare. A supply of 200 Psalm books in Hebrew and German, a festival gift for the soldiers from the community of Frankfurt am Main, was completely exhausted within three days. If time and room permit I stay companionably with my comrades after the service for a while longer. Then I let them tell me of their experiences and adventures in the field, or I tell them about my own. Religious and political questions are posed and discussed until all opinions always unite in the wish that the war should soon progress to a decisive victory and to peace!

I would gladly also gather my French co-religionists for a religious service. But coincidence has it that in our army's domain, with only one exception, there are no relatively large cities with Jewish communities. Only in Longwy, with the ready approval of the Rear Echelon Commander, have I held a service for the Jewish civilian population, but it was very poorly attended. However, I regularly look up a Jewish family in Montmédy and have, with a Jewish comrade quartered in their house, enjoyed many Friday and Festival evening meals at their table. Domestic tranquility is not broken by the fact that our hosts cling to their own French Fatherland with the same fervent love as do we Germans to ours. At their request, on Yom Kippur I sent field prayer books to Russian Jews in a prisoner-of-war camp who could not take part in the service. I received a letter of thanks from the Christian officer in charge: he wrote of his admiration for the religiosity of the Russian Jews that had pleased him so much that in each book he had written a pious German saying in dedication.

The high points in our religious life in the field are of course the festivals which are all, in sequence, celebrated by us. There was Chanukah: in the bare schoolroom of a poor town the familiar candles of six menorahs shone. Everyone in the room lit his own candle. Accompanied by a harmonium, the song *Maoz Tsur* echoed from the throats of fifty Maccabees and at the end the heroes of today, like the children of yesterday, received their gifts – food or clothing or something to smoke from the almost inexhaustible charitable donations with which friends from home had overwhelmed us for this purpose. After the cloudy, oppressive winter came Pesach, festival of spring and freedom. Loins girded, like the Army of Israel at the Exodus from Egypt, our soldiers in field grey sat, man beside man, around festively lit Seder tables. In front of each stood a glass filled with wine and each received a piece of the 'bread of affliction'. We lacked only the 'bitter herbs' (should that not have been lacking?) but all the more eagerly did everyone grab for the children's joy: *charoset*! A 15½-year-old volunteer, being the youngest, asked without hesitating '*Mah Nishtanah?*' Why is this night different from other nights? And the 'master of the house' answered: 'If God had not saved us so miraculously, we and our children would still be slaves.' And then the old, wonderful melodies of the eternally young night of freedom echoed. On the second night we could see in the light of the full moon a column of armed men leaving from the church in Grandpré, each with a large package of unleavened bread under his shoulder. They marched towards new deprivations, but as free men fighting for their holy homeland. What for us until now were only historical memories from hoary prehistory became all at once direct experience during these world-historical days.

Who could not have not been seized by images of horror that Jeremiah's *Lamentations* over the destruction of Jerusalem, recited on *Tisha Be'av*, unrolled before our eyes? Mass murder, devastation, plundering, horrible torment of old people and children, defenceless women and those driven out of their homes, hunger and plague as a result of the sword – these were no images but everyday reality and it is our own brothers and sisters who are struck down most terribly, as hostages to this war. Every sunny summer day that rose over meadows and forests was an incomprehensible contradiction: there is so much light, so much warmth, so much beauty in the world; why also so much human misery?

Gradually autumn approached and with it the 'Days of Awe'. The year before, I had just arrived in the field and, with only a few congregants, had celebrated in a makeshift small town room. This time, on New Year alone, I was able to assemble 1,500 comrades for six services divided into two armies, and for Yom Kippur half of that number in three armies. The mass of people – no service had less than 200 participants – both uplifts and carries responsibility. But we were lucky to find, for almost all services, a professional prayer leader, who recited the incomparable prayers worthily and intimately. In cases where gaps appeared in the small field prayer books printed by the Verband der deutschen Juden the larger *Machzor* helped, and no essential parts of the evening or morning services were left out. Naturally the magic that these highest of holidays spreads over the homeland is irreplaceable and our surroundings, despite all precautions, were anything but models of home. In Grandpré we had to share the church with a contingent of Frenchmen who had been captured in the Argonnes that morning. They sat silently, antiquated steel helmets on their heads and flanked with bayonets, in the dark background of the spacious hall. In the front on choir chairs, many who had participated in the bloody attack only a few hours before prayed by flickering candle light. And during the silent devotion the crashing of the bombs which French pilots were dropping onto the nearby railway station could be heard. In Ch—, the church had been shot into rubble by enemy artillery the previous evening, leaving us only an empty dark barn into which 200 men crowded. But even our loved ones at home could not have prayed more fervently than we did, thanked The Lord, and recited the *She'hecheyanu* prayer to Him who has kept us alive: Our Father, Our King (*Avinu Malkeinu*), frustrate the plans of our enemies. But the great climax came on Yom Kippur. Understandably I could not make a tour through the army section of Str— on that one day, so I requested, by telephone or in person, leave for the Jewish soldiers to travel to Metz. Where this could not be permitted, I asked that they be freed from duty for the day. In the narrow confines of our own army I scheduled for each of the *Kol Nidrei*, *Mussaph* and *Ne'ilah* prayers a service for several divisions. A single assembly with everyone in one place was out of the question because of the distances involved. What a powerful day it is, when the soul is shaken in its innermost core and at the same time redeemed and reconciled. Not a few soldiers here experienced this for the first time in their lives. It was like a second celebration of the revelation of the Torah on Mount Sinai; as if, desert around us and at the foot of a Heavenly Mountain, contritely confessing the heavy blame of the entire world, we heard the eternal word of God's mercy and loving-kindness through the thunder of artillery. When the day ended it was as if we had received new Tablets of the Law from Sinai instead of those which had been destroyed, with the proud battle cry of '*Shema Israel*', a cry for peaceful battle, for the perception of One God and one mankind: the ancient nation that argues with God still lives. His Prophets are no more, but he who on a starless night looks on holy watch and announces the Messianic Morning of Nations has himself become a prophet.

The meaning of our field services lies first and foremost in the fact that Jewish soldiers see and feel that they are cared for exactly the same as are the others. Their self-respect as Jews, the requirement for their respect from others, demands Jewish religious services as a right. Just like Protestants and Catholics, they want their own field chaplains. Not a few men pray with us without deep religious needs, but to show their solidarity. In these field communities a unanimity prevails which confirms the Kaiser's oft-quoted words [see Note 11]: There are no more parties here. Liberals, orthodox, Zionists, assimilationists: no matter how differently they may consider their Judaism, they feel one with each other as Jews. Without being able or wanting to enter into controversy, they get to know and respect each other as comrades. By this means not only do parties become closer but also social classes, rich and poor, academicians and artisans, the big city and the country Jew. But in most cases both services and an ardent need come together for religion, which in many cases has only in the field awoken from a deep sleep. I am admittedly speaking of soldiers at the Front and not at the rear; an entire world divides them in every respect. Only those who really fight the fight, who daily and hourly look death in the face, experience a religious rebirth. It appears simply as a belief in one living God, but their faith is deeper and more profound exactly because it is experienced. It is not difficult to dress it up in Jewish forms because in most cases it has remained preserved in the heart as comfortable remembrances of childhood. And if even in these believers there is no desire to brood, so much greater the need to learn and to know what Judaism and Jewish history and religion really are.

It is hoped that Jewish field services remain more than simple war memories for the many who have participated in them; they should be remembered also as their part in training a new generation of Jews for approaching peacetime. Parties will revive again and fight each other but the fight will be with nobler weapons. They will all merge closely, and nobody will stand aside indifferently any more when the old *Judenhaß* rears its head again. But what appears to us to be the most important: the new generation will no more exhaust its strength in defending itself. During this age of iron, the foundation has been laid for building anew, for Jewish knowledge and piety. We see the future of our German Fatherland with the same confidence as we see our German Jewry.

Jewish Chaplain Conferences[32]

Who would have dreamt that the war would make this possible: Jewish chaplain conferences! And yet conferences of professional associates, physicians and military officials, whether in one army or several, are a natural result of the long static war in the West. Christian chaplains have repeatedly held meetings, and Protestant chaplains of the entire Western Army have on one such occasion been received in the Kaiser's headquarters. For us Jewish chaplains, the necessity for regular gatherings has been even more urgent: we have neither a *Feldpropst* [chaplain provost] like the Protestants and Catholics nor a central religious authority. Even more, we lack any traditions, preparatory work and standards in our specific areas of responsibility. In the beginning it was only through the Verband der deutschen Juden, whose negotiations with the War Ministry must be recognized, that approval for Jewish chaplains was obtained. We remain in continuous contact by mail, so that the one can experience the essentials of the other's work.

First it was necessary to seek personal contacts and discussions between each individual Jewish chaplain so that, at least for Jewish spiritual care in the Western Army, a unified approach could be arranged, permitting homogenous organization. Next, two or three of us from adjacent armies got together for informal discussions. By February 1915 we were already six, and on 14 March at my suggestion the first choice was the little town of Hirson, on the crossroads of the French northern and eastern railways and approximately in the middle of the line that connects the extreme north of the Front with the extreme south.

Northern France is classic rabbinical conferences territory. In the middle of the twelfth century, under the chairmanship of the famous Rabbeinu Tam, Rashi's grandson, a considerable number (up to 150) of rabbis attended rabbinical conferences in Troyes, Reims, Ramerupt, and other communities in northern France.[33] The decisions of these conferences, which were not limited only to ritual and religious subjects but also concerned civil rights and community matters, influence the shaping of Jewish community life through to the present day.

I will not forget the sunny early spring day which I experienced in Hirson. Sauntering along the main street I had unexpectedly met three of my colleagues. The feeling of solitude which sometimes stalks us in our lonely locations gave way at that moment. Here I was amongst *Amstbrüder* [brother ministers] – the designation had nothing stiff any more but sounded so pure and profound that we really could have been brothers.

In my modest hotel room we chatted while awaiting the arrival of the others. It was afternoon before our meeting could begin in the comfortable officers' room of the field hospital that had been made available to us by Rear Echelon Command. The procession of chaplains with a *Magen David* on their caps made quite a sensation in the streets of Hirson. We were: Baeck (Berlin), Baerwald (Munich), Chone (Konstanz), Italiener (Darmstadt), Emil Levy (Berlin Charlottenburg), Lewin (Leipzig) and myself. Baeck was the chairman and Italiener kept the minutes. We succeeded in concluding a general orientation, which was the objective of the meeting, and discussed preparations for celebration of the upcoming Pesach festival. At 4.00 p.m. the meeting was concluded. We parted with the resolution to get together regularly every ten to twelve weeks.

The conferences which followed were more substantial and productive, even though the subject matter for the order of the day naturally remained the same. A group of questions concerned arrangement of the field services. For a large participation to be made possible, the announcement must occur at the correct time, in the right way, and with proper emphasis. Celebration of religious festivals requires, in every case, careful preparation. For Rosh Hashanah and Yom Kippur, a special field prayer book and commemorative publication were published. A second group of questions dealt with generation and procurement of appropriate Jewish and particularly Jewish-religious reading material to be handed out to the participants in religious services and patients in field hospitals. The role of the Jewish chaplain led to many questions. Our presence was originally only authorized, and we were only provided with, a monthly military allowance at the proposal of the Verband der deutschen Juden. These allowances were provided by the municipalities in Germany and had to provide for the costs of a living standard commensurate with our position and also the practice of religious duties. However, since 1 August 1915, and by *Reichstag* decree, we have been made equal with volunteer Christian chaplains in so far as we now receive the same monthly allowance from the state, which is greater than the usual stipend. Actual equalization of rights for which we still must strive, has not been fully solved: problems include involving a Jewish chaplain on official occasions such as dedication of memorials or cemeteries, and appointing rabbis or rabbinical candidates as chaplains assistants to share the load. Finally, we discussed new ideas which we hope will survive the war: a memoir containing experiences of Jewish spiritual care in the field would be valuable material to future generations, so too an endowment founded by Jewish chaplains and supported by comrades in the field to help alleviate the need of the bereaved.

In individual cases differences in the way of practicing our respective professions are revealed, according to the character of the personality and his specific circumstances: the size and extent of the army to which he has been assigned and the strength of his connection with the Command to which he belongs affects the degree of his freedom of activity. But we are united in recognition of our technical difficulties, which have increased significantly due to limitation of automobile traffic.[34] And we are also united in appreciating help from military authorities and colleagues of other faiths; united in our pride in the bravery and competence, moral gravity and religious self-determination, of our Jewish comrades, and in our love for our German Fatherland and for the unique task which has equally been bestowed upon us German Jews.

The second conference of Jewish chaplains took place in Lille. It was a ghostly sight to see the rubble around the railway station rising up in front of us from the dark of night. I had seen many ruined towns, but in this city the horror of destruction was more overpowering. The richest and most beautiful business premises around the station had been flattened by well-aimed German fire; however, the public buildings, the station itself, stock exchange, and the theatre had all remained unharmed. Admittedly these buildings had come within a hair of becoming sacrifices to the fierce fire of the memorable night of 14 October, when after the flight of the French garrison a German reserve company entered the conquered city.

The German Gouvernement established in Lille is strict but just. Like everywhere else in German-occupied areas it tries to keep the machinery of civilian life functioning or return it to normal, but at the same time also secures all military necessities against disruption. The local police have been strengthened by military police. Every insurgency leads to large fines or other considerable punishments. I was astounded when, on the stroke of 6.00 p.m. in the broad light of day, all inhabitants disappeared post-haste into their homes: it was the result of just such a penalty. When night falls no civilian is allowed to be seen on the streets at all. The city looks dead and only from window to window does one hear women chattering and laughing.

For German soldiers who are quartered here for months at a time, the large city conceals many dangers. Command successfully endeavours to offer healthy nourishment for spirit and heart to men and officers alike.³⁵ In the new theatre, classical performances with first-class artists are staged. And this all 10 kilometres from the Front! The art gallery can be visited daily by presentation of a ticket issued by Command. French supervisors guard the many valuable paintings.

For our next meeting, we met in Lille on 26 May in the large veranda of the elegant hotel in the Rue Nationale where Colleague Baerwald lives. This was a real 'conference' because it lasted from 10.00 a.m. to 5.00 p.m. with an interval during which we dined in the shady garden. Lille has a rich Jewish community.

On 5 August 1915 we travelled to the third conference in St Quentin. Colleague Levy had taken care of our lodgings through Command. St Quentin doesn't give the impression of a busy industrial city of 55,000 inhabitants. But its history, which it visibly incorporates, makes it venerable to the visitor. Outside in the northern cemetery lie holy mortal remains as well: they are the bodies of fallen soldiers from 1870/71. A new military cemetery has been created with modest wooden crosses erected at the head the graves of 1914/15. Dedication of the memorial that likewise honours German and French heroes took place a few months ago in the presence of the Kaiser.³⁶

In the bright hall of a former pension for young girls, eight of us Jewish chaplains assembled. The last planned conference was convened in Sedan for 18 November. I had visited the city with the world-famous name on many previous occasions. It was supposed to have changed a great deal since 1875, when it was abolished as a fortress and the fortress buildings fell. It still looks dark inside as if burdened with old humiliation. The city has been spared the destruction of this war except for the bridge over the Maas which the French, as elsewhere, blew up before their retreat. A German is overcome with proud memories when he looks around at the Maas valley and the surrounding heights. But one feels that they pale in comparison to the more violent current conflict and intuits that Sedan Day will in the future make way for an even more glorious victory.³⁷

In a sitting room of the pretty synagogue in which colleague (Reinhold) Lewin regularly holds his field-services, we sat, German rabbis all. Our French colleague is in the field. I once sought out the prayer leader who leads services here every Friday evening and Sabbath morning. I heard from him that the community consisted of no more than twenty families out of a total of 20,000 inhabitants, but they are apparently well-off.

At our last sitting we were without Colleague Baeck, our former chairman. His work as Jewish chaplain in the West had been exemplary for us but he had been transferred to the East [see Chapter 5]. Perhaps he will succeed there as well, despite much greater difficulties, in making contact with colleagues in the other armies. Our Jewish chaplains in the West have become so used to regular conferences that we would like to repeat them more frequently than hitherto. They mark particular episodes in our work and allow retrospection and perspective. Photographs keep alive the memory of our meetings in Lille, St Quentin, and Sedan and are at the same time an enduring expression of the solidarity and sincere understanding that exists amongst us across various religious directions. We have come together in all seasons, each time in another part of occupied France, and have marvelled at the intertwining of the solid structure of an entire army, standing like a wall of steel and iron from the North Sea to the Swiss border. This wall cannot be toppled but can certainly come to life one of these days and swoop down to destroy the enemy. The longed-for day will come, and will make further Jewish chaplain conferences impossible, but also superfluous.

Pesach in Front of Verdun[38]

Now the longed-for mobile war started up again. We had seen it coming for months: endless columns of ammunition, heavy and heavier artillery and troops, troops, troops. Narrow and wide gauge railways had been brought up near to the Front and whole forests of encampments erected. Existing field hospitals were emptied and new ones built. No-one could say with certainty, but everyone felt that it would be a mighty blow against the stronghold on which the chain of our Western Front had remained hanging as from a hook.[39] Stormy and rainy weather did not allow for reconnaissance by enemy airplanes, and this was welcomed even though it didn't facilitate encampment and work in the open air became less pleasant. Everyone was overcome by feverish tension which increased daily. Now final preparations had been made. The battle, one of the greatest in history, must begin tomorrow or the day after. A miserable steady rain developed, an execrable ally for the enemy. All roads were flooded and rain penetrated systematically and unceasingly into all the burrows, dugouts and foxholes which we had prepared, destroying everything. No tent could withstand its incessant onslaught – man and horse surrendered to its paralyzing effects. In addition there was the agonizing uncertainty: has the Frog guessed at or been told about our plan? Has he gained time to prepare his defences?

Eventually, on a Sabbath, the sun triumphantly broke through the clouds and the weather remained sunny. A quiet Sunday followed. On Monday morning 21 February at 8.00 a.m. our bombardment began. It only lasted a few hours, less than one tenth of the time which the French used in artillery preparation for the autumn offensive in Champagne, but was overwhelming. The murderous thunder of thousands of guns could be heard for miles. They had stood there for weeks, like unleashed beasts in the arena ready to attack their prey as soon as the command came – and we breathed again. Despite the horror of the battle that followed, a battle of man against man for every forest, every town, every valley and every hill; despite the terrible sacrifices of our opponents and equally terrible losses to our own troops, it was nevertheless exhilarating to experience how it progressed. Soldiers from all corners of the *Reich* pushed in an incredible frenzy against the ever-renewed and strengthened living wall of humanity, of fire-spewing cannon and machine guns. They pushed their adversary ever further back toward the fortress which they should have protected, but now lay almost completely in ruins.

But the enemy knows that it is not only fighting for the castle nor for a piece of earth, but for the big picture, and they fight with the courage of desperation. They throw ever new divisions into the giant bowl that is Verdun, also Blacks and Negroes [see Note 18] and their Russian friends. Every foot of ground is defended with utmost tenacity and, if eventually it has to be conceded, no sacrifice will have been too great in the attempt to reconquer it. The countryside changes appearance, although a human being is hardly anywhere to be seen. As in the words of the Prophet (but certainly differently from what he had prophesied), 'the valleys are raised up and the hills become valleys'.[40] What is happening here is so gigantic that only the visionary power of a prophet can intuit it, only the fantasy of a great poet can recreate it. All those who call themselves 'well-travelled', who have fought in Russia and Serbia, in the Carpathians and in front of Ypres, declare that everything is child's play compared with Verdun. The wearing and tedious monotony of trench warfare has gone; but it is also not the mobile warfare of which so many who experienced the first weeks of the war have for so long dreamt: the carefree attack through open countryside. By comparison the action, the real attack, is comparatively easy here, because of thorough artillery preparation. Stormed trenches are levelled, empty, dead. But to keep and maintain them against the heavy enemy fire directed upon them, and to fight with hand-grenades and bayonets against the immediately following enemy infantry attack: this type of positional warfare is something novel, unknown, demonic. Friend and foe agree: Verdun is hell, a hissing, howling, bursting, crashing, flaming hell, a suffocating, crunching, devouring hell. Who, after 1½ years of gruelling battles, could have thought it possible for the human eye to see, the ear to hear, the brain to grasp and bear, day and night, for weeks and months, what has happened here? It is an undreamt-of triumph of the human spirit, which here commands the will of man. You must not succumb; you must win. Awe is the only suitable feeling toward every one of these great heroes who resist all the horrors with which they are continually attacked, and who, defying the terror in their own hearts, endure at their posts. Each one of them a complete man.

I could only listen to the stories: tales of the wounded and those who returned from the Front for a few days' break taught me the language of the trenches, which could be heard all around. What I saw were wounds and mutilations of varying degrees of severity, that all the iniquitous weapons of this war had inflicted on young human bodies. The danger of the commonly encountered and often deadly gas gangrene [see Note 17] is supposed to be diminished by the presence of air. In the beginning it was difficult to stand the sight of its effects, but shameful comparison with what these poor men have seen and endured made me overcome my horror. Spiritual care has also become more difficult because early enthusiasm has disappeared. No-one doubts that we will win. But fighting is too bitter and stubborn to stop one longing for peace. The number of those taken ill has increased and the continued upheaval has weakened their mental resistance. I encountered quite a few Jewish sick and wounded in war and field hospitals. Many showed a naïve joy that I found them among so many others. But I had the clear feeling that they all felt reassurance and moral strengthening when their own chaplain came to talk to them, bring food or something to smoke, read to them, or write for them. How many reunions have I experienced there! The same men who I had seen amongst my field community filled with joyful confidence lie here now, shot through the chest and breathing with difficulty. But their will to live, the doctor's art and the nurses' care direct the bobbing little boats of their fate more swiftly and securely than those outside generally believe. Their little boats are led past the dangerous rocks and one day, when the chaplain comes calling, the information is: 'Sent back to Germany in the hospital train', which is the wish of those who first become conscious, on their hard bed of pain, of how foreign their surroundings are and how alone they feel.

In the meantime regular exchange of letters between next of kin and Jewish chaplain often develops. Sometimes this is the first news that a son, husband or brother has been wounded: also what type of wound had occurred. But no matter how scrupulous and thorough, this news is obviously inadequate.

Worried loved ones at home desire more and more information: Is there really no danger? Could the patient's father not come for a visit? Could the patient not be brought to a field hospital at home? What could they send him? Etc., etc. Fearing that people like us do not dare to tell the next of kin the complete truth (a widely spread but false assumption) an uncle, teacher, or rabbi from home may contact us and request 'more truthful' information. The intimacy of Jewish family life can nowhere be denied. How gladly we tell these people that really and truly things are not going badly, and justify the prognosis of complete recovery. How gladly we would send them news daily if time allowed us to visit the patient daily. And how difficult it is to give them news of a surgical intervention, a necessary amputation. How infinitely difficult it is to take away from a mother, father or wife the last hope of the survival of a loved one, because God has taken him. There is no need to describe this to any sensitive soul. All of these changing situations naturally increased during the weeks and months of the Great Offensive, and there were many mortalities amongst Jewish comrades in the field hospitals. As far as it is possible, I am informed about such cases telegraphically by someone in the relevant army section so that I can organize burial and if possible attend it. In most cases many dead have to be buried at the same time, so a Christian chaplain makes a common funeral oration. There have already been two occasions when, at their request and in their presence, I have performed this office. This unity of faith in the face of death, which is the same for Jew and Christian, like the womb of mother earth which takes both in, contains something wonderfully conciliatory in the middle of all the suffering in this war.

The arrival of Pesach after our difficult work came to all of us as a real festival of deliverance. For three months there had been neither time nor opportunity for collective services in the field: this would now be compensated by our most beautiful religious family celebration. After the decision of the Jewish chaplain conference in Gent (29 February) matzoth and Pesach wine for the entire Western Army had been ordered some time ago. The festival meal arrived carefully packed in ten large crates, which the Women's Association of the Frankfurt Lodge had collected for us: 100 kilogram boxes of vegetables and fruit, oranges and macaroons, wine and honey. The main course was still missing; but despite the lack of meat during these days, Rabbi Dr Nobel's[41] energetic efforts had secured for us an entire hundredweight of kosher smoked meat. A reliable Jewish butcher took over the preparation and now, in my kitchen, the cooking in kashered pots began which would have done honour to any Jewish *Hausfrau*. My concern that something of the enormous quantities would be left over disappeared rapidly. I didn't yet know what it took to satisfy several hundred stomachs, and soldiers' stomachs at that. Also the battle situation did not allow for even a rough estimate of the number of participants.

The army command, which according to my plan was made known eight days previously, announced the fixed location, day and hour of the religious service and the Seder to follow, had unexpected success. On Monday 17 April at 7.00 p.m. at the church in St—, the only large space that could be put at our disposal, about 500 congregants assembled: among these five Jewish nurses, two officers and several physicians. Four Russian co-religionists from the nearby prisoner of war camp were, at my request, allowed to take part; they looked very dignified in their dress uniforms and obviously felt for the short hour of the service as if they were free men. We did not have a Cantor – our excellent previous prayer leader had fallen a short time before, so I had to lead the evening prayer. The sermon followed the prayers. The large assembly, which completely filled the centre nave of the church and which, in the semi-darkness of the background appeared even larger, was for me the most impressive sermon of all. They came from all parts of the Fatherland, and here, on foreign soil, they had united into a single community. Most were filled with terrible pictures of past days, their souls searching for lovely images of their parents' house; many were lost in thoughts of their brothers, cousins, friends now resting in French or Russian soil. But all of them are fighting, witnesses of the great time when God, as He did long ago in Egypt, provides miracles and signs that the yoke of slavery, which the powerful enemy – moved by arrogance and fear – wants to force around the necks of a free people, will be broken into pieces.

In this entire service, the living present was intimately connected with hoary remembrance, and the distress and uplifting of our German Fatherland with the suffering and pride of Israel's history. The entire service was in accordance with ancient traditions, framed by two patriotic songs accompanied by the organ. Because of the large attendance, I had to give the subsequent Seder meal in the roomy but insufficiently large hall of the church forum for three separate groups and the reading of the *Hagadah* had to be appropriately shortened. On the table which connected lengthwise-arranged simple tables, sat the 'master of the house' between two lights. In front of him lay the three-tiered Seder dish and to the left and right of him were the nurses, officers and physicians. The 'master of the house' led only the first part of the Seder. The second part he assigned, happy that for once he could listen (and didn't have to recite), to an old reserve soldier and the third to the younger son of Rabbi Meyer from Regensburg. Each celebration was attended by 150 men. Certainly many from religious households would have sorely missed the dedication during that evening. But the austere sobriety that originally belonged to the night of the bloody Pesach offering, and the haste with which our ancestors, staff in hand, walking shoes on their feet, ate the bread of affliction, was without doubt nearer to the spirit of our modest celebration in the field. Otherwise I am sure that no-one fell short in physical enjoyment: instead of the requisite four cups of wine, the same number of draughts were taken from their own cup which had been brought along. At the end of each celebration I handed out newspapers and periodicals with Jewish content, mainly the Pesach celebratory issue for our soldiers in the field which had been donated by the Verband der deutschen Juden. It was exactly midnight when we parted from each other to the strains of *Vayehi Bachatzi Halailah*. Some groups remained together on the street: there were comrades from the same region, friends, brothers who, by pre-arrangement or coincidence, met each other here and celebrated a happy reunion. A father with his son were also present. Gradually it became quiet in the dark, rain-dimmed streets of the little town. Far from danger, our brave soldiers surely rested well this night in the shelter of the quarters which had been prepared for them. The following morning a number of soldiers joined together in praying *Shacharit* before they returned to their positions.

A similar and yet different picture was seen at the second Seder. Tuesday evening shortly before 7.00 p.m., about 300 men marched in closed ranks from the town hall in L— to the motion picture theatre. Their number increased rapidly to about 400, so that I had to 'branch off' and direct them to the adjacent café which had been provided to cover this eventuality. There they had their own prayer leader, with their own Seder plate, wine and matzoth. The main community, consisting of 320 souls, filled the festively lit theatre hall which had been decorated lovingly and tastefully down to the last seat and standing place. Four Jewish nurses, physicians, officers and deputy officers were seated in front. A golden *Magen David* on a white background shone by the light of the candles behind the raised prayer-stool. Comrade Glast, a practiced singer who had already proved himself as *chazan* on the High Holidays, stood on the pulpit and sang the melodies of the *Ma'ariv* service, well-known to most present, with a beautiful voice and delicate understanding. With the counting of the first night's *Omer* I ascended the 'pulpit' to give words to the experience of this unique hour. Many who sat before me had, just a few hours ago, crept out of their trenches and hide-outs and travelled in constant mortal danger to the rear, along constantly shelled streets, until they successfully reached the narrow-gauge railway or another means of transportation. And now they were enfolded in solemn silence, bright shining light, in an atmosphere of human kindness and Godly peace. It all happened 'as in a dream', so one soldier told me in the name of them all. I began the Seder with a general reflection on its meaning and significance. With the assistance of Herr Glast and Herr Levy – who with his wife deserved our special thanks for the realization of this celebration – I read from the *Hagadah*, translating and interpreting from time to time. Not everybody could partake of the symbols of the immaculate Seder dish, which I handed round in the sight of the entire assembly; however everybody partook spiritually, and the child's questions, read by a member of the Jewish community of Frankfurt am Main, were answered in detail by the 'master of the house' with the greatest attentiveness. More than one person must have been moved by half-faded memories of the golden days of his childhood, and resolved no longer to withhold the deep spiritual value of this poetic celebration from his own children, that is if God allowed him to return home safely.

Normally the meal takes place in the middle of the Seder evening, beginning with eggs and matzoth dumplings. But despite all the celebration we were reminded that we were gathered together under abnormal conditions. The meal, the same for everyone, consisted of meat and potatoes and, as dessert, fruit and coffee. The non-commissioned officers and men 'tucked in', as the military says, in a company kitchen with the eating utensils which they had been ordered to bring along with them. Sergeant First Class Steigerwalt from Heilbronn had prepared everything most carefully. And then everyone returned to their seats. The nurses, officers, physicians and sergeant majors, and whoever else had come without knife, fork, spoon and plate, were served in the café that had been emptied out for that purpose. After that, Grace was recited. All participants, apart from those called to duty in the interim, again filled the cinema down to the last seat. Here we finished with the second part of the *Hagadah* (with the old, familiar, lovely songs) in enough time to be in our sleeping quarters before midnight.

The next morning we again had a full prayer room when our *chazan* graced us with *Shacharit*, Torah reading, and *Mussaph* with no less beautiful and worthy reverence than he had done previously. And then the last soldiers, cartridge belt around their waists and rifles slung over their shoulders, returned to the solemn period of the *Sefirah* to do their difficult duty as German soldiers. *Leshana Haba'ah* [Next Year],[42] from the Seder evening still echoed in their ears and each thought of the place that was holiest to him because it held father and mother, wife and child, and because it surrounded his soul with peace and joy.

And this most violent of all battles thunders on. It has already cut down several of those who had prayed and sung hopefully with us at the Seder evening, others have been more or less severely wounded. We will never remember this evening with joy. But it was an experience that, during the most dreadful period of this war, gave us new courage and new faith and will, if we are permitted to return home, long be remembered, even in far-off future days of peace. Pesach in front of Verdun.

Relearning[43]

This war is becoming an immeasurable tragedy for the individual as well as for the nations of the world. Nevertheless, it is true that it can be an incomparable school for us humans. But only he who has retained a receptive heart and the will to learn is able to learn something: not dead and sterile, but living fruitful knowledge, which can only be learned in the hard school of life. In most cases this learning will be a relearning: this is essential as a remedy for our distorted reason and the impoverishment and perversion of our will.

The man in the battlefield is placed into a world completely different from the one he has known before. Time, which previously meant money, even life, signifies little or nothing here. Days, weeks, months, fly away here monotonously; there is no haste or unrest, as if one could squander and lose an hour. One has time in plenty. Space, by contrast, takes on undreamt-of significance. Formerly, space was easily overcome by means of modern communication. But now almost every stretch of road must be travelled on foot; one must summon all one's strength in order for each foot of earth to be wrested from the enemy. Spatial things acquire a new face. The soldier knows every tree, every stone in front of a trench or on the road, he observes plants growing and the animal life around him. Sunrise and sunset, the stars in the night sky, become as familiar to him as streets of his home town to a city-dweller. There is a general return to nature.

It hardly needs to be said that such relearning connotes a true healing for us Jews. Most of us come from the cities, engaged one-sidedly in intellectual, abstract knowledge. We are seldom engaged in pure contemplation. From a centuries-long purely logical education which has been forced upon us by conditions we return to the biblical educational goal of *Daath*.[44] This *Daath* corresponds much more with our 'perception' than with our 'knowledge'.

This perception is disproportionately more important for real learning of all things than 'knowledge' alone. Our peacetime civilian profession directs us to countless people: how few of them do we really know and understand? In the field, where the soldier stands, lies, eats and sleeps with his comrade day and night and perhaps for years, one sees the other through to the depths of his heart. Hollow phrases are frowned upon, masks fall, and the man is valued by his innermost core. Parties, social status, religions come nearer to one another than would be possible at any other place or time. Existing prejudices between certain classes are ironed out; we also understand the good in different people and do not deny them the right to exist any more.

Despite our ability to think and judge, we Jews have not always looked at our surroundings with an unclouded gaze. The mistake which we so often make with respect to ourselves, that the exception proves the rule, also sometimes applies to us with respect to others. But it is only natural that the majority in whose midst we live are much less well informed about us than we are about them. The same thing has happened to my Jewish comrades as has happened to me. They have found, during conversations with Christian soldiers and officers, even the otherwise well educated, an astonishing ignorance about the history and nature of Judaism. Hardly anyone knew how many Jews live in Germany; their number is generally overestimated six- to eight-fold. Even the well-meaning are permeated with the thought that Jewry aims at commercial and spiritual world domination, to say nothing of other often-told fairy tales. How much useful explanation can a soldier amongst soldiers, an officer, a physician amongst officers and most especially a Jewish chaplain, disseminate to a wide audience by open dialogue.

I have therefore greeted the fact that Division and Corps Commanders repeatedly visited our religious services with great joy. First, one of these gentlemen came, quite unexpectedly, accompanied by his Adjutant. On another occasion and at his instigation a second Commander came with his Adjutant, etc. The result was that, during a period of four weeks, four generals honoured us by their visits. They all spoke of the feelings that these services had awakened in them in the warmest words to my community and myself. Apart from the sermon, they could understand the liturgy only through translation. But a prayer like *Kaddish* for our fallen brothers, introduced with a few suitable words and recited by the entire congregation, even in the original language deeply and visibly affected them. These men, who possess unusually open eyes and incorruptible judgment, have only taken their first brief look into our religious life. But the image that it impressed on them may remain decisive for their future ideas about the Jewish religion.

I should like to mention a particularly impressive experience. Jewish comrades mainly from Frankfurt am Main had felt the need for their own prayer room and erected a 'forest synagogue'. Halfway up a wooded hill, they levelled off a floor around a sturdy, German oak tree. A birchwood railing fenced the area off facing the valley. Steps led to a higher area with a narrower handrail made of delicate birch branches with the inscription 'The Lord is my banner'.[45] The wide oaken table was covered by a tent-cloth and topped by a raised pulpit. Lifted above even this high pulpit one saw a shrine, the 'Holy Ark', which leant on the tree-trunk that appears like the pillar of a temple. Behind this, the forest continued to the top of the hill, greeting the high ridges of the Argonnes across the broad valley. And over everything arched God's heavens like the mighty dome of a giant temple. The oak's knotty branches did not hide the heavens: they more resembled outstretched arms with which to receive the sun-lit pure blue of the day and the star-shone night splendour, before collecting them up and bringing them down to the consecrated piece of earth.

Consecration of the first forest synagogue in our army section, perhaps in the entire army, was to be a solemn occasion. Long before the set time about eighty participants, including officers and physicians, had gathered at the site, indicated from the road by a signpost. At my invitation the Commander of the division in question, a former China warrior and wonderful old warhorse, appeared, followed by his adjutant. The regimental band had been commandeered for this special occasion. The beautiful Dutch benediction,[46] carried afar by the sounds of the music, opened the ceremony. A short *Minchah* service followed and then the Torah scrolls were raised into their ark accompanied by communal singing. Pastor H, who had rendered outstanding service by making the occasion possible, said a few words of blessing. I myself gave the 'celebratory sermon'.

The deep silence of an autumn day reigned in the forest around us. Instead of the *Ner Tamid*, the same world-light shone that the Eternal has kindled over the firmament. Cannons thundered on the other side of the valley. Bloody battle in the midst of the holy peace of nature. In seemingly eternally peaceful nature, powerful forces battle for victory everywhere, and everlasting Godly laws are revealed even in the thundering struggle of nations. And we humans, who are placed equally into nature and in history, what else could be our ethical duty other than to overcome this conflict in our own breasts with the iron law of duty? As our religion commands us to do for ourselves, our community and our Fatherland? Only unswerving and loyal fulfilment of our duty can give us the inner peace that stands above even ardently longed-for external peace.

Those were more or less the thoughts that overcame me on the quiet heights of this hill and which I attempted to put into words. The hour, unforgettable to all who attended, concluded with *Deutschland über alles*.[47] His Excellency, in his short and powerful speech, expressed his joy at having attended our service to the assembled participants. He advised them to come here whenever their hearts were heavy with worry or sorrow, so that they can find, by praying to their God, new strength and confidence for the hard battles which lay ahead for all of us. A real celebratory mood was felt by all who attended, long after our beloved General had bade us farewell.

The interest of influential members of our military shown by such visits has a second effect that should not be underestimated: it has raised Judaism and our Jewishness in our own eyes. We suffer from an underestimation of our common religion in the same way as from an overestimation of our personal abilities and achievements. Correct self-awareness, learned from observing others and comparing ourselves with them, is an important asset gained in this school of war. We already know that our mental capacity, sobriety, diligence and dependability is properly appreciated even by those who do not wish us well. A well-known General once said to me in conversation: 'We need thinking soldiers, and we find them in your co-religionists.' But a pressing lesson for all of us was that even the bravest Jew achieves the respect of others only by personal modesty combined with pride in his faith.

Relearning (Continuation and Conclusion)[48]

'Happy is the man who learns, even from the days of his youth, to bear the heavy load, who sits alone and patiently bears it because it has been laid upon him.'[49] I am reminded of these deep words untold times in the field. It is true that the young generation, now fighting and suffering, has been cheated out of the carefree gaiety of the best years of their lives. The heavy yoke of a long and bitter war weighs heavily on our youth. But nevertheless, and maybe even because of this: 'Happy is the man...' applies to them. Here too we must relearn. The 'century of the child' believed that wisdom's noblest end was to let young people live out their lives, and where possible clear all frustrations and obstacles from their path. But now it has been proved how right were the wise educators who warned that character can only be shaped by fighting against the world's stream. In their misguided, blind love, Jewish fathers and mothers in particular were most keenly concerned in making their children's economic and social careers as comfortable and smooth as possible. They did not even shy away from showing their lack of character by baptism, just so long as their loved ones would suffer no inconvenience as a result of their faith. The smoothness of their life's path was thus impeccable; but how many have stumbled and fallen exactly because of this smoothness? We do not require the century of the child, but rather that of the man, and apparently the foundations for this can only be laid by this World War.

Initially, we speak about physical fitness. Even considering the great upswing of sport amongst the youth during the last decade, who would have believed that our young men could be able to bear the strenuous efforts that are required from a soldier these days? It is possibly even more difficult for the young Jewish man. A hundred years of freedom cannot compensate for damage that years in the ghetto has done to our physical development. Additionally, the Jewish home has spoilt men and made them soft. The young child had to be anxiously protected from every draft of air. And now that same youth stands outside day and night, in wind and weather, without roof or blanket to cover him. The mummy's boy who left his parents' house perhaps for the first time rests no more on soft cushions. Like Jacob in that first night in the desolate field a stone must serve as a cushion,[50] and he sleeps on such a hard bed as soundly as did our ancestor, with equally pleasant dreams. There is no doubt that the war makes thousands into cripples, makes thousands ill and infirm for the rest of their lives. But it cannot be emphasized too often that an even larger number are hardened and invigorated, even become healthy because of this war. This applies to those affected by all types of nervous weakness, in whose number we Jews have a frighteningly high contingent. Fresh air activity, physical labour, and unflagging obligation, heal better than any medicine the nervous complaints of modern man who works inside a small room or at a desk. Morbid irritability is overcome by focusing the will on a simple, clear, near goal, and the will is thereby infinitely strengthened and steeled.

This strength of will is most easily tested when it has seemingly been abolished because subordinated to the will of another. In this respect, military influence manifests itself most clearly in discipline, unconditional submission to the command of superiors, and silent obedience. The characteristic power of subordination begins only where constraint is recognized as beneficial and commands are obeyed willingly. We Jews have achieved a great deal already when we, who are so inclined towards criticism and dissent, are forced to join together in silence, limiting our individuality.

Nevertheless, subordination of the person to the cause cannot mean decline of individual personality. Every man must hold his own at his post. No other man will stand in for him: he stands wholly responsible for himself. But nevertheless, within this tightly organized system a great amount of individual freedom is still permitted: a soldier's presence of mind, ability to take decisions, courage: these are as contagious as their opposites, and on them depends success, in small and large undertakings. This is an excellent school for grumblers, doubters, weaklings and the hesitant. Here words, however great or beautiful, do not count: the deed alone is decisive. With all their praise of study and delving after truth, our sages also praised the deed as the highest goal. The warrior is schooled in independence, drive, and the healthy self-assurance that these provide. As many precautions as are provided, in the end each man must look after himself. 'If I am not for myself, who is for me?' But we are not speaking about canonization of the ego here. On the contrary, nowhere as much as in the field can we understand Hillel's wise words: 'But if I am *only* for myself, what am I?'[51] Indeed, that person who acts only for himself and plays no part in the joy or suffering of others should feel like a lost soul and a pariah. Soldiers in the field judge a comrade with the same certain verdict as do school comrades: according to his goodness or heartlessness. 'The heart is weighed there.' Teachers and superiors may delude themselves, but he who has suffered at the hands of comrades is himself to blame. What is said and written about the spirit of comradeship amongst our soldiers at the front, not the rear, is not exaggerated. Is it then any wonder that when men, day-in and day-out, stare death together in the face, they feel bound to each other in life and death? Everyone experiences first hand that he relies on the assistance of others, as they do on him. 'Do unto others as you will that they do unto you.' The practical application of the commandment to love one another,[52] which appears to most people today as incomprehensible and impossible to accomplish, is hereby illustrated. Thus, in the community of soldiers in the field, in this part of human society, the balance between individual rights and duty to the whole is accomplished, one could say automatically.

It is therefore not too much to assert that, for eager students, the school of war breaks new ground for an improved attitude to life. The great demands on the externals of life are lowered to a very modest level. 'Bread for food, clothes for protection, and a peaceful return home to one's parents' house': in these three requests, which our ancestor Jacob made on that first night in the open field, his descendant sees everything that is worth striving for. For what purpose have we really lived? For money and material things? How small and useless these now appear, where rich and poor have the same fate! For enjoyment and comfort? But what do these mean to him who daily puts his life at risk? And why would he have died? He doesn't know.

The materialistic 'philosophy of life' in which members of our faith often indulge, reveals its hollowness here. Death, which has become a daily appearance and now hardly feared at all, puts overestimation of life back in proper perspective. Life, short or long, has no value and is not worth living if man does not fill it with meaning that outlives him. Man must work towards a goal higher and more inclusive than his small individual existence; he must work for the community, he must fight for *Volk* and Fatherland.

The enthusiasm during the first months of the war was, in the real meaning of the word, a God-like filling of the heart with all that is great, good, and true. What a religious service before battle or thanksgiving service after victory meant then! Like women and children in places of worship back home soldiers in the field streamed in droves to communal prayer, driven by an inner urge. All faiths were united as brothers and one did not ask whether the next man was Catholic or Protestant. Jews visited Christian field services to satisfy their religious needs when they were still deprived of chaplains of their own faith. A new day seemed to have dawned, when faith blossomed.

But then came the gradual setback. Wings that had raised up and carried the soul became paralyzed. The longer the war lasted, the more hope disappeared and with it the desire for spiritual uplift. There are always those, not a few in number, who have found God once and for all in the silence of many a long night. But the majority, if they were not religious at home, have gradually been overcome by fatalistic belief: their fate has been decided and no matter what they do or suffer, they cannot escape it. A faith of resignation that does have some practical advantage but has little in common with the humble confidence of the faithful one 'who sits alone and bears his fate with patience, because it has been laid upon him'. The length and nature of this war are to blame for this setback, but who would assert that it would not have occurred if we had won a rapid peace?

What I observe with heavy heart about the failure of religious obligation (which obviously cannot be laid at the door of the religion itself) applies in the same way to Christians as to Jews. But what can be of some comfort to us Jews is that our Jewish soldiers have become more Jewish. This is a sign that outside, or rather beneath, our faith there is something that binds us together: the past, present and future, in brief our common history. A solid bond of memories made flesh and blood, of living experiences, hopes and fears, enfolds us all. The Jewish soldier in the field feels this more strongly than ever without any lessening of love for his German Fatherland. One of the motives that compels the Jewish soldier, even the 'irreligious', to attend religious services is the need to meet together with his fellow-Jews. The prayer room here becomes a true *Beit haknesset*, a house of assembly, like the synagogue was once called. Although members of this community come from the most different regions of the *Reich*, the feeling of being a stranger is never present even for a second: all recognize each other as brothers. This strengthening of community spirit creates and also raises a noble Jewish self-consciousness. I am not saying that all Jewish soldiers in the field experience this transformation. There is certainly a smaller residue which shuts itself off from the Jewish community, partially because of fundamental rejection of everything that is particularistic, partially due to ignorance and lethargy, but mostly because of cowardice: they harbour the childish delusion that they are not recognized as Jews if they take pains to avoid every Jewish association.

But even this remnant must have its conscience shaken by the new anti-Semitic movement that, for many, has come completely unexpectedly. *A priori*, it cannot be comprehended why such base suspicions and endless calumnies have been voiced so loudly against a portion of the nation which is surely second to none in its readiness to sacrifice and offer up blood and material possessions for the Fatherland. Where justice has not prevented this, intelligence should have. At a time when more than ever before a united nation is needed, not only has the artificially maintained civil truce been broken, but mistrust and discord have been sown and have even reached our fighting forces. Every patriot should be filled with deep pain and shame, that also here the noble spirit present at the beginning of the war, as signalled by the Kaiser's words: 'I no longer recognize parties' [see Note 11] have been forgotten and denied so quickly and thoroughly. Even if the *Judenzählung* sprang from the well-meaning intention that it could counter domestic mischief-making and agitation, its effect has been the opposite. Not so much because of the results of the census: we Jews certainly would have had nothing to be afraid of, indeed we would have liked the public to have been informed of its results if statistics had been presented in a less one-sided and incomplete fashion. Every Company Clerk received the 'secret decree', misunderstood it or had to misunderstand it, and acted as if he himself was from now on authorized, even duty-bound, to investigate his Jewish comrades, even Jewish officers and physicians, for slacking. And this too was calculated to undermine harmony, if not authority as well. The chasm between Jews and Christians, which had once been bridged, opened up again. The Jew felt marked. We know well that some of our Jewish comrades are slackers, just as are some Christians, and we want all of these to be strictly dealt with. But we are justly indignant that the offence of one single person is imputed to all of us, such that all Jews – whether serving in the rear because they are ill or wounded or, because of education or ability, they are commandeered to clerical or other positions without having any say in the matter – are reckoned amongst cowards and those who have forgotten their duty. The Jewish soldier sees the memory of thousands of his brothers who have given their lives for the Fatherland reviled, and his own military honour deeply wounded. He did his duty as a German man. Clearly, it was no more than his duty to do so: he didn't ask for thanks or reward, but he also did not expect such ingratitude. No-one will believe that this bitter experience has raised the Jewish soldier's joy in serving the Fatherland.[53]

One good thing has resulted, however: it has welded Jews together. Antagonisms between liberal and orthodox, Zionist and 'assimilationists' had already receded greatly. But now, in the field, in the face of our common distress, everything which separates us has been forgotten. People who before wanted to know nothing about their Jewish faith are at once emphatically reminded of it. The *Judenfrage* is put to them personally and demands from them a personal decision. The better ones amongst them eventually declare themselves decisively and unreservedly part of our community, precisely because it is under attack. An awareness of solidarity has been awakened in us now that we are faced with stress and hostility, which we would not have experienced in times of happiness and freedom. And thus, as so often in our history, it is shown that *Judenhaß* is that 'strength that always wishes to do evil but always does good'.[54] Our lot has not yet become the pure blessing for which Israel (Jacob), 'he who wrestled with God',[55] so often had to fight in his nightly battles with the world. But men who have gone through this school of war have attained the moral maturity to understand that the question: 'Am I my brother's keeper?'[56] is no question any more. 'All Jews are responsible for one another.'[57] In this profession of moral responsibility, the young generation of Jews is united in the spirit of their forefathers. This is no confession of faith; it is, however, only one step from this, not only to the old faith that has been handed down to us, but to a living faith in The Lord God, the God of Israel.

It is a foolish and presumptuous endeavour to prophecy the future. Will we German Jews be better or worse off politically and societally after this war than we were before it, or will everything remain the same? Which thinking person could predict this with any certainty? But our old Jewish optimism, tried and proven in thousand-fold sufferings, safeguards us from thoughts of the future that are too dark. Already clear signs bear witness to the fact that we Jews will not remain the same. Our returning sons and brothers will be like a living stream, a new and firmer will to be Jews will arise. And this will pull the indifferent and the half-hearted, the faltering and vacillating, along with it; a will which guarantees Jewish renewal. [end of diary]

*****

In a 1975 interview with Rolf Vogel the then 93-year-old Georg Salzberger described the occurrences of 1 August 1914 as follows:

When war began, a call went out from the Verband der deutschen Juden to German rabbis, asking them to report for service as chaplains. I reported at once and received a uniform, a certificate from the War Ministry which I could show everywhere as proof of my vocation, and a horse and cart. But I did not see the latter: they would have been superfluous because in the field, transportation could only occur by automobile. I then travelled in uniform to the French border; there I disembarked and waited. After a while an automobile in which one man in civilian dress and one in uniform sat stopped to pick me up. We started talking and until today I still hear the officer saying: 'How good it is that the destruction is occurring in France and not in Germany.' Suddenly the officer asked me: 'To which church in Frankfurt do you belong?' 'I belong to no church: I am a rabbi', I answered. I noticed that no more words were directed to me throughout the rest of the long journey. Whenever I was given a lift I waited for the question, and answered proudly: 'I belong to no church, I am a rabbi.' The impact differed and in one case was especially curious. A cavalry officer, who had to travel around a great deal, asked me: 'Tell me, Herr *Pfarrer*: you are travelling all over the army. What are you really doing?' 'I am not a pastor, I am a rabbi.' 'Rabbi? that is really interesting. They also exist.' He was delighted that I was a rabbi and not a military pastor, and very often gave me a lift![58]

About his daily work as chaplain, Salzberger related:

My work consisted of going to the various divisions and after a previous request holding services for the division's Jewish soldiers. On our High Holy Days all Jewish soldiers of the entire Fifth Army were involved. We were loaned large localities for this purpose, often immediately behind the Front. We were told repeatedly to pray quietly because the enemy is on the other side and can hear you: a fight can start on this account. I was naturally in the trenches with the comrades. Part of my work consisted in visiting field hospitals or larger army hospitals where I cared for not only Jewish soldiers but soldiers of other faiths where possible. I well remember an incident in southern France where I arrived for the first time in a barracks in which the seriously wounded lay. I simply asked, without caring about religious adherence: 'Can I help you write home, comrade?' 'Yes', they answered. They were happy when I took the postcard, noted the address and then sent a reassuring answer to the family back home. My first visit in that type of field hospital was a terrible experience: how they lay there groaning, man next to man, in a church, bleeding in a foul-smelling room. I thought that I couldn't endure it. But precisely because I learned to react with each individual without regard for his religion, to ask him about his personal affairs, about his family and also to write correspondence for him, I learned to work as minister in field hospitals as well.

Often they came in large numbers, sometimes their numbers were very small. I was very pleased at the visit of non-Jewish officers at my services on several occasions. Once a certain Captain von François asked me if I would like to get to know his father General von François.[59] I was introduced to the General who asked whether he could participate in a service. 'Naturally Excellency', I said. As thereupon agreed to, at exactly 12.00 noon the next Sunday his automobile arrived in front of the church. After the service he had highly commendatory words not only for the sermon, but for the service in general, and made everyone who had been awarded the Iron Cross step forward.

My relations with Catholic and Protestant chaplains varied. I had very good contact with some, especially with the Catholics. Jewish soldiers told me that the Protestant chaplain said at services: 'Yes the Jews: I cannot tolerate them, the Jews.' I lodged a complaint about this at Command and thereupon the authoritative officer asked what he should do and whether I wished to make an incident of the affair.

'Not at all', I said, 'I just want the gentleman to be told what the Kaiser said: "No parties any more, only German soldiers"'. And this occurred. I was, together with the Catholic and Protestant chaplains, awarded the Iron Cross Second Class by the German Crown Prince.[60]

Author's Summary

Georg Salzberger is shown to be a kind and compassionate man, with a deep sense of *Pflicht* [duty], to faith, *Volk* and Fatherland. He volunteered immediately, despite only recently having taken up the position of rabbi at the newly built Frankfurt West End synagogue, thinking of his country before personal advancement. All his writings are informed by a sense of patriotism and the justice of the German cause, and a sense of superiority (however gently expressed) of his own German culture over others, such as those of France and Russia. His deep sense of loyalty to the Kaiser and royal family may seem exaggerated today, but were typical for the time, especially amongst German Jews attempting to emphasize their German patriotism and their feeling that they were Germans first, and Jews second.

Descriptions of conditions in the field hospitals, particularly the infectious disease hospitals, are typical of the state of military medicine at the time, with emphasis on wound-related and non-wound-related infectious diseases. Whatever the attempts to combat these, lice were ever-present in the trenches and louse-born typhus was common. Polluted water-supplies due to poor trench drainage during the wet season led to diseases such as typhoid, cholera and dysentery, and the nature of trench warfare led inexorably to wound sepsis, gas gangrene and tetanus. Bacterial pneumonia commonly followed wounds, and venereal diseases were common. No antibacterials were available to treat infections, with the exception of the newly discovered salvarsan against syphilis.

Salzberger's description of the holding of large Pesach services in the midst of the Battle of Verdun contrasts strikingly with the surrounding slaughter. These services, together with the improved Seder rations, must have been a great comfort to the stressed and shell-shocked soldiers. No greater contrast between war and faith can be imagined. The longer the war lasted, the more the Central Powers suffered from the British sea blockade and the more difficult it became to obtain adequate rations. In this regard, Rabbi Salzberger's enterprise in collecting so much food, especially meat, from various sources for both Pesach Seders was no mean feat.

In contrast to many other chaplains, Salzberger directly refers in writing to the *Judenzählung* of October 1916 in his memoirs and realizes how dangerous this is to future German-Jewish relations. The last chapter ends with a very sobering view of the future and the full realization that this might not be as bright as he would wish.

NOTES

1. G. Salzberger, *Aus meinem Kriegstagebuch. Von dem Feldgeistlichen bei der 5 Armee.* (Frankfurt am Main: Sonderabdruck aus der Monatschrift *Liberales Judentum*, 1916), pp.1–134.
2. Salzberger, *Aus meinem Kriegstagebuch.* pp.1–11.
3. The battle of Mars la Tour (16 August 1870). Two Prussian corps encountered the entire French army on the Rhine and forced them to retreat into the fortress of Metz.
4. Psalm 144: 4. Also recited on the High Holy Days.
5. Genesis 22: 2. The story of the *Akeda*, or Binding of Isaac (Genesis 22: 1–19) is recited on the morning of the second day of Rosh Hashanah.
6. Jeremiah 31: 15–17.
7. Rosh Hashanah is variously referred to as 'Yom Hadin' (The Day of Judgment); 'Yom Hazikaron' (The Day of Remembrance); 'Yom Tekiat Shofar' (The Day of the Blowing of the Shofar), which is sounded on all days except the Sabbath.
8. A communal list of confession of sin read several times during the Yom Kippur service.
9. Leviticus 16: 1–34.
10. Isaiah 57: 14–21; 58: 1–14.
11. The Burgfrieden (civil truce) declared by the Kaiser on 4 August 1914, proclaiming that he knew only Germans, irrespective of faith or party.
12. Formula from 1 Kings 18: 39 repeated seven times at the end of Yom Kippur concluding service.
13. Deuteronomy 32: 1–52.
14. Salzberger, *Aus meinem Kriegstagebuch*, pp.12–23.
15. Ibid., pp.24–44.
16. The German word Typhus does not differentiate between typhoid fever (Bauchtyphus) and louse-borne typhus (Flecktyphus).
17. Antibiotics had not yet been discovered and, despite careful aseptic techniques, wounds became infected (or were infected on admission). Gas gangrene commonly resulted from penetrating shrapnel wounds and could only be treated by wide excision or amputation. Abscesses were treated by incision, and if limb infections did not heal amputation was the only resource. Bacterial pneumonia, typhoid fever, typhus, scrub typhus, dysentery and cholera had no cure and their mortality was high. Tetanus was uniformly fatal in the first months of the war until prophylactic anti-tetanus serum was made available. However, many still died from fatal serum anaphylaxis and no vaccine was yet available.
18. French colonial troops from Africa and Indo-China.
19. Psalm 121.
20. At the start of the war, French soldiers wore the same red trousers (*pantalons rouges*) as they had done during the previous century, until they became such targets that their uniform colour was changed to a dirty blue.
21. Literally 'nation of the world', Hebrew and Yiddish for an uneducated person.
22. A word of terrible irony. The National Socialists were to bind all Germans deemed suitable into a single *Volksgemeinschaft*, from which Jews and other undesirables were excluded

and had to be purged. The word 'Volk' is untranslatable: it is an exclusionary national concept.
23. Salzberger, *Aus meinem Kriegstagebuch*, pp.45–54.
24. Alfred Dreyfus (1859–1935), an Alsatian Jewish captain in the French General Staff, was convicted in 1895 of treason by espionage for Germany, stripped of his rank, and exiled to Devil's Island. He was released from prison and pardoned in 1899 and later totally exonerated. L'Affaire Dreyfus tore the fabric of the Third Republic apart in its cradle. The irony is that this could never have occurred in Germany, because Jews were not allowed in the Prussian officers corps.
25. Rabbi Salzberger's viewpoint reflects those of the most patriotic German confident in the rightness of the German cause. The unlikelihood of remuneration, as described, does not seem to have struck him and he appears not to have much sympathy for the plight of civilians under German occupation.
26. 27 January.
27. Salzberger, *Aus meinem Kriegstagebuch*, pp.55–61.
28. Russian prisoners of war were often used for road-building on the Western Front.
29. Salzberger, *Aus meinem Kriegstagebuch*, pp.62–79.
30. Malachi 2: 10.
31. Ten adult (post-Bar Mitzvah) Jewish males are necessary for a quorum or minyan before a service containing all the prayers can occur.
32. Salzberger, *Aus meinem Kriegstagebuch*, pp.80–96.
33. Rashi: Acronym for Rabbi Shlomo ben Yitzhak (1040–1105), a French rabbi, born in Troyes, author of a comprehensive and definitive commentary on the Talmud and Old Testament. Rabbeinu Tam (1100–1171): Rashi's grandson, and another renowned scholar. Around 1150, Rabbeinu Tam, his brother the Rashbam and others convened a synod to discuss conditions of Jewish life after the Crusades. In Germany soon afterwards synods were convened by the three communities of Speyer, Worms and Mainz. The regulations issued at these synods are known as the Takkanot (legislative enactments) of Shum (the initial letters in Hebrew of the three towns).
34. Due to inclement weather and increased troop and munition transports.
35. Venereal disease was very common amongst soldiers during the First World War. Antibacterials did not yet exist, but Paul Ehrlich had recently introduced salvarsan for the treatment of syphilis.
36. St Quentin is the largest city in Picardy. Heavy fighting occurred around and in it during both Franco-Prussian and First World Wars. The city endured a harsh German occupation during the First World War, and lay in the centre of the war zone: 80 per cent of its buildings were damaged or destroyed by war's end.
37. The Battle of Sedan on 1–2 September 1870 resulted in the capture of Napoléon III together with over 100,000 of his troops, while attempting to break through and relieve the besieged city of Metz. This battle for all intents and purposes decided the war in Prussia's favour. In 1871, 2 September was declared Sedan Day and a German national holiday. Its celebration was the cause of French bitterness.
38. Salzberger, *Aus meinem Kriegstagebuch*, pp.97–111. The Battle of Verdun was fought between German and French armies between 21 February and 18 December 1916. The exact number of casualties is unknown but was at least 700,000 on both sides, with over 100,000 French and Germans killed or missing. Although the French ultimately repulsed the Germans, it grievously debilitated both armies.
39. Fort Douaumont was captured by the Germans on 25 February but retaken by the French on 24 October 1916.
40. Isaiah 40: 4.
41. Nechemiah Anton Nobel (1871–1922), a noted rabbi in Frankfurt am Main.

42. Leshanah Haba'ah Biyerushalayim, 'Next year in Jerusalem': recited towards the end of the Hagadah readings.
43. Salzberger, *Aus meinem Kriegstagebuch*, pp.112–19.
44. A Hebrew word without exact English equivalent best translated as 'knowledge'.
45. Exodus 17: 15.
46. Probably the German translation of the old Dutch Prayer of Thanks (*wir treten zum Beten*) by Adrianus Valerius (c. 1575–1625), a potent symbol of the Throne- and Altar-alliance of German civil religion until 1918.
47. This only became the German National Anthem during the Weimar Republic.
48. Salzberger, *Aus meinem Kriegstagebuch*, pp.120–33.
49. Lamentations 3: 27–8.
50. Genesis 28: 10–11.
51. Ethics of the Fathers 1: 14. Hillel said: 'If I am not for myself, who is for me? But if I am only for myself, what am I? And if not now, when?' Hillel the Elder (c. 110 BCE–10 CE), also called Hillel the Babylonian, was considered the greatest sage of the Second Temple period.
52. Leviticus 19: 18.
53. The Judenzählung refers to the Jewish Census decreed on 11 October 1916 by the Prussian War Minister, ostensibly to confirm that Jews were not slacking front-line duty as was asserted by a minority of anti-Semitic extremists. Questionnaires were completed and sent back, but the census was discontinued in early 1917 and results were never published.
54. *Faust* Part 1, line 1336. Johann Wolfgang von Goethe (1749–1832).
55. Genesis 32: 24–32.
56. Genesis 4: 9.
57. Talmud Bavli (Shavuot), 39a.
58. R. Vogel, *Ein Stück von uns: deutsche Juden in deutschen Armeen, 1813–1976: eine Dokumentation* (Mainz: von Hase & Koehler Verlag, 1977), p.136.
59. Hermann von François (1856–1933), an Infantry General who played a major role in the German victory at the Battle of Tannenberg (26–30 August 1914).
60. Vogel, *Ein Stück von uns*, pp.133–4.

CHAPTER THREE

Martin Salomonski: Zola in Chaplain's Uniform

Martin Salomonski (see Plates 3, 4 and 5) joined the army as chaplain in 1916 and served with the First Army on the Somme and elsewhere. He published two booklets: the first in 1917 of his experiences during a year on the Somme,[1] the second a compilation from the first book, representing a small manual to describe the spiritual needs of soldiers on the Front.[2] Translations of the first book follow:

To the Western Front[3]

At midnight I took sad leave of my deeply-rooted views about the construction and condition of modern methods of transport. The Prussian-Hessian express train has always been an emblem of our state machine – durable, expedient, comfortable, always in the best of condition. One can say the exact opposite about the Belgian train which we now took, without falling prey to gross and conscious exaggeration.

Now we travelled to Herbesthal in a darkened, overfilled military train. All seats taken, and in corridors man pressed against man. Standing, squatting, lying: everyone trying to sleep. 'Everyone get out!', soldiers and conductors cried on the dimly lit platform at 2.00 a.m. We were at the German border and went together under strict supervision through the customs hall and then back to the train. 'Just like the shepherd who musters his sheep',[4] I thought. Everyone was in a hurry, trying to grab a precious space in the train. He who returns first finds a seat, and the law of 'love thy neighbour' is not much followed on trains. An hour by train before their arrival, soldiers already begin to feel a joyful anticipation when they are travelling eastwards, and from Lüttich onwards nothing more can mar their happiness! Even if the train dilly-dallies towards German soil, after a delay of many hours soldiers remain in good humour. The only problem is that each one is a little afraid, with dreadful fear of the border crossing, and wishes (with a certain uneasiness) the customs examination (which is more than perfunctory, by the way) that 'forgives seven times' to be over. Yes, one is happy to go home, whatever happens!

Eventually we travelled on. Day was already dawning and the train, as if pilot-led, glided slowly onwards, through Belgian territory. The allegedly great destruction caused by the war in Belgian regions was less obvious on our journey. Certainly, the much-pitied land had, in 1916, two peaceful years behind it. While battle raged around it, and other peoples were burdened with sacrifice, suffering and deprivation, almost the whole of Belgium had remained untouched since the end of August 1914, and could experience the orderly hand of German administration. Flemish and Walloon peoples were given great freedom and enjoyed many advantages. If small discrepancies did occur, may this not have been the result of over-generous German concessions?

I do not dispute that I have seen a few shot-up houses along the railway embankment, but otherwise nothing reminded one of war. On the right section of track we met one goods train after the other, all of great length and with an amazing number of axles, such that the eye searched longingly for the last carriage. The brakesman was enthroned on an open seat smoking his pipe. We waved amicably to one another, then one could once more see the heads of telegraph poles, which are of green glass in France, mixed with our large German white porcelain ones. We travelled through tunnels and well-guarded bridges, where many a bearded reservist held faithful watch, and over rivers, canals and serpentine creeks. Anglers were plying their traditional trade in the quieter waters of the sacred early morning, and nothing reminded us of war. Monsieur squats with dignity on the bank of the river in pagoda-like stillness, his rod horizontal to the water, defiantly for hours and days. Next to him stands Madame's blue kitchen bucket in which the fish will swim once caught. And twenty metres away squats his competitor. This picture belongs to the waterways of France and Belgium, as do the beautiful trees fringing the waters, obvious guideposts for aeroplanes of friend and foe.

At Jeumont we arrived on French soil. Each of us had already travelled many times in spirit to France and to Paris. The German knows and values the achievements of his Western neighbour, his education and character, and we always have a word of apology when the French undervalue us. We resemble a couple unhappy in love. One recognizes the fruitlessness of his feelings but wastes them anew on new pleasantries and cordiality. It will remain so after the war and is, in the end, a product of German power of intuition which predicts for both peoples more level, if not identical, paths.

While we were crossing the French border I dreamt with open eyes of my old schooldays. I saw them before me, worthily represented by my teacher Professor Ferdinand Lamprecht, head of the Berlin Gymnasium 'Zum grauen Kloster'.[5] He was telling us again about 1870/71: As a young officer he had served in the campaign of the Third Ulan regiment. While I was preoccupied with these happy memories, the northern French industrial area came into view: the conquered stronghold of Maubeuge, the chimney and factory-rich Hautmont slid gently by, and the train left behind Le Cateau, Busigny, Bohain – three towns in which I was later often quartered. Then, to the north-west, a huge building emerged, which I did not recognize at first. I identified it because it dominates the landscape. It was the cathedral of St Quentin, proudly dominating hills and valleys, ruling unchallenged over houses and towers, field and forest. Everything appears small before it as it towers imperiously over the town. Now the brakes were applied and the train stopped punctually in St Quentin station, my final destination.

In the Theatre of War[6]

How many generations have worked on the glorious St Quentin Cathedral! And now it stands there, strong and defiant, strong enough to withstand the strongest explosions and well-aimed direct hits. English pilots and giant cannons could not lay waste to it in the first year; if indeed they have in the meanwhile damaged it, it remains no act of heroism and has not been made easy for them by our Supreme Command. Our army has done everything it can to protect this church during this time of war, perhaps more than the French state did during the last years of peace. They are probably responsible for clear signs of deterioration and lack of care inside the building.[7]

A strong team of white horses was waiting for me and I made the acquaintance of my staff: Privates First Class Aach and Koppe. We have got along well until now, and it will be a sad day when we have to part. The two comrades are the solid assistants of the Jewish chaplain in Supreme Army Command. My circle widened during the Battle of the Somme and the great strategic retreat thereafter. Young theologians were commandeered from the Front to support me, but always only for a short time! The number of Jewish chaplains who have entered the field of battle is gratifyingly large, but the sacrifices they have made are also great. Eight chaplains known to me have already fallen, three of them in the Battle of the Somme. We honour their memory![8]

We travelled to our quarters with the Widow E. This worthy lady had spent the last five months in bed but my arrival got her to her feet. Apart from the desire to eat, unexplainable in one so thin, and her continual need to change servants (it is different at home!), she showed no signs of illness and seemed much more cut from wood which can grow to a hundred years old. She worried only about herself and not about the house that she had inherited. She obligingly left the cleaning of the rooms to us and generously ignored the spiders' webs and dusty curtains, as well as the window panes which had taken on a field grey colour. She got up late and therefore went to bed early.

Marie Blanche (for these were her names) had her good sides as well. In the crowd of gossiping neighbours she was the most restrained chauvinist and stood second only to a formidable '*Madame L'Econome*', the little mistress (powdered in the French manner) of the neighbouring girls' school. For good pay, this dragon taught German officers French and paid court to every doctor who had the bad luck to be quartered with her. Like other French women she admired German medicine, which did not stop her from spewing poison and bile on everything German. She laid claim to a high level of education and (oh, how rarely one finds this in France) even understands German. Her hatred had something ingrained about it and one must unfortunately generalize that the upper echelons of French society, especially, are completely uneducable in their unreasonable complaints at everything 'Prussian'. How much more harmless was the good Madame Moisson, even if she called the Kaiser a brigand and appeared determined to kill him with her own hands. But apart from this talk, which translates into admiration in our own quieter idiom, she incorporated healthy bourgeois characteristics and accepted Germans as human beings.

Having arrived in this world of women, I must also introduce an old spinster, Fräulein Viktoire. She was significantly large, lacked all charm, and was contemptuous of the male species. She only became friendly if one called her 'the Maid of Orléans'.

All these ladies visited one another daily and drank good coffee (the French were also, to the last, plentifully supplied with these and other provisions) while they crocheted the most beautiful blankets, collars and borders. Their meetings were marked by both agility and eloquence.

It is high time that I bid farewell for a while to the female world of the 'revenge' quarter: the streets named after Metz, Strasbourg, Alsace and Lorraine![9] On the afternoon of my arrival I reported for service at High Command and was received by the Commander-in-Chief with friendly, kind words. In the evening I was introduced into the large mess hall, and upon arrival there experienced the natural shyness that everyone feels in completely alien circles. The touch of embarrassment which accompanies us from childhood on such occasions is nature's merciful gift. It warns all those who have inherited their rank of the deeply-rooted duty of benevolent comradeship (particularly strong in the officers' corps). And it is in the end better for all who maintain a sense of reserve when they join a group than it is for the man with 'enviable self-assurance'.

I had that afternoon received the map of the camp area. The first message from the Front arrived, calling me to a burial the following morning. At 7.00 a.m. the next day the truck arrived for me: we travelled westwards through the still sleeping town (it was still only 6.00 a.m. according to French time and the French are not early risers).[10] The truck was driven to the chain of watchposts with moderate speed, but after that it showed what it could do. We stormed forward, flew over, sucked up and swallowed the undulating countryside. We were still bumping steeply downwards when the wall of a steeply-rising street stood before us. Again we were on the heights; valley after valley disappeared from view. The truck, given its head now, sped through further towns and villages, past woods and rich farmsteads, past fields of ripening crops well cultivated by our soldiers, further and further on. The truck remained, however, very obedient, tractable and docile in the driver's hands, as he steered it through the swelling host of wagons and marching columns.

In both directions, the further we got, the stronger grew the stream of artillery and vehicles carrying munitions and provisions flowing in both directions. And in the middle of all these, trucks appeared and with amazing dexterity broke through the path that to the human eye seemed too narrow to pass, and flashed by. Behind the town of Nesle my companion, next to whose seat two rifles sparkled, took map in hand for the first time and soon we swung in a southwesterly direction; after 15 minutes we reached our destination, an advance field hospital. The comrade whom I buried there in a well-tended German cemetery in the presence of a senior surgeon and a few lightly-wounded comrades was a 40-year-old grenadier guard, killed by a bullet while assisting a wounded comrade in a trench. The wounded men listened to me with respectful attention when I talked about the dead man's old mother who, while we were burying her son, had still not heard the terrible news. I ended with the unfortunate and grossly premature hope that the deceased would be one of the last victims of this war and felt confident that I had not said anything amiss to his comrades.

With greater justification than before I addressed my funeral oration in the field to the living, in an attempt at giving them comfort in the suffering and danger which was renewed and increased every day. Clearly no extensive praise would bring the dead back; the biblical words: 'weep not for the dead, weep rather for those who remain behind'[11] assume increased relevance. The compassion shown by our comrades in arms is a great deal more honest than that seen at home from acquaintances and so-called friends, because each feels that he is representing the Homeland and wants to dispel the crushing thought, 'No-one can be with him' by pouring out his soul to God, praying and feeling: 'He was my brother!'

After the burial I visited a seriously wounded Jewish soldier at the same field hospital. He lay there with chest shot to pieces, trusting and waiting to hear something that would give him hope. The poor young man had to suffer in vain for four more long weeks. I resolved to inform the immediate family whenever I became acquainted with cases of death or illness. This was a hard burden to carry, the heaviness of which could not be measured at the time. But a great satisfaction developed out of it for me, and whenever I could I also sent a short message back home about meetings with healthy comrades. Because even if a letter from the Front from a son or husband arrives saying 'I am fine', does not gnawing worry remain in every loyal heart, robbing parents, wives and fiancées of sleep? Their hearts continue to beat at the same feverish pitch and they want to know: 'How is he doing at this particular minute?' Therefore it is always good to obtain a new endorsement of one's cautious hopes, even from a stranger, someone who does not whitewash the news.

My perceptions even of the positive side of the war having become considerably toned down, I travelled the first part of the journey back home. Like many others I could hardly wait for my conscription and had always worried about coming out too late. In Nesle I witnessed a dreadful event that froze the blood in the veins even of those who accompanied me. North of the city, high up, were three German field balloons, looking in their plump yellowness like decorations in the shining blue morning heavens. And then: a wild fleeing of the women and children into the houses, an anxious milling around and staring up by the men! An enemy airplane appeared high above the first balloon, dived sharply and shot it down. We saw a tiny column of smoke and soon the entire proud giant shell became a sea of fire. The observer plunged from the basket head over heels into the depths. An outcry rose to heaven but the plane rose proudly like a bird of prey that has mauled its booty and sped off to invisible heights. I can still hear the crowd's cry of pain at the horrible sight of this act of destruction. It was an indictment before God by French men, women and children of those to whom the judgment of world history will attribute the blame for this war.[12]

Reflective soldiers often debate over whether death is evil. There are sufficient men in the German army for whom nothing is more enticing, despite healthy love of life, than the call of war. Such men are happy to sacrifice their lives to protect the Fatherland, and would rather die than wish to fade away in an infirm body or an enslaved Homeland. But all of us revolt against each pointless murder that tears innocent citizens to pieces in a fraction of a minute, with no human help available. The vindictive transplantation of the air war into peaceful towns far away from the Front is an invention of our enemies that could be demonstrated even before the war started. Our air forces have gone to war against the armed enemy following only justifiable dictates of necessity and resistance, and they treat the enemy with conciliatory chivalry. More than one vanquished opponent has been thankful for this, or experienced it with inner embarrassment. By contrast, the abuses and attacks upon our prisoners of war, especially in France, by officers, physicians, nurses and the inflamed masses, often at express command of their superiors, are well known. At sea this degeneracy has been surpassed by the British, who are ever more avidly learning new tricks.[13]

Beginning[14]

An artillery man said that the French were firing heavily today. On Tuesday at dinner, where everyone wants to hear something new, someone asked what that bunch were planning now: 'The French are shooting again!' 'Still shooting', the artillery officer corrected him. On Wednesday the constant roaring was taken to be the announcement of an attack. Now I, the outsider, could see – from the serious demeanour of the officers, their increased activity, and their short stay at table – that the enemy was announcing not only the arrival of American missiles,[15] but that they intended to do worse. I found other signs of emerging battle in my spiritual care. A religious minority in the field yields accurate information about the ebb and flow of the combat operation, of the rising or falling numbers of losses. The town's field hospitals filled up surprisingly rapidly and in almost every one I found badly wounded Jewish soldiers. One had lost an eye, another was stunned by gas poisoning; bullet wounds in head, jaw, shoulder, lung and abdomen, shrapnel in knee and thigh, all devastating results of artillery and trench fighting, were evident. The wounded rested pale and bloody in their beds and soon also in the broad corridors, even lying on the floor. Ambulances rolled in day and night without pause. The heavy omnibuses, which in German cities are used for such peaceful or enjoyable pursuits, brought in the lightly wounded, and closed automobiles pulling several cleverly built two-wheeled trailers brought in the seriously wounded.

On Friday 30 June I was called to Bapaume, which had until that point been easily reached by rail, for the burial of a Württemberger. But when in St Quentin the scheduled train was cancelled and I attempted to get to my destination via Cambrai. I had the same bad luck: from Cambrai only munitions trains and troop trains were travelling through. I used the enforced waiting time to introduce myself in the field hospitals, and returned to St Quentin in the afternoon without having accomplished my mission.

That evening I held the first religious service in the synagogue. It was a dilapidated and badly damaged building lacking all beauty, but one that over the years of battle had attained honour and been visited many times. In addition to the usual liturgy I added some interpolations: a prayer for each comrade who had fallen or been badly wounded during the course of the week and the extended prayer for Kaiser, Princes of State and *Reich*, in which God's blessing is beseeched: 'For our army that is used to winning in battle, and is now fighting the harsh battle that has been imposed upon it by others.' My sermon was based on the words of the Prophets: 'Like a man whom his mother comforts, so will I comfort you',[16] because spiritual comfort that stems from faith seemed to speak so convincingly through this.

In fact, the soldiers in the field lack nothing so much as the warming, loving breath of upright womanhood; and nothing depresses them as much as the impossibility of entrusting their cares and hopes to a sensitive heart that understands and forgives all. It makes no difference whether this happiness that is denied in the field takes the form of wife or mother: true manly love venerates both.

Generally, when night falls and one prepares for sleep, one's longing flies eastwards; one looks across as if into an unearthly but sharply defined time of youth and peace. The man on his bed is like a boy; the worry-lines on his forehead smooth out; anger and passion dissolve like a fist unclenching; the imagination, often numbed during the daily battle, stirs its wings, and softly rocks us to sleep and dreams.

After wild games and happy larks
The evening bell to tired child talks
I happily lay me down to sleep
Mom tucked me in, my soul to keep.
Who covers me now 'ere I sleep?

The faithful hand upon my head
Took all the fear from me instead
My mother had to be with me
For me to sleep so happily.
Who covers me now 'ere I sleep?

I became a man and went to war
With no thought now for Homeland's door.
I looked for joy a long, long time,
Repented sins and all my crime.
Who covers me now 'ere I sleep?

Now here I lie in the foe's land
On cold, cold earth and hard, hard sand.
Abandoned now, and quite alone,
With nothing dear, just cold hard stone.
Who covers me now 'ere I sleep?

O that a wonder could occur
And mother's softness 'fore me stir!
So that I, led by mother's hand

> Could then return to childhood's land
> To cover me here 'ere I sleep.[17]

In such hours, which are not spared anyone in the field, one learns to pray. One is enfolded in humble devotion and spiritual purification, and is not far away from Goodness or from God. When a soldier comes to services, his innermost soul is filled with high expectation, not with humdrum daily events of life in the field, be it cinema or church. Woe to anyone who disappoints him and sends him away empty! No community is more willing and yet more demanding than comrades at the Front. One must always consider that, under the shot-up uniforms, the dented helmets, that make them seem all alike, the noblest hearts beat, the most glorious thoughts weave. One is soon disabused of the belief that education goes along with a clean-shaven face. Here, the chaplain has the glorious role of raising the spirit and that is more than just arousing *Andacht* [devotion, silent prayer]. I now know that our German word *erbauen* [uplifting, edification] is a shining jewel and the best resource for curing a soul's despair. Edification makes enduring deliverance possible and is not as fleeting as enthusiasm or so-called 'mood'.

We must take the latter word in its strict meaning. It should be a firm foundation on which an enduring task is performed. Who does not feel happy when he succeeds in this: to equip those who fight such that greatest joy and new hope speaks to them from our work; that they devote themselves to God and His teachings as does the farmer (whom we do not call *Bauer* for nothing)[18] to his earth, the master to his house. Just as both will never believe that floods will carry away their fields, that lightning will destroy the roof under which innocent children sleep, soldiers' hearts must be filled with the inner certainty: 'God is with me, I fear nothing',[19] and this must stay with them. The longer the war lasts, the more difficult it becomes to lift the spirits of our heroes, and there are no hard and fast rules. But according to my limited experience one does better, where possible, putting some distance between the war and religious contemplation. German soldiers do not need to be reminded to do their duty. Furthermore, it is better to discard all pious sayings. Waving the hands about and staring upwards (I am aware of my exaggeration) are also useless. Grab the man's heart and show him his salvation, his happiness and his peace! Then he leaves comforted and will remain so in life and death.

Next day I was sitting for a bit in my easy chair (I have so far not seen a real German sofa in France) and had nodded off to sleep having made myself tolerably comfortable in the uncomfortable chair – probably for more than 15 minutes. Suddenly a massive blast woke me with a resounding crash. The walls of the flimsily built house shook, the many pictures shook on their nails, window panes shattered, doors opened. It is astounding how the soldier, not losing his head, instinctively takes cover when this happens. Children especially learn very easily. They recognize the barely visible aeroplane in the sunny sky, often identifying the exact number of planes, cleverly work out their direction of flight, and differentiate German from French machines by the whirr of their propellers.

On that day, St Quentin glaziers could have become wealthy if they had had sufficient supplies of putty. Many window panes broke and many houses, roof and all, were badly damaged. The cathedral received a friendly nudge, which is now on the conscience of a stupid 18-year-old English flier. We shot him down, and when he was taken prisoner he was quite proud of his success, which was, however, significantly diminished by the bravery of our engineers. Railway traffic, the great aorta, remained uninterrupted.

In the field, when one meets somebody whom at home one would have walked past with indifference three times a day, it is as if the sun has risen in the evening, and friendly embraces occur without either party having to curry favour. The clouded lenses of prejudice fall away and one sees clearly and joyfully that every single person has his good points. How many, especially those who have fancied themselves good judges of character, have badly misjudged their fellow-men in the field and have learned better! After valuable time together, usually only brief, they part having learned something of permanent value from one other.

Yes, war also has its good points! I have also been especially fortunate to meet very many acquaintances and also former pupils from my time as a teacher in Berlin. I have also met not a few of my congregants from Frankfurt on the Oder[20] or people from Brandenburg, and also soldiers from other German contingents. This results from the fact that during the five months of the battle of the Somme a large part of the German army has, for shorter or longer periods of time, been stationed in my sphere of activity. When I speak to officers and men, our discussions become less formal and we start to build bridges of mutual understanding.

Kant on the Somme[21]

My memoirs are not designed to, and should not, have anything to do with strategy of the Battle of the Somme,[22] but there are limited areas on which I must touch. To defend ourselves against the enemy's furious deployment of all available means and power, and the use of their main armies and best troops in a small area, proved, at first, a difficult task for our numerically inferior army. German soldiers achieved great things at the beginning of the enemy's advance; what they endured was beyond comprehension and much heroic blood was spilled. But what the Entente considered impossible was achieved: the brunt of the attack was checked, the offensive brought to a halt and broken into smaller battles. The enemy's blood and that of their allies flowed for naught; they made no headway and achieved nothing.

July through September were the three months of sacrifice, with harvest for field hospitals and cemeteries. Almost on a daily basis, I participated in communal burials in both St Quentin and on the Front. Each chaplain held his service and gave his sermon, and each tried to highlight all that united us and leave no room for divisions. Psalm 130, read out at the open graves by Catholic chaplains, had a poignant and lasting effect. 'Out of the depths I cry to you, O God.' Standing near the depths of the tomb and from the depths of his pain, man begs for relief from suffering and fortifies himself with faith in a better future both in life and after death. I wish that this song of the Lord, which pours balsam into hearts of all who pine, could be recited at each bier, like the *Kaddish*: this prayer of noble self-conquest that praises the Lord in the midst of suffering and ends in yearning for God's kingdom and peace on earth.

Religion should lose no opportunity to bring to life the concept of peace, this iron component of its inventiveness. It should not make us wait until war teaches us the meaning of peace and what a threefold blessing it is. No less worthy than the ceremony by which often twenty or more comrades are committed to the earth are individual burials at the field hospitals. Although military salutes and music are lacking, the soothing compassion of the wounded is always present. Propped up on crutches, bent over by wounds and frailty, they honour their dead brothers. Even in the midst of their illnesses, where everyone is at their service and no-one commands them, they demonstrate moving humility, a prime virtue of the German soldier.

I experienced a very moving example of this among the hospital occupants when a Jewish soldier was being buried [Plate 29]. They stood back indecisively and awaited my invitation to participate in the natural though mistaken assumption that their presence might be unwelcome.

> At the castle Vélu, through its broad avenue
> The misery on wheels is on public view.
> The wagons roll on and briefly stop,
> And more and more are loaded up.
> In white beds in the mirrored hall
> The heroes lie there pale and small.
>
> And now they bring another in
> With terrible wounds and no voice within.
> His bloody clothes don't have his name
> And death is near, his life to claim.
> No nursing helps him, but steadfastly
> A young nurse stands by him calmly.
>
> Because just 'ere the soldier gives up the ghost
> He calls to his dear one, whom he loves the most.
> The nurse stands by till the midnight hour,
> Until his mouth opens with death's final power
> And rattling he stammers, one time withal:
> 'War-ventured, worker, Rosenthal.'
>
> Because Rosenthal was a German Jew
> A rabbi was ordered, the last rites to do.
> He stood before the open grave
> To relieve the pastor in the small enclave,
> And many soldiers were standing aside:
> Should they now leave, or should they abide?
>
> The chaplain thinks: this cannot be right --
> I stand here alone, with no soldier in sight;
> The dead hears not, but he surely is worth
> A comradely honour in his final berth.
> 'Come comrades' the rabbi loudly cried,
> 'He was a worker, war-ventured: then he died!'

> They all stand together as if mesmerized
> Their caps in their hands, sadness in their eyes.
> The evening sun shines warmly in
> And the feeling is heavy, so heavy within;
> They knew him, and caring held them in thrall:
> War-ventured, worker, Rosenthal.

When a wounded man is in the field hospital and can hope to remain alive, he feels as if he is in Paradise and the Biblical words shine out of his eyes: 'I am too small and unworthy of all the mercy which You have shown to Your servant.'[23] Yes, he is thankful, yet he must often still bear and suffer so much. I will not speak here of the terrible mutilations that the battle inflicts which make the man fearful at the thought of his difficult future, even though everything is done at home, even for older invalids, to prepare them for easily-learned work that can earn them a living. May a time come in our Fatherland when a happy race takes up this duty with ease, and when no saviour looks like a beggar!

The loss of limbs is a lesser evil than blindness, facial disfiguration and permanent loss of speech. And then there are the smaller irritants that make defenceless patients despair: oppressive summer heat and its companion plague of flies. Very few effective remedies exist against the latter, which in many cases make the last hours of the dying even more miserable.

The path to death is quick. How often have I sat at the bed of a suffering man, spoken to him about an approaching good future and speedy return home, knowing that in a day, maybe even in an hour, he will have crossed over into the unknown. And how difficult it is with the mentally ill, who have been confused by the din of battle but nevertheless remain conscious of their clouded condition. I have also been called to the beds of attempted suicides, men greatly depressed by domestic strife, or by breaks with parents or siblings. Each bed holds a new task for the chaplain. It is best to tread very carefully, initially ask very little and let the poor patient speak himself if his strength allows it. One must always proceed in such a way as to gain his trust and lighten his spirit: only then will he be willing to accept words of encouragement. It has never seemed wrong to me for a human being to seek the goodwill of others, because it only comes to him who is worthy of it. Thus the guiding principle for all chaplains, if they are to be most useful to those entrusted to their care – make yourself well-liked! It makes no difference whether the patient is old or younger. Each one must feel: 'That man is my friend, he does everything for me, and I can rely on him.' Also don't imitate their superiors, because you are not one of them. In other words no rudeness; but also no softness!

One stands before young Kantians: even if they do not know his name, the categorical imperative pulses through their veins:[24] there are no mercenaries, none can be bribed by the enemy's money, none can be lured to defect by a trench poster: they are all sons of duty!

This well-deserved praise extends, in our context, into three specific groups: like the soldier at the front, they do their best and, when necessary, sacrifice their lives:

Respect all physicians, nurses and medical orderlies! They have saved hundreds of thousands of men's lives for their families and for the Fatherland. They have either prevented or nipped in the bud infectious diseases such as cholera, typhus/typhoid,[25] dysentery and malaria. They have laboured day and night for long months in the midst of the cannon's thunder. Think of the valiant stretcher-bearers who faithfully search the churned-up battlefield to fetch the wounded and dead. Oh, if only you could see the nurses: their gift of angelic patience, not shunning the horror, how no work is too lowly for them! How they stride from camp to camp as tender comforters, how even their presence has a healing effect. The final secret of medical success remains organization and our sense of order.

In this war a second band of people, apart from the men and women of the Red Cross, have stepped forward. These people hurry to their brothers without weapons and build protective habitations for them with spade and hoe, even under fire. Hauliers [*Schipper*] are also soldiers, and real ones at that! Their achievements have been recognized at the highest level and the sensitivity of the German is again demonstrated by the fact that he regards the man who helps supply the soldiers as an equal comrade and wishes him well.

Druckposten [cushy jobs]: what a stupid word! I do not assert this in order to whitewash it. The hauliers do not serve in *Druckposten* and the old reserve army men certainly do not either. I politely request that the word *Druckposten* not be mentioned to describe these groups. And the same applies for the sutlers, telegraphists and administrative personnel. The soldier behind the counter, with the many hundreds that crowd around him on a daily basis, performs gruelling work that requires a high degree of strength and skill. Telephone operators are all heroes, deep in their dugouts. I can think of three who I looked up in March 1917 shortly before our strategic withdrawal towards Sailly: patching cables and remaining calm, establishing conversations for hours on end. This requires men as reliable as precision machines, but also with independent thought. Nerves of steel are too weak for them: they must have no nerves at all! It is no different for clerks who are so often maligned. A red cross hangs in front of their little rooms. They also convey messages and must do their job to keep the troops in order in their accounting books. Every single one of these has done his duty and in every one of them glows the holy 'You must!' Kant has his part in the German victory at the Somme.

But They Cannot Escalate Things[26]

The French and English calculated that the war would be decided on the Somme in 1916. They knew that our troops were constrained in all parts of the European Front, especially in the East, and didn't believe that we had the necessary reinforcements of men and arms both for the Somme and everywhere else. They underestimated the elasticity of the German army. When it was necessary a second great defensive army arose, as if conjured from the earth, but in reality brought in by rail in the normal way. At that time the more astute among the enemy began to have misgivings: was it at all possible to overcome German power? Then they began to bring over other nations – even the 'neutrals' – to their side. But this didn't help them at all and to this day has not led to victory, because Germany nourishes and defends itself by its own efforts. We can use gunpowder as long as there is still air, we have cannons and railways as long as there is iron, we can steer the vehicle of victory as long as there is coal to mine.

The German soldier has shown his superiority, and what was interpreted as errors has on the contrary proven to be the secret of his success. Oh ever-mocked German thoroughness, milked like a cow in different comic papers, which now overflow with patriotism, you have shown your worth! Daily drill has taken thousands upon thousands of railway trains safely to their destination: it has taught machinists and stokers to remain in their locomotive even when ten flyers circle above them and drop bombs. But the German spirit has not remained static: from tiny beginnings great creations have unfolded. The U-boat, weapons in aeroplanes, the use of gas, the machine-gun and much, much more which we shall only be able to talk about when peace has come.

Romania led off the dance of our new enemies. Before these disloyal allies openly betrayed us, enemy pilots had already entertained us by dropping slips of paper saying: 'Romania, the ally of the Central Powers, has declared war on Austro-Hungary.'[27] And still they could not force escalate things! Not one necessary man marched away from the Somme, the battle carried on as before. German soldiers knuckled down even more determinedly than before, protected by their new steel helmets.[28] Yes, we still had enough forces to bring in the harvest behind the front, where our big guns stood, and everywhere else in the occupied areas.

Harvest of death and harvest for the living! For a long time to come the farmers in Northern France will find bones and skeletons when they plough.[29] It is better that these last remains of the Battle of the Somme have no distinguishing markings of nationality, because otherwise one would have to fear that they would be desecrated. This is already happening at the hands of the enemy who fire upon cemeteries and memorials erected in the cleared areas by Germans for friend and foe alike, just because their aesthetic sense is insulted.

The summer of 1916 brought a great deal of rain but the harvest was not adversely affected because the downpours usually changed to dry warm weather under influence of the nearby sea. Also, no enemy's greedy desire to cause starvation could destroy the corn in sheaves, ricks and barns. Incendiary bombs missed the corn, and as at home, nobody starved on the Somme. And still, the enemy could not force us out: the German sword saw to it, just as the Lord God would have wanted.

Autumn Celebrations[30]

Three weeks before the start of the Jewish New Year celebrations and through a special decree of the Commander-in-Chief, a directive was issued to all troops involved outlining the place chosen for services and the guidelines for exemption from field duty. As a result, individual units were enrolled punctually and one week before the holidays I already had 1,400 comrades on the list; eventually this number reached 1,600 [see Plate 26].

I had started with the necessary preparations in a timely fashion: initially, after having rented a piano, I formed a choir, which practiced the traditional hymns twice a week. The Berlin Jewish community kindly provided the necessary sheet music; the Verband der deutschen

Juden and the Vereinigung für die Interessen des orthodoxen Judentums provided many prayer books, and donations were sent by the German Rabbinical Association as well as from my home community and other benefactors. All assistance was voluntary, and this noble attitude filled me with special gratitude. I was also able to use previous donations, sent from the homeland on sad occasions, to cover costs.

The military authorities put a large theatre at our disposal for the six services, and also provided a fire extinguishing service. A factory building furnished with electric lighting was allocated to feed the men and equipped with tables and benches. Furniture was brought in from a distance on six large trucks. These fixtures would, according to the usual orderliness of our military authorities, serve other purposes at a later time.

Mass quarters were prepared for soldiers' accommodation: only morning coffee was provided, because I had undertaken to arrange the ritual catering myself, with approval of army administration. The commissariat provided a large part of the necessities which had been discontinued for each man on the three festival days, once his troops had arrived. The meat supply lay in reliable hands and I borrowed the necessary cutlery. Four large field kitchens, three cooks, seven female workers and a large number of willing comrades helped with food preparation.

Large notices showed arriving soldiers the way to the registration office and the area where services were to be held. Upon entry each man received a coupon and identity card. At the conclusion of each service men were conducted to the dining room in military order. The dining room could feed 350 men at a time, so that with the men divided into five groups, each meal ended after a total period of 2½ hours. With the exception of Yom Kippur, only warm food was served (soup, vegetables, meat, potatoes) and there was no lack of bread, beer, cigars and coffee. The many officers and physicians, who ate at a special table, had the same food as the troops, and everything was free. Cost price was charged for taking of a group photograph of everyone who participated in the celebration and, by this means, a not insignificant sum of money was obtained for army coffers. Before commencement of Yom Kippur soldiers were given a snack, consisting of sausage, bread and beer, in the theatre hall. Because many comrades only arrived at the last minute, and some had to leave for their units immediately at the end of services, each received at the end of the day a well-packed parcel of cold meat to take back with him.

Spiritual nourishment was also provided. Great piles of army newspapers, religious writings, weekly papers, army prayer books and sermons, and books which both taught and entertained were laid out and received with special joy by our field-greys.

Services were dignified and solemn, held according to traditional rites. At the centre of the service was the sermon and a prayer for the Kaiser. Additionally *Yizkor* was recited on Yom Kippur, during which we commemorated the many soldiers who had been killed on the Somme.

The beautiful and edifying recitation of the comrades who led the prayers, the powerful singing of the strong choir and congregation, and the uplifting sight of so many soldiers, young and old, created a solemn atmosphere of wonderfully stirring power.

When the first service on the eve of Rosh Hashanah began at 7.00 p.m., the entire large gathering, which filled the house, packed together head to head, rose up; every soul dedicated itself to the power of the moment. Sixteen hundred German soldiers far from home, separated from wife and children, mother and father, united in the worship of God. Even during better times our holidays do not lack dedication and majesty, but we could only properly experience their real meaning and inner liberation during this Great War. Every written word and many prayers gained a new and more certain meaning and equipped us with unbending determination to remain faithful to our Kaiser and German Fatherland; willingly to sacrifice our blood and lives in the certainty of God's merciful guidance.

May the memory of these solemn days of dedication, for which we thank our faith and our Kaiser's care, remain with us and not disappear during better times! They remain alive to me and I think of all the young and tender comrades on whose head I would have liked to place the hand of blessing; I think of the steely soldiers and old reserve men: each time I looked at them, my dear departed father's picture appeared before my soul.

The Great Weeping[31]

Even though autumn starts out warm and golden, it isn't summer any more. It only gives the year which is coming to its end deceptively clear days to which it has no right, in order to demand its own rights without mercy. Then rain pours defiantly from a cloudy sky, wind whistles scornfully through badly-built chimneys, streets and ditches silt up, and the spectre of mourning and hopelessness raises its head. Even the jokers in the troop become melancholy; the guards hide their extinguished pipes in coat pockets and warily examine the rivulets under their soaking boots. Cars wickedly splash filth and water on officers and men alike. Each man hangs his head like an exhausted horse and rails against the harsh fate of war. That is the time of the great weeping and one broods a lot about death and dying, and whether the dead of August 1914 are not much better off than we are.

During this time I buried a dear student whom I had met when I was still fresh and joyful at the end of July. Now he lay still in his coffin: comrades had decorated the box with fading greenery, and held in their hands laboriously created wreaths, autumn's last adornment. The faithful minstrels stamped across the meadow covered with enemy artillery, playing him a last goodbye, and the enemy flyers (who have learned to defy all weathers) flew circles above in the disconsolate afternoon hour. An old sergeant major with the Iron Cross First Class whispers a word to his lieutenant, who says: 'We also have in our midst two Jews, both of whom would surely like to speak with their chaplain.' There is such a thing as wordless thanks and I thanked both friendly superiors, for the words 'very kind' did not seem to suffice. And then I went to the two pale 19-year-olds, who told me that they were doing very well in their company. Soldiers do not throw superlatives around. Suffering men approach one another more easily and during these times one quickly gets to know comrades in the escort unit: men whose nature or military careers set them apart and who awaken heartfelt sympathy.

On another occasion a Bavarian infantry lieutenant entered my room and requested that I attend the funeral service for a sergeant major: 'We can take for granted agreement of a father who has lost his only son and we want to make sure that our dear dead comrade is sent to Munich. Sergeant Major Johannes will accompany him. Please write to the rabbi and ask him to prepare the family.' Is it not noble to take the sting from the deepest pain and grant cathartic tears? These are not exceptional cases! And just as good deeds call out to be emulated, this loyalty and love which transcends death taught me to ensure that a number of the fallen were sent home with approval of command and military escort, in the dead of winter, and also to raise others from their graves before the retreat so that they may rest in German soil. The sight of decomposition has not frightened us; in many cases the bodies are relatively intact. They seem to sleep in their coffins, as if waiting to be sent home. In one open coffin which comrades had decorated five months earlier, we found a fresh green branch, lush and full, in the hands of a lad from Mainz: he was the second son that his mother had given up.

Our efforts are not always successful. When the dead lie one on top of the other or in mass graves, wrapped in sheets because wood is lacking, piety forbids that their peace be disturbed: so the poor family must let go of the last hope to which wives, mothers and brides have ardently clung.

I cannot leave this sad section without saying something about grave memorials because the faithful German soldier's soul speaks out of them as well. Wherever the fighting has allowed, signs of love and memorial stones stand, moving marks of friendship, both touchingly beautiful and awkward. Inscriptions which no poet could improve upon tell of the dead man's acts of heroism and, when the troops move on, soldiers take a quick photograph or pluck a leaf from the little mound and put it into their breast pockets.

As is the case with all field chaplains, I place great importance on the erection of grave memorials and recording them photographically [see Plate 30]. When I consign both tasks to my comrades, I always find helpful support, so that, in most cases, something permanent has been created for the bereaved at home.

Everyone's temper depends on the weather, and November rain does not improve the mood in the field. It is the transitional month of discontent and petulance, and has a considerable effect on the men's physical state. Even practical and sober men show signs of unrest and impatience, irritability and asperity. Only a minority are able to remain their normal selves, especially in war. All others, irrespective of whether their exhaustion is expressed in hypersensitivity or indifference, are healed only when the first real day of frost drives the infection from their veins. But so long as it still rains, one can easily cause offence, even when one resorts to rumours of peace simply to cheer up good acquaintances. Then it is important to be offended by nothing, even if the other party is very coarse. Each man needs and finds friends, even if it is a four-legged friend.[32] Moods change and spread as quickly as fashions. During these critical times in the autumn my work was not affected and I became quite a maid-of-all-work. The demands upon me increased and my office became an inn, a restaurant, cigar store, bank, book store, photographic art academy, hand luggage desk, information desk, complaints office, and almost a tailor's workshop. A Pomeranian came to me, held forth about his trousers and would not permit interruptions. When he finally finished and I advised him to go to a tailor, he opined innocently: 'Now I have come here and I thought that you would understand this as well!' I gradually became well-versed in the different German ethnic groups, and, even more easily than by their dialect, I learnt to differentiate among them by their character. The Bavarian is down-to-earth; the Silesian clever; the Saxon good-natured; the Badener trusting. That leaves the Berliners: they are just Berliners.

On Vacation[33]

The first morning of the vacation! The journey starts today and tomorrow we will be home. Some men sing, whistle and make a noise. Others are silent during the train journey. Some look out of the open window, allowing the biting wind to whistle around their faces for long stretches of journey. Although it is forbidden, many descend from the home-bound train at every stop and stomp on the platform until the train leaves again. Only a very few can sleep.

The journey home is beautiful! One is young and fresh, and will change places with nobody. All the soldiers' accumulated longing is unloaded and their deep yearning will soon be fulfilled. Fear and worry come to rest. How ardently the heart greets German soil, the starry sky and dear moon, which here do not contain French flyers. Many comrades love surprises: they did not announce their leave, and become living festive gifts to their wives and children. The vacationer rightly becomes the honoured focus of family and neighbours. He strolls, led by his younger relatives, and disappoints his acquaintances because, having been warned not to, he will tell nothing about the Front. Instead he fills concert halls, theatres and stores, makes pious pilgrimages to places of worship and cemeteries. But he doesn't remain anywhere for long. During quiet conversations and even in sleep he lingers secretly with his company and sees himself already on the train back. Only the journey home is beautiful!

Leave is like a dream, unreal and shadowy. Everything as it was! During my vacation I spoke with some grumblers who bewailed the undeniable economic hardship and admittedly high price of geese, and I almost gave them a piece of my mind. I preferred to tell them that in many villages and towns in the occupied territories no Frenchman may leave his house after 9.00 p.m. or 10.00 p.m.; that almost all are restricted to their own area and may not travel; that every day they must be prepared to be taken away from home and hearth, bundle in hand, and taken to wherever the exigencies of war dictate. After I told them this, these gentlemen quickly changed the subject and when they spoke of sacrifices of blood, we were of a similar mind.

Once upon a time a soul rose to heaven and stood before God's Throne. God saw that it was troubled and said: You are now free of the earth but your heart remains below and you worry about the sufferings of mankind. This war is necessary. Everyone had it too good, wanted to rise too high. Men didn't honour their daily bread and worshiped gold. My children require a hard lesson! When all nations long for peace and one does not wish to rule over another, then the war will end. But also now, be comforted, dear soul! I will not allow the innocent to starve. I will give rain and harvest at the proper time and watch over the ripening fruit. The naked will be clothed and the freezing will be warm. I will give comfort to the afflicted and not punish anyone too severely, I will send fathers to the orphans and succour to the widows. But also those who are called to me according to My will, who rest on foreign soil or in the depths of the sea, they will live again. And all hearts, which like yours are silenced by grief, will beat again. Children will be named after husband and son, mother and father. Their dear souls will reside in them, each child will be doubly dear to me, and no name will be missing. And when the wicked desire war again, then these children will be grown up, rise up and say: 'Heaven forbid that we should draw our swords against others! We have fought once: never again!'[34] And the wicked will blush and be ashamed.

The Kaiser's Birthday[35]

On the morning of 27 January 1917 the Kaiser's birthday was celebrated with a beautiful service in the cathedral of St Quentin. Pastor Eschenroeder began his address with a reference which brought special honour to the Jewish faith: 'In one of the oldest synagogues in Germany, that of Worms,[36] one sees two crowns over the lectern on which the Torah is read. They are called the crowns of priesthood and that of royalty. But over them hovers a third, the crown of a good name.' In an effective performance, the speaker adorned our Kaiser with all three crowns; when he spoke of his piety and justness, his good and pure conscience and the heavy burden of his office, he touched the feelings and sensibilities of all present. The old sentence of Rabbi Shimon in *Pirkei Avoth* was heard for the first time in the basilica and during the course of the day many officers asked me about this text.[37]

At noon, in sunny winter weather, the military in St Quentin gathered on the large city square. From here the Commander-in-Chief made a pithy address to soldiers who had come from the Front, and gave them the saying, 'The citizens are the wall'[38] to think about. Then troops marched past while a pilot flew overhead and each soldier demonstrated old-fashioned Prussian correctness. Half-mockingly and half-anxiously, the French peered out of their windows and listened to the blaring music which had reminded them once a day since war's beginning that German walls were firmly established in France.

Winter Joy[39]

The third winter in France was extremely cold and lasted a long time. The exceptional cold affects the French more than it does us, because the petit bourgeois stratum of society, the farmers and workers, know little about protective winter clothing. Prosperous Frenchmen do have beautiful fur coats, but they disguise the coat's outside and, at a distance, the wearer may be confused with a leaping carnivore.

Music, theatre and cinema unite to make pleasant the hours of recreation which the harassed soldier certainly deserves. The most popular and prevalent form of entertainment is the motion picture theatre, whose domain has extended right up to the Front. Soldiers prefer films of a light nature. They want to have something to laugh about. During these evenings one could speak of a double *Bombenerfolg* [smash hit]. The walls boom with thunderous applause and also sometimes with the echoes of explosions. When I look at the cheery crowd I have the reassuring feeling that a nation which can still laugh so heartily must be healthy in its innermost core. But even our comrades' laughter was sorely impeded. The French theatres in our area have highly defective seating: this was even the case during peacetime. Sitting on such seats for hours at a time causes physical strain.

A brief remark about music in religious services: Even within the different faiths, divergent music is heard during important sections of the services, so that soldiers thrown together from all sides cannot unite as a powerful choir. This problem can also be found in Jewish field services. The melodies of Jews from the east and west of Germany differ, and it would be desirable to unite these, even in peacetime.[40] The Dutch prayer of thanks has shown the value of unified communal singing during services. It has become the common property of army and home, resounding like thunder in church and synagogue. 'We step forth to pray': everyone knows and loves this song.[41]

Germany remains the country of bookworms. Despite being fed richly, the hunger for reading material in the soldiers cannot be sated. One sees lines like those queuing for eggs[42] in front of army book stores just as at home, and newspapers from home arriving by fast train are grabbed out of the hands of soldiers who distribute them. The demand for daily newspapers does not decrease, even though the army provides its own well edited and illustrated newspapers to satisfy the comrades' thirst for information. Army administration pays for this endeavour out of its own pocket. Approximately 100,000 papers arrive weekly, to be distributed amongst our troops free of charge, and a staff of field-grey workers, in particular the down-to-earth listening-posts, keeps the soldiers in a good mood and abreast of the news.

Educational or sociable meetings and counselling sessions also feed the soldiers' soul. Students have in many places taken up again their professional memberships, and medical, clerical and technical meetings have taken place, often in Brussels, a city which constantly operates at fever-pitch and still has a raised temperature even in the midst of a depressing war. Jewish chaplain conferences have taken place there as well [see Chapter 10] and provided their participants with enjoyable hours of collegial meetings and valuable exchange of war experiences.

Most soldiers are not teetotallers but there are some who are abstemious. But how good alcohol tastes, and how good it makes one feel! It can be said that moderate enjoyment of beer and wine as counterbalance to bodily and psychological strain is beneficial for some and indispensable for others. Give a man exhausted by the hardest combat a mouthful of beer, give a wounded man something hot (even if it only has the colour of coffee), and they gain new strength and optimism. In winter, a convinced proponent of alcohol will also stress its warming qualities. This also applies to cigars and cigarettes!

Playing cards are another source of conviviality for soldiers in the field, and give the men something of that inner sense of self-esteem which The Lord of Creation cannot renounce. The company billiard championship at headquarters is also a favourite. However, our cosy circle soon flies away and is scattered to the four winds. Small pleasures don't last long during war.

Country and People[43]

Before the war much was said in Germany about the degeneration of the French nation; also about their two-child policy and increasing celibacy rates which would soon lead the country from an already static population count to an inexorable population decline. In truth, apart from the fable of degeneracy to which the excellent French soldier gives the best answer, all of the above observations are correct. The nation is healthy, but its future is darkened by terrible losses in this war as well as unrecovered losses during the Napoleonic era.

Their striking lack of objectivity and logic, the combination of chauvinism with optimism, especially in questions of war, are old racial characteristics with no hint of degeneration. They still dream of *la grande nation* [the great nation], and each French man and woman can give an ornate speech with the key words *liberté* and *lumière* [liberty and light], whose headquarters and sun are in Paris. Objections or attempts to disprove this are fruitless, and at the end of the day we let it go.

Each nation, including the French, has its merits. Their patriotism is well-known and will be worth emulating in our future party-political battles, which must be fought with emphasis upon the unifying love of Fatherland. As far as religion is concerned, France's condition is less favourable. The separation between church and state was simply the result of an internal detachment of these related institutions one from the other. During war religion, otherwise the refuge of matrons, has apparently won. Adversity teaches one to pray! Now, men and young women also go to church, and there they find comfort in their suffering and in the agonizing uncertainty of their loved ones' fates.

Much necessary change in education of the young has taken place in France during the past few years. One sees, in all medium-sized and larger towns and cities, fine schools and boarding schools, with plenty of gymnasia on the German model. This expenditure is easy for cities and communities because France is rich in natural wealth: cultivation of grain, fruit and vegetables, as well as other branches of agriculture which are well-developed. The country has beautiful forested areas and the famous abundance of wine that the land cannot consume on its own. In the north, industry is well developed and functions under favourable conditions. Travel is facilitated by the many canals, and a thickly woven network of excellent roads which even the war has failed to wear down. By contrast, French railways are much inferior to our own. Old stations, few and too short siding tracks and switches, small shunting facilities, unprotected signal boxes, and level crossings without overpasses complicate and endanger operations which admittedly do not have to reckon with the density of our service and the length of axles of our goods trains.[44]

France's prosperity is also shown by the décor of their homes. One has to enter, and not judge them by their narrow street entrance which has an average of two windows (because each window is taxed). Inside one sees adroit exploitation of space and cosy furnishing. Rooms are decorated with beautiful old furniture, valuable paintings, marble fireplaces with high mirrors and wide ledges for objets d'art, bronzes and clocks, lace drapes, and candelabras contribute further to the effect. The comfort and good furnishing extends to the kitchen, and concludes in the ubiquitous wine cellar. The above description applies especially to old houses, real jewel-boxes which contain much more than their outside appearance would suggest. They show much feeling for style on the part of the old master builders and the owners who have often lived there for many generations, and their value is further increased by adjoining well-tended gardens. The double and triple cellars of these old buildings have provided good shelter during this war. Northern France and even the Paris area is a land of catacombs and caves. Kilometres-long passages connect city neighbourhoods, and German science in service of the army has taken these features into proper consideration. Wonderful country estates and farms make everything even more beautiful: every village has its own chateau with a large park and a farmyard.

The houses of the poor do not make a happy impression as far as hygiene is concerned; however, one cannot claim that the corresponding living conditions in Germany are everywhere things of the past.

The Frenchman has, through the centuries, been a symbol of grace and tact in Germany. His polish, spirit and language are worth emulating. There is something genuine in the elegance of this nation and its living expression. Women and children, but also men of all circles are graceful and courteous. Certainly their politeness is excessive and I can imagine that even the executioner says: 'I am sorry' to the condemned man before he pulls the guillotine's lever. It is reported that pickpockets in the St Quentin Champs Elysées utter the latter phrase before they run off.

The combination of grace and dignity is especially expressed in the education and good works of the clergy. They preach to their congregations with impressive eloquence and fiery language, and their entire being shows something rounded off and balanced in everything that they do. This endearing manner is also found in the common people. A young woman walks up to me in a crowded street, an infant in her left arm, stretching out her open right hand: 'Charity, sir, my babies are starving.' This has the same effect as if the Madonna were to rise out of her picture frame: she would have disarmed even the most hard-hearted. Begging, so common in war, is quite comical: children climb high on the low windows and cry out: 'Bread, bread or a sou.'

Enough has now been said about country and people. But it must be added that our administration has afforded them all the freedom which may be permitted and that the population has accepted leniency with self-interest and as if it couldn't be any other way, and has put up with the unavoidable with dignity. Their hatred of Germany is the same, irrespective of how strict or lenient the regime may be.

Through Night to Light[45]

The long winter provided increased opportunity to hold regular field services. Military activity had waned significantly and comrades could be given leave more easily. I held services in each division once a month, and in a period of four weeks travelled throughout the entire division. I also held weekly Friday evening prayers in St Quentin, which were well attended by soldiers returning to the Front and those going on leave. Notification and approval of services were given telegraphically and dissemination amongst the troops was by word of mouth in the usual way. To facilitate longer trips, the Quartermaster General often placed an automobile at my disposal. I have always been thankful for this special concession because I know that frugality in rubber and gasoline use are primary commandments in war and that spiritual help in the field has its limits. Non-commissioned officer Röber always drove me quickly and safely on these trips. Only once, in March 1917, when we were visiting a neighbouring army, for whose Jewish chaplain I was to substitute, during a muddy thaw and thick fog, our car was swallowed up in an especially deep crater, though without damage to the vehicle. We had the crater to thank that we were not captured, dead or alive, by the British. Our situation out there was unenviable and we didn't think much of our chances of getting out alive. But we both worked on the car until it was lifted out of the hole. That was the main thing! Then, with necessarily long intervals in shelters, we travelled back.

It is not always easy to get around in wartime, even on the railways. Until now, enemy aircraft have disturbed me less than cancelled or suddenly changed connections. Once I had no other choice but to jump out of a decelerating train, and many a time I could only travel forward thanks to the friendliness of the engine driver who let me ride with him. One must always travel forward when funerals or services have been arranged and the comrades are waiting: their travels are also no walks in the park but may represent heavy exertion and dangers, depending on the distance travelled and nature of the route.

> Forty men are trudging through the snow
> Grope from icy peaks and heights below.
> Into valley in which churches stand
> Push their column towards God's command.
>
> Even if this is not their faith's true home,
> Yet the soul rests here from faith alone.
> Pious words of courage exalt souls
> As a path that leads to heaven's goals.
>
> One man rallies up and speaks of right:
> God, let us journey to Your light!
> See, the foe still wishes war's dismay
> Give us victory and peace today!
>
> And with voice which broke on heaven's vault
> His last word did echoing assault.
> And like roaring storm it thunder'd down
> Evermore beyond, beyond and down!
>
> Forty men all heard the noble sounds
> And trembling turned away from icy bounds.
> When the last one hastened through the door
> A wave howled through the air and sounded more.

And the roof and walls they did collapse
And crashed down, burning stone and apse.
Forty men they saw this all occur
And none of them dared near destruction's jaw.

Forty men all thanking on their knees
Their God in silence, who all creatures sees.
One man rallies up and speaks of right:
God, let us wander in Your light!

Forty men are trudging through the snow
Climbing up towards the ice's glow.
On the mountain's slope a flyer sank
And of death quite suddenly he drank.[46]

We have prayed in shot-up churches, in which sometimes a corpse still lay; in barracks and barns; but also in town hall rooms, in soldiers' homes and reading rooms; in summer (as has already been mentioned) under the heavens or the green roof of the forest. After services we hand out reading material, the beautiful field bibles of the Verband der deutschen Juden, and tobacco donated by my home community.

On one occasion I was able to refresh 150 comrades with hot chocolate and on another with liquor (who is shocked?), biscuits and crisp gingerbread cookies. Often we took a group photograph and, after long conversations with all the comrades, I went on my way again. My questions centred mainly on their family circumstances, age, homeland, occupation and their wishes. The comrades' wishes were mostly of a personal nature and so cannot be repeated; but one can well believe that many asked for intercession so that they could be moved from their quiet positions to the active front or to their old regiment. 'I have little prospect of promotion here and wish to return to my regiment.' – 'I have already applied twice for a transfer but my company won't allow me to go.'

I had no influence in such cases and all I could do was to repeat our old adage: 'This too is for the best',[47] and recommend that the comrade be content with his present circumstances. I myself have often enough experienced the deep truth of this admonition. Once, when I was worried about bad news from my family, I attempted later that evening without hope of success to arrange a telephone call home. The connection succeeded within a few minutes, it was as clear as a local call in the city, and the news it brought calmed me down. How thankful one is at such a time and how one hears one's heart beating! Then one goes up to the telephone, holds it, and says: 'What a great invention!'

Then came the retreat in 1917,[48] my farewell to St Quentin, to my quarters and to my landlady. Before I left, I visited all parts of the Front once more, most especially the beloved graves which we now had to leave behind. I saw for the last time Noyon and its mountain Saint Siméon, from whose peak one could see through a telescope, when the weather was clear, the Eiffel Tower, delicate as a knitting needle. Then we took the five Torah scrolls of the St Quentin synagogue which the Chief Quartermaster (who thought of everything) had entrusted into my care, and off we went. We left with mixed feelings of pain and the joy that spring brings with it.

Spring came late in the third year of war but didn't disappoint. It brought no frost and didn't destroy any blossoms. We celebrated the Festival of Spring (Pesach) in another location, in which we also built a house for God. The synagogue, intended to be used for some time, was erected in a room which, with its cold walls, made an ugly initial impression. A friendly effect was rapidly created by covering these surfaces with white material. In the middle of the wall, facing east, the Holy Ark was built. It was my task to give special character to this central point of God's house. Over the ark a board with the Hebrew inscription 'Holy to the Eternal' was fixed. On the outside it was further decorated by a curtain with golden edging, with a crown and an image of the Star of David. The latter also appeared in the middle of the prayer lectern, on which two candles were placed. The erection of the *Ner Tamid* was not easy. We certainly had an excellent source of light due to the provision of electricity in all rooms, but couldn't find anything that could be lowered down from the ceiling far enough to receive a translucent bulb. Necessity is the mother of invention! We hollowed out a petroleum container from an old table lamp made of pressed clear blue glass and hung it up on brass chains [see Plate 31]. Now we only needed the benches to complete the preparations. The glorious words of our recent services encouraged me: 'On the first day of the first month you shall erect the tabernacle of the tent of meeting. And you shall put in it the Ark of the Testimony, and you shall screen the ark with the veil. And you shall bring in the table and arrange it, and you shall bring in the lampstand and set up its lamps.'[49]

At the beginning of the service the seats had to be removed because the large number of participants allowed for standing room only. During the long drawn-out turmoil of war, nothing had given me greater joy than completion of this task. As with the execution of all good plans, I had willing and capable helpers, old and new benefactors. The comrades thanked me at the end of the two-day celebration with voluntary donations for those blinded by the war.

The days have now become ever longer and now in June it is still as clear as day at 10.00 p.m. because we now have summer time, and thus gain almost two hours in France [see Note 10]. It seems as though it will never grow dark again, as if night must give up the game. A rosy glow, which keeps watch from sunrise to sunset, lights up the northern skies and unites the blush of dawn and dusk. Until the fireball breaks out! The sun of peace, announcing itself after three years of war, will not allow another darkening. As Zola (no average Frenchman) wrote: 'Truth is on the march, and nothing will stop it.' Yes, truth is on the march![50]

Author's Summary

Martin Salomonski must have been very conversant with the novels of Emile Zola. His descriptions, especially of the petit-bourgeois level of French society, are shot through with sarcasm, wit and penetrating insights. As was the case with so many of his generation, German patriotism apparently blinded him to injustices perpetrated by the German army on the occupied French population and led to a feeling of the superiority of German *Kultur* over all things French and a falsely high opinion of the Kaiser, a deeply flawed man who in reality did not exercise meaningful military leadership at any time during the war.

He glosses over the scorched earth policy of the German army when they retreated from the Somme to the Hindenburg line in 1917 and doesn't show much sympathy for or understanding of the French civilian population. This inherent German sense of superiority and the rightness of the German cause does not stop him from describing the French countryside and the beauty of French country houses and cathedrals in loving detail. The last few sentences of his diary, quoting Zola's letter to the President of the French Republic on behalf of the unjustly convicted and jailed Alfred Dreyfus, are unbearably ironic, given the history of German Jewry after the First World War.

The memoirs do not contain any direct description of anti-Semitism in the German army except for an allusion to promotion difficulties (p.112). Interestingly, no mention is made of the entry of the United States into the First World War in April 1917, although this would one year later play a major role in Germany's defeat. It is possible that Rabbi Salomonski made the common mistake of under-estimating the power of American arms when fully mobilized. The initial Russian Revolution of March 1917 is also not mentioned, perhaps because the Eastern Front was so far away.

Rabbi Salomonski's memoirs are unique amongst Jewish chaplains in containing poetry – much of it moving – which the author has attempted to translate into English. His sympathy for the plight of suffering German soldiers is obvious from his frequent visits to the Front and local field hospitals which were choked with wounded from all sides during the climax of the Battle of the Somme. His descriptions of Rosh Hashanah and Yom Kippur services for approximately 1,600 men, and of Pesach celebrations (including Seders, pictured in Plate 27 but not described) after conclusion of the Battle of the Somme, need no elaboration except to emphasize his ingenuity and dedication in obtaining such large amounts of food at a time when Germany, both at home and in the field, was suffering greatly from the effects of the British sea blockade. The willingness of the German General Staff to approve such large Jewish religious gatherings is also a point to be noted. The last paragraph of 'On Vacation' (p.105) is a memorable plea for future peace and understanding which was not heeded.

After High Holiday and Succot services in 1917, Rabbi Salomonski received letters of thanks from the soldiers who attended. Translations of a few of these follow:[51]

> The days that I recently spent in L.C. will remain in my memory for the rest of my life. The first sounding of the Hebrew melodies on the first evening was a solemn moment for me. The first thought which flashed through my mind was the same as you expressed in your address to us: 'We are brothers'. I see the great merit of these services in the field in the fact that they encourage religious perception. I gauged the warmth of our prayers in the fact that, ever and again, they rapidly directed all my feelings back to my home. My parent's house stood clearly before me. And I am not ashamed to admit that tears came to my eyes when I thought how mother and father would be sitting alone at table

thinking with frightened anxiety about their only child. In such a way my thoughts that were concerned about Judaism blended with those of my loved ones back home, and this service became a great experience for me. I believe that now rather than earlier I will be able to bear all the personal problems that the war brings to every individual.

A truly good speaker goes along with the mood of his audience and receives new impulses from them. Did you notice the devotion of your 800 listeners, we rough men, some of whom have been fighting for three years, others very young, made men before their time by hard destiny? Certainly yes. Those listening to you have all, in spirit, shaken your hand; the powerful men's chorus which followed the excellent prayer leader was also a source of heartfelt joy to us. And we cannot leave unmentioned the other organization of the festival, the exemplary, plentiful provisioning, for which we thank your facilitation and the cooperation of the commissariat.

During services in the field I was reminded ever and again of the earliest times of our nation: the wandering in the desert, which resembles this war in more than one way. Then too our forefathers led a wandering existence as pronounced, more or less, as we do in this war. Then they also will have lacked 'the comforts of the modern age' and yet the visitor was offered, then as now, a picture which gives rise to the call: How beautiful is it when so large a number of co-religionists find each other together here in the field.[52] How different it is, despite all the great differences, from day-to-day gathering with comrades of other faiths, no matter how peaceful and pleasant this is. How beautiful it is to see acquaintances and friends again, regardless of whether our quarters are better or worse than those far from where we live in peacetime, or if the festive meal does not have its accustomed character. Those who think alike find themselves together and create, in the framework of what is offered, their own festive day, which after all must come from inside of us. Before this war we did not recognize the advantages we enjoyed, and that the comforts of home are by no means something that can be taken for granted. The more so do we naturally enjoy the beautiful days that are offered to us and the more so will we enjoy the festivals when we will be able to spend them, hopefully in the not too distant future, at home. For me, at any rate, the festivals in the field will remain a life-long memory.

Martin Salomonski. dedicated German patriot, could never have imagined what would transpire in his beloved Fatherland less than two decades after the end of the Great War.

NOTES

1. M. Salomonski, *Ein Jahr an der Somme* (Frankfurt an der Oder: Verlag der königlichen Hofbuchdruckerei Trowitzsch & Sohn, 1917), pp.1–105.
2. M. Salomonski, *Jüdische Seelsorge an der Westfront* (Berlin: Verlag von Louis Lamm. Ueberreicht vom Centralverein deutscher Staatsbürger jüdischen Glaubens, 1918), pp.1–36.
3. Salomonski, *Ein Jahr an der Somme*, pp.13–24.
4. *U'netaneh Tokef* [Let us now relate the power], one of the holiest prayers in the High Holiday liturgy. The image is of God counting his flock and judging each one for deeds during the past year.
5. 'At the grey cloister', an elite Berlin Gymnasium attended, amongst others, by Otto von Bismarck.
6. Salomonski, *Ein Jahr an der Somme*, pp.25–33.
7. St Quentin is the largest city in the Aisne Department of Picardy. Heavy fighting occurred around and in it during both the Franco-Prussian and First World War. The city endured a harsh German occupation during the First World War, and lay in the centre of the war zone: 80 per cent of its buildings (including its cathedral which dates back to 1195) were damaged or destroyed by war's end.
8. No details of these rabbis are available. An unknown number of rabbis and assistant rabbis entered the war as soldiers, medical orderlies and assistant chaplains, and many died. Examples are provided in the introductory biographies.
9. French towns and regions that felt vengeful towards Germany after the 1870/71 war, when they were annexed. The street names would have been given this sobriquet. The Germans made a lot out of supposed French vengefulness during the war.
10. French time differed from German time by one hour and the Germans instituted German time in occupied areas of France and Belgium.
11. Jeremiah 22: 10, modified.
12. The French crowd's feelings may well have been mixed. Nothing is said about what happened to the other two balloons.
13. Identical charges and exaggerations were levelled against Germans by the Entente. As in all wars, propaganda was a powerful weapon.
14. Salomonski, *Ein Jahr an der Somme*, pp.34–45.
15. The United States sold munitions to both sides until it entered the war on the side of the Entente in 1917.
16. Isaiah 66: 13.
17. All poetry in this chapter was written by Rabbi Salomonski and has been translated by the author.
18. A play on words. *Bauer* in German means 'farmer' while *erbauen* means to 'edify' or 'spiritually uplift'.
19. Isaiah 41: 10.

20. There are two Frankfurts in Germany: the much larger Frankfurt am Main, and Frankfurt on the Oder (where Rabbi Salomonski's congregation was located).
21. Salomonski, *Ein Jahr an der Somme*, pp.46–52.
22. The Battle of the Somme (1 July to 18 November), an offensive between the British and French against the German army. By the time fighting ceased there were at least one million casualties. The Allies had penetrated a total of six miles but the offensive helped bleed German forces from, and contributed to the end of, the battle of Verdun.
23. Genesis 32: 10.
24. Immanuel Kant (1724–1804), seminal eighteenth-century German philosopher. The categorical imperative is one of Kant's most famous statements and a central foundation in his philosophy: 'Act only according to that maxim whereby you can, at the same time, will that it should become a universal law.'
25. The German word *Typhus* does not distinguish between *Bauchtyphus* [typhoid] and *Flecktyphus* [typhus].
26. Salomonski, *Ein Jahr an der Somme*, pp.53–60.
27. Romania signed a treaty with the Entente on 17 August and declared War on Austro-Hungary on 28 August 1916 by invading the southern Carpathians and Transylvania. Its war aim – acquisition of land from Austro-Hungary – was successful and Transylvania, part of Bukowina and the Banat were added to her territory after the war.
28. The new German *Stahlhelm* [steel helmet] used a harder silicon/nickel steel than did the British or French. The *Stahlhelm* had to be formed in heated dies at a greater unit cost than the British helmet, which could be formed in one piece, but with correspondingly greater protection.
29. This still occurs.
30. Salomonski, *Ein Jahr an der Somme*, pp.61–5.
31. Salomonski, *Ein Jahr an der Somme*, pp.66–71.
32. Dogs or cats significantly help soldiers' loneliness in times of war.
33. Salomonski, *Ein Jahr an der Somme*, pp.72–5.
34. Terrible irony, given the fact that these two words now relate to the Holocaust.
35. Salomonski, *Ein Jahr an der Somme*, pp.76–83.
36. Jews lived in Worms from around the early eleventh century until the National Socialist era.
37. *Pirkei Avoth* 4: 13.
38. Gaspard II de Coligny (1519–1572), a French-Huguenot admiral during the French wars of religion, was entrusted with the defence of St Quentin in 1557. *Civus muris erat*: 'he was the citizen's wall'.
39. Salomonski, *Ein Jahr an der Somme*, pp.84–91.
40. German Jewry consisted mainly of Ashkenazi Jews but Hamburg also had a sizeable Sephardi community. Ashkenazi Jewry was divided into many sects, each with their own liturgical melodies. The organ was used extensively in non-orthodox services.
41. The German translation of this prayer (*wir treten zum Beten*: Adrianus Valerius, c. 1575–1625) was a potent symbol of the Throne- and Altar-alliance of German civil religion until 1918.
42. The British sea blockade rapidly led to food shortages throughout Germany.
43. Salomonski, *Ein Jahr an der Somme*, pp.92–7.
44. The excellent Prussian railway system was a key factor in their victory during the Franco-Prussian war and facilitated troop movement between the various fronts during the First World War.
45. Salomonski, *Ein Jahr an der Somme*, pp.98–105.
46. This poem seems better suited to the bloody Alpine battles fought between Italy and the Central Powers.
47. A saying attributed to Rabbi Nachum of Gamzu, a Talmudic teacher of the first century CE.

His name is explained as referring to Nachum's Hebrew motto *Gam zu le'tovah* [this too is for the best].
48. Between 9 February and 15 March 1917 the German armies on the Somme carried out a strategic withdrawal to a shorter and more powerful line of defence, the Hindenburg Line. They left behind a trail of scorched earth and torn up railway lines.
49. Exodus 40: 2–4.
50. Emile Zola (1840–1902), the most important exemplar of the French literary school of naturalism and major figure in the political liberalization of France and the exoneration of the falsely accused and convicted army officer Alfred Dreyfus, encapsulated in the renowned newspaper headline *J'Accuse*, of an open letter to the President of the French Republic in George Clemenceau's newpaper *l'Aurore* (13 January 1898). The original reads: '*La vérité est en marche, et rien ne l'arrêtera.*'
51. *Bericht über die Jüdischen Herbstfeste 1917 bei einer Armee im Westen in Form von Feldbriefen. Druck der Armee-Druckerei.* Jerusalem, Central Archives for the History of the Jewish People, P 24/10, pp.1–8.
52. Psalm 133: 1.

1. Jewish Chaplains Conference of the West, St Quentin, 5 August 1915. Standing (left to right): Rabbis Baerwald, Italiener, Cohn, Lewin, Salzberger. Sitting (left to right): Rabbis Wilde, Baeck, Emil Levy. Copyright: Jewish Museum, Frankfurt.

2. Jewish Chaplains Conference of the East, Riga, February 1918. From left to right: Rabbis Hanover, Tänzer, Arthur Levy, Baeck, Sali Levi, Rosenak, Sonderling. Copyright: Jewish Museum, Frankfurt.

3. Jewish chaplains of the West. Standing (left to right): Rabbis Baerwald, Salomonski, Salzberger, Lewin. Sitting (left to right): Rabbis Klein, Chone, Italiener, Wilde. Copyright: Jim Herzog.

4. Jewish Chaplains in front of the B'nei Brith Lodge hospital train. Standing (left to right): Rabbis Klein, Levi, Lewin, Wiener, Cohn. Sitting (left to right): Rabbis Salomonski, Lazarus, Wilde, Italiener, Salzberger. Copyright: Jewish Museum, Frankfurt.

5. Rabbi Martin Salomonski with his brother Moritz (left) and cousin Hans (right), both physicians. Copyright: Jim Herzog.

6. Rabbi Leo Baeck flanked by Catholic and Evangelical chaplains. Copyright: Marianne Dreyfus (private collection).

7. Rabbi Leo Baeck with soldiers. Copyright: Marianne Dreyfus (private collection).

8. Rabbi Aron Tänzer in uniform with medals. Copyright: Leo Baeck Institute, NYC.

9. Rabbi Aron Tänzer at a Seder in Pinsk. Copyright: Leo Baeck Institute, NYC.

10. Rabbi Aron Tänzer with soup kitchen board members. Copyright: Leo Baeck Institute, NYC.

11. Rabbi Aron Tänzer flanked by his sons Friederich (Fritz) on the left and Paul on the right. Copyright: Uri Tänzer (private collection).

12. Burial site of Rabbi Aron Tänzer. Copyright: Uri Tänzer (private collection).

13. Rabbi Leopold Rosenak. Private collection: courtesy Rachel Aber Schlesinger.

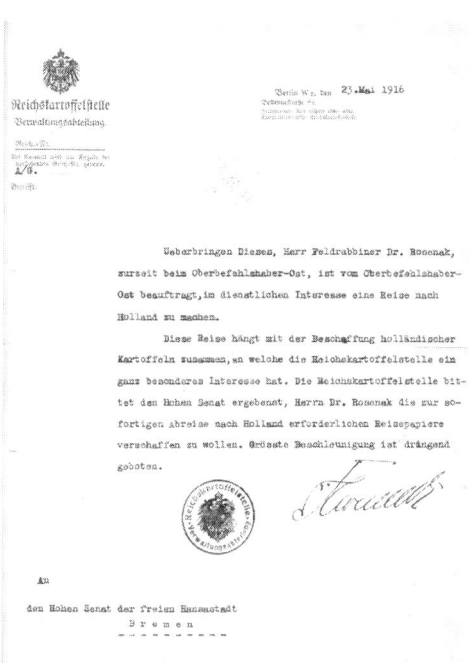

14. Letter from 'Reich Potato Department' (Reichskartoffelstelle) permitting Rabbi Rosenak to travel to neutral Netherlands to obtain potatoes. Copyright: Leo Baeck Institute Archives, Jerusalem.

15. Rabbi Leo Baerwald with horse, cart and young assistant in France, c. 1916. Copyright: Staatsarchiv München and Jane Vogel-Kohai.

16. Rabbi Jacob Sonderling distributes gifts to Jewish children in Poland. Copyright: Jewish Museum, Frankfurt.

17. Rabbi Alexander Winter, flanked by Protestant (left) and Catholic (right) chaplains. Copyright: Naftali Winter (private collection).

18. Rabbi Alexander Winter with Reb Chaim Halevi Soloveitchik, also known as the Brisker Rebbe (1853–1918). Copyright: Naftali Winter (private collection).

19. Siegfried Alexander during the war. Copyright: Hannah Goldwyn (private collection).

20. Rabbi Paul Lazarus. Copyright: Alte Synagoge Essen, Archiv, AR.4004.

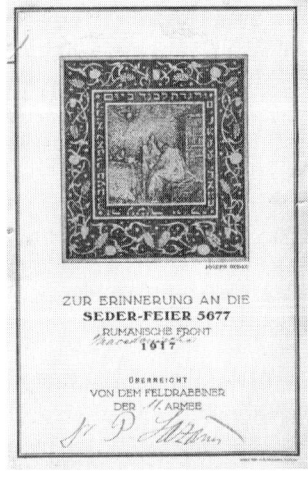

21. Invitation signed by Paul Lazarus for Pesach celebration in Macedonia, 1917. Copyright: Center for Jewish History, Jerusalem.

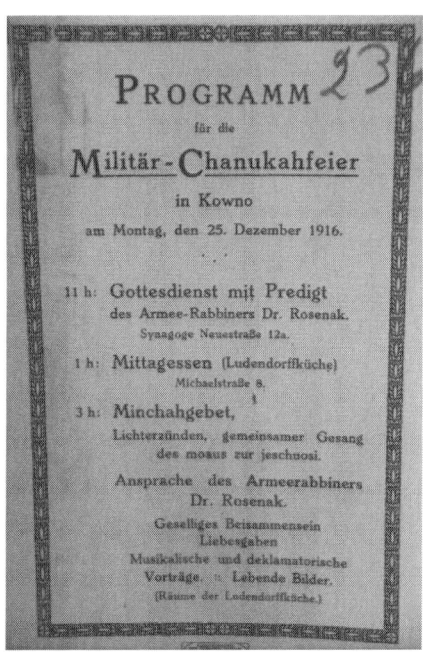

22. Chanukah programme in Kowno, 1916. Copyright: Centrum Judaicum Berlin, CJA 1, 75, Ve 1, Nr. 397, #13020, Bl. 221.

23. Yom Kippur service in Brussels, 1915 apparently organized by Offizierstellvertreter Baum. Copyright: Leo Baeck Institute, NYC.

24. Chanukah 1916 on the Eastern Front. Copyright: Jewish Museum, Frankfurt.

25. Seder in Riga, 1918. Copyright: Jewish Museum, Frankfurt.

26. Rosh Hashanah in Brussels with 1,600 Jewish soldiers. Copyright: Jim Herzog.

27. Seder on the Western Front, 6–7 April 1917. Copyright: Jim Herzog.

Pessach-Feier.
Zur Zeit des grossen Krieges
St. Quentin
29. und 30. März 1915 (14. und 15. Nisan 5675)

1. Sederabend.
Eier mit Salzwasser
Suppe mit Mazzeklössen
Rinderbraten mit Kartoffelbrei
Kaffee
Torte

2. Sederabend.
Eier mit Salzwasser
Rinderbraten mit Kartoffelbrei
Gemüsebeilage
Mazzeklösse mit Backobst
Kaffee

28. Hand-written menu for both Seder evenings in St Quentin, 1915. First evening: eggs in salt-water; soup with dumplings; roast beef and potato puree; cake; coffee. Second evening: Eggs in salt-water; roast beef with potato puree; vegetable accompaniment; (dessert) dumpling with baked fruit; coffee. Copyright: Centrum Judaicum Berlin: CJA 1, 75, C Ve 1, Nr. 380, Bl. 127.

29. Jewish burial on the Western Front. Copyright: Jim Herzog.

30. Jewish headstone on the Western Front. Copyright: Jim Herzog.

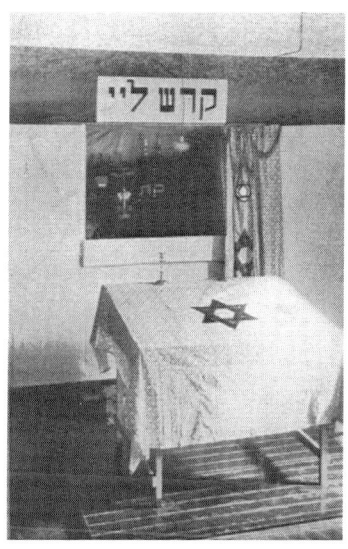

31. Pulpit, Ner Tamid and Aron Kodesh, France. Copyright: Jim Herzog.

32. Burial site of Rabbi Saly (Sali) Levi at Berlin Weissensee (author's collection).

33. Rabbi Siegfried Alexander at a memorial service in Berlin Weissensee cemetery in 1936 commemorating the 12,500 Jews who died for Germany during the First World War (after propagation of the Nürnberg racial laws). Copyright: Bildarchiv Pisarek / akg-images.

CHAPTER FOUR

Bruno Italiener: Hope, Patriotism and Kindness

Bruno Italiener (see Plates 1, 3 and 4) volunteered for service at the beginning of the war, was appointed Jewish chaplain for the Seventh Army on the Western Front, and served there throughout the war, also taking part in the Rabbinical conferences. During 1914–16 he wrote war reports, published in 1916 under the title '*Vom Heimat und Glauben*'.[1] Translations follow:

We Must Win (August 1914) (Sermon)[2]

'See, I lay before you today both the blessing and the curse.'[3] Thus we read from the Torah today. These words have never appeared more meaningful. Blessing or curse, that is what our German Fatherland must now contend with. Blessing or curse, that is what will befall each and every one of us during this battle.

We do not fight this war for half-measures, but for *das Ganze* [the Big Picture]: great good, or else great misfortune. And that is the power, and beauty of this war! Yes, war can also be beautiful. A war so taken up, as it has been begun in our Germany, will bring blessing: despite the terror that it brings to all of us, despite all the wounds that have afflicted us and will afflict us in the future.

We have already been at war for three weeks. Would we have missed these weeks? Is there one of us who would delete these weeks from their lives despite terrible tension that has burdened us, the upheaval that this time has brought to all of us? Would we wish to have missed these days of enthusiasm, when a wave of one great will took hold of our entire German *Volk*; these days of courageous and happy faith in victory of *unsere gute Sache* [our good cause]? And at the end of the day is there one of us who does not feel that these three weeks of war have improved us spiritually, who does not feel that he has become more mature, freer, better?

Yes, we have become better. I do not wish to invoke the shadow of the past during the momentous time in which we live. But have we not always wished to make real experiences inherent in the words

Einigkeit und Recht und Freiheit für das deutsche Vaterland [Unity and right and freedom for our German Fatherland] which hitherto had been mere words?[4]

Moral strength guarantees this, the strength that lies in our German *Volk* and has perhaps never showed itself more clearly than at this time. A people that discards with such humility the scythe, pen, book, and instead takes the sword into its hand; a people that with such fervour accepts as the most natural thing in the world separation from wife and child, father and mother, sister and betrothed and departs from them, perhaps forever; a people that marches with such a sure step, such shining eyes, such clear and happy song, such as one sings at festivals – such a people carries in it a guarantee for the future, and will not forget when peace comes what it promised quietly and unspoken to itself and to others.

But each one of us individually has also become better. Are these the same people who thought only of themselves and their own comfort, who now bear every discomfort, solely to bring help to others, to permit a certain lightening of their burden; are these the same people who guarded their money mean-spiritedly and distrustfully, who tried in a thousand ways to increase their wealth? And now these same people in an instant, when everything becomes uncertain, when it is certain that they will suffer grievous loss – despite all this, they are happy, despite all material worries that filled them previously: these same people step back behind one great thought: will Germany be victorious, will our nation as a whole survive and live on?

And are these really the same people who worried anxiously that invisible barriers between themselves and others should not be moved by even a hair's breadth? Are these people not beginning to tear these barriers down so thoroughly that they will, God willing, never exist again in the same form? Yes, it is as if the Kaiser's words, 'I know only Germans', have flown like a spark from his palace and penetrated into every German house and heart, and have burned out all pettiness, prejudice and bitterness that previously separated the children of one people, sons of one Fatherland, from one another.[5] Whence did these new and strength values spring?

There is only one answer. The strength comes from FAITH. Our German people BELIEVES. There is nothing greater than when one can say of a people that it is a people of faith. Because to have faith means to have strength, it means to be strong both in happiness and misfortune. Our people have this faith. Obviously, there are those among us who cannot yet find the way back from the shallow waters of disbelief, from slogans of the years of peace, to the holy depth and silence of God's Faith. There may be some amongst us who are wondering whether the real God is the cold modern God of a philosophical system or is still the old God of the Bible. But for our German people these last few weeks have sufficed to find again that which they never really lost. Even for those few who had forgotten, our German people believe again; they feel, now that everyone is unsure and afraid, that there is only the One: He who is enthroned in quiet majesty, from millennium to millennium.

Our German people who see all artificial prognostications, all individual expectations collapse around them, pray once more and speak the words of the ancient Psalm: 'I will lift up mine eyes to the hills, whence cometh my help?' And they answer confidently: 'My help comes from the Lord, Creator of Heaven and Earth. He does not let your foot falter, your Protector does not sleep!'[6]

Yes, we pray again! For we were unable to pray properly for so long – it seemed as if superficial pleasures of the day bound our movements, that we could not ascend higher! These days of holy need have liberated our souls. We pray again: not only to our Father in Heaven to keep us and our loved ones at home safe, but more: that in the storm and roar of battle, our Great and Powerful God of peace and justice will help our German cause, that He will help the cause of truth and justice to victory.

Whether God will hear our prayer to protect us and our loved ones we do not know: we hope for this in the depths of our hearts. But we do know that God will hear our prayer for justice and truth, we believe and know it.

Yes, the words that we so often hear during these days, that we so often read, are true: we *must* be victorious, Not only because otherwise our nation would cease to exist and we would lose our material wealth, our lives: that would be a miserable 'must'. We must be victorious in a higher sense, because with our battalions march faith and justice. And these cannot be conquered. Whether a few or thousands fall, Germany *will* live. Germany *must* live! Amen.

The German Song (October 1914)[7]

Many comrades feel that one can show bravery only when facing the enemy. But there is also bravery behind the Front, often no less great than in the most dashing assault: this is the bravery in the field hospitals. Anyone who goes through our field hospitals with open eyes and feeling heart really gets to know us Germans: only then does he understand why we Germans must conquer, even if a world of enemies gathers against us.

One sees heroism there as great as that at the Front, and sometimes even greater because it is quiet. Our heroes in field hospitals do not boast, they remain quiet. A large room with twenty to thirty beds one next to the other, in which wounded men, many badly wounded, lie. But almost none speaks. Sometimes a muffled whispering, a slight moaning when the pain becomes too intense; otherwise nothing. Deep silence: silence of strength.

A powerful secret strength flows out of these beds of pain, shines from the eyes and faces of each one: this power is called patience! Our wounded and ill are all patient. It is as if they unconsciously know what a great thing patience is, as if in all their pain the deep truth has been revealed to them that, like everything great, victory in this great and honourable war can come to us only through tenacity, persistence and patience. It is as if the wounded know what a service they are doing for the Fatherland when in their sickbeds they draw to themselves this great, secret power: patience.

When they leave the field hospital, those who return to the Front assist comrades who might lose patience when an attack doesn't succeed immediately or an expectation doesn't get immediately fulfilled. And those who return home must now be patient with those Philistines who are dissatisfied because they cannot read at breakfast every day about at least one fortress stormed, one army corps captured, or a dozen English warships destroyed.

It is no coincidence that our wounded and sick are so patient. The patience comes from a deep well of strength that we Germans possess in large measure: its source is our faith. Every right-thinking German has faith, but none is as conscious of it as our wounded.

In the deep, holy silence of field hospitals one's feelings become clear; and every German becomes more profoundly aware of God than before. Therefore every story of each wounded man ends with the simple and often moving profession: 'I have found faith again'.

This is why what I recently saw in a village church which had been converted into a field hospital does not appear to me as a coincidence. When I entered the semi-darkness of the church, a large, beautiful house of God that contrasted strangely with the midday sun shining outside, I found that same deep silence. On the floor of the church, on mattresses, lay thirty to forty severely wounded men. Then the organ began to play, and the sounds of the old German song burst through the high, wide rooms of the church – a French church: 'Wait, O my soul, wait for the Lord. Commend everything to Him, because He helps so gladly.'[8]

We were all, at that moment, at home: not Protestant, Catholic or Jew, but simply Germans. We felt that this was not just *a* song that just happened to be echoing in the hospital, but *the* song that resounds on the great battlefield, where our brave young German soldiers lie suffering. This is the song that sings in every German heart, in the trenches, in battle, at home: The song of power, the song of patience stemming from faith, the German song!

Soldiers Graves (November 1914)[9]

There is no better medicine to strengthen a real German soldier's mind than a pensive stroll through our military cemeteries. In the solemn silence of the graves he can find the peace, the inner strength that he needs in the tumult of battle.

Comrade, do not pass by any military cemetery without thinking. March there in rank and file, spend a minute in thankful faith thinking of those who, with ringing step and cheerful song, passed by before and now rest there quietly in the cool earth. And listen to the silent speech of the grave.

Each grave tells a story. Each grave is different but the same. Each tells of a young man who hung onto life, who had a loving family at home just like you, and who left everything that was dear to him when the Kaiser called: he did his duty, fought, and fell like a man, for Germany's protection and honour – a true German soldier, a hero! Our dead are heroes each in their own way, whether they fell in battle or died in a field hospital. They were brave in life and in death.

Only the most beautiful place in each area is good enough for a military cemetery. Some cemeteries lie high above on the towering heights, where the first rays of the morning sun shine while everything below still sleeps in darkness; some are hidden in a valley, away from the street noise, still and peaceful as a child nestling in his mother's arms; others are found at the edge of a forest, where the wind whistles through the treetops.

And the decorations on the graves! Hardly one without a flower, a sign of remembrance, even if it is only in the form of two willow sticks bound together in the form of a cross, on which a loving friend's hand in the haste of the advance has noted deceased's name and regiment.

Friend and foe rest together, often in the same grave. 'Death reconciles', says an old proverb. Nowhere is this shown more movingly that in our military cemeteries. I read a moving inscription in a Belgian churchyard in the middle of German war graves: 'Here rests a brave Belgian soldier: dedicated by German comrades.' Thus do German soldiers honour their fallen enemies. If photographed, these signs would be a holy memorial to our own dead for those at home, and bring solace to many a grieving mother or wife that their child or husband, despite lying in foreign soil, also lies in his homeland. Because a grave is only foreign when no-one knows it or cares. A fallen soldier whom even one human heart remembers wistfully and faithfully, whose last resting place is decorated by only one human hand: that soldier does not lie in foreign soil but at home, in his Fatherland!

The Nurses (November 1914)[10]

We all awake to life in our mother's arms and, when we part from the world, a kind female hand usually closes our eyes for eternal rest. Caring woman's love surrounds almost all of us throughout our lives: so it is in peacetime! In war it is otherwise. We are alone, surrounded only by men. So many sons, so many husbands, so many brothers, and yet there is no German mother, no German woman on the field of battle.

There is one exception: the nurse. She has come along, left home and hearth to do her duty in a foreign land, just like us – a brave German girl! Therefore there is no German soldier who does not treat a nurse with respect. Many greet her as a comrade; the more so as a symbol of home. The young German woman in the enemy's land seems to us like a greeting of the best of what we have at home. The pure look of a real nurse, from which the hidden deeds of unselfish love and care shine out, is for the German soldier a memory of his beloved family at home: of mother's goodness, wife's love, sister's tenderness. He knows again why he fights, why he suffers: for their protection, their purity. And the hand grasps the rifle butt instinctively and more strongly and the will to victory is steeled. We must be victorious for our loved ones at home!

Every man improves near a pure woman but perhaps none more than we Germans. It is no coincidence that our most beautiful German song, dedicated to the glory of our Fatherland, begins in the second verse: 'German women, German loyalty.'[11] The best that we Germans have, our loyalty, we owe to our women. Therefore for many wounded and ill soldiers, a period in a field hospital leads not only to bodily improvement, but also to inner purification. He returns to his unit more mature. He sees that the simple German woman is as strong and as brave as he, perhaps even more so.

She knows no danger, illness may come in whatever form it will. She goes to every bed and nurses and comforts. She knows no fatigue, no impatience, only her duty. And together with that, what femininity, what concern! Whoever has seen how a nurse arranges the pillows of a wounded man, how she gives him food, how she mops his fevered brow, so that he dreams that her hands belong to his mother: that person truly understands the meaning of the word 'sister'.[12] Every one of our wounded would like in his own way to thank the nurse who looked after him. But she wants no thanks.

One often hears it said that German discipline protects foreign girls and women from violence. I believe that the German soldier does not need to be compelled to do this. He is too honourable a man, has too much respect and love for mother, wife, sister: he will not harm foreign mothers, women, girls. He has too often sung or heard people sing German song: 'He who does not honour female sensibilities is not worthy of love or friendship.'[13]

We want to keep it so! For the sake of the German girls here, who by their selfless care give so many blessings to our wounded; for the sake of our loved ones at home, most of all for our own sakes! We want to return home with clear consciences, we want to sing at the victory celebration, if God wills it, 'German women, German loyalty!'

A New Year (January 1915)[14]

New Years' bells have never rung out as solemnly, nor with such iron resolve, in our German Fatherland as during this year! The terrible anger of a nation against a people that has out of pure envy disturbed us from our best and most useful pursuits and thereby given us the unshakable will and determination to state our own terms for peace and righteousness.[15]

But next to this war song the bells also sang another song, softly and jubilantly: a song that has never rung out so purely in German lands: the song of the beauty of the German people. For never has our people been as beautiful as on this New Year's Eve. The entire German people prayed! And there is nothing on earth more beautiful than a nation at prayer.

The individual who faithfully turns his gaze towards heaven wears an unforgettable expression. But an entire nation at prayer – over sixty million – otherwise so different in their desires and opinions, are, in this respect, all identical, with heads bowed before the one great God in heaven! Comrade, that is a picture so great, so beautiful that when one sees it one can only do one thing: pray with them with folded hands, asking God that he protect such a people. And God will protect us. Our best people in Germany have never experienced times more joyful or more confident than in these past weeks.

A people that enters the New Year with such humility cannot be destroyed, even if a throng ten times greater than we are assembled against us. Because we Germans carry a strength within us, from our Kaiser right down to the last man, on which the greatest army must break because it is a strength that comes from faith! That and only that, is what our enemies are right to envy.

They do not need to envy us for our readiness to sacrifice because we also see in them great strength, see their sons willing to dedicate their blood and possessions to their Fatherland. And they do not need to envy us for our brave young sons, because we too see in them examples of bravery and contempt for death that no real soldier can fail to recognize.

But this simple faith in the Lord, which not only one or two but the entire German people possess – man, woman, and child, all together, strong in faith in the one great just God – they must envy us for that strength, which will destroy all their plans! This has never been clearer to me than on the first day of the New Year at the organ concert in the church at Laon.[16]

It should have been an hour of musical attention but it was much more. It was the New Year celebration of the entire German people. Everything seemed to be a reflection of something larger and nobler. That glorious House of God, in its solemn beauty, now in war without any images, doubly effective because of size and breadth of the room and the quiet yet passionately loud speech of the pillars, which lift even the most recalcitrant human soul up to the Eternal! A reflection of deep, simple German faith.

The thousands of people crowded together, all faiths mixed: Catholics, Protestants, Jews, of all ranks: nobles, officers, men, all

German – a glorious reflection of our great, united German *Volk*. And that great, united German nation sat with us in the church for the entire celebration. It joined in when the song of thanks rose up thunderously to heaven:

> I inscribe this on my memory:
> The Lord hath done great things for us
> And graciously has helped us.[17]

The German people dreamt with us of the German homeland, as Beethoven's: 'Holy night, pour heaven's peace into my heart.'[18] And the German people joined us in silent prayer, trembling with Körner's battle prayer: 'Father, I praise You! It is not a battle for the riches of the earth, but we protect the most holy with our swords!'[19]

We felt this during the entire evening, but most of all at the end when we all stood up to sing the old Dutch prayer of thanks![20] The old French church, many hundreds of years old, has surely never heard such singing like the song of our young German soldiers the first day of 1915. It was as if they wanted to make the church burst with their song! This was not simply the singing of more than 2,000 people, it was a call to battle, the vow of an entire people who had for the New Year only one wish: to be victorious; only one faith for the New Year:

He does not make the bad serve the good; His name be praised; He does not forget us.

Liebesgaben [Gifts From Home] (November 1914)[21]

A few days ago I saw a vehicle with gifts from home. I confirm here, comrade, that as I walked in amongst all the chests and boxes, in the unadorned goods vehicle, I was as moved as if I were in a house of God. How much love and care, how many good wishes were in each package, even the smallest thing!

A note fell into my hands: 'Whoever receives this should please send me a post card.' A clumsy child's hand had written those words, the hand of a schoolgirl who felt all the love that a young heart can have for Germany: she had put all this into her small gift that now daily waits for a greeting from a great soldier in a foreign land!

Therefore the word rings so true, so reminiscent of the Homeland: *Liebesgabe*! But not only, comrade, because it reminds us of so much sweetness, warmth and love at home, but also because it reminds us of what makes us Germans true Germans, the German spirit. Each gift is consecrated by German sensibility.

Two packages: One from the parents! Well packed by father! How mother has once more thought of everything, and so much more! And even gloves! Dear, good mother! And this? Tied up so tightly and each time smaller? Wait, you naughty sister, for when I come back home!

And the other package! I see by the handwriting it is from a wife. The faithful soul! She also forgets nothing, just like mother. And here is the photo of our youngest child! Heavens, how big the girl is growing!

That damned wind! It blows the cigarette smoke into my eyes! ... And thoughts wander homeward ... And the longing gaze sees the German village: healthy, vital, like the German soil, dreaming in evening's peace: with its blast furnaces in which German steel glows, forging German strength! With its schools, where everyone learns the German spirit; with its houses of worship, in which they pray with German faith!

Look now in war! They speak only of us, live only for us. And thousands upon thousands of women, young and old, at work in palace and hut! They sew and knit for us! And with each stitch a thousand wishes and with each thread a thousand greetings for the son, husband, father, brother, no, for us all! For the Fatherland! And the French, Russians and, dearest friend, the English!, wanted to break into these homes, burn down these houses, make these people suffer, violate and kill them!

Comrade, they want to! But we thank God that they could not! We thank all the courageous men who have thrown themselves against the enemy! And you are one of them, comrade! You will make sure that they will not be able to invade us in the future! That is your *Liebesgabe*, comrade, for the loved ones at home, for the Fatherland!

Ich Hatt' Einen Kameraden (December 1914)[22]

In a place of foreigners: foreign houses, foreign streets, there is a dull roar. It's coming nearer. A song: A German song. Our soldiers on the march. They sing. And then it becomes clear: '*Ich hatt' einen Kameraden, einen bessern findst du nicht*'.[23] And meanwhile you stand there and this stream of strength, of life's fullness, flows past you, and a picture rises in you that slumbered and now has awoken, that you will not be able to forget as long as you live.

The first days of mobilization, summer's glow. A tightly packed crowd in the streets, waiting; and then a deep silence. Everyone listens: they are coming! And then they are here! How powerful the thunder! How the eyes sparkle! How the flowers shine on their breasts, on their rifles, as if they knew that they are parting from wife and mother, sister and betrothed! And a call rises up, ever louder, ever louder! And a thousand arms are raised and wave, and a thousand windows open and greet! There! Again the song! Who started it? No one knows: *'Ich hatt' einen Kameraden …'*

I recently visited a field hospital. The wounded and sick were singing, *'Deutschland über alles'* [see Note 4]. We read the newspapers and are not ashamed to weep. Our soldiers' songs vary according to the region and age. Volunteers sing more war songs, both young and old. *'Ich hatt' einen Kameraden…'* That is the song of the German soldier, the song of comradeship and loyalty. And it is also the song of war! What did we know about comradeship in peacetime? Now we all know what it is!

The comrade is our brother, who shares his last morsel with us. A comrade is a friend who warns, spurs us on, who dreams of home with us at quiet times. A comrade is the father who carries us with strong arm, wounded from battle, puts us to bed carefully like a child, and when, if it is necessary, closes our eyes for eternal slumber.

Not only will you see the hundreds of thousands who have left for battle to protect Germany's honour. But you will also feel the spirit of all the millions who in former times left home and hearth, wife and child, to protect their German soil, to protect the Fatherland. Long dead and yet so alive, a proud and immeasurable throng, and all of them – comrades.

You see the columns of Spicheren and Wörth, hear the thundering hurrahs of the heroes of Vionville, see the shot up flags under the mountains of corpses of the victors of Gravelotte.[24] You see our dead of the Napoleonic wars: men and women, giving their money, their wedding rings, their hair, their very lives, for the Fatherland.

And Fichte[25] greets you with a grave nod and Arndt's battle song: 'The God who made iron grow did not want slaves.'[26] This song thunders around you. And Lützow's wild and bold hunters storm past you.[27] And far off in the distance old Fritz with his grenadiers, and the victors of Rossbach and the pious soldiers of Leuthen.[28] And all are comrades!

And you feel now, perhaps as never before, what it means to be a German; the entire heavy burden, what it means to be the protector of your heritage, to be a comrade of such comrades.

And an iron will grasps you: to be worthy of them, and one thought takes hold of you, to conquer, or else die in such a way that you will deserve the highest praise on your gravestone: '*Ich hatt' einen Kameraden ....*'

Home (July 1915)[29]

We all dream of home. We live, we fight, and if need be we die for home. I have never felt the same strength radiating from our Homeland as when I saw it last. It was late afternoon when we crossed over the border: we didn't need to ask where Germany was. We recognized our Germany by the women and children who stood in the fields and streets, in front of the houses, who waved and greeted us with such warmth and kindness, as it was in the first days of mobilization, perhaps even more so. The greeting had become quieter, and we all felt that the greeting was not only for us but also for sons, husbands, fathers far away who wear the same uniform as we do, and for whom hearts and thoughts have yearned day after day, for months.

We recognized our Germany from the quiet order in the life at railway stations, in restless stamping of machines, fire and smoke of furnaces, factories that we passed. We also recognized it from the solemn quiet in the towns and villages, dreaming in the peace of evening.

You have helped to ensure that our Germany looks as it does. Your watching and waiting, your privation, care, longing, has not been for naught! It is your strength that swings the hammer working in the factories! It is your loyalty that protects the houses that stand there so peacefully! And the German forests sing of your patience and courage, as do the German trees which grow towards heaven so proudly! And yet, comrades, I have not yet shown you the real Germany!

It does not lie outside in the land that one can see passing by, its fields, factories, cities and towns; it lies much deeper, buried in hearts that beat and care and hope for Germany's welfare. I got to know them when I saw the homeland once more. In the beginning I was disappointed. But when I saw life and activity in the streets and theatres, when I saw the beautiful shop window displays, it seemed as if the war were something strange and distant, happening far away from our Fatherland.

But when I looked at the picture of home more carefully, the many women dressed in black; German mothers looking into the eyes of German wives, who despite all the longing, the care that plagues them, still bear their fate with such quiet patience, such brave and quiet faith; when I spoke to German men who despite all offerings of blood, strength and treasure were still ready for future sacrifice for the greatness and honour of our Fatherland; when I saw young German men and girls with only one desire: to contribute to the sacrifice for the Fatherland, with only one pride: to be German – only then did I feel the complete and true greatness of our Germany, only then did I realize that I had beheld the true Germany.

Comrades, let us pray to God to save Germany. We feel even more strongly than we did a year ago, when the war began, what we have in our Homeland, how we love our Germany. We feel it especially at moments when a picture of the Homeland appears before our eyes and greets us: with its order, beauty, strength, and purest virtues, its courage for sacrifice, patience, piety. We want to carry the picture of our Homeland in our hearts. It will uplift and comfort us and give us the strength to carry on and bear up and prove that we are worthy of our German Homeland.

Hospital Thoughts (December 1915)[30]

There is hardly a place that imparts more moral courage than our field hospitals. One must properly understand its language, to better learn from it. Perhaps nowhere does one feel how weighty our time is, than in the quiet of the sick room. At the Front in the trenches everything is too loud, the ramparts usually speak a language too violent for us to be able to think things over quietly.

But he who goes through the hospital with seeing eyes, feels with trembling the greatness of our times, the existence of great men. All the virtues that we otherwise only read about in books and in which we in our own day did not wish to believe: steadfastness, thankfulness, brotherliness and more than anything else patience, here they come to meet us, one and all!

What appeared to me fourteen months ago, when I first set foot in our field hospitals, as characteristic of almost all the sick – their inspiring patience – I have had confirmed again and again on each new visit.

I have stood at many beds and looked into many pale faces, but almost never found one who has lost patience. And what images I have seen! After how many long months have I found many wounded and sick still here, always lying in the same place and, when I ask how they are, always giving the same patient and satisfied answer.

Do not believe, that this is the patience of indifference. What a brightening in the eyes one usually sees when one relates a story of victory! What interest in all that is going on out there! No, they have not become blunted by what they have lived through, only more serious and mature. And this maturity shines out of their countenances.

One sees that they have had much time for reflection. And, now that the cool breath of death has stroked them, they have turned their eyes questioningly and searchingly on the meaning of life. That is why almost all have become devout. Not filled with that external piety that people like to see, but rather with pure and quiet piety that prays secretly and is therefore doubly visible, because it shines from the eyes of the sick with that deep and mysterious look that one cannot easily forget.

True piety and thankfulness are closely linked. I have not found such thankfulness as I found in the field hospitals anywhere else. Only the sick really know how to value life's riches because they must do without them. What is natural for the healthy man – that he can move an arm, see, breathe – is a joy for the wounded man, for which he is deeply grateful.

What is destroyed at the Front in the trenches by the nature of war is built up again in the sacred silence of the field hospital, namely spiritual values and relationships between man and man. Nowhere else is there such true comradeship. One has to see with one's own eyes how the more lightly wounded assist the more seriously wounded, how they nurse each other.

May something of that spirit of comradeship penetrate into our German Fatherland and remain there, long after the war ends! That is one of the deepest wishes of us German Jews for our Germany. Because only a Germany inwardly and truly united would make the terrible sacrifice that this war demands worthwhile.

May something of the spirit of the hospital fill all of us now, during the war! I believe, comrades, that this would be the only thanks worthy of those who must suffer for us in hospitals, the only thanks that would make the name 'German' and the name 'Jew' names of honour.

Great Is My Strength Through The Lord (September 1915)[31]

I should write down what I would like to tell you on Rosh Hashanah, comrade. But I can do this only when I think of our services in the field, how you entered the room in which we so often have had services, with confident tread, still carrying on your uniform traces of the trenches; how you laid down your rifle, took in your hands the prayer book that I held out to you. And when I look into your eyes, which tell me of standing guard and battle, suffering and hope, but also of longing for the Homeland, for father and mother, wife and child, then I know what should appear in these pages on Rosh Hashanah. A short and devout word in which the experiences of the past resound and give power and faith for the coming days.

I find them in the reading of the Prophets for the first New Year's day. In Hannah's prayer of thanks that begin with the words: 'Great is my strength through the Lord, my mouth is enlarged wide over my enemies, I rejoice in Your salvation.'[32] 'Great is my strength through the Lord!' Is there one amongst us, one in our entire great Fatherland, in whose heart these Biblical words do not echo?

'Great is my strength through the Lord.' Yes, how great has our strength been proved to be! When they rose up against us in the first August days when the war began, one enemy after the other, you know, comrade, how despite all enthusiasm that filled the streets, despite the proud and steady tread with which you marched out, that the question still beat quietly in our hearts: 'Will Germany endure?'

And how we have endured! What a string of victories during the first weeks, what a strong impregnable rampart, through the long months! Again and again they ran up against us, always new enemies, new places for battle in West and East! And what resulted?

Our entire great German Fatherland is, except for a very narrow strip of border in the extreme southwest, completely free of the enemy.[33] By contrast, our troops in East and West are deep in enemy territory. Is that not wonderful, comrade? Against such a number and such brave opponents who do not fear death! Yes, it is like a wonder! And the longer one considers it, the more thoughtful one becomes, the more shatteringly the conviction penetrates into our consciousness: 'Great is my strength only through God, and I rejoice in His salvation.'

And what our German people as a whole experience, how much more strongly do we feel individually! Each of us has come nearer to his God during the past year. Obviously, we cannot constantly pray, cannot constantly live in a devout mood as we did during the first days of mobilization. But we all feel that we stand before God differently compared to last year! God has helped us so often through a thousand perils and dangers. 'Praise the Lord, O my soul, and forget not the good that He has done':[34] never have these words from the Psalms awoken an echo in our hearts as now. Too often we have felt the breath of God but not of *El hagadol ve'hanora*, of that great, noble and powerful God who speaks to us out of the storms of war, out of blood, strife and suffering; but also the breath of *El rachum ve'chanun*, the merciful and compassionate God, He who speaks to us through acts of love.

We have felt his power when we saw hospital trains rolling, when we stepped through the rooms, seeing doctors and nurses at work. We have, almost all of us, changed spiritually during the past year. When one looks at people superficially, in the field and at home, one might believe that everything is the same as it was. But when one has the opportunity to look a little more deeply, behind the mask that every human being carries, then one recognizes many changes! We have all become more sensitive.

The words 'father' and 'mother, 'wife' and 'child', have attained a completely new sound. Only now, in the midst of this terrible dying, can we really appreciate one another. And we have become more brotherly. Not only our ears, but our hearts hear others' suffering. Common need and care have brought us together. Many who walked past each other with indifference have found one another in friendship and do not wish to lose one another again. Therefore we look to the New Year with such confidence. 'Great is our strength through the Lord!' We will receive the New Year with this call. Certainly, in earlier years we did not wish to begin any great thing without God; and many who looked like a heathen on the outside wrote secretly in his work books: 'with God', folding his hands faithfully at important decisions in his life. But those were exceptional. Usually, he depended only on himself and on other people. We have all learned now to think differently.

Now, when all predictions have proved to be wrong, all calculations about nations and individuals false; when one so-called good friend after the other deserts us, now we Germans experience as never before the words of the Psalms: 'It is better to take refuge in the Lord than to put trust in princes.'[35] We pray more faithfully than ever with

Hannah: 'Great is my strength through the Lord, because I rejoice in His salvation.' And this faith in God's help lives out here among us in wondrous devotion.

But it is not only during religious service that we see this faith, shining out from all the young faces who look so seriously, and can pray with such rapt devotion; we encounter it in the trenches, we read it in letters of our brave young men to loved ones back home. We encounter it above all in the field hospitals. I have stood at so many sick beds during the past year and looked so many in the eye, old and young, fathers of families and near-children. We did not ask about background or religion, we felt ourselves united by belief in the One God, to whom we say: 'I rejoice in Thy salvation.'

And the same faith lives at home. We encounter it again and again with deep emotion in the letters of our loved ones, in every line, every word, we read it often with great feeling in the pain-filled faces of so many fathers, and many wives who have been called here to the sickbed of their child or husband, and now sit at the bedside for long and fearful hours, caring and still hoping for help from the only One who can help.

And what each individual in our Germany feels, the voice of German news reports testifies to every day with growing power. One must really read the war news properly. There it is written that not only have we made progress here and there, we have fought off this or that attack; but much more must be understood from these words. How much heroism, firm persistence, patience is found behind each sentence, each word! One feels it involuntarily, that these simple unadorned sentences are written with the heart's blood of the German nation and behind them stands the secret of our strength and our indomitability 'Great is my strength through the Lord, I rejoice in His salvation.' That must remain our belief. None of us knows what the New Year will bring, whether a long fight, whether victory and a peaceful homecoming. But we all feel: with confidence in God we will be able to bear what comes more lightly.

'Great is my strength through the Lord.' With this resolution we fight, and may we be victorious in the coming year!

Friendship (August 1915)[36]

Never before has the section from the prophets that was read yesterday in our home synagogues appeared as meaningful as this year. Because it tells of friendship, the friendship between David and Jonathan: between Jonathan, the king's son, and David, the simple shepherd boy.[37] Often this bond of friendship that bound the two youths together is set as an example for young people but I believe that it has seldom had more to teach us Jews and Germans than during the past year.

How many young men are there who can find a friend for a lifetime? What previously bound one to the other was usually certain common, often very superficial, interests. At best there was some similarity in spiritual direction, but this was not the same as two hearts that beat as one, which alone creates a true and lasting friendship.

Two hearts seldom beat together in days of peace. It happens mainly in moments of extreme emotion, when the deepest and most noble characteristics of humanity come to the fore. And this is perhaps nowhere truer than at times of danger, such as in wartime.

It was thus with David and Jonathan. The two had been drawn to one another for a long time. But the oath of true friendship in life and in death was made only when the greatest danger threatened, when King Saul's hatred threatened to destroy them both.

So it is again! It is what the German spirit expresses in the well-known folk song *'Ich hatt' einen Kameraden'*, friendship unto death: 'Remain my good comrade in eternal life' [see Note 23] – that has happened countless times in this war.

Thousands upon thousands of such pure, selfless friendships have been formed recently. The German spirit is especially receptive to friendship. It was a German poet who coined the words, 'Whoever has had the great fortune to be a friend's friend.'[38] And this has happened to many: in the trenches in which many German youths stand guard – they feel that war has brought them together, and cannot tear them apart again. They have found each other in the face of death: that moment which, otherwise, given differences in the social circles from which they came, would have made such a friendship impossible.

The Great Equalizer has in this way brought many blessings in the midst of war. When grenades fall, when bullets fly, the small compartments that society artificially erects between man and his fellow fall away. Then there are no factory owners, labourers, employers and employees, there are only men, only comrades. Even the difference between Christian and Jew, which appeared unbridgeable before the war, has become significantly softened, and in some circles has almost completely disappeared.

Just as the king's son Jonathan forgot that David was in fact a simple shepherd and only saw in him the hero who overcame Goliath, the noble youth to whom his heart reached out in wonder, so too have Christians now forgotten with what little esteem they regarded Jews before the war. Christians have seen the heroic deeds that Jews have performed against the enemy, with the same, in some cases greater, courage than their Christian comrades; they have realized that Jews have always been brave, and that the spirit of the Maccabees has never disappeared from us. The Christian soldier is now partly ashamed and surprised to recognize that the Jew, as far as human feeling is concerned, does not differ from him at all in love of Fatherland and willingness to sacrifice.

If this war were to bring us Jews nothing else but greater understanding from, and greater inner closeness with, our Christian fellow-citizens, then that would already be a prize that we German Jews would receive with special joy. Because inward appreciation of our Christian fellow-citizens is much more important than the receiving of external rights, of certain higher civil service positions that have until now been denied us, especially in the army.[39]

Let us use the time well that has been given us and brings us into such close contact, as perhaps will never occur again. Let our comrades recognize that in the face of the enemy a Jew is not to be bested by a Christian when it comes to courage and enthusiasm against the enemy.

Let us make them see in our bearing that we are fully conscious of the deep responsibility and holy duty of being a Jew. But let us also show through our deeds, through worth, tact, refraining from the extremes of emotion and bellicose imposition, that we should be recognized only by our own sheer humanity, by our deeds. Let us, by the faith with which we adhere to our religion, make them understand that we can be as good and faithful Germans as they, simply because we are good and faithful Jews.

Then perhaps a time will come; and if we do not experience it ourselves, then our children and children's children will experience it. A time when a true friendship may develop, like that between the powerful king's son Jonathan and David, the simple shepherd boy, not only, as now, between individual Jews and Christians, but between *all* Jews and *all* Christians. May there come a time when a Jew may call a Christian as David called Jonathan: My brother! Amen.

[Rabbi Italiener sent two reports of his wartime activities to his home community in Darmstadt during the first two years of the war:]

19 April 1915

Up till now I have held a hundred services in the field. The men are very happy with this and come from the most varied units. When I am not there, as at the Front, where I can usually visit only once a fortnight, services are held for about thirty men on their own. I hold services here in Laon on Saturday afternoon, and recently Friday evenings, and we have acquired a harmonium played by a Christian school teacher. I held the recent Seders here in Laon in great style, with excellent cooperation from Command. After services the participants, more than a hundred men, marched in closed ranks, led by a sergeant major, to the festive hall, decorated with green pine branches and flags from the different German states. The Seder plate lay before me and each man received a *Hagadah*. Several Christians, as well as a Professor of History from the University of Freiburg in Breisgau, also attended. In the middle of the celebration we had a hot meal with two courses: peas with sausage, smoked meat with potato salad, oranges and coffee. I gave a talk during the first part, followed by the prayer for the Kaiser.

The second part of my duties consisted of field hospital visits, also burying two dead Jewish soldiers. In both cases the care of the physicians and other medical personnel was wonderful. In the face of death there are no Christians or Jews – only human beings! The consciousness that the deceased has a rabbi present during his last hours of life gives some comfort: exchange of correspondence with family members is one of our most thankful tasks. As thanks, I often receive many packages of sausage, baked goods, cigars, etc. which I distribute to all irrespective of religion. Books (especially those containing short stories with cheerful themes) and periodicals are also most welcome.

The mood of the men remains confident; despite everything that has happened to them they have not become hardened: in fact, the opposite. The camaraderie between Jews and Christians is very good, and cooperation from Christian superiors, allowing men from quite far away to attend Jewish services, is excellent. Here and there I do hear complaints of mean anti-Semitic affronts by superiors, but I have not yet determined how far these complaints can be justified.[40]

2 November 1915

My duty area has enlarged and now comprises a large part of beautiful northern France. Despite all difficulties, the moving gratitude of all the men fills us chaplains with the happy feeling that only consciousness of doing one's duty can bring. Churches are usually the only indoor places with enough room for our services, but we sometimes hold them out in the open and when necessary in bomb-proof shelters. Recently we held our services in a cave: a wooden table which both Christian faiths had used as an altar served as a Torah-reading stand, two candles on each side of the Torah scroll, the cave's dim light, the comrades' faces hardly recognizable in the half-dark, the distant glow of the noonday sun at the cave entrance: what a unique picture! We also took part in the dedication of a memorial for fallen German and French soldiers, all faiths united together. Where possible, Jewish graves are decorated with a Star of David or a Hebrew and German inscription.

We held High Holiday celebrations according to tradition (including sounding of the Shofar) in the Great Hall of the Palace of Justice near the location of Army High Command. About 400 men attended and we raised our voices to our Creator with the songs and prayers of our youth. On Rosh Hashanah eve we had a good meal of kosher Frankfurter sausage, potato salad and beer. On the afternoon of the first day we enjoyed coffee and cake and rested in well-deserved relaxation after a strenuous first war year.

Another service in France was held, upon approval of High Command, with about thirty Russian Jewish prisoners of war. They decorated the room festively with two candles, a white tablecloth, a hand-painted Star of David and inscribed the words 'Blessed shall you be when you come in' (Deut. 28: 6). One of the prisoners held the service. After the service they all voiced the wish that I send them prayer books. One of them said to me: 'German Jews have a Fatherland, we Russian Jews have none.'

We have had two more Chaplains Conferences, one in Lille the other in St Quentin. I continue with my field hospital visits and my relations with the Christian chaplains continue to be good.[41]

Author's Summary

Bruno Italiener was a young man when he entered the army and youth is reflected in his uncomplicated idealism and certainty in the justice of Germany's cause. His is a world of compassion and simple justice, and care for his fellow-men in need. His sermon in August 1914 (the ninth in the series) idealizes war to a point that would be unthinkable today, but must be taken with the tenor of the times. His knowledge of German history and literature, sometimes of a quite obscure and secular nature, is striking and assumes that an educated reader will know what he is talking about without his always having to spell out the details.

The sermon preached on the theme of David and Jonathan, as applicable to Jewish and Christian Germans, is beautiful in concept. He takes for granted the fact that Jews will be better off in a post-war Germany because of lessons learned on the battlefield. As with other Jewish chaplains, he takes equal treatment of all religious groups for granted. He mentions but does not elaborate on anti-Semitism in the field in one of his reports (see p.140) and describes services and celebrations in the field including services in the caves of northern France similar to those reported by Rabbi Leo Baeck (see Chapter 5). Bruno Italiener's faith in the German spirit and his conviction that Jewishness and Germanness were so connected as to be practically one and the same thing echo the beliefs of many Jewish thinkers and philosophers of the time. Unfortunately, his writings end in 1916, so we have no direct evidence about the impact of events that may have challenged his optimistic assumptions – about the ultimate German victory, and about the growing solidarity between Christians and Jews.

NOTES

1. B. Italiener, *Von Heimat und Glauben. Kriegsbetrachtungen* (Darmstadt: H.L. Schlapp Buchhandlung, 1916), pp.1–46. The first seven reports were written during the first year of the war and published in the war newspaper of the Seventh Army. Number 8 was also published in Feldrabbiner des Westheeres (eds), *Sabbathgedanken für jüdische Soldaten* (Leipzig: Verlag von M.W. Kaufmann, 1918) (see Chapter 6); Numbers 9–11 were, apart from the first sermon (no.9) which was preached at home immediately after the outbreak of the war, sermons in the field. Sermons are not numbered in this text.
2. Italiener, *Von Heimat und Glauben*, pp.27–32. Although this is the first chronological entry after the war began, it is listed as no.9. It is not clear whether this sermon was preached in Rabbi Italiener's home congregation.
3. Deuteronomy 11: 26.
4. Beginning of third verse of *Deutschlandlied*, later *Deutschland über Alles*, written 1841 by August Heinrich Hoffmann von Fallersleben. During the First World War, the German anthem was 'Heil dir in Siegeskranz' (sung to the melody of 'God save the King'). The third verse of the *Deutschlandlied* comprises the text of the modern-day German national anthem.
5. The *Burgfrieden* (civil truce) declared by the Kaiser on 4 August.
6. Psalm 121: 1–3.
7. Italiener, *Von Heimat und Glauben*, pp.5–7.

8. *'Harre, meine Seele, harre des Herrn!/Alles ihm befehle, hilft er doch so gern'*. Lyrics: Friederich Räder (Röder) 1815–72, Music: César Malan 1787–1864. The first two lines of the song were prescribed for all sixth grade Prussian schools, until the First World War.
9. Italiener, *Von Heimat und Glauben*, pp.7–10.
10. Italiener, *Von Heimat und Glauben*, pp.10–13.
11. *'Deutsche Frauen, deutsche Treue'*. *Deutschlandlied*, first two lines, second verse.
12. *Schwester* in German means sister (sibling) or senior nurse (sister), as used by British (but not Americans).
13. *'Wer des Weibes weiblichen Sinn nicht ehrt/Der hält auch Freiheit und Freunde nicht wert.'* From: *'Stoßt an'* (Let us drink to), German university students' song, by August Daniel von Binzer (1793–1868).
14. Italiener, *Von Heimat und Glauben*, pp.13–16.
15. He is probably referring to the English and French.
16. It is unclear whether Rabbi Italiener knew of the 'National Day of Fast and Humiliation' held in England on 2 January 1915, when the entire people there joined in prayer as well.
17. *'Bis hierher hat mich Gott gebracht/In mein Gedächtnis schreib' ich an Der Herr hat Großes mir getan/Bis hierher mir geholfen'*. Ämilie Juliane von Schwarzburg-Rudolstadt, (1637–1706); several melodies exist.
18. *'Heil'ge Nacht, o gieße du/Himmelsfrieden in dies Herz.'* From *'Hymne an die Nacht'* (traditional Christmas song, author not known), music by Ludwig van Beethoven (1770–1827): Theme from piano sonata nr. 23.
19. *Gebet während der Schlacht* (Theodor Körner, 1813 [1791–1813]: killed during Prussian wars of liberation): *'Vater, ich preise dich!/`s ist ja kein Kampf für die Güter der Erde/Das Heiligste schützen wir mit dem Schwerte.'* Original music: Friedrich Heinrich Himmel (1813).
20. The German translation of this prayer (*Wir treten zum Beten*), written by Adrianus Valerius (c.1575–1625) became a potent symbol of the Throne- and Altar-alliance of German civil religion until 1918.
21. Italiener, *Von Heimat und Glauben*, pp.16–18. *Liebesgaben* means 'gifts sent with love'.
22. Italiener, *Von Heimat und Glauben*, pp.19–22.
23. *'Der gute Kamerad'*, or 'The Good Comrade', is a traditional lament of the German armed forces. Text by Ludwig Uhland in 1809 and set to music in 1825 by Friedrich Silcher. 'The Good Comrade' plays an important ceremonial role, and is an integral part of a military funeral. The first verse follows:
    'Ich hatt' einen Kameraden [Once I had a comrade]
    Einen besseren findst du ni(ch)t. [You won't find a better one.]
    Die Trommel schlug zum Streite [The drum was rolling for battle]
    Er ging an meiner Seite [He was marching by my side]
    In gleichem Schritt und Tritt.' [In the same pace and stride.]
24. Sites of battles during the Franco-Prussian war. The battle of Mars la Tour took place near Vionville.
25. Johann Gottlieb Fichte (1762–1814), one of the founding members of German idealism.
26. *'Vaterlandslied'* [Fatherland song] by Ernst Moritz Arndt (1769–1860), German author and poet of nationalist works: *'Der Gott, der Eisen wachsen ließ/Der wollte keine Knechte.'* Written on the eve of the Prussian wars of liberation against Napoleon (1812).
27. Ludwig Adolph Wilhelm von Lützow (1782–1834), a Prussian general chiefly known for the *Freikorps schwarzer Jäger* [Black Huntsmen] named after him.
28. The Battles of Rossbach and Leuthen were fought in November/December 1757 under the leadership of Frederick the Great ('old Fritz') (1712–86) as part of the seven year Silesian war.
29. Italiener, *Von Heimat und Glauben*, pp.22–4.
30. Ibid., pp.25–7.
31. Ibid., pp.33–6.

32. 1 Samuel 2: 1. Original: 'My heart rejoices in the Lord.'
33. This was the case on the Western Front throughout the war. In the East, a brief Russian incursion into East Prussia was reversed at the end of August 1914 by the Battle of Tannenberg.
34. Psalm 103: 2.
35. Psalm 118: 9.
36. Italiener, *Von Heimat und Glauben*, pp.37–40
37. 1 Samuel 20: 18–42.
38. *Wem der grosse Wurf gelungen/Eines Freundes Freund zu sein*: An die Freude [Ode to Joy]. Friederich von Schiller (1759–1805).
39. Jews were not allowed to become reserve officers in the peacetime Prussian army, nor were they permitted to join the civil service.
40. B. Italiener, *Berichte des Herrn Dr. Italiener aus dem Felde an den Vorstand der israelitischen Religionsgemeinde Darmstadt* (London: Leo Baeck College, 1915), ITL/BER: 1.
41. Ibid., ITL/BER: 2.

CHAPTER FIVE

Leo Baeck: Chaplain and Neo-Kantian Philosopher

Leo Baeck (see Plates 1, 2, 6 and 7) is the best-known German-Jewish chaplain of the First World War. Reports on his activities as chaplain during the First World War are published sequentially in the *Gemeindeblatt der jüdischen Gemeinde zu Berlin*. Translations of some of these follow, including a published war sermon.[1]

27 September 1914

I have been directed to visit battle and field hospitals, and divisions with fixed positions, for two half days each. My greatest difficulty lies in the wide geographic extension (40–70 kilometres) and isolation of the Jewish soldiers. Additionally, it is not always possible to reach the men, who are currently almost all in the trenches. I have found Jewish wounded in almost all field hospitals and my visits seem to be a great blessing for them. I have given all the Jewish soldiers I met news by letter.

I have already made all dispositions to hold Yom Kippur services on Tuesday evening and Wednesday morning (29, 30 September). On my request, High Command has issued an order of the day that all Jewish soldiers, so long as the war situation permits it, will remain free of duty from Tuesday 5.00 p.m. through Wednesday 7.00 p.m., so that they may gather for communal prayers.

15 October 1914

On 30 September I held Yom Kippur services in a church in Chauny. Thirty to forty men of various ranks, including physicians, attended. The middle section of the church was put at our disposal, away from the altar and the other sacramental locations, and lit with candles. I recited prayers – including *Yizkor* – and delivered the sermon, from the lower pulpit: in front of it chairs for participants had been arranged. To my joy, several members of my home community were amongst the small crowd. I had the feeling that the day was close to all of us.

In each service the sentences of *Avinu malkeinu* were repeated aloud; *Kaddish* was repeated by a few men at the end of *Yizkor*; and at the end of the *Ne'ilah* service the sentences of the Confession of Faith (*Shema*) constituted the service's end.

The journey to surrounding field hospitals is sometimes significantly facilitated by my having a vehicle at my disposal for a few days. These field hospital visits have proven an important part of my work. The wounded are brought a piece of home and their confidence increases. Morale is raised by the fact that a Jewish chaplain visits them as well, as is the case for those with other faiths. Additionally, regular news can be given to the family of the wounded; often I have conducted quite an extensive written correspondence.

In many cases I have unfortunately also had to send sad news to the family. At burials, where the dead are mostly interred in one mass grave, I have spoken at the graveside together with a Protestant or Catholic pastor and afterwards alongside them I have followed the funeral procession. I have invariably notified the bereaved family about the funeral, its place and time, and news of the deceased.

I devoted the whole of last week to beginning a general tour of individual divisions, and spent every three days at two divisions. I held two small services out in the open, to give spiritual care to those Jewish soldiers who felt isolated in their unit. Additionally I made enquiries about Jewish wounded in field hospitals and aid stations. This back and forth travel has been associated with many difficulties and exertions. Many towns in which I spent the night have been destroyed by shells and the few houses that still have a roof and a few windows are already occupied by other soldiers.

I have succeeded in getting in touch with only one Jewish chaplain colleague thus far: he has made the main rear echelon position his permanent base. According to my experience gained thus far, the latter severely limits the field of activity. Despite all difficulties it is absolutely necessary to visit all sections of the army. Only thus is it possible to give the soldiers (if not all, then at least as many as possible) the personal impression and certainty that a rabbi is amongst them. It is very important that not only the Jewish soldiers, but also those of other faiths experience this. This is clearly of importance for recognition of the Jewish religion and is also important for the attitude of Jewish soldiers that their religion stands alongside the others.

30 October 1914

I have continued visiting individual divisions and brigades. The number of soldiers participating in these services varies between eight and twenty-four. Services are usually possible only in the early morning or late evening under the cover of darkness, to allow troops to come out of trenches and return to them after services. Locations are determined by local conditions. In Noyon the City Commandant allowed us to use the large cathedral; however, I requested rather to use a small room in the house in which I was quartered: the small number of soldiers would have been greatly disproportional to the huge cathedral space, and changed the service's tone. In one location a schoolroom was placed at my disposal, in the others three services took place in the open. The order of the services was as follows: Reading of a Psalm and a small Torah or *Haftarah* section of the week (Hebrew and German); after that the sermon; then an abbreviated form – based upon the field prayer book – of *Shacharit* or *Ma'ariv*; a free German prayer after that; conclusion with the priestly blessing and *Kaddish*. After the service I stay companionably for a while with the troops: I obtain the addresses of their parents, to be able to give them a short report about their sons. In order to present a picture of the external conditions of such a service, I give the following example:

In Carlepont the area has been almost completely destroyed by fighting in previous weeks. Because of this I chose for services a small tree-bordered square in the castle park which leads from the main street to a hilly slope. A pulpit was quickly erected by sappers and decorated with sheets and branches. The meeting place was given as the town's church square, and a notice posted there, to show them the way. I awaited the men there and we went together to the candle-lit pulpit: the soldiers stood around the pulpit in a semi-circle. Dark night surrounded us, and the sickle moon broke through the clouds for only a few moments, shedding its light on the surrounding groups of trees. Nature's silence alone, interrupted from time to time by the rolling of distant gunshots, was earnest and reverent. The service took about forty-five minutes and I stayed with my small community for about an hour in a house in which I had found a large table and chairs in the disorderly rubble, to discuss questions and worries which moved them all. Thereafter the men were led by their superiors back to their different positions.

For one service the local brigade commander had arranged for the cooperation of a regimental band and I had arranged some non-denominational pieces of music with them as introduction and end to the service. However, a few minutes after the service started enemy bombardment of a nearby steeple began so that, upon request of the officer present, the service was broken off; I resumed it in another more secure place and it ended modestly.

All the officers I have met during the past six weeks have unconditionally praised the aptitude and reliability, the fearlessness and ever-present voluntary preparedness, skill and military intelligence, of their Jewish soldiers. A certain pride to do their duty, courage, ingenuity, and clear open glance can be found in almost all of them. I was also able to observe that they prove themselves not only as comrades, but also as superiors; also how rapidly sons from well-off families get used to deprivation and effort, and the peculiar sensitivity which Jewish soldiers demonstrate towards the indigenous population. During the coming days I wish to visit some of the larger field hospitals again and then continue my way to the individual units.[2]

4 January 1915

My routine work day is as follows: I leave my permanent quarters early in the morning and arrive at divisional staff quarters for whose area a service has been arranged, around 9.30 a.m. I discuss all necessary issues with an adjutant. It is easiest if the day is prearranged at least three to four days in advance so that the written command can reach everywhere and proper leave of absence is granted. It is sometimes difficult to find a suitable place because of the present army positions, or alternately to decide whether parallel services are necessary. Likewise, the hour that most suits the troops to allow them to leave their positions and return to them again must be examined. All possibilities must be considered, not only the place in question but also the way there, the hour, and whether the place appears safe from bombardment, whether night quarters can be used if necessary, etc.

When the chosen place is a large town which lies almost in ruins, it is necessary for me to travel there at once, to find a suitable place for services. The unfavourable weather only rarely allows services in the open. In the neighbourhood of the troop position, regimental staff is usually accommodated in a farm house. I go there, and discover in the town hall a small undamaged room which is arranged, cleaned in good time, and illuminated for the appointed hour, 8.00 p.m.

The journey to the town serves another purpose. A few kilometres away the grave of one of our soldiers lies in a field. The family of the deceased requested me some time ago to arrange care for his last resting place. I ascertained this, and with the help of an attendant erected a memorial tablet and recited our ancient prayers over it. A tree which our comrades have planted on the hill will turn green early in the year.

From there the way leads to the permanent position of another division where, as before, I prepare a service for our men. Towards evening I arrive in my quarters, after which I travel to a few field hospitals and enquire about the wounded and sick.

Work requirements are considerably easier for Protestant and Catholic chaplains. There are usually more of them closer together and each of them has therefore his easily surveyed work area, in which goals can be achieved relatively quickly and the most favourable time can be found for their work. In addition the possibility of sharing and eventual substitution of the work is available. Each pastor belongs in a specific circle of men with whom he can coalesce. The Jewish chaplain has difficulties of distance, because his field of work extends over an entire army; he provides care in many areas: This is especially great in the widely extended First Army. All the same the rabbis in the West, where the fighting has become static, have it easier than their colleagues in the East with its war of movement.

The number of those who gather together for services is steadily increasing, partially because the number of Jewish soldiers has increased through replenishment of volunteers; for example in one division it increased threefold.

17 January 1915

The first three services which took place near the Front were held in the evening, as precaution demanded. It was not easy to find a suitable protected room in Audignicourt, and cloudy weather made holding the service outside inadvisable. But eventually an appropriate room which was occupied by troops was freed up and prepared for a few hours. It was Friday evening, and when we remained together for a while after the service in a comfortable room in whose midst stood a table with a white cover and two candles, it seemed like Sabbath celebration at home, especially since donations from home made a small meal available. It was a cheerful get-together that ended too early for all, when the time to depart arrived. We said farewell at the town's exit; individual groups disappeared in the wooded roads which led to hills, and then I myself returned to the town.

The evening service in Carlepont commenced at 8.00 p.m. Through deep darkness we searched, from the square where we assembled, along destroyed walls, for the way to the house in which a small room had been prepared for us. Warmth and light surrounded us there. A small pulpit was erected and next to it the room's decoration, a large glued mural affixed in place of the shot up window as protection against wind and rain, on which was written the Declaration of the Rights of Man, which the great French Revolution announced as its Declaration of Faith.[3]

In Bezaponin, the town church was chosen to be the site of the service, which was fixed for 7.00 p.m. But in the meanwhile it became apparent that it needed to be equipped as a field hospital, and so a regimental orderly room, the largest other room in the small town, was prepared: Pine branches and ivy tendrils were affixed to the walls and to the hanging lamp. The soldiers who were quartered in the house sat together in the room next door; the door remained open, and thus a second small community participated in the service. For several amongst us – so I heard during our hour long social get-together – the service was particularly solemn; there were some volunteers amongst us who had just arrived at their regiments a few days ago and now, during this night, would be moving into their protected positions for the first time.[4]

2 February 1915

Our soldiers have been situated for five months in the area of the places where we gathered for services and a description of this region might therefore be of interest.

The scenery in all the above-mentioned areas is charming: a French Thuringia.[5] During many sunny days, such as we have had during the past weeks, the stark contrast stands out between the soft, lovely natural beauty and the hard difficulties of war.

France has a network of excellent roads; but the heavy munition and provision vehicles which have crossed over them day after day for many months have taken their toll, and the prevalent change to cooler, humid weather has done its own damage. We must retain a clear vision of the area before us, in order to be on our guard against overly torn up roads. The watch posts which have been erected with necessary prudence point the way forward. On many roads travel by vehicle is prohibited, and on others advised against, due to danger.

Successes of our encounters with the enemy during the past few weeks have allowed us to reach many places more calmly and comfortably. Thus, one can travel by cart to the area of Chivres, where the last service took place. From there the communication trenches continue. Exact signposts give directions in the criss-crossed trenches; to the left and right one sees the protected underground, often quite roomy habitations of our soldiers. Most of the town lies in ruins. The cellars serve as lodgings; one of the few undamaged rooms was used for a service. The inhabitants have long since left town, and with them the coming and going of daily life has moved away: the silence of the abandoned and lost lies over everything.

I describe one place more, which during the past few months has become a communal place for us, as an example of others. Épagny lies secluded from the graceful valleys and hills on a bare high ridge, over which grey rain clouds seem to hang perpetually; a meagre place, even if it is one of the larger towns in the area. The small church has been turned into a field hospital; in the houses each room is full of soldiers; it is as if one noticed the proximity of the battlefield. From the heights, the streets can be seen stretching out leading to defensive positions, to places that everyone here knows. Roads are mostly unused: everyone knows how much they are threatened, and the town from which they extend also reflects something of this anxious seriousness. In such a way the town has retained something solemn and stern, even when the sun shines and the grey of the clouds disappears. But it is especially in such a place that one can experience how much warmth and almost joy is brought by a religious service.

20 February 1915

The number of men taking part in the services varies between ten and fifty-five. After many efforts I have finally found suitable versions for communal singing. Even when our circle is small a song begins and concludes the service and we all experience how much these communal songs uplift us, regardless of whether those that sing are few or many.

The service in Noyon took place in the local cathedral, in a side chapel separated from the main aisle. An old beautiful columned passage which opened into a garden on the other side led to the chapel from the nave: this seclusion led to great quiet. It was a morning Sabbath service and even here, where there is no recess in the uninterrupted course of daily exertions and duties, the thought that it is the Sabbath day brings its special tone to the service from the very beginning. The quiet, peaceful room, into which nothing of the day's noise and battle penetrated, had its own atmosphere.

During *Shacharit* especially, the thunder of our bombardment penetrated and made the windows of the church clatter to the ground. But this restless roaring can, like quiet, produce a strong, even solemn, experience. It acts almost like accompanying serious music, that speaks of the solemnity of each hour. It does not disturb the service but brings it a new atmosphere. And the almost sombre feeling which arises from gathering together which enters devotions during the hour of prayer loses nothing by it; rather it gains a certain ardency, in the midst of the turmoil and thundering that penetrates from the outside.

Two cemeteries prepared for our fallen warriors are described. In Le Mesnil, a town near Audignicourt, a quiet meadow has become a military cemetery during the past few months. It lies, just like many of our old Jewish cemeteries, on the slope of a hill, surrounded by fields and trees. A low wall of boulders, artlessly put together like part of nature, has been erected around it by medical orderlies in their spare time. Each of the deceased has found his own special place and each grave is faithfully tended. A soft peaceful mood of fulfilment and completion lies over it in nature's stillness. The gaze wanders far over the fields and streams to the dark woods; fields stretch upwards and downwards in soft lines, and the heavens vault over everything, as if protecting and calming.

Another cemetery, which has been prepared during the past weeks, is isolated and almost hidden, but just as peaceful. It is isolated from the main road, and a narrow path leads below to a deep valley floor that, ever more narrowly, ends in a woodland. The cemetery hill lies here on both sides of the road between the trees. All who are buried here have most probably often looked down while they were alive. No wall surrounds the gravesites. The woods themselves are the cemetery: its trees surround and traverse it and the hilly walls that surround the valley make up the protecting walls. All turmoil seems to withdraw and below there is only quiet.[6]

2 March 1915

I am responsible for more than seventy field hospitals. They extend over a very wide area, some near the Front, others far behind it. An equal number of Protestant and Catholic chaplains are occupied full-time with these. It is difficult to be in contact with all these hospitals from one location, but experiences of the last few months have gradually made many things both possible and easier, most importantly that regular news of the delivery of the wounded and sick can reach me. So it is to be hoped that each one has received a visit from a rabbi.

In all its diversity, the same [German] order appears that is found everywhere else. In the cities, field hospitals are located where hospitals and large spiritual educational establishments – often found in France – are present; apart from these, factories and theatres must supply their rooms. In the smaller towns and villages churches and schools, and here and there châteaux, serve as hospitals. Even under unfavourable conditions much has been achieved. In the beginning straw or a mattress on the floor served as beds, but now proper beds are available, arranged in equal rows with a chair and small table next to each. Churches turned into field hospitals present a strange picture. The building keeps its character and receives those who enter with its paintings, statues and shrines on which the daylight falls shimmeringly from narrow colourful windows. But in its rooms living spaces have been established, divided by the columns with their shafts and pillars. The stone floor is covered with planks, stoves are brought in, and there are thick curtains in front of the doors. Here and there is a table, around which those who are allowed out of bed sit; warmth enters the house's solemnity.

15 March 1915

In St Léger the service was special in that it took place inside a cave. The French battle area, especially in countryside north of the Aisne, is rich in caves, both natural and those which have gradually arisen through stone bridges penetrating into the mountain. Some of these caves have room for many hundreds of men and have served as secure living spaces for entire units. After I had often held services in the town, it had been bombarded several times and on request of Division Command a more secure location was sought. All the rooms in a solitarily standing manor house were too small, so a nearby cave was designated. We entered through a wide door and gradually the eye differentiated serpentine jagged walls, vaults and domes, side passages and niches. A pulpit was erected on a back wall; on it stood two candles which lent the space a certain semi-darkness, so that one's gaze looked down on the rows of praying men. In the dark silence inside the mountain all of us experienced the silent dedication that dwells in quiet, prayerful assembly. We were about fifty men who had gathered together for Friday evening services: many were often seen at services during the past six months, others had been in the field for only a few weeks and the exceptional location in which our ancient prayers were intoned had the greatest effect on these recent arrivals. When we exited the cave it was almost night, and outside under a starry sky we were filled with a new ardour.[7]

18 May 1915

Jewish prisoners of war in a nearby camp, currently used in street work, have participated in some of my services. I readily received permission upon request, and was told that these were the 'cleanest and most useful' of all the prisoners. The prisoners themselves were full of thanks when they told of the friendly treatment which they had received, allowing them everything possible under the extraordinary circumstances. They were led to the place where services were held by a guard and the expressions on their faces spoke more clearly than words what it meant to them to be present in the circle of the devout. And we all experienced the blessing of being able to render a kindness to one another during difficult times. These were men whom war had led into a foreign land but despite this they felt – as may be observed almost everywhere by our soldiers – the same wish, to overcome war's difficulty, wherever possible, by goodness and friendliness.[8]

More than anything else this great measure of kindheartedness and nobility of heart which so often resides in the modest, simple man is revealed. Men share everything with each other: great sacrifice, effort and difficulties as well as things such as small gifts which they receive. The crucial thing in camaraderie is that they get to know each other in both virtues and deficiencies and so get to know and value themselves, often for the first time. This is something under which we have often suffered in the narrower sense: the last decade has erected many partitions, so that many in our country know little or nothing about those who live near them. It is understandable that much that prevailed over a long period does not disappear overnight; there is a law of inertia. But one thing will endure: that people who until now had just walked alongside one another have now thought about the same things during solemn moments, and speak to each other about their hopes and longings. That is the real sense and value of comradeship.

Jewish soldiers have, by order of High Command, been given necessary leave for the festival of Shavuot as far as military necessity permits. I have, both during and after the festival, held a large number of services and I hold descriptions on these over for my next report.[9]

6 June 1915

Near the village of Chiry, which lies on the road from Noyon to Compiègne, a newly established military cemetery was dedicated on Sunday afternoon. Many of our own graves as well as those of French soldiers from the time of the great battles are scattered in the fields and meadows.[10] Each one is cared for, but units who have been in the area for a while have expressed the wish to prepare a common graveyard for all who have fallen for the Fatherland. Each individual contributed a few pfennig, and a quiet, peaceful meadow was purchased, standing on a gentle slope with a view far over the rolling hills. All who have lain scattered here and there, both friend and foe, have now been moved over and buried next to each other, each in his own grave. The field was dedicated on a fine late afternoon which gilded the low gravestones with its shimmering light shining in the flowers and branches which adorned the low hill. A dense crowd surrounded the cemetery: next to generals there were numerous officers and other representatives. All experienced what this place related of the solemn and difficult days through which we lived, and the good days for which we hope. This could be heard amongst the dedication speeches, but the quiet cemetery itself spoke the most poignant words.

In one of the towns in which I have held regular services for many months, a soldiers' home has been erected to facilitate social gatherings – which the narrow quarters do not allow – also during unfavourable weather. A roomy barn has been renovated, windows and doors erected, benches and tables brought in, and adroit hands have decorated the walls with inscriptions and drawings. Here we, who came together for services, have remained together for periods of a few hours. Amongst us there are those knowledgeable in recital and singing, and they present old and newly-acquired ability in singing and recitation. Communal singing alternates, with a glass of beer and cigarettes donated for each man. Guests who enter the open doors participate in our cheerfulness, until the appointed hour warns of parting and a short speech ends our gathering, as it began.

18 June 1915

One of these services took place under the impact of heavy fighting at Moulin sous Touvent.[11] Each day and each battle site had its own threatening solemnity; everywhere soldiers anticipated the thought that they might have to give their lives. Those who gathered together for prayer greeted each other with these modest words. We had assembled in a village near which individual units stood in reserve waiting for the hour when they might be led forward. A small number of troops from these rear positions was able to assemble at services for a short while. Everything around that penetrated the ear – the rolling sound of bombardment and wounded who could be seen being carried to aid stations, the anxious tumult – everything seemed to command solemn prayers. We assembled in a small protected space for a service and sermon, and these were for all of us a continuation of thoughts that had filled us outside. It was a beneficial gathering in a difficult time, to be together in body and especially in spirit. The wish 'for a good *Wiedersehen*' with which we parted quietly included all the comrades.[12]

Hören und Hoffen [Hearing and Hope] (Sermon for upcoming New Year)

There are few of us in our country for whom the year has simply passed like a play that one likes or dislikes. We have all experienced the year: it has encroached on our experiences and hopes, it has become the essence of our existence. Our world has posed new questions to all of us, which the thinking man cannot avoid.

It is the deepest demand of our religion that we do not pass by any question that touches our lives. Its introductory word is therefore, always and again: 'Hear!'[13] 'God speaks to you!' For our faith it is a godless quality when the ear is closed: he who has turned away stands before it as a sinner. It has given its many commandments, but they are all, to begin with, a simple word; they become reality only when these words have called to men from life quietly or loudly, and they have heard. The world around us speaks, admonishes and asks, and only insofar as there are people who hear will truthfulness and loyalty, righteousness and love descend to earth.

Recent days have conveyed a new piety into our country, and this year has spoken to us more loudly and forcefully than all others before it; it has penetrated ears and souls of those who previously went on their way satisfied and undisturbed. Its essence has spoken more clearly and with another sound; what was self-evident has become extraordinary, and the extraordinary self-evident. People who have accepted their togetherness without comment, like the air that they breathe, have been separated for months; concern extends more widely than space which separates, and fear extends its gloomy sway. But this separation has much that brings one nearer to the other, people have learned to listen to one other. The thought that they live, this most natural of things in the world, has now become something great and special for them. The day itself has become an answer to questions and fears: it has its own sound and its coming and going speaks to people. This great occurrence, with its heroism, danger, need, dedication, sacrifice: all have entered, and peoples' ears have been opened, their souls hearken.

Will this new piety remain, will it penetrate through the daily routine that will and must return? Or will it be like before, that we speak more than we hear and pass by questions that await us? Only the future can answer. But we already recognize something crucial. It will not all be different and new, but it will also not all remain old. Because this solemn time has powerfully disrupted our lives. What has for so long dominated life's view has collapsed. What was the appearance and glittering life climax of a superficial culture, to which people aspired; self-satisfaction that saw every new milestone paved on the way to humanity and knew how to offer constant congratulations; belief that everything has already been achieved, that there is so much civilized behaviour, education, religion in the world: all of these peaks and crests to which one looked collapsed when the first solemn day of war placed its oppressive heaviness on it and when what really stood firmly was demonstrated. We recognized how little that is strong, straight, and secure has been built up despite all the frameworks of ascent, how little faith really exists on earth despite all reigning, beckoning religions. War has brought great disillusionment with the bitter question: where is justice that binds men together, where is faith, where is loyalty and truth?

Perhaps we Jews are the ones who dispute this the least. We have known this feeling from the days of our forefathers: of standing alone in the family of nations, not understood or respected – this feeling of loving without thanks, being forgotten and abandoned. Since time immemorial we have been able to tell of wisdom that wants to keep abreast with power and majority; perfidy that is ready to be set aside to elevate life; the sound of beautiful phrases ready for inviting and invited. For us no dream has been destroyed and for this reason our hope is strongest.

One hope arises out of the weakness. He who is tired or does not wish to bestir himself temporizes and waits on others, on their tides of action and talents. Most stay away, and their lassitude enters their souls even more: with it comes pessimism that drags darkness in front of and behind it and in the end signifies that we have already seen it ourselves from the beginning. Only confidence that drives us to expect the best and the most from ourselves is consistent and true. Only he who fights truly hopes. He has heard what the times have spoken and what conscience announces, and wants to answer through his own struggles and efforts. He hears the call: Be the future yourself!

So our religion signifies hope. It is a wisdom that sounds obvious, but must be repeated continuously: justice, goodness and morality give us only as much as they withstand the test. The first evidence for religion is the man who possesses these qualities. He who wishes for goodness must, in his own existence, start with it himself. We have once again experienced how little real godliness has entered into the world thus far. It will always be little and weak where man is intent in preserving the virtue of others and therefore has forgotten progress towards his own virtue. He who wishes to broaden faith must start with himself. That alone is real religion and only personal will, courage, hope and vigour affect the future.

A New Year begins, and we look outside with our desires and our longing. We must not expect fulfilment of the coming days from others – we must expect it all from ourselves! Then we possess the confidence, then we build up that which will last. Many hollow words and empty images have collapsed, and we can hear the voice of our lives that much more penetratingly. It speaks of the reality that surrounds us, of the future for which we ourselves should struggle: that is the New Year of our religion.[14]

7 August 1915

The longer the war lasts, the more men I see from all parts of Germany. An image of the structure of German Jewry appears in miniature to the observer, in a variety revealed in its own particular way. Inside the Jewish community there is an unmistakable difference between soldiers from north and south Germany. But each province also has its own distinctiveness. It is precisely the smaller circle, reflected by the communities in the field, in which the variety which exists within German Jewry is revealed. It speaks in the type of devoutness by which their need for religion is expressed.

In a small village in which I have often held services on Sabbath afternoon, people from the same area usually gather. It is more a family than a community that assembles. All know about each other and their families, and many have known one other for a long time. But the manner of experience, type of participation in services is the same for all. The former inn room in which we gather transforms itself into a *shul*, into the synagogue of a small town with its atmosphere and warmth. One of the older men knows how to lead the service, in the ancient melody of Sabbath afternoon, with ascending and descending cadences containing so much that is calm and contented. All the rest join in responsive sentences of the prayers and on their faces is reflected something of this experience, with which at home each one was filled in hours of rest after days of work. After services, questions and opinions are voiced: loudly, sincerely although a little muddled, expressed as they surely were at home during quiet Sabbath hours. One of them knows how to quote a Bible text in line with the sermon as proof of his opinion and hope; another mentions a sentence from our sages, which he has heard from his grandfather. Conversation and contradiction, question and answer go back and forth, sometimes serious sometimes cheerful. It is Sabbath afternoon in a small German town, here in the field.

Another service has the characters of a Friday evening in the synagogue of a larger North German community; a teacher knows how to intone the familiar melodies of Lewandowski.[15] And when thoughts are exchanged before parting, they almost all carry the sober, scrutinizing character of home. Alternatively, a clear Rhineland or south German accent sounds. The richness and variety of Jewish life in Germany appears ever and again, in its human and religious features.

20 August 1915

What has this year brought to the individual, in his existence and character, in his life and *Weltanschauung* [world outlook]? This question has another answer in the West than in the East, where movement and change present new events and experiences. Here, even if particular weeks of battle have continuously come but where each quieter day has no turmoil or worry, experiences have retained the same spatial horizon. For many in these areas during the past ten months a dangerous, difficult existence has played out, in the same section of trench in which the soldier stands opposite the enemy and in the same town.

This static situation imposes stronger demands on ethical characteristics. Little festival atmosphere remains in hard daily work: the difficult courage of patience, ability to resist inner tiredness must be proven. Individual soldiers transferred from Eastern regions opine that the task imposed here is more difficult than the hard, exhausting push forward in which individuals see a specific goal for which they fight and the enthusiasm of marching forwards drives them on. Here the goal is the same daily duty, the same way and same place. There, it is the constant necessity to overcome physical tiredness; here inner exhaustion is the danger that must be conquered. Every man in the field has become manlier, more self-conscious in the good sense, and therewith more modest and humble. He has learned to understand the seriousness of sober demands, the daily duty of standing firm. Because daily routine, with the same dangerous duty, stands in place of great days with great victories, moral strength must be even stronger. This strength has grown in many men, who will also understand, during the years of peace, how to go their way and stay in their position, and know who they are. The men and youths who stand in the field are our future. We must confidently hope that they will be able to do justice to whatever future duties God gives them.[16]

21 October 1915

I am writing this report on my way to the East, the new operational area to which I have been directed. This report expresses some of my thoughts from my past year in France.

There were no Jewish communities in any of the French towns which I frequented. Only a few individual Jewish families lived here and there, and for the citizens a *'pasteur israelite'*, as I was called there, is a new phenomenon. They looked on my military quality with a mixture of wonder and regard for German order which cares for everything. Only larger towns in France have Jewish communities; an extension across the provinces, with which Germany has created a rich Jewish religious life, is lacking. Added to that, the number of Jews in France is small. Loss of Alsace-Lorraine has become fateful for French Jewry as well as for France itself, because these provinces were the source of population increase. In their desire for the lost provinces the thought of *la revanche* [revenge] is expressed as much as the wish for that region with greater human fertility.[17]

A meagre spiritual life occurs together with this external isolation. A minority must not become too small, otherwise it dries up and atrophies. French Jewry has been in danger of this occurring for decades. For them it has been especially precarious that embittered France has erected walls hindering spiritual contact and separating themselves from Germany. For the spiritual life of French Jewish communities much depends on a free path again being opened between the two countries: the future of the French nation also appears to depend on such connections, so that honest communication may be created between the two peoples.

The small number of our co-religionists in the West stands in contrast to their abundance in the countries of the East. It is an abundance that calls for and awaits shaping, a further fertile base that awaits a new creative hand. This future speaks of great effort but promises great things: it is full of possibilities. Here too tasks are presented to German Jewry, powerful tasks, in which they can both give and take.[18]

5 March 1916

The region to which I have been transferred has no large town: the largest of these had, in peacetime, about 8,000 inhabitants but is now empty. The entire population, amongst them the entire Jewish community, was led away during the retreat of the Russian army.[19] All other market towns and villages, together with many meagre villages and scattered farmsteads, are mostly smaller and many places with barely fifteen low wooden houses and a church are called villages, which is why Jews were allowed to live there.[20] Here fate was kinder to most Jewish inhabitants in that they could avoid forced expulsion to the East. This was partially because the places lay secluded from roads and forgotten, and partially because on the day of expulsion most could hide in the deep forests that extended everywhere. When the storm passed, they were able to return to their homes.

Almost everyone here has his own wooden house that is sometimes smaller, sometimes larger and grows with the increase of his meagre possessions or growth of his family. Sometimes on this side and sometimes on that a little part is built on, as his property permits or the need arises. Almost all have a horse in the stable, a cart and a sled, without which in the wide countryside without railways one would be like a prisoner in the town, and also cut off from livelihood. Many also have a family cow so that they have their own milk and prepare their own butter and cheese. Many of the women, for those who do not know them, look at first glance like German farmers.

There is no wealth in these areas and no proletariat. Poverty and need are present, especially where the usual earnings by handicraft and trade are hindered or limited and the usual assistants, those who are better off, have mostly been led away or fled. But conditions are always more bearable than in places where many thousands live crowded together in large towns. During peacetime many of these places, situated between trees and water with their nature and people, must be a quiet idyll. But now the turmoil and compulsion of war, constant coming and going, has penetrated and people must now share their small house with those who war has led into their country.

On my way, because of the long distances, I have only remained in one or the other village for a few hours or a single night and self-evident hospitality is always present in Jewish homes. As small as the house is, a special room is always available for the newcomer, and as limited as provisions are, there is always something offered him. For these people, all cares and needs are contained in the one word: God! A future can be built on such a foundation![21]

6 July 1916

During the course of the past months, paths to the places where services are held have become better known, but nature has given them another shape and colour. The further north in this country, the stronger the contrast between winter and summer. Winter is followed by summer almost without transition, without spring. Almost immediately after snow begins to disappear under the sun's rays, budding and blossoming has begun. With summer the long days and bright nights arrive. In order to be able to use the far-away railways for a portion of the way, it is sometimes necessary to start at 2.00 or 3.00 a.m. and often only possible to return to quarters across long, sandy roads at the same time one or more days later. The night is light most of the time and only dark for an hour. The simplest person here feels like being in another country, and longing and love for home are therefore doubly alive. Novo-Alexandrovsk is the only town of any size in my new area.[22]

6 August 1916

Apart from regular services, I have also been able to gather Russian prisoners of war for services in two camps. The external impression of these Jewish prisoners of war is favourable; they are impressive upright figures with intelligent eyes looking out clearly. There are men from different parts of the huge Russian Empire, of differing professions and all military age groups: academics, artisans and merchants, younger men who this war has drawn out into the world for the first time and older men who life has caused to travel widely. One man distinguished himself in wars against Japan, China and Germany; fate has now made him a prisoner. Almost all understand or speak German and they continuously express the wish for a sermon in the German language, and to discuss their thoughts and hopes after the service. One thing is striking: they express, almost without exception, a Russian feeling of country and patriotism that one would not expect to be so vibrant in these men: a pride of country, faith in its power, strength and future. Not only do they speak with pleasure and self-consciously about the particular home from which they come, but also with strong faith in Russia's significance and its relevance. They repeatedly say that what is bad is the fault of bad officials; that much good lies in the heart of the people, and with the optimism that is part of every Jew they declare that good will prevail and Russia's future will be great. But none have any clear perceptions of exactly what will be or will happen.

Their wishes for the future of the Jewish population are clear and specific: especially an expectation and yearning for greater freedom, and longing for improvement of their educational system. One overriding thought appears: an extension of childhood. Each life bestows and preserves a bright, warm school-time, even where gloomy cares cast their shadows over their parents' house: a piece of childhood and youth, which allows freshness to come into being and grow, from which one must live for a lifetime. In small villages where children roam free in the streets, fields and meadows, nature is always childhood's bright, broad parlour. But in the larger towns here in the East, the most poignant part of the hard fate of the Jewish population is that shown by the children who know only one school, the hard school of life which lacks childhood. He who has once seen a little girl of four or five swathed in a white kerchief sitting next to odds and ends in a cellar window denoting a store, keeping an eye out for customers with eyes in which childhood appears to struggle with old age, has experienced the issue. A real school, in which childhood has room to exist, is a necessity of life here. Yearning for knowledge and light hardly needs to be awakened, it is spontaneous and informs everything. What is essential is a childhood for all, a place in which free air may be breathed during formative years.

22 August 1916

Many assembled for services have lived two years of war almost uninterruptedly in the field, and become older, by two fateful years. They appear old and experienced compared to those who have only been here for a few months. Many Jewish chaplains also belong to the older age group and, like so many others, have been confronted with new tasks during this time. What was at first seeking and groping, often pure looking and hoping, has gradually become regulated work, an office with its specific, ordered course. None who entered the field at that time were purposeful in their actions. Only after trial and error, attempts and new beginnings, has each achieved his goal, according to his own idiosyncrasies and personal predisposition. All achievement goes back to what one must first approach as what Goethe called the *Pflicht des Tages* [Duty of the Day].[23] Jewish chaplains in the field must preserve the courage to achieve today what can be achieved today and not stand and wait, nor to fear the new, perhaps unsuccessful path.[24]

20 September 1916

During the third week of the month, a conference of Jewish chaplains on the Eastern Front was held.

These meetings with exchange of experiences and reciprocal instruction give us Jewish chaplains in the field the possibility of shaping our work uniformly. For chaplains of other faiths, this cohesion has been ensured from the outset by organized leadership through the Catholic and Evangelical *Feldpropst* [Chaplain Provost]. Relatively early, common pastoral activity in individual regions was further facilitated by designation of one of them as *Referent* [consultant] to facilitate familiarization with everything necessary to divide tasks and interlock duties. But even then the necessity for meetings soon became apparent. Spoken words and personal feelings can have a stronger and more inspiring effect than written explanations. Jewish chaplains have lacked such facilities. The distance between individual colleagues in the East is proportionally greater than desired – and much greater than in the West – and neighbourly relations are impossible. Therefore conferences, with their debates and stimulation, to initiate common tasks, are a significant need.

Meetings in West and East have so far all fulfilled their purpose. It has been an implicit policy that rules and principles should not be determined by majority but rather by general consensus. This is always achieved despite differences in views and temperaments. The necessary amount of discipline – without which rapid and ordered cooperation is impossible – has always occurred. Every viewpoint demonstrates that a goal can be reached only when collective thought and commands for common good exist in all. Care about individuality with its idiosyncrasies is valuable and necessary in nurturing of mind and spirit. However in our own work, which can only be cooperative, individuality – if it is to be a blessing – must be combined with a strong sense of cohesion and solidarity, to achieve optimal results.

21 October 1916

Size of the service area and difficulties with roads as well as lack of a large town to allow accommodation of a large number of men did not allow assembly of our soldiers in one place during the High Holy Days. It was decided to divide the entire area of the Front into three sections, to which one day each of the two days of Rosh Hashanah and one of Yom Kippur was dedicated. Additionally, a service was held on the two days during which I could not be present at the section concerned. According to reports, this did occur as arranged thanks to the efforts of all concerned. In this way, each man was provided his one festival day.

During the first day of Rosh Hashanah a roomy log cabin in the woods was prepared. Around us was the usual camp picture, a coming and going of soldiers at work, and over everything the peculiar silence of the camp area. Individual community groups, who gradually assembled, were already standing in front of the house and it seemed as if there was something festive in their attitudes, something that spoke of the special day and reflected the spirit in a house of prayer. Nature contributed to the atmosphere: trees looked into the windows, between them the rays of the sunny autumn day played on long rows of benches, on the table placed in front of them, on spruce and birch branches that decorated the walls. The service hour began and the house became filled with worshippers: a real festival lustre entered with them.

On the second day of Rosh Hashanah in the other area the service took place in a large barn in the middle of a field that had been festively prepared for us. Long rows of rifle pyramids were arranged in front of the barn, soldiers waited in circles in the warm sunshine, a picture of peace and quiet contentment. In the corner of the barn stood tall wreaths of the last wildflowers and grasses; bunting was extended over boxes lying on top of one other to make a pulpit in front of which the considerable community positioned themselves. The wide door remained open to let light in and with the light came the soft autumn wind and the odours of field and meadow wafted in, covering everything like a festive sheen.

We got together on Yom Kippur in a small town, a town but not really a town, abandoned by its inhabitants, which had become a military camp. A high room, previously erected from strong, unhewn tree trunks, was given to us and decorated festively. A few lamps fastened to the ceiling and a row of candles illuminated dense rows of worshippers in the semi-darkness, bench behind bench. The autumn rain, which played a monotonous unchanging tune on the roof like a song of farewell to summer, was forgotten during prayer but then heard again. It appeared to the eye as if it still saw the sun of a festival, which shone over everything.[25]

19 August 1917

During past weeks, days of battle in this region have left their mark. Thus, hospital service has represented a greater demand than field services, and with it many memories have awoken of the same paths trodden during the past three years.

One thing has remained the same: the special kind of camaraderie which exists in the field hospitals. Pain and illness tend to make people selfish, and each one who is suffering is inclined to think first of himself. It is different in the field hospital: here the patient feels secure, far from continual danger: sheltered and protected, almost saved. Thoughts of his wound or illness recede, especially during the first few days, behind these other soothing thoughts: that he is now beyond the line of threatening destruction, far from the place of horror. It seems to him that he has already taken the first steps back home and almost has the feeling that convalescents have at home, those who are allowed to return home cured so that they may regain their health and strength. A quieter, softer comradeship begins, a gentler helpfulness, a desire to care together for others begins to stir in each one: for both those who lie in their beds and even more for those who are able to walk around in their striped robes. Perhaps nowhere else does one hear the word 'comrade' uttered so softly and with such emphasis as here in the field hospital.

The physician's work can be very personal. As much as rules and regulations have given all field hospitals the same form, each still retains its own countenance through the men who work in it. Until now too much has been written about stories of war and too little of its history, too much of externals and too little of essentials and for this reason hardly anything has been said about military physicians. Much has been told about the work that they perform, but almost nothing about their personalities, the humanity which they bring to their positions. This is also valuable for our narrower circle, our Jewish community from which so many military physicians have emerged. Both technical and human talents are required from all who lead and decide. But to the physician in particular the ability is bestowed to combine both harmoniously. He is of significance not because of all that he is in a position to order and accomplish, but also because of what he is able to give of himself. Here in the field he has his own place.[26]

20 December 1917

During the past month the first certain sounds of peace have sounded promisingly in our services here in the East. Everyone is thinking that a bridge to a new shore is being built.[27]

These words of confidence also resonate in our Jewish community – strong faith in our Jewish future. We both need and wish for Jewish youth, youth of thinking and experience. The essential thing is people who will come in the future: not institutions, rights, places – as much as these might mean – but we ourselves, we are the living, growing reality. The best spiritual care and best task for our Judaism today, both at home and in the field, is to find people and bring them together: people who do not simply walk along, but who see each other approach. We will become what our future becomes. And it seems that the act of looking forward to it may uplift us. Our community promises a time of renewed youth.

We live in days during which the prophetic words of peace become true again, that path of 'He who will proclaim liberty' will become perceptible.[28] The future is coming; he who wishes to receive it must believe in it, and we can believe in everything that we also treasure in ourselves.[29]

March 1918 [no day given]

Spring has arrived for the fourth time during this time of war, with joyful sunshine after grey, frosty months. During these weeks, a door has opened to the East. The status quo, preserved for over two years by defence and protection until we could advance, is behind us. It is a peculiar feeling now to be able to travel comfortably through this now abandoned region, which was for so long the site of fighting and watching, care and sacrifice, and to look across from beyond, the side which belonged to the enemy, to the trenches and habitations in which our soldiers lived and had their whole being during this time.

Those who now walk there have one thought: how much it would also mean in a spiritual sense to acquire the view of the other side, to see our world from the situation of the other. This war has led all who fought into foreign lands. At first strangeness confronted us; but this was only the smokescreen that hid the light; when strangeness gradually dissipated and vanished into the earth, warm rays appeared. When initial mistrust with its anxious fear and stifling hesitation disappeared, how rapidly did a vitality, a wish to support and manifest friendship, break through! Every returning soldier can tell of this – how he experienced helpfulness and goodness from people of other countries. Humanity penetrated through everything that separated us, and every distinctiveness and difference served only to strengthen what we had in common. Even if nations were far away, people came closer to one another.

Preconceived notions and words were, more than anything else, the main things that separated us. Nations are often only a simple word to one other. But feeling for objectivity always wins. All hate in men and nations usually dates back to faith, speech, presumption, and seldom to facts and occurrences, and mainly exists through conscious or unconscious renunciation of the latter. The characteristic of hate is, as our sages said, that it is without real foundation, that it originates in 'mine' but not in actual experience. Therefore, when actual events are understood, hate is overcome. Thus, the battle of arms is accompanied by a spiritual battle, this contest between delusion and insight, word and reality, blind faith on the one hand and clear sense on the other. Development and progress depend upon which one of these wins.

The question is often asked whether after this war, which desired to create an abundance of hate between nations and in fact did so, these nations will ever find each other again. There is no doubt that dark depths and many chasms have opened during these years. Because the future will command so many empty, desolate places, only collective labour will be able to accomplish needed work. In such a way nations will, despite all, discover each other. Faith in humanity will become stronger than belief in the mere word.

When the day will come where we may all look back from the other side, the riverside of freedom, on the years of war, when nations will attain the right outlook, then they will embrace the reconciling sentiment of peace. Life is stronger than destruction and resentment, and will rise out of the rubble. Historical development occurs and nations become ever stronger and directed to one another. None can remain alone any more, neither externally nor inwardly. The will to life will have to become the will to live together. Every nation will find a place for its tasks only when it is capable of self-awareness and justice.[30]

Author's Summary

When the neo-Kantian philosopher Hermann Cohen lay dying in 1918 and students were lamenting his loss, Cohen responded: 'Be of good cheer, you have Leo Baeck.' And indeed, Leo Baeck's reports on his war activities contain more philosophical thoughts and musings than those of any other Jewish chaplain. Baeck likened his duties to the soldiers with those of a rabbi to his congregation: his concept of duty fills his reports. He describes services in every type of location and weather, including in the trenches; his description of an evening service in a cave in north-eastern France (pp.153–4) is particularly moving. Reports of visits to field hospitals and activities there abound (in France more than seventy hospitals lay in his area of activity) and several moving descriptions of military cemeteries and burials are included, as are Holiday services on the Eastern Front.

Leo Baeck played a leading role in organization of the Jewish chaplains conferences in the West and later in the East, starting in 1915. The minutes of one each of these meetings, which dealt with all aspects of life or Jewish soldiers, are provided in Chapter 10. Baeck was a leading figure in the Verband für deutsche Juden and was entrusted by them with the issuance of a special field prayer book which was distributed to all Jewish soldiers.

Reports which he sent to his community in Berlin on a regular basis are free from any form of religious chauvinism. They are marked by a strong sense of German nationalism which viewed Germanness as a civilizing force for good, and other peoples, for example the *Ostjuden*, as different and in some way inferior to forces of German *Kultur*. Baeck felt preservation of Jewish identity to be key and at the centre of this *Gruppengefühl* (group feeling) stood affirmation of the Jewish religion. He described achievements of Jewish soldiers in a positive light and emphasized their leading role behind the lines, because of their high education levels, as translators, clerks and other roles which were often wrongly described as *Drückebergerposten* (cushy jobs).

Baeck avoided effusive interest in the *Ostjuden* showed by some of his contemporaries: he describes the poverty and suffering of the civilian Jewish population, before and during the war, in a moving way, but his descriptions are tinged with the superiority of German *Kultur* and the need to 'lead' the *Ostjuden* by German example. His reserve against Chassidic 'piety' compared to his positive characterization of Russian Jewry, is striking: 'Chassidism, with its poetry and its danger, its mood and its delusion, its softness and effeminacy, has not gained much access here.'[31] By contrast, he held the Jewish Russian soldier in high regard.

Moral force is regarded as the most important guarantor of a good and peaceful future after war's end. Behind descriptions of life at the Front lies a certain alienation with real conditions at home, its difficulties and shortages. As a Kantian, Baeck was convinced that ethics, and not aesthetics, form the foundation of life and that people who fight for moral principles are more likely to grow spiritually from the burdens of the war. A certain detachment from reality is apparent, and with the passage of time, his reports become more philosophical and less grounded in reality than they were at war's onset.

The regard in which Leo Baeck was held by the soldiers in his charge is shown in a letter home from a field hospital in France in December 1914 by Walter Herrnstadt, who died in 1920 of wounds received during the war:[32]

> With God for King and Fatherland ... yesterday's service with Dr Baeck was very uplifting! We used the front room of the church, in which about twelve comrades and one Christian non-commissioned officer (who had requested to attend the service and was completely carried away) used the first two rows of benches. Dr Baeck first read Psalm 91 and then combined it with a masterly sermon that lasted approximately forty-five minutes: Now we must hold out, be patient, and trust God, who will direct everything to the good. Many men found God only at this moment. Dr Baeck gave a moving description of a service held a few weeks ago in the open-air after darkness had fallen directly behind the firing line, after which all prayed silently for quite a while. After that, a soldier was inspired to come forward and say that only now, in silence, had he found God and learned to pray. After the German sermon, which concluded with a definition of 'With God for King and Fatherland', Dr Baeck chanted the *Shmoneh Esreh* and then said *Kiddush* before *Kaddish*,[33] followed by Psalm 121. Then a silent prayer for the Kaiser and the priestly benediction in conclusion. We were all very moved by this magnificent hour, which will never disappear from our memories.

Leo Baeck's hopes for peace are those of a decent and moral man who tried to see the best in all people. He does not express himself directly on the prevalence of anti-Semitism in the German army and shares the contemporary hope and wish that German anti-Semitism was a thing of the past which would disappear after the nation had been purified by war.

NOTES

1. The digitized original which I used has been discontinued; originals are available in the Deutsche Nationalbibliothek: https://portal.dnb.de/opac.htm?method=showFullRecord&currentResultId=Gemeindeblatt+der+j%C3%BCdischen+Gemeinde+zu+Berlin%26any&currentPosition=1.

2. L. Baeck, *Gemindeblatt der jüdischen Gemeinde zu Berlin*, vol.4, no. 11 (13 November 1914), pp.140–3.
3. The Declaration of the Rights of Man and of the Citizen (*Déclaration des droits de l'homme et du citoyen*), a fundamental document of the French Revolution.
4. Baeck, *Gemeindeblatt*, vol. 5 no.2 (12 February 1915), pp.16–18.
5. Thuringia is a free state in Central Germany known as 'the green heart of Germany' because of its dense forests.
6. Baeck, *Gemeindeblatt*, vol.5, no.3 (12 March 1915), pp.32–4.
7. Baeck, *Gemeindeblatt*, vol.5, no.4 (9 April 1915), pp.48–9.
8. It is likely that these prisoners were from England and/or its colonies and dominions (Canada, India, Australia, New Zealand, South Africa). The German army used prisoners of war from all countries (including Russia) for road work.
9. Baeck, *Gemeindeblatt*, vol.5, no.6 (11 June 1915), p.73.
10. Probably refers to the First Battle of the Marne (5–12 September 1914), and the German retreat thereafter, and the First Battle of Ypres (October/November 1914).
11. A village in northern France, site of fierce fighting in 1914 during the German retreat from the Marne.
12. Baeck, *Gemeindeblatt*, vol.5, no.7 (9 July 1915), pp.84–5.
13. In Hebrew, *Shema*, the opening word of the Jewish confession of faith 'Hear O Israel, the Lord your God, the Lord is One.'
14. Baeck, *Gemeindeblatt*, vol.5, no.9 (8 September 1915), pp.111–12.
15. Louis Lewandowski (1821–94), German composer of synagogue music, choirmaster of the *Neue Synagoge, Berlin*. Many of his pupils became prominent cantors.
16. Baeck, *Gemeindeblatt*, vol.5, no.9 (8 September 1915), pp.113–14.
17. Many people living in Alsace-Lorraine before the Franco-Prussian War moved to France after the territory was conquered by Germany. Loss of these mineral-rich territories was a source of French bitterness.
18. Baeck, *Gemeindeblatt*, vol.5, no.11 (12 November 1915), p.142. Baeck's low opinion of French compared to German Jewry is reflected in writings of other chaplains.
19. Lithuanian Jewry was particularly oppressed during the First World War. The attitude of Russian military authorities toward Jews was one of suspicion and hostility; rumours were spread that they were traitors, and pogroms occurred. Early in the war many Lithuanian Jews were expelled from their homes.
20. Jews were generally excluded from or limited in large cities and towns.
21. Baeck, *Gemeindeblatt*, vol.6, no.4 (7 April 1916), p.46.
22. Ibid., vol.6, no.8 (11 August 1916), pp.92–3.
23. *Was aber ist deine Pflicht? Die Forderung des Tages* [What then is your duty? The demand of the day]. *Wilhelm Meister's Wanderjahre II*. Johann Wolfgang von Goethe (1749–1832).
24. Baeck, *Gemeindeblatt*, vol.6, no.9 (8 September 1916), pp.105–6.
25. Ibid., vol.6, no.11 (10 November 1916), pp.128–9.
26. Ibid., vol.7, no.10 (12 October 1917), pp.107–8. Reports which would have dealt with the Russian Revolution and entry of the United States into the war are missing from the digitized database.
27. Immediately after the Bolshevik revolution on 6–7 November 1917 (New Style), Lenin sued for peace. The treaty of Brest-Litovsk was signed on 3 March 1918.
28. Isaiah 52: 7.
29. Baeck, *Gemeindeblatt*, vol.8, no.3 (8 March 1918), p.29.
30. Ibid., vol.8, no.5 (10 May 1918), p.53.
31. U. Sieg, 'Empathie und Pflichterfüllung. Leo Baeck als Feldrabbiner im ersten Weltkrieg', in *Leo Baeck 1873–1956. Aus dem Stamme von Rabbiner*, ed. G. Heuberger and F. Backhaus (Frankfurt am Main: Jüdischer Verlag im Suhrkamp Verlag, 2001), pp.44–59.

32. Reichsbund Jüdischer Frontsoldaten (ed.), *Kriegsbriefe gefallene deutsche Juden* (Berlin: Vortrupp Verlag, 1935), pp.28–9; M. Berger, *Eisernes Kreuz, Doppeladler, Davidstern. Juden in deutschen und österreichisch-ungarischen Armeen. Der Militärdienst jüdischer Soldaten durch zwei Jahrhunderte* (Berlin: Trafoverlag, 2010), p.60; M. Berger and G. Römer-Hillebrecht (eds), *Juden und Militär in Deutschland. Zwischen Integration, Assimilation, Ausgrenzung und Vernichtung* (Baden Baden: Nomos Verlaggesellschaft, 2009), p.95.
33. In Hebrew, the three root letters for both words *Kiddush* and *Kaddish* (see glossary) are identical and mean 'holy' or 'sanctified'.

CHAPTER SIX

Aron (Arnold) Tänzer: Mover, Shaker and Creator of Soup Kitchens

Even though Rabbi Aron Tänzer (see Plates 2, 8–12) was 43 years old when war started, he volunteered and as soon as permitted served on the Eastern Front (first on the Polish border, latterly also in Ukraine) from 1915 until the end of the war. His war reports are in two parts. The first one (war memoirs) is in the form of a typescript dealing with the time before and during his call-up to the end of September 1915 (pp.175–96); the second part (pp.196–238) is in the form of a handwritten war diary in Sütterlin script, dealing with the period 2 October 1915 until the end of the war and his return home.[1]

Chapter 1. The First Year of War[2]

The hours through which we lived during those first August days were solemn, carried by the purest sense of fulfilment of duty to Nation and Fatherland. It was this alone which inspired me as well, a 43-year-old man with feelings deepened by profession and life experience, so that I knew only one care, one love: the German Fatherland. When during the last days of July prospects for preservation of peace dwindled ever more, and when they disappeared completely on Friday 31 July after the tension of the preceding days, which had become unbearable, the Kaiser's decree felt like a release. This decree, identifying a 'situation of impending peril' over the entire *Reich*, made me decide firmly to participate militarily in any future war, although at an earlier time I had been found medically unfit for duty.

Expression of patriotic sentiment reached its climax when, in late afternoon of 1 August, the three Göppingen newspapers published a special edition containing the mobilization decree. Now the dice had fallen and all political, social and religious barriers had disappeared. The Kaiser recognized in us only Germans.[3] That fateful 1 August was the Sabbath. At its hour of conclusion, late in the evening, almost my entire congregation was assembled solemnly in the synagogue. The service was actually that of the Ninth of Av,[4] which already carried in it a deeply serious character.

On 4 September I received a negative response to my request to the Jewish Oberkirchenbehörde for posting as Jewish chaplain. When I assumed activity in the field the following year only a few days sufficed to convince me that the objection raised at that time did justice neither to duties, nor to the area of work of a Jewish chaplain. I recognized a definite need for more Jewish chaplains, because the six Jewish chaplains in the field at the time could not possibly suffice for a war on two extended Fronts. I therefore decided to submit a new application if the war were to continue for long.

Chapter 2. Enlistment and Departure[5]

After the Oberkirchenbehörde rejected my first enlistment application, the Verband der deutschen Juden, to whom I turned simultaneously, placed me on the priority list submitted to the Prussian War Ministry of those deemed suitable for appointment as Jewish chaplain. But I could not be considered because as a Württemberg rabbi I could be appointed only by the Württemberg War Ministry. Through summer 1915, the latter showed no inclination to do this, and the Oberkirchenbehörde had not responded to my second application of 16 December 1914. During the course of the first years of the war the number of Jewish chaplains had increased and all large German states were represented. Jewish chaplains from Baden, Hessen, Hamburg and Bremen were in the field and only Württemberg was still not represented.

In a further submission on 26 May, I again applied to the Oberkirchenbehörde, and requested its support at the Württemberg War Ministry for my appointment as chaplain. Happily, this time the Oberkirchenbehörde decided to recommend my petition to the Württemberg War Ministry, which then forwarded their recommendation to the Prussian War Ministry. I was informed of this on 13 July. The granting of my request was fulfilled in short order, because the new formation of the 'Army of the River Bug'[6] during the first half of July created the need for an extra Jewish chaplain.

At the time, no uniforms were prescribed for Jewish chaplains, only the right to carry the Geneva Red Cross as an armband was recognized. The first Jewish chaplains who arrived in the field were forced to wear a uniform which they chose for themselves, and bore only partial resemblance to those of Christian chaplains. Military Administration refused to bear any costs for equipment and payment of Jewish chaplains. This was also the case for Protestant and Catholic volunteer extra-budgetary chaplains. But these chaplains were soon provided with a monthly allowance of 150 marks by the Army Commissariat. However, rabbis and other clergy such as Old-Lutherans who were chaplains not belonging to the two main Christian denominations were not included.[7] A few commissariats carried their costs without further ado, and gave the Jewish chaplains the same monthly allowance as was received by chaplains of other faiths. But because there was no corresponding decree, at first Jewish chaplains were granted neither reimbursement of equipment costs nor a monthly allowance. Costs had to be raised by Jews of the individual German states. On 13 August I received the news that the Israelitische Zentralkirchenkasse had approved an equipment allowance of 600 marks and a monthly allowance of 150 marks, on condition that if I received financial assistance from another source its contribution would be reduced.

Soon thereafter, the question was newly ruled on in a decree of the Prussian War Ministry that Old-Lutheran and Jewish pastors would be issued, retroactive to 1 August 1915, a monthly reimbursement of 300 marks and a one-off payment of the same amount. I was informed of my appointment as Jewish field chaplain on 6 August by the Prussian War Ministry, together with travel approval and instructions, allotment of a wagon and two horses, free accommodation, free travel to the army, rations for the horses, and use (where possible) of the service automobile.

Although I was completely inexperienced in all military matters and had no-one knowledgeable from whom I could request advice, I was ready to travel in a few days. The equipment allowance was insufficient and I had to contribute a considerable amount from my own pocket. But I made this small sacrifice gladly, because now finally I could travel to the field. The initial strange feeling of being dressed in the new and unfamiliar uniformed clothing was soon overcome. To know something about services in the field, I read different well-respected publications, took riding lessons at a Stuttgart riding arena – which gave me considerable saddle ache – bought a revolver, and took shooting lessons, something that later on proved very useful.

Saturday 15 August I took leave of my community and family on my way to Breslau. Parting was very difficult. I blessed all my children before I left and bound them to love and obey their mother.[8] An enormous burden now rests with my wife. May she be equal to the task! The long journey, mostly in company of officers, allowed me to gather myself and gave me a welcome opportunity to acclimatize myself to my future companions.

On 16 August at 10.00 p.m., I arrived in Breslau and was directed to reasonably good quarters. I was sent to the baggage replacement division, which provided me with a wagon, horses and a driver. I was scheduled to depart to the Bug Army with the next transport, to Uhnow on the Galician border.[9] Because I was informed that the area was rife with cholera, I used my enforced stay in Breslau to get my first inoculations against cholera and typhoid.[10] I supplemented my personal equipment with various things, and continually inundated Command with requests for information as to when my transport would finally depart. As I found out later, transports to the Bug Army had been discontinued for a few days, because of redeployments.

Monday 23 August at 8:00 a.m.: I finally departed with a large transport. Thanks to the individual transport number, I obtained a second class compartment for my exclusive use. Immediately before departure five railway and postal officials, transferred from the Western to the Eastern Front, came to me with the request to allow them to travel to Uhnow in my roomy compartment, and I at once agreed. In Brocken a longer train with Bavarian troops was connected. Their youthfully happy mood and love of singing throughout the entire journey acted as a blessing in the face of the increasingly 'asiatic' appearance of the countryside and ever-increasing accumulation of depressing signs of war. The landscape had little beauty: neglected, dirty, although with mostly pretty girls and women, all barefoot, in the nearby coal mining area. The more miserable the conditions in the regions east of Breslau, the larger the families are. Via Kattowitz and Myslovétz, we arrived via Oswiecim,[11] in Cracow at midnight and in Tarnow in the early morning hours.

Here we were already in the war-zone, as could be seen with every glance through the windows. We travelled through the terrain of the breakthrough battle at Gorlice-Tarnow, so fateful for the entire Russian campaign.[12] Before our eyes we could see the terrible destruction wrought by the Russians, here as elsewhere, during their retreat. Destroyed railway stations, long rows of houses turned into ruins, blown up bridges, etc. Everywhere we could see railway bridges lying in rivers like dismal wrecks, abandoned trenches, cable insulation, shell holes, and – most harrowing – lone soldiers' graves on the roadside, some with a modest cross very often only recognizable by a bayonet or a wooden post bearing a helmet. Russians had resided in this area for nearly ten months but the destruction was the work of the last few days, even hours, when as a result of the breakthrough it became apparent that they could remain here no longer. The civilian population, mostly Jewish, who swarmed around each train in crowds, told terrible tales of the Russians' hasty withdrawal. The impoverished impression made by the Jewish population was striking: hunger, misery and disease could be seen on every face. At each station we heard the same hundred-voiced plea for bread, which we distributed in generous quantities.

During the early morning hours of 23 August we arrived at Rova-Ruska station, which was still surrounded by signs of fighting. At 8.00 a.m. on 25 August, after a journey of forty-eight hours, we arrived at the little station of Belzec, on the Russian border. Without knowing it, we had reached our destination, because the command had gone out for all transports, including those which had been destined for Uhnow, to change course for Chelm, to which the Main Rear Echelon position had been moved.

Chapter 3. Belzec-Chelm-Vlodava[13]

I stood at Belzec station where our transport to Chelm ended; at that time there was no railway connection to and from Chelm. I was left completely to my own devices and had to act on my own initiative. To start with I got the horses and wagon ready for the impending trip to Russian territory. Then I took provisions for myself and my batman, as well as two-days' provisions for the horses, and secured several bottles of mineral water, because it was out of the question to drink well water in that infected area.[14] Then I tried, by gathering information and with the aid of my map, to find the present position of our Bug Army and orient myself on the right road to take.

The only road that could to some extent be used was, according to my map, the one via Tomaszow-Zamosce-Krasznostav-Chelm-Vlodava to Brest-Litovsk. So then forward in God's name into the Kingdom of the Tsar! After a few minutes, I travelled past the Russian border post with uplifted feelings, not only as a member of the victorious German army but also as a Jew, for whom before the war entry into the Russian state was possible, if at all, only after overcoming the greatest difficulties.[15]

The state of the Russian roads, justifiably notorious, proved at first better than their reputation. According to the map, I was travelling along a first-class main road, and my horses had not really begun to feel the difference between these roads and those of Breslau's paved streets. At first they moved forward well, although roads bore many traces of having been used during the Russians' hasty withdrawal. This retreat was also indicated clearly by ruined houses and heaps of rubble, from which a chimney usually remained standing, towering like a gravestone. After about two hours we arrived in the first reasonably large town, Tomaszow. Although they shone in the August sun, the mostly whitewashed houses made quite a gloomy impression, because a 'cholera' notice had been affixed to almost all of them.

My wagon stopped in front of a fountain, from which my batman and the horses wanted to drink. Hardly had he attached a drinking bag to the fountain pipe,[16] when a crowd of Jews of all ages gathered around and wanted to help him. Because of danger of infection, I had to turn people back but at first was unable to do so because they appeared not to understand me. Then I had the good idea of using Hebrew. The amazement on their faces was delicious. A man in German officer's uniform who spoke Hebrew: this had not happened to them before. Eventually one of them shyly asked me if I was a Jew. When I confirmed this and added that I was a German Jewish chaplain, signs of joy and pride could be unmistakably observed on their otherwise careworn features. The Russian War Administration knew nothing of spiritual welfare for its Jewish soldiers.[17] I could only escape from the many questions which then started by rapidly moving on.

The nearest field hospital was in Zamosce, where we were forced to pass the night out of consideration for the horses. Conditions were more favourable here because the results of German administration could be felt. The little town had not suffered much from battles that had been fought nearby a month previously, because in their haste to retreat the Russians had not had time for the usual arson. The largest hotel in the square was already equipped as a kind of hostelry for officers passing through who were prepared to try and fight with every kind of vermin that came to disturb their sleep. I was shown to a room at the back of the house which was covered a foot high with filth and garbage that remained from the Russian period.

I had my room cleaned by Russian prisoners of war, and in the meanwhile took a bath in a facility that our valiant reserve men had erected. I valued this greatly because for several days I had not changed my clothes. In order to make a start on my pastoral work, I sought out the infectious disease hospital where I found among many seriously ill comrades a Jewish volunteer whose condition appeared to be nearly hopeless. The following year, to my joy, I found him healthy again in Pinsk. In the narrow dark alleyways of the small town, whose inhabitants were mostly Jews, provisions were plentiful, but any purchase had been strictly forbidden because of the danger of cholera. There was a kind of restaurant in my 'hotel', so that at least I didn't need to take up battle with the vermin with a growling stomach. The vermin sought me out until dawn broke the next morning, when I hastily fled the battlefield.

The following day, 28 August, I got as far as Krasznostav, past several towns that existed on the map but not on the ground; piles of rubble, partially still smoking, were all that remained of them. The Russians had come through here during their retreat and had practiced upon these small places for their forthcoming masterpiece in Brest-Litovsk. On one of these rubble heaps I saw a silvery-haired farmer sitting with his small grand-daughter, both a picture of complete despair. Perhaps they were lamenting their home, incinerated by their fellow countrymen.

Hard battles had been fought near Krasznostav during 21–30 July, as could be seen from the shocking condition of the destroyed buildings in the town centre. It was no better in the side streets, where entire rows of houses had been destroyed. All of this was the Cossacks' handiwork before their withdrawal. As I heard from desperate Jews who stood around on the street, many human lives had been destroyed during the havoc. Added to this was the terrible fury of cholera, which claimed more sacrifices daily.

A canteen had been established for the troops on the ground floor and for officers on the upper floors, reached by a rickety staircase, in a ragged little house that the Cossacks did not appear to have considered worth burning down. Upstairs and downstairs there was, apart from tea (and what miserable tea!), army bread, and a small quantity of hard, old cheese; there was nothing else to eat or drink. Fairly large numbers of officers of all ranks assembled in the upper 'dining room' by the light of tallow candles; their mood was good, inconvenient though the highly primitive board and lodging was. Sleeping accommodation was also very poor. One could either crawl somewhere under the straw that was stacked up on three walls of the dining room, or, if one was lucky, as I was, find a leaf sack which had been laid out in a nearby tent. However, as I will soon relate, my leaf sack took me out of the frying pan into the fire. It must have been midnight when I groped for my place of rest. It had become very cosy above in the officers area: stimulating discussions and eyewitness accounts about the fighting of the past few weeks held the group together for some time, and I found several gentlemen who I had got to know during the train ride.

Soon we started to speak about the culture of the now-conquered land and we came to the subject of Polish Jews who were a peculiarly favourite topic of conversation amongst officers. This on its own was surprising to me, but even more so was their apparent ignorance of Jewry, its religion, history and customs; despite this it didn't in any way hinder the astounding certainty with which they spoke about and judged these things. Most officers rightfully acknowledged the terrible general plight in which Jews lived under the Tsar's regime. Only one older major could not accept the Jewish-German dialect. He believed that this language reflected their character: as the latter people is patched together, so is their language composed of many languages. I offered lengthy explanations of the individual nature of this unique language, of its history and its special significance for the German language.[18]

Around 9.30 p.m. our numbers were happily increased by two young lieutenants, who brought along with them a small bottle of Moselle wine. Soon a special atmosphere, merry with wine, developed that made us almost forget that we found ourselves advancing in enemy territory, surrounded by a severe cholera epidemic. I did not do justice to the wine, because at that time I was still a teetotaller. Nevertheless, I remained in the cheerful circle until around midnight, when I sought out my leaf bag, upon which I immediately fell asleep. I awoke soon because my neighbour to the right was groaning in heart-rending fashion. I asked him repeatedly whether I could be of any help but received no answer. Eventually the groaning ceased and I thought that he had fallen asleep. Because it was pitch dark in the tent, I couldn't confirm this.

In the first morning light I saw a lieutenant stagger to the tent's exit through rows of sleepers. I hurried after him and found him outside almost unconscious with terrible shivering fits, writhing in pain. I immediately woke up my batman, got him to bring my small travelling pharmacy, and shook a goodly amount of cholera drops between the lieutenant's teeth which opened with difficulty.[19] In the meanwhile the lad brought hot coffee from the nearest canteen, which

I dribbled into his mouth as best I could. Soon the shaking ceased, and I could wrap the sick man tightly in my horse blanket; with my batman's help I was able to take him back to his leaf sack. A few days later I met the man, healthy again, in Chelm, where he returned my blanket with words of thanks, and told me that during that night two officers, one of them my poor neighbour to the right, had also fallen victim to cholera.

I continued my journey to nearby Chelm, which I hoped to reach in a few hours. I was able to continue my journey very slowly and with many interruptions, because after crossing the railway lines I had blundered into one of the large troop transports which was at that time, under the command of Mackensen, on its way to Serbia.[20] Vast columns of German and Austro-Hungarian munitions and baggage trains took up the entire width of the road and its adjacent terrain. To wind through them was possible only laboriously, sometimes by asking, sometimes with violence. Hungarian baggage drivers especially did not want to consider making way. Only when I supported my lad's complaints with a few straightforward expletives in Hungarian was I able to reach my destination. The valiant sons of Hungary were so perplexed by the presence of the Hungarian language in the German army that they stopped their wagons for a moment and allowed my own wagon to squeeze through. I repeatedly heard the remark in Hungarian: 'These d____ Germans can do everything!'[21]

It was already late in the day when, after traversing countless trenches, barbed wire emplacements, military graves and wandering Jews, we eventually arrived in Chelm. It was already evening when I finally arrived at the German Regional Command and was assigned accommodation among the prevalent bee-like bustle. My accommodation was exceptionally primitive in a bare little room at the dismal rear of a building, but at least I could finally get out of my clothes and obtain the night's rest that had eluded me for so long. The next day my first port of call was Rear Echelon Inspectorate, where I hoped to obtain instructions about the nature and extent of my duties. As was the case during the following years in all senior army sections, I found a helpful reception and complete willingness to support my official assignment in every possible way. However, I was informed that my duties themselves fell within the framework of general service regulations, and would be left to my own judgment. The Armee Oberkommando –AOK [Army High Command] alone was responsible for issuing any service instructions, and I should therefore contact them. But the AOK was on its way to Brest-Litovsk, which had been occupied three days earlier. I wanted to set off there as quickly as possible but was forced into a three-day delay in Chelm, because my horses needed rest and my cart needed repair.

I therefore began my spiritual duties there and then, obtained information about the existing three Chelm field hospitals, and arranged to conduct a field service in the main synagogue, commandeered from the Jewish community for this purpose. All divisions that could be reached were told of this through official channels, and the Jewish soldiers invited. Because the service was to take place two days later, I devoted the intervening time to field hospitals, where I visited all the wards and, as I would do in the future, went from bed to bed and made myself available to comrades without first asking their faith. I found numerous Jewish comrades, some wounded and others ill, in two overfilled hospitals. The third makeshift field hospital had been set up in a church. Here I was urgently requested by comrades to give them a lengthy report about the current war situation. I was happy to be able to report only good news. At this time I also received my second typhoid inoculation.

On Sunday 29 August at 10.00 a.m. I held the scheduled field service in the spacious main synagogue which the Jewish community administration had prepared for this purpose. Because of danger of cholera the Jewish civilian population was forbidden from entering the synagogue during the service, but all the more eagerly they crowded outside at the windows. Apart from a large number of Jewish soldiers, several Christian officers arrived for services. Before services commenced (as I always did later) I handed out the field prayer booklet which had been published by the Verband der deutschen Juden at the beginning of the war and was made available free of charge, so that comrades could keep it permanently.

I saw hardly anything of the town, and what I saw I didn't like at all. Almost everything – streets, houses and people – carried, in filth and squalour, unmistakable traces of the sufferings of war. The miserable, haggard appearance of the civilian population, almost all of them Jews, was especially conspicuous. On Monday 30 August, I started the journey to Brest-Litovsk, where I supposed the AOK to be located. The next station that I had in prospect about half-way there was Vlodava. This time again the going was slow, both because of the many columns of baggage trains and also because of the bad state of the roads, which passed through fighting areas. The Russian army, which since the breakthrough at Gorlice-Tarnow [see Note 12] had been continually pushed back northwards by the Bug Army, had, near Vlodava, settled masterfully into expanded positions and resisted stubbornly. They had been forced into this because meanwhile, in the first week of August, the Weichsel fortresses had fallen, and the Russian troops who were flooding back eastwards feared being cut off by the Bug Army. The Russian defence plan included comprehensive destruction of the road which, in an almost straight line, led northwards to Vlodava: this was carried out with blood-curdling efficiency.

I had to abandon my plan to travel on to Brest-Litovsk the next morning, because the horses needed a rest day, and because I felt the signs of developing dysentery. In the first morning hours of 31 August I called in at the nearby field hospital, where I received a sound portion of cognac and rice soup to swallow and, after a 24-hour sleep, woke up feeling fine. I looked at the half-destroyed little town, in which long successions of streets now presented nothing but a chain of rubble heaps which in many places were still smoking. My request to hold a field service there was turned down because it was not possible under current circumstances. There could be no question of regular provisions yet, because replenishment of supplies had come to a complete standstill and nothing could be obtained from the hungry civilians, even for money. German efficiency and order, justly admired during the entire war by friend and foe, had not yet been established. Something resembling a refreshment station had been set up in what had been a pharmacy on the corner of the market square, where nothing but 'tea' was available, which everyone could ladle out of a large barrel.

On the same day I received the telegraphic request to proceed to Jablon – where AOK was located – with my batman and wagon. After I had ascertained on the map the way to Jablon, which lay halfway between Vlodava and Radzyn, I set out early on the morning of 1 September hoping to arrive in Jablon by midday. With inexcusable blind confidence I depended on the map, on which a decent road was marked. What I in fact discovered was a typical Russian country road without any foundation, a real sand wilderness, in which from time to time single trees indicated something resembling a road. Around 9.00 p.m. I was eventually able to drive up to the small Jablon hunting lodge in which the AOK was located. I reported immediately to the officer on duty who was extremely busy, so meanwhile I arranged housing for my batman and the horses, and eventually was assigned a room for myself, in which I was given a simple dinner. I did not even open the large bag of mail brought to me from AOK, even though I had been without news from home for weeks. I was content to have finally arrived at my place of service; everything else could wait until the next day.

Chapter 4. At Armeeoberkommando[22]

First thing next morning I looked through my mail. Apart from satisfactory news from home I received a great many publications of all sorts, for distribution during the forthcoming High Holidays. After a short walk through the pretty park surrounding the hunting lodge, I arrived around 7.00 a.m. in the staff dining room, to which I was assigned for meals.

Soon thereafter I introduced myself to His Highness Prince zu Wied, adjutant to General von Linsingen, who was my advisor in service matters. He explained my official duties thoroughly, answered questions concerning my obligations, and gave me the opportunity that same day to report officially to the Chief of Staff, General von Holzmann, whose friendly reception encouraged me to ask if I could begin my full official duties with the troops. He made accommodation available to me at AOK, whence I could more frequently visit the troops who could be reached. I declined this offer with thanks, as I did often in the future, because I feared that to reside at such a distance from the troops would hamper my work. I decided to depart the following day for Brest-Litovsk, which for the time being I would make my headquarters and the centre of my activity.

Chapter 5. Brest-Litovsk[23]

It was still very early the next morning when my horses again took up their battle with the Russian sandy desert. With great difficulty, we reached the town of Slavatvocz on the Bug River at 2.00 p.m. The small town consisted only of one long street, and its aspect was terrible to behold. Right and left were only smoking piles of rubble, all handiwork of the fleeing Russians. At the end of this nightmarish alley of ruined houses, I caught sight of the only house still standing, belonging to the local Polish Catholic priest, and next to it two charming small churches, the badly damaged Polish and almost undamaged Russian church. I found the Catholic priest's house, whose inhabitants had fled. Room was made for me there alongside four officers and I was invited to share their frugal luncheon.

After lunch, I was invited to join a small mounted contingent who were about to requisition horses on the other side of the Bug River. A small Lithuanian horse carried me courageously across a narrow bridge over the Bug. Six horses resulted from this sortie, won in the face of all the farmers' cunning and, on one occasion, of armed resistance. My revolver, always hanging on my belt, saw action for the first time with harmless warning shots. I noticed at that time that almost all the farmers understood and spoke German.[24]

The piteous picture of a very old woman, whom we found sitting on the floor of a house in complete despair, made a deep impression on me. Little by little, in-between continuous sobbing, we learned her harrowing history of suffering. A native south-German, from Augsburg I believe, she had married and moved here decades ago and lived happily for a long time. Early deaths had diminished her family circle: at the beginning of the war her entire family consisted of two grown-up grand-daughters. And these too had fallen victim to the bestial Cossacks who had dashed through. The old woman's house had been plundered as well. We could discover nothing else about the whereabouts of the young girls or the criminals from the old woman, who seemed psychologically disturbed. Unfortunately we could not help her.

Around 4.00 a.m. on 4 September I started on the journey to Brest-Litovsk. I had been warned of the bad quality of the road on the left-hand side of the Bug which led through Terespol, so I used the right-hand road through Domaczov-Stradecz. Again we passed the terrible road of ruins. At the end of this, a kind of bridge across the Bug had been created, which later became the 'Linsingen bridge'. Only with great difficulty could horses and wagon be brought to the opposite river bank. After about two hours struggling through deep sand we reached the large road leading from Vlodava to Brest-Litovsk, and at least we were on firmer ground. But the road had all the characteristics of a route taken by a large army. Masses of troops, marching to and back from Brest-Litovsk, endless baggage columns, wide ditches opened up by the Russians, and in addition horse cadavers lying on both sides of the road, decomposing in the oppressive heat. A huge cloud of smoke hovering over a distant place indicated far and wide the location of Brest-Litovsk.

After having almost been run over by an automobile, I finally reached Brest-Litovsk in the evening around 7.00 p.m. I stood with my wagon in the midst of a great crowd of troops and wagons of every sort on this side of the Mukhavets River, and could look into the smoking world of rubble on the other bank. But how was I to get across with horses and wagon? Although only a few narrow planks had been laid across the river, this difficulty could be overcome with the aid of some comrades, so that I was able to drive up to the Commandant's house when darkness fell. A tremendous explosion had occurred three days earlier on the nearby terrain near the Russian airship hangers. A long line of German mass graves in the cemetery on the right side of the Polish church is now the final resting-place of this explosion's many German victims.

I will always be haunted by the terrible experience of entering this immense burning and smoking heap of rubble which, only a few days earlier, had been the great, rich, thriving city of Brest-Litovsk. Paralyzing horror struck me. Everything that had happened before paled into the background before this act of incomparable destruction. Anyone who managed to enter Brest-Litovsk saw for the first time a large city, furiously eradicated in a way that only small towns had been up to now. Hundreds upon hundreds of human homesteads pulverized to their foundations or mutilated into a senseless ruin harbouring nothing but rubbish and ashes, with at the most one staircase rising into the air. And this was not even the effect of the gradual, nagging fury of a long siege. No: a Russian city was, from yesterday to today, ruined on command and by the hand of its own provincial government. Only about one-quarter of the city remained completely or partially habitable

The destruction of the city had no purpose: neither in the case of eventual surrender, nor to limit enemy operations: The destruction of peaceful possessions only deprives innocent civilians, in this case, for the most part Jews who, since the founding of the city, had comprised easily three-quarters of the population. And precisely this fact was, given notorious hatred of Jews by the wild Russian gang of soldiers, of decisive importance, urging them on in their destructive work.

On 15 August 1915 the Russian City Commandant announced that the entire civilian population had to leave the city during the three days of 17–19 August. For this purpose, the city was divided into three districts from north to south, with evacuation of the area in the direction of the citadel[25] on the first day, and the other two on the following days. At the time the city had about 40,000 inhabitants, amongst them 30,000 Jews. At the same time, it was announced that trains would stand ready at the railway station, to take the population into the Russian interior. But only a small number of open trucks were at the station and very few passenger cars, in which one could obtain a place only with a large *bakshish* [bribe]. The railway in Brest-Litovsk at that time was supposed to transport the entire crowd of unhappy departing inhabitants into interior Russia. Because of this, many inhabitants had obtained small farm wagons at exorbitant prices, but the great majority went into exile, and unknown misery, on foot. Many weeks later one could see these unhappy victims of their own heartless government wandering ragged and starving on country roads and in the forest surrounding the city. Images of horror, inextinguishably imprinted on the memory.

Large quantities of supplies of all kinds, worth millions of roubles, were available in Brest-Litovsk. But already in May the Russian commandant had forbidden any export of goods out of the city. And even when they were forcibly expelled, those who possessed goods could take nothing with them. Russian *Kultur* had other things to do with the supplies, and trains already stood at the station, after the ravening hordes had carefully chosen what they wanted. During the designated three days, evacuation of the city took place, as recommended. Those who left on the second and third days witnessed appalling things. Hardly had the inhabitants left their houses, and often earlier, the Cossacks stormed in and threw everything within their grasp – furniture, linen, beds, clothes, valuable weapons of every sort – out of windows into the streets where previously-invited farmers waited with their panje wagons[26] to have their share of the booty. The most valuable items could be bought for a few kopecks. What could not be sold – and given the huge amount of material offered, that was not a little – was torn into pieces, demolished, destroyed. An endless robbery and plundering took place, accompanied by howling and yelling which may have represented for many Cossacks the greatest party of their lives.

But the climax of the Russian *Kulturarbeit* [cultural work] was reached in Brest-Litovsk on 24 and 25 August. On these days, the Cossacks were commanded to go to a certain square to receive precise instructions, then with hand grenades and incendiary material they went from house to house and street to street, staging a terrible blowing-up and burning-down of beautiful rows of streets; four-fifths of the city fell victim. Not a single house would have been left standing if the Russians had had their way, and the rapid penetration of soldiers of the Central Powers had not forced them to flee and abandon the destruction.

There could be no question of sleep during the first night, and very little during the following nights. Not only because the half-broken, narrow sofa which had to serve as my bed made any prolonged rest at night impossible; but even more because this reasonably intact house, which stood like an oasis in the wilderness in this area of ruins, lay near the main thoroughfare from Mukhavets, where there was a very loud coming and going of soldiers day and night during the first weeks. It was impossible to keep the house gate and doors locked; everyone came and went as he wanted. Even brief rests resulting from overtiredness became a torment because of the prodigious plague of flies which had developed out of this world of rubbish and rubble. Like a black cloud they covered every wall, every surface; food and drink couldn't remain uncovered even for a moment. Later I often had to suffer from such plagues of flies in all parts of Russia, but never in such vast numbers as in those days of my first sojourn in Brest-Litovsk. Any attempt to combat them proved useless, and in the end they had to be accepted with patience, as in the case of so many things – for example the dreadful 'rations'. These consisted, for the many officers who did not belong to a local formation, of a single 'meal', available only at noon, consisting of a kind of vegetable soup that would have been too much even for a Spartan. To accompany this there was – nothing, not even any bread. But flies there were, in unlimited numbers. I soon abandoned this soup and preferred to live on tea and army bread for more than a week, until order was restored.

Next morning I went in search of the field hospitals. Throughout my entire time as a Jewish field chaplain, I found in this my most important and cherished work. It was not difficult to find them. I simply needed to follow the many panje wagons travelling through the city carrying the wounded. A small, relatively undamaged synagogue, a Russian church, and a nearby large grammar school had been turned into primitive field hospitals during the first few weeks. In the synagogue I found only those ill with cholera and typhoid, lying in straw on the floor; in the Russian church only the lightly wounded and those less seriously ill; and in the gymnasium sick of every kind. Very few beds were available, and the building was terribly overfilled. I clearly saw the dreadfully harrowing circumstances that obtain during war even in the victor's camp.

It is recommended that those who have stayed at home and (unfortunately there are many of these) who in their comfortable patriotism were, and still are, enthusiastic advocates of war, should at least once experience such field hospitals, especially the large field hospital in Brest-Litovsk. This soon became the only hospital in the square, and I worked together with my Christian colleagues to carry severely ill comrades from the wagons into this one building (the former grammar school). We were pleased when we could at least find a place for them somewhere on straw in the corridors. Packed tightly together, these wonderfully patient men filled every corner of every room and passage. Eventually the hospital held 1,200 patients: bloodied, wounded, maimed bodies. Nobody worried here about religion or social status, only suffering men spoke and functioned unintentionally as the strongest protest against the horrors of war. The sick and wounded were continually carried along the passages to the operating room in which surgeons worked ceaselessly.

Because of the great personnel shortage, I helped, like everyone else, wherever I could and arrived back at my quarters only late that night, where a very unpleasant surprise awaited me. Both my horses and my cart were gone. There were well-built unused places in a large courtyard opposite my quarters. I had sheltered my team in one of these and secured the door with a padlock. A guard had been placed in the courtyard itself, and my batman had the key because of the need to care for my horses. According to the guard, a lieutenant had come to the courtyard in late afternoon, asked what was contained behind the locked door, and, after obtaining an answer, had broken in and made off with my team. All he said was that he needed the horse and cart for urgent official business and that he hoped to be able to return them soon. Because the wagon did not belong to the collective company and because the guard had not been particularly instructed to watch my team, he had not worried further about the matter.

Naturally I reported this to the local Commandant's office and was issued with a voucher, which I sent to AOK from whom I received new transportation a few weeks later. The forcing of locks and appropriation of property was no rare occurrence in Brest-Litovsk at that time. During the same period, a large amount of money had been stolen from the locked chest in the local Commandant's office. In addition, a non-commissioned officer tried to break open my locked room with his sidearm. My attempt to chase after him, assisted by several comrades, was unsuccessful because the rogue, who jumped through the window, easily found a hideout in the darkness in a heap of rubble.

On 6 September I began the preparations for Rosh Hashanah services, to be held on 9 and 10 September. Firstly I worked on the necessary orders of the day for formations that could be reached; then I looked up the main synagogue, which was the only place I considered suitable for these services, not only because it stood out as a stately and externally less damaged building in the surrounding world of ruin, but also because the clear yellow of the external walls shone from a long way away. Of approximately fifty other places of prayer, only three had escaped destruction.

The central main entrance of the Brest-Litovsk synagogue led into the prayer room, with 600 places for men, and both side entrances to the two women's galleries. Opposite the entrance, on the east wall, the artistically fashioned Holy Ark, in which the Torah scrolls are kept, predominated. Two large marble plaques containing prayers for the Tsar in Hebrew and in Russian, were situated on the north and south walls. Many high-arched windows let a good deal of light into the wide room, which was lit at night by spirit lamps.

In the anteroom, two chests stood which had previously been full to the top with Torah scrolls and nailed shut. The fleeing Jews had left them behind, trusting that these ritual objects, of great value only to pious Jewish sentiment, would, because of their holy purpose, be spared from destruction. I found the chests broken open and their content, partially torn, scattered on the floor, an indescribably painful sight to a religious Jew, for whom it is a thousand-year-old tradition to treat Torah scrolls with the utmost respect. As in this ante-room, all the chests in the inner room that had contained Torah scrolls and religious books had been broken open and their contents scattered on the floor. In several places the synagogue's roof and ceiling had been broken through, so that previous days of rain had left several puddles on the floor. Fragments of window panes, not a single one of which remained unbroken, covered the floor a foot high, and filth of all kinds filled the entire room. The rows of seats, overthrown and piled on top of one another, were in complete disorder. It was necessary to clean up and restore order before any thought could be given to holding a religious service. With the help of several Russian prisoners of war and the cooperation of my batman and a few Jewish comrades, I was able to set the synagogue in reasonable order over the following two days.

The unique picture of this ruined city, in which no civilians lived and only soldiers were milling around, was completed by the sight of many soldiers with odd equipment: fireplace pokers, iron rods, small shovels and similar implements, all tools with which they could burrow in the rubble. Soldiers acted like treasure hunters, looking eagerly for objects of value, which the fleeing inhabitants might have buried. Vast quantities of books of every kind were found, mostly in Hebrew and Yiddish but also many in Russian, and educational and literary texts in German. Various versions of ready-to-send letters printed from the mostly illiterate Russian soldiers to their families at home were found, reporting their excellent health, heroism and the victorious campaign of the Russian army. This is a very convenient method of correspondence, because only names of sender and recipient needed insertion.

That day, I was called to Regional Command about something that had been found. I encountered a significant amount of all kinds of synagogue silver piled up on a large table. The men present wanted information from me about the age and value of individual pieces, because they had to be declared as war booty. I was able immediately to determine the age of each item, but evaluation of each item's worth was more difficult. I argued with the gentlemen that all were *Kirchengut* [church property] that in no way fell under the heading of booty; and I urged them that all the items, of which I would make inventory, should remain in safe keeping under official lock and key until High Command (whom I would inform at once) made further provisions. My suggestion was accepted immediately and carried out with my assistance. I will explain later how I was able to deliver these and other synagogue silver found later safely from Brest-Litovsk to Germany.

Amongst the plethora of Hebrew writings of all kinds which our soldiers had tracked down and which lay around in piles on all sides I found a small Torah scroll which would be easily transported for use at my many later services in individual divisions. Austro-Hungarian Jewish chaplains had all been equipped with such small Torah scrolls by their army administration. With approval of Regional Command, I took possession of this scroll, which has served me very well. I later informed the Brest Jewish community of my acquisition in writing and till today preserve it as a cherished war souvenir.

Announcement of the upcoming Rosh Hashanah services had rapidly been disseminated, and ever more Jewish comrades called on me in my quarters. On both festival days I held very well-attended services lasting several hours. A valiant musical comrade officiated excellently as prayer leader. I gave two sermons and tried to transform the homesickness that filled our hearts, especially on such festivals, into a mood of devotion to God and joy in duty. After that I spent several stimulating hours with a number of the comrades in my quarters. The Rosh Hashanah services went off significantly better than I had hoped.

I wanted, whatever happened, to celebrate the highest Jewish holiday, Yom Kippur, a week later, with the fighting troops. I intended to assemble the Jewish soldiers in the area in a suitable location somewhere between Kobryn and Antopol. Because of the loss of my horse and cart I was provided for this journey with a small open panje-cart and also two small but unbelievably untiring horses, and with much difficulty I travelled the 50 kilometre long distance to Kobryn on 14 September. I crossed the Mukhavets, swaying wildly on the planks which had been laid loosely across the river, the regular bridge having been blown up by the Russians. The sight of refugees, who in their neglected, starved state resembled animals sheltering in the woods and on both sides of the road, was terrible. Passing German troops gave all provisions that could be spared to these unhappy people.

In Kobryn I received the news that my plan was not feasible, because troops were already more than 120 kilometres away from Kobryn and in rapid advance, so that no services were possible for the moment. An urgent telephonic request to AOK resulted in a directive to hold the service in Brest-Litovsk for troops who could be reached. After a brief visit to the small neglected town, in which almost every house bore notices of an epidemic, and an almost sleepless night spent in a miserable hut, I had to return to Brest-Litovsk the following day, and make preparations there for services on Yom Kippur. During the next two days, 16 and 17 September, the Brest-Litovsk field hospital was especially full, and I therefore had many opportunities to be of assistance; I remained there almost until the start of services. I held three services on Yom Kippur, with sermons and *Yizkor*. About a hundred comrades and a few Russian prisoners of war participated. We all fasted the entire day, according to ritual. I shared leading of the service, which is especially extensive on this day, with the aforementioned prayer leader, and an extremely devout atmosphere was created.

Chapter 6. Biala: Rear Echelon Headquarters[27]

The fixed quarters from which I wanted to visit the individual divisions had a vehicle which was permanently at my disposal. AOK had ordered me to go to the Warsaw Gouvernement. However, during those days, to travel from Brest-Litovsk to Warsaw was extremely difficult because the railways in this area, which had only recently been occupied, were being reorganized and tracks had to be changed to German width.[28] I learned that on the next day, 19 September, the first train with the wounded and sick would depart from Terespol, close to Brest-Litovsk, in the direction of Warsaw. I was able to obtain a panje wagon as far as Terespol, where I was told that this first train would depart at the earliest sometime during the evening. I therefore decided to go to Biala and await the train there.

The railway station at Biala was a pile of rubble. I shortened my expected long wait by visiting the nearby infectious disease field hospital. Talking with the sick, writing postcards, etc., made the afternoon pass quickly. Toward evening the long-awaited train finally arrived. But at first our travel could be continued only as far as Luckow, where we had to wait the whole night in appalling cold. I still have not completely recovered from the severe chill which I caught there.[29] When the train eventually started up again at 7.00 the next morning, I had to be content travelling in a filthy dog kennel, next to four other people, opposite the baggage section. It was not possible to stand properly, but at least we did not freeze. The short trip to Warsaw took our train nine hours. Around 4.00 p.m. it arrived at the outskirts of a Warsaw suburb. I quickly decided to disembark and found a hackney which took me to Warsaw and the *Kommandatur*. I ruined my stomach by eating too much roast in my kosher hotel, and became very ill.

I had to remain there until 29 September, in a state of severe suffering which confined me to bed most of the time, so that I didn't see much of Poland's capital. But I did see enough to perceive the easily recognizable enmity of the Poles towards the Germans, which was visible to the sharp observer, hiding behind hypocritical friendliness. And yet it was only a few months ago that, without Polish cooperation, German blood and German bravery had liberated the Poles from their hated Russian yoke.[30]

I visited the great synagogue in Tlomackie Street.[31] Dr Poznanski, a shy Polish-Jewish man,[32] was very kind but he preached in Polish, which was horrible. Here the rich Jews, about 20,000 out of a total of 300,000, are the leaders of the congregation. They are assimilated, and also unfortunately feel themselves to be genuine Polish nationals and greatly damage the general Jewish population under German administration. One had heard terrible tales about barbaric deeds of Russians against the Jews due to denunciation by the three-times wretched treacherous Poles – cursed enslaved souls![33] Just before I left I was honoured in the great synagogue and bought many things in this large city, in which everything is available.

I found every cooperation at the Gouvernement. I was fitted out after only a few days with a wagon and two horses, and was the guest of honour in the Jewish Folk Theatre. Despite the Yiddish, it was very enjoyable. If only there had not been such restlessness in the sold-out house! On 29 September I left Warsaw where, if I only had been healthy, I could have had a very enjoyable time. But I was plagued with stomach pains and bronchial catarrh. The return trip from Warsaw to Brest-Litovsk (where I had duties to take care of) took 36 hours.

On 30 September I arrived again in Biala, headquarters of the Rear Echelon Inspectorate. Here, until further instructions by AOK reached me, I wished to establish permanent headquarters, being heartily tired of the continuous haphazard wandering about that had already lasted for six weeks. A large field hospital with almost 2,000 patients was located there, and because it was not difficult to reach the front soldiers around Pinsk as well as the rear echelon troops, establishment of regularized spiritual care with plenty of activity beckoned. My accommodation in the small town, almost exclusively inhabited by Jews and overflowing with German troops, was extremely primitive. The Jewish owner of a small, low house near the market square operated a kind of hostel for foreigners in the form of a bare, miserable little room, which was now taken over for accommodation of German officers. Basic amenities were lacking, and one had to make do with upside down crates, wall shelves, etc.[34]

On 2 October I travelled to AOK in Jablon; because of my batman's ignorance of how to drive on bad roads, the trip took 8 instead of 5 hours. Further, because my horses could make no progress in the deep sand, I had to requisition a new horse amongst the many animals grazing without supervision. My reception in Jablon was very friendly. In place of my batman, I was given an experienced driver. My purchases have been made, payable from the rear echelon war chest to the amount of 300 marks monthly expense allowance;

daily subsistence allowance: 1.20 marks; daily contribution money: 7.50 marks; equipment: 30 marks.

4 October. A farmer came and said that I had requisitioned his horse. He said he was poor. I returned the horse to the farmer. Today the war chest in Biala paid me expenses of 300 marks for each of the months August, September and October. I remarked to the paymaster that I had departed only on 15 August, but he pointed out that in his instructions about me a date of 1 August was clearly stated and I was therefore to receive 300 marks for August as well.[35]

9 October, Biala. Today I send Bertha a postal order for 600 marks to invest. Bertha has written to me about how expensive everything is at home and that she cannot make do with what she has, so I immediately tell her in my letter to use 300 marks for housekeeping.

10 October. Smallpox vaccination. At the request of Felddiakon Fischer, I have become greatly involved in establishment of the soldiers' home. I am also wholly responsible for the establishment and administration of the library and will travel to Brest-Litovsk next week to set it up.[36]

No news from home for five days. My activities – a) Forty-first Reserve Corps; b) Field hospitals (almost daily); c) Soldiers' home; d) Evenings at Rear Echelon Inspectorate. According to army commands given on 11 October 1915: I may be reached at all times through Rear Echelon Inspectorate so that I can be notified of all Jewish burials and be asked whether I can attend and so that I can receive news of admission of the seriously wounded Jewish men to field hospitals.

12 October. Another arduous day in the large Biala field hospital with no differentiation according to religion! Work piled up: reading, conversation, telling stories, hearing stories of their suffering, for hours on end in the most miserable ventilation. I am often half-dead after such a day. I have already made good friends with a number of Protestant pastors who have also worked together with me in field hospitals.

14 October. Burial this afternoon of Naftali Levi, who died of dysentery in field hospital no. fifty-eight. The Secretariat of the Stuttgart Oberkirchenbehörde informs me that I have to pay back 450 Marks to the Zentralkirchenkasse. I answer at once, so that nothing be deducted from the sum I sent to Bertha; instead, 50 marks should be kept for a synagogue hostel, and I send 400 marks at the same time by postal order to the War Chest.

18 October. I hear that all the civilian inhabitants of Brest-Litovsk who had since returned were expelled again within 24 hours. I haven't even got a piece of bread and I'm freezing. May God watch over me.[37]

24 October. Celebratory service in the main synagogue of Biala. Very good participation by soldiers from the town and surrounding area. I gave a good sermon – numerous local inhabitants were present.

27 October. Diverse duties. The many *Schnorrers*,[38] male and female, from Biala frequently cost me almost 10 marks in one day. Large amounts of work for the existing Jewish population. Upon request and with written approval I hold a conference in my quarters on 4 November. Suggestions for discussion: organization of the community administration and charity organizations – school – suggestion to Major Funcke: decrees in Yiddish. I plan establishment of a school for children of 6–12 years of age.

Daily conferences: establishment of the soldiers' home; library, 300 volumes, established by me. Formal opening: many senior officers and at least 200 soldiers.

10 November. Travel with Frau Mun to look at a soup kitchen for the poor, there a conference with all participants, a meal followed by Grace.

11 November. One horse in the stable is dead. The lodge sends 100 marks for charitable purposes. My library in the soldiers' home is flourishing magnificently. During the first four days, sixty-five readers have borrowed ninety-one volumes; 306 volumes are available to be lent out. Talk at 6.30 p.m.: 'War as Educator'. Unger came despite a terrible snowstorm. Daily discussion of all kinds in matters related to the soup kitchen and school.

13 November. I receive the written license for the soup kitchen, mentioning my name, as Major Funcke graciously agreed to. Wood is provided free of charge, and potatoes partially free by a local inn. Many hours of work daily in this soup kitchen. Daily conferences on all matters relating to the soup kitchen and the school.

21 November. Because many penalties have been incurred due to ignorance of official decrees, on my initiative and under direction of the local rabbinate, official decrees are now read out in Yiddish in synagogues and other locations.

23 November. Grand opening of the soup kitchen in the presence of officers, dignitaries, the Oberrabbiner and the Kronrabbiner. All full of praise. The enterprise has succeeded: May God watch over it further.

26 November. Arrived in Brest[-Litovsk] at 4.00 p.m. Quarters with the officers. Very good but noisy, and the food is terrible. Brest is without any civilian population, a completely dead city. Snow benevolently covers the ruins.

27 November. Synagogue service. Lucas leads the prayers in front of sixty-eight soldiers, three officers, two staff surgeons. The synagogue was dreadfully cold, with a snowstorm and a temperature of -18 to -20°C. I commemorate the mass grave in which Ludwig Goldschmidt is buried, and write to his father. I write to Dr Minden about the synagogue silver (from Brest-Litovsk) and the soup kitchen in Biala.

28 November. Travel to Kobryn by train; very comfortable but cold. The Rear Echelon Command car is waiting at the station. Kobryn is now clean and with a beautiful synagogue: magnificent and fifty years old, with a beautiful three-story high structure in carved wood over the Holy of Holies. Eight Christian officers and one woman are present. Many Jews. I spoke very movingly and was congratulated. During the afternoon and evening the local Jewish population invaded the soldiers' and civilian living quarters. Oberrabbiner David Grünburg appears with a large deputation. A civilian committee enters with eleven other petitioners. There are about 3,000 Jews from Brest as well as 2,000 more homeless Jews in Kobryn. I write immediately to the Verband der deutschen Juden that I wish to establish a soup kitchen here as well. The Oberrabbiner writes too. The difference between Russian and Polish Jews is enormous, with Russians having a higher culture. My room is cold, with broken windows, and the food is awful.

30 November. Arrival in Pinsk. The large railway station is a ruin. Numerous German restoration efforts. Russian Jewry is on a higher level than Polish Jewry [perhaps due to the proximity of Galicia to Poland].[39]

1 December. I am requested to give a sermon at the Chanukah celebration in the great synagogue in Pinsk. Agreement of Command and placement of placards [to inform the local population]. The destitution in Pinsk – ration coupons for bread and flour. The beautiful Chanukah celebration. The large '*Klezmer*' choir[40] with over 3,000 people in the synagogue including the Commandant and several officers. Deputation of the people from Brest: countless petitioners; my advice to them. More synagogue silver to be stored.

3 December. Approval of new soup kitchen.

4 December. Distribution of gifts in the trenches and dug-outs. In the evening a gathering in the hall of the citizen's committee. I establish a soup kitchen for 1,000 people as well as a society to maintain it. Darkness in the streets. Searchlights with quivering flares.

8 December. Service for soldiers in Biala and distribution of gifts.

9 December. The board in Berlin wishes to hold the silver from Brest in safe custody. Letter to the Rear Echelon Commandant in Brest regarding my trip to Berlin.

10 December. Censorship of letters in Yiddish or Hebrew from prisoners of war.

13 December. Send off the first large report to the AOK in Jablon. Night celebration in the mess. Receipt of 200 marks from the Jewish Women's Association; 150 marks given to the soup kitchen in Biala; 10 marks to the poor; submission of requisite receipts.

16 December. A non-commissioned officer writes me a letter requesting a Christmas package for twelve people who would otherwise receive nothing from home. I go to the package depot; the delegated representative Licht, an old Berlin bachelor, refuses because according to regulation X each soldier must receive one package. I speak to the actual person who has been delegated with this who absolutely agrees and makes twenty packages available to each of the three chaplains.

On 18 December I wish to have the packages brought to me according to the advice of Major von Gemmingen. Licht refuses. I hand the matter over, as I did before. The Jewish Aid Organization sends me 2,000 marks for my three soup kitchens. On 19 December I give 500 marks to the soup kitchen in Biala and send the receipt to Berlin. I receive twenty gift packages for soldiers, and distribute them.

27 December Monday. Departure to Berlin.[41] Sleeping car as far as Berlin. Donations from all sides: benevolent societies. At 11.00–11.30 p.m. that night: fast train back.

29 December. Arrive in Biala and go straight to the civil administration. The four chests from the Göppingen women's society and the distribution list.

1 January [1916]. I stand in as a deputy in Brest-Litovsk. 400 marks from the Benevolent Society. One chest of blankets, linen, provisions.

2 January. Meeting regarding matzoth for the civil population.

26 January. Sermon in Brest-Litovsk. Service for the Kaiser's birthday[42] in the prayer room of the soldiers' home in Brest-Litovsk.

30 January. Celebration of my forty-fifth birthday. Dinner: good food in the mess with champagne – Major Funcke honours me with three cheers.

7 February. I finally receive written permission from Rear Echelon Command for establishment of a Jewish soup kitchen for boys and girls. The German Jewish Benevolent Society sends me 5,000 marks for distribution. I give 1,000 marks each to the Biala soup kitchen and the Brest-Litovsk refugee committee in Biala; I deposit 2,500 marks against receipt at Rear Echelon Command in Biala because of my morning trip to the Front, and take 500 marks with me as well as 690 marks of my own money. Yesterday's benefit concert for the soup kitchen was a great success. Rear Echelon Command today provides free of charge to the Brest-Litovsk refugees: 2,500 kg sugar; 1,000 kg salt; 500 kg grits; 1,350 kg wheat.

9 February. 9.00 a.m. departure to Kowel by train. Enjoyable trip, one mishap, much swampland – frozen – arrival 2.30 p.m. in Kowel. Friendly reception at General Command. All services arranged at the Twenty-second Infantry Division. Excellent board and lodging. Kowel is a large, beautiful town. With God's help I will return there.

10 February. In the morning at Kowel railway station: to the Wolczek Front railway station. Strict control under Austro-Hungarian supervision: unfortunately unheated second-class car. Very slow trip, especially where the wire fences lie deep in the swamps. Wolczek Front station – a small town of noisy but artfully designed shelters. Woeful refreshment in the Austro-Hungarian officers quarters – no food, only tea.

Colossal snowstorm: telephonic cancellation of services at my destination because travel there in an open panje wagon is impossible: 43 kilometres. And could not have taken place in any case, for military reasons. Services at 10.00 a.m. in underground canteen of Army Battalion 109-68. Many soldiers go there direct from the trenches: wonderful service, ditto the sermon. Then distribution of an entire chest of gifts: great rejoicing! Two hours together before return to the trenches. In the afternoon return by train to Kowel. I am transferring to Kowel because of proximity to the Front.

18 February. Travel by car to AOK in Jablon to report in person: firstly in the morning before Prince von Wied and then at 4.30–5.45 p.m. before Major General von Stolzmann, who is very satisfied. Prince von Wied tells me that the Iron Cross is on the cards. Very friendly welcome from everybody. Wonderful evening in officers' mess.

24 February. The properly equipped soup kitchen: its three month existence. My photograph with initials decorated – the celebration – my talk and the authorization of another 1,000 marks. About 17,000 people have been fed in three months.

27 February. According to the distribution book, two receipts to the sum of 1,500 marks sent to the Benevolent Society. Rear Echelon Command in Biala to be provided with a written report on *Schechita* matters.

3 March. Arrival of Austro-Hungarian contingent in Kowel. Evening reached Biala by fast train with dining car. Sent off 600 marks to Kobryn Rear Echelon Command by postal order as a donation for the Benevolent Society for distribution amongst the needy Jewish community of Kobryn under supervision of the Chief Rabbi. Similarly, 400 marks to Pinsk Regional Command. Evening: departure to Warsaw, and then Vilna for the Rabbis' Conference on 7 March.[43]

5 March. Vilna beautiful city, but huge amount of Jewish begging in the streets. Moral admonition of officers. Rabbinical Conference (in Vilna): Baeck's wisdom, Rosenak's speculation [pp.246–9]. Visit to the synagogue of the Vilna Gaon.[44]

9 March. Return to Biala. I receive the requested vacation and depart on 11 March.

30 March – 9 April. At home. I am ill with a high fever.[45]

8 April. Departure for Berlin.

10 April. Meeting with Drs Nathan and Kohn in the Benevolent Society office. I receive another 10,000 Marks.[46] I support my plan for a *Konzentrationslager* for the homeless and will supply a written explanation of the need for this.

11 April. Arrive back in Biala. Have immediately to submit a long report on the nature of burials in the field.

14 April. Departure at 5.00 a.m. for General Command in Iwanowo. I arrange services for the Second Cavalry Division (Pinsk, 18 April); Second Infantry Division Ljubatschevo (22 April); Brest-Litovsk (24 April). Evening: arrival in Pinsk.

15 April. Appeal after appeal to me for money. I will give 1,000 marks to the Jewish elementary school tomorrow. Evening: discussions with the two Mayors Drs Lurie and Wohl. I offer 2,000 marks for immediate distribution to the poor. Command requires assessment of the statutes for a workers' association for vegetable-growing and fishing that is to be founded: this is given to them. According to Lurie's opinion, this association has socialist tendencies. The committee

requests an article from me for the Pinsk newspaper about the Pesach celebration: I will provide this.

18 April. Pesach festival service [see Plate 9]. Over 3,000 soldiers from all over the district. Repeated discussions with Command. Captain von Bissing, who is called the *Judenbeschützer* [protector of the Jews]. Beautiful Seder evening in the rooms of the civilian committee – excellent atmosphere; sixty-two soldiers, four non-commissioned officers, two lieutenants. Long table with white cloth, eight silver candelabras. Lieutenant Steinfeld toasts me, and I toast our Homeland. Young girls serve the very good food, for which I will pay. We sing Hebrew songs. The soldiers are exceptionally enthusiastic and thankful. They wish to publish my morning sermon at their own cost. The civilian committee presents me with the bill for the very basic soldiers' Seder dinner; 240 marks. Extraordinary impertinence, but I pay everything immediately. At 4.00 p.m. departure to Iwanowo.

19 April. Tomorrow at 6.00 a.m. I depart with the light railway: a trip of about 4 hours to a local reserve infantry division: fifty-eight Jewish soldiers of differing ranks are stationed there. I hold a very nice service, with a sermon, in the Christian chapel and afterwards provide a simple dinner for all, with matzoth and wine which I brought along with me, costing about 36 marks. The return trip was terrible in an open little carriage during a rainstorm. Overnight in Iwanowo.

20 April. I travel for 8 hours on light railway to Ljubatschevo, to the Eighty-second Reserve Infantry Division: a true journey from hell. I find a very friendly reception and stay in a monastery. I visit General von Spessart of Division Command and am invited to dinner, where I am treated very honourably. The General praises the bravery of the Württemberg troops in the West. I receive an example here of the small regard for us shown by my non-Jewish colleagues.[47] The horrible return journey: flares, slogan, war cries, etc.

22 April. Beautiful service in the Russian church; about seventy soldiers, physicians, officers present; a meal follows the service. It was wonderful. I bring a consignment of postcards with me: joy and gratitude on the part of the soldiers. In the afternoon an 8 hour journey back to Iwanowo on the light railway from hell. I spend the night in a field hospital at the railway station because I feel unwell.

23 April. Return to Biala. A mountain of mail awaits me. Complaint upon complaint about the mistreatment of Jewish civilians working in the lumber mills daily without pay: women and children go hungry. Cries for bread and potatoes – Mass regulations, punishments,

imprisonments rain down. Very stupid politics, which spares Poles at the expense of Jews. I am unhappy not to be able to help, but only to complain. – I am almost becoming a Zionist here, my heart weeps for these unhappy people.

26 April. In the mess I introduce the topic of a sign: 'Entry for Jews forbidden' in one of the streets, about which all the Jewish soldiers are upset. Commanding Major von Teichmann promises to get rid of it.

27 April. Many enthusiastic thank you letters from soldiers for services and the Seder.

1 May. Dr Feuchtwanger asks me by telephone to come to Radzyn to set up a soup kitchen. I agree and travel there today and from there to Warsaw to the Rabbis conference [see Chapter 10]. Arrive in Radzyn at 8.00 a.m. Written approval for Jewish soup kitchen immediately obtained from Regional Command. At 6.00 p.m. meeting of men and women at Rabbi Chaim Fein's home. I establish the soup kitchen and give them 1,000 marks, and 500 marks for the Jewish refugees.

2–4 May. Rabbis' Conference in Warsaw with myself as secretary.

6 May. New accommodation in Brest-Litovsk. Sent Bertha 300 marks.

19 May. Sent nine parcels with differing contents to the Front. I received an old horse-drawn wagon and also two horses that have scarcely been cured of mange, but am happy with them. Instalment of a telephone in my lodgings.

20 May. Service in Brest-Litovsk: sixty-eight participants. The Torah was read. I preached a very moving sermon and received many compliments, including some from Christian officers present. The cash department at the Royal German Regional Command in Lodz sends me 351 marks on behalf of the local Jewish Benevolent Committee for the refugees from Brest[-Litovsk]. I will travel to Biala tomorrow to hand this amount over to the Board for Brest Refugees, and then send the original receipt to the cash department in Lodz.

21 May. Trip to Biala and visit the soup kitchen. Dr Jakobsohn receives 500 marks against receipt for the soup kitchen. The inhabitants of Brest receive the 351 marks that I received from Lodz. Mass crowd of poor people with petitions to me in Dr Jakobsohn's house. I distribute 38–40 Marks.

22 May. Over thirty consignments to the Front. Announcement of Shavuot services at AOK and General Command in Iwanowo. Sent Bertha 100 marks.

22–29 May. Daily field hospital visits. Major Heubes, Commander of Military Railways Division Six, requests a presentation from me which I agreed to for 1 June at 7.00 p.m. on the topic: 'Concerning the culture of the Jews in Poland.'

30–31 May. Trip to Warsaw to obtain prayer books for the soldiers.

1 June: Presentation at the Military Railways Division Six in Brest-Litovsk. On 29 May Major von Nostitz recommends me for the Iron Cross. Well-attended presentation about 'The Jews in Poland' given at the officers corps of Military Railways Division Six and their guests in the large mess hall. Present: 120 men and two women. At the end I answered questions, followed by a festive meal at which I stayed until 1.00 a.m. Today the Military Railways Division told me through Major von Nostitz that they wish to have the presentation printed at their own cost and it will be as they say.

3 June. Bad attack of nettle rash.

4 June. Departure to the Front: Pinsk, Ljubatschevo, and vicinity.

4-10 June: Stayed at the Front. Day and night the thunder of cannon, bombardment, grenades whistling over Pinsk.

7 June. In Pinsk. Service in the synagogue, overcrowded as always. The Austrian breakthrough. The unbelievable mass *schnorrering* [see Note 38]. I manage monthly payments of 5,600 marks from the Benevolent Society. Evening in Iwanowo.

10 June. Services – night trip to Brest, arrival 11 June at 5.00 a.m.

12 June. I am awarded the Iron Cross Second Class. General accounting to the Jewish Benevolent Society. Evening: innumerable congratulations. Mass distribution of all kinds of gifts: newspapers, cigarettes, books, writing paper, etc. Wounded in field hospital from the Russian breakthrough in Volhynia.[48]

14 June. Great, continuous worries about the Russian breakthrough. Innumerable congratulations on my Iron Cross, also from the Stuttgart Oberkirchenbehörde and Stuttgart lodge. Daily huge amount of work in the field hospitals – and in the same way the ever greater daily dispatch of gift parcels to the Front. Daily distribution of books, cigarettes, newspapers in the nearby field hospital without regard for faith. Terrible wounds due to the Russian offensive, amongst them many badly wounded Jewish soldiers. My field hospital book: the arguments at home: Paul [see Plate 11] has reported to the army too soon because he sadly does not believe that he has a home any more.[49] All Jewish soldiers from the entire Rear Echelon, in the Gouvernement, local field hospital, and Austro-Hungarian service area, are invited to attend the service in Brest-Litovsk to be held on 29 June.

16 July. In Kowel at AOK. Distribution in the streets to the poor. Terrible anxiety about the bad relations between Bertha and my children.[50]

23–26 July. Vilna. Rabbis' conference [see Chapter 10]. Evening of 26 July around 11.30 p.m.: return to Brest-Litovsk. A telegram has arrived to Reserve Field Hospital 116 regarding the burial of Vice Sergeant Major Oscar Sandherr from Mannheim.

28 July. After repeated telephonic requests from the Brest-Litovsk Gouvernement Provost Marshall, I report to his office on the same day at 11.00 a.m. A clerk or secretary is already there. I have no idea what this is about. The Provost Marshall picks up a thick pile of papers and informs me that, on order of the defence counsel of colleague Dr Sänger,[51] I must give testimony whether it is 'the duty of Jewish chaplains to concern themselves with welfare of the Russian or Polish Jewish civil population'. Sänger has apparently asserted that this was so in a letter of July 1915 to an Austrian official and accused him of partiality, which is why the official has accused him of libel. I tell the Provost Marshall of my experience, how I only concern myself with the civil population according to the wishes or with approval of military authorities; also how because of this and at the wish of AOK I have transferred my site to Brest-Litovsk, because there is no Jewish civil population there. I also inform him of the AOK decree that permits humanitarian care for the civil population only after that of the army has been attended to. I am told to dictate my testimony to the secretary and give the following declaration: 'I am of the opinion that Jewish chaplains, as can be inferred from the exact wording of the identification card that they have been given, are only appointed to give military spiritual care. Their assistance in matters of welfare for the civilian population can only follow a request in special cases from the military authorities, and in some cases can be approved later on. In no way is it their duty to concern themselves with the welfare of the Russian or Polish Jewish population unless this is requested.' The secretary minutes this, and I must sign the document and swear to its truthfulness. Sänger has doubtless exceeded his competency most imprudently.[52]

29 July. Very well attended service in Brest-Litovsk, complete with Torah reading: I had *Yahrzeit* for my dear departed mother. Oh, how anxiety intrudes during the past weeks about the fate of our Bug Army since the start of the new Russian offensive! The news is unfortunately not good. May God stand by us!

1 August. Our mood in Brest-Litovsk has been elevated. Hindenburg, Ludendorff, and the entire Eastern Front General Staff are here and will remain here. Hindenburg, who is for the moment living in the new railway car, is taking over Supreme Command from Dunaburg to the Romanian border. Day of the most anxious expectation. Large troop transports to Kowel.

7 August. Sent Bertha 150 marks today, as full payment for the account.

8 August. Sent 130 marks to Bertha. Huge amount of work daily.

19 August. Today I sent 150 eggs home.

20 August. Trip to Berlin.

21 August. Handed over the second shipment of liturgical objects from Brest to the Board of the Berlin Jewish Community [see Note 41].

5 September. Trip to AOK in Kowel. Meeting with the new Chief of Staff, who awards me with the Knights Cross First Class of the *Friederichs-Orden* with swords. Afternoon: travelled further to Lemberg, where the Austrian offensive has failed. At night return to Brest: again I find there a very large pile of mail.

22 September. *Preparations for the most difficult and most beautiful Rosh Hashanah.*

27 September. First festival evening in soldiers' home, Brest-Litovsk, service for the rear echelon: 224 men, five officers, four physicians, two sisters. Went off wonderfully. Afterwards I entertained the physicians in my quarters. My fever, still 38.5°C in the afternoon, disappears.

28 September. Service for Eighth Division in Kowel Main Synagogue: about 800 soldiers, amongst them 200 Austrians of the Twenty-first Division. Reading of Torah – refreshments impossible, because there is no food. The mice in my bed – sleepless night.

29 September. Vladimir-Volynsk. Beautiful service: 600 soldiers, 200 Austrians. The latter are unruly.

30 September. Sokal. Nice service, with soldiers and forty Austrians as well as the civilian population. The *Chassidim*. Departure at 1.30 a.m. during a rainstorm – God protect us – a one-and-a-half hour wait in Sokal in the train.

1 October. Service for Russian prisoners of war in Brest-Litovsk: their enthusiastic affirmative interruptions during the sermon. Services on first and second days of Rosh Hashanah held in my absence for the soldiers in the Brest-Litovsk soldiers home, per

order of the day. Went off very well. Telegram from the Forty-first Reserve Corps advising me that Jewish soldiers from the Eight-first and Eighty-second Infantry Divisions are being sent to Brest for Yom Kippur, although they no longer belong to the Bug Army. Colleague in the nearest town cannot make the journey to perform his spiritual duties, and leaves the soldiers to their fate. There are all kinds of *Zaddikim* in the world![53]

6 October. Yom Kippur evening – Brest-Litovsk; 350 soldiers – very solemn, 6–8.30 p.m. Good prayer leader; many men from Forty-first Reserve Regiment; eight physicians, three officers, two nursing sisters.

7 October. Yom Kippur in Kowel synagogue. About 700 soldiers, many officers. Austrian physicians and sisters. Service from 11.00 a.m.–6.30 p.m. In the evening 150 men: good evening meal: cost 271 marks. The four-filed march of the troops through the dark streets of Kowel: 800 marks for the poor and for the soup kitchen. My health is somewhat better. At night return to Brest-Litovsk.[54]

15–16 October. 18,940 cigars, 40,800 cigarettes, 1,807 books, 1,162 packages sent to the Front (without linen), tobacco, etc.

19 October. Service in Brest-Litovsk, thirty-eight soldiers, luncheon for all in soldiers' home.

20 October. Service in Kowel: eighty-two soldiers. I am based at AOK over the festival period.[55]

23 October. Start of vacation through 27 November. Everyone at home healthy. I spent ten days in bed.[56] Frl. Von Quistorpp, nursing sister in rear Echelon Command in Brest-Litovsk, sends me a hundred eggs. Otherwise, the usual unpleasant things. I have already consumed my December income in advance paying the domestic bills to the sum of 800 marks. May God assist me further. Fritz moved to the artillery on 16 November: First Regiment in Ludwigsburg, arranged by me.

16 November. Presentation about 'The impressions of a Jewish chaplain' in the Stuttgart open lodge: about 500 men and women present. Exceptionally successful.

23 November. Another visit to Fritz and Paul in Ludwigsburg. Wonderful young men. Photograph taken of us together [see Plate 11]. Bad atmosphere at home, wavering between hunger for money and food.[57] The usual problems with Bertha: because of this I depart (early) for Brest-Litovsk on 3 December. On 30 November I received the Knights Cross of the Order of (Kaiser) Franz Joseph, recently deceased.[58]

10 December. Today informed colleague Baeck of the following: In a recent Army Ordinance under the heading 'Family payments etc. for families of medical and chaplain personnel due to enemy constraint' the following sentence has been added to para 2: 'Among the *chaplains* the Military Oberpfarrer [Senior Chaplains] are majors, all others have rank *equal to captains*.'[59]

17 December: Great preparations for Chanukah services: for the 24–26 December in Kowel and Brest-Litovsk, including rear echelon and prisoners of war. Mass consignment and distribution of gifts in the field hospitals.

22 December. Following my written suggestion to the Gouvernement about collection of Hebrew books in Brest-Litovsk, Graf Waldersee has requested an oral presentation about this. My suggestions have all been accepted. Graf Waldersee is very kind and wishes to invite me to dinner soon. From all sides Christmas gifts for the wounded, etc. are given to me for dispatch to the Front. Dispatch to field hospital 3/VI of 150 cigars, 300 cigarettes, twenty-five books. Twenty-five books for Austrian patients. Additionally, diverse items of linen, and about 400 cigars and 1,800 cigarettes. Further distribution to all Jewish as well as Christian soldiers.

24 December. Large Chanukah service with the prisoners of war in the area of the Gouvernement: about ninety participants, very moving.

25 December. Very solemn, beautiful service in the Kowel main synagogue, about 300 soldiers. Everyone sings *Maoz Tsur*. A very moving sermon. Return about 2.00 a.m. in an awful snowstorm.

2 January [1917]. A Jewish civilian worker for Military Railways Division Six had an accident and is due to be buried today in the military cemetery next to two Russians. His brother (also a civilian worker in Military Railways Division), did not tell me but I was simply requested by the administration of field hospital 3/VI to officiate at the funeral. At the same time one German Catholic soldier and two Russian soldiers were buried. When we had gathered at the field hospital chapel, the victim's brother arrived and complained that his brother was not being buried in the Brest Jewish cemetery, but it was too late. So the Catholic chaplain and I walked behind the cortege with the four coffins and musical accompaniment, a column of soldiers, and about eighty Jewish civilian workers, in the driving snow to the military cemetery. There the Jewish man's coffin was carried to his appointed common grave with the Russians. He

was about to be lowered into it when his brother and all the Jews started to weep bitterly because the deceased was not being buried in a Jewish cemetery. I put this matter to the representative of the Military Railways Division Board. He complied with my request and the body was loaded up; the funeral cortege then travelled to the Brest cemetery. On my command a number of Jews went there as well; while night was falling a grave was dug, I prayed and said *Kaddish* – a moonlit scene. Continued work at field hospitals and gift distribution.

22 January. Today a great celebration in the Rear Echelon Command mess in Brest-Litovsk.[60] Twenty men and two women are present, among them many dignitaries. I was the only one to whom Excellency von Waldersee raised his glass. The liquor donated by myself was so greatly appreciated by his Excellency that he drank three bottles.

27 January. Very nice service at 9.00 a.m.: officers, 120 soldiers, physicians, sisters. Distribution of field bibles. Larger distribution of cigars and cigarettes to the German and Austro-Hungarian troops who visited me.

30 January. My birthday: spent quietly and soberly. Friendly letters from Bertha and all the children made my birthday joyful. I hide my birthday from men in the mess.

31 January. This evening, at an already late hour, the rear Echelon Commandant mentioned accidentally (I believe) in the mess that yesterday was my birthday. Geheimrat Professor Müller from Rostock, the consulting surgeon at AOK, immediately sent for two bottles of champagne at his expense, made a nice speech honouring me, and all raised their glasses. I responded deeply moved.

12 February. In Biala. Soup kitchen inspected – various changes made. Large distribution of money, and mass begging.

16 to 21 February. Sick, in bed with tonsillitis. Paul is in Belgium – may God watch over him. My nerves are beginning to fail – sleeplessness.[61]

3 March. Nice service in Brest-Litovsk – about eighty participants. Colleague Baeck requests me by cable to make a presentation about the official position of Jewish chaplains at the next Jewish Chaplains' Conference of the East [see Chapter 10].

5 March. Rabbinical conference in Bialystok. My presentation: 'The Offical Position of Jewish Chaplaincy' was enthusiastically received. I had to depart early at 5.00 p.m. for a burial in Chelm.

6 March. Burial of Hermann Reichelsheimer from Reichelsheim. Died in field hospital 132, from asthma and bronchitis on 4 March 1917. Solemn burial in the German Heroes' Cemetery in Chelm. Visit at AOK. As always, warm reception. The night horribly frozen over. Awful weather.

1 April. *Hagadah* purchase in Warsaw. The phenomenal prices of everything – But everything is invariably available, and in abundance.[62]

6 April. Departure for a Pesach tour. A room in the officers' overnight lodging in Kowel. Noisy: music and the rumpus in the house until 1.00 a.m. – The cars outside also made a racket – so no sleep. Bought 40 lb of matzoth for the Seder from Kreisrabbiner Goldschmidt in Kowel at 4 kroner (105 marks) (per lb): a swindle! Evening service in the main synagogue. The benches are back thanks to my protest. About 800 soldiers participated. I am allowed only Front soldiers, and only the most religious, to the Seder: 140 men, all crowded together, but beautiful atmosphere. I made many speeches, dinner, and the wine was good.

7 April. Large service with sermon, about 800–900 soldiers. Very solemn. Afternoon departure to Vladimir-Volynsk – there evening service with about 600 soldiers and many Austrians. I can only allow 104 men to the Seder, because I can find neither space nor provisions. – Very nice. Food good. The perceptibly worsened mood of the soldiers.[63]

9–12 April. Sick in bed.

24 April. Scandalous burial of the Jewish civilian worker of Military Railways Division: Isak Nagel of the first Replacement Command. Strong petition to Military Railways Division with my suggestions on 25 April.[64]

25 April. Housing of 265 volumes of Talmud, etc. in the main synagogue of Brest, whose renovation was requested by the Gouvernement.

1 May. I receive my complete gas mask equipment. I immediately test this in a stink room after release of a stink bullet. A brilliant technical achievement.

3 May to 15 June: Home leave.

23 May. Trip to visit Paul in Kientzheim near Colmar in the Vosges Mountains. He looks wonderful despite strenuous duties.

27 May. Sermon in Göppingen. Fritz is home on leave.

11 June. Two hour presentation at the lodge. Very large attendance. Theme: 'The Jews in Poland and Lithuania.' Otherwise (unfortunately) *the usual* at home!

13 June. Departure from home.

15 June. Arrival in Brest-Litovsk. Plenty of work. Preparation of my memorandum about organization of Jewish spiritual care in the German army, for the forthcoming conference in Vilna.

1 July. Burial of Battalion Physician Dr Hermann Baer von Euskirchen: he fell dead from his horse due to a heart attack – also belonged to the Seventh Infantry Division, Ninety-seventh Artillery Battalion. Very solemn burial under the thunder of artillery fire – the offensive begins.[65] That night in Brest once more.

2 July. Morning departure for Vilna. My memorandum about the organization of Jewish spiritual care in the German army is received most favourably. Famine in Vilna.

12 July. Service at 10.30 a.m.: well attended, about ninety men – atmosphere was very good. Arrival in Brest 11.00 p.m. – Fritz is not there yet.

15 July. Only *one* letter received since 15 June from my so loving and dutiful wife.

17 July. Departure to Osiekrov for a service. I arrive in a most wretched hamlet, where the entire Division Staff is located. Very friendly reception by the staff, in whose mess I dine and sit next to His Excellency Division Commander Lieutenant General von Wencher. His Excellency is prepared to allow Paul to be transferred to Ulan Regiment 20, First Squadron (the divisional Ulans). Fritzi is on the way from home: he will be in Brest-Litovsk on 19 July, as I have been telegraphically notified. I organize good staff quarters for him.

21 July. I arrange for half a day's leave for Fritz from the firing line: we have some happy hours together. May God watch over us further. Paul's transfer is initiated.

24 July. Two hours visit in field hospital no. three. Apart from a few Jewish civilian workers, not a single Jewish soldier in any of the four sections. The hospital is actually almost empty. I distribute two boxes of cigars and 250 cigarettes amongst the comrades. The insolent letter from the chief physician of Reserve Wunderlich, is answered dismissively. A fanatical, *meshuggene* monster and fanatical Zionist from the Frankfurt orthodox community. Miserable rabble.[66]

9 August. Relocation to Kowel, where I am living in the German and Jewish section. I have small quarters, whose meagre facilities cause me much trouble and expense. The Rear Echelon Commander is very friendly, but the officers under him do as they wish.

13 August. Burial of the Russian prisoner of war Pejssa Glossmann. Visit to Württemberg field hospital 501. Daily uninterrupted work from morning to evening. Sent off a copy of my pamphlet describing the activity of Jewish chaplains which was sent to the Verband der deutschen Juden, also to the Royal Oberkirchenbehörde in Stuttgart – plus three additional copies. Visit to all Kowel field hospitals and daily dispatch of packages to the Front.

20 August. Service in Osiekrov. Pleasant reunion with my dear, brave Fritz. Daily field hospital visits, large amount of correspondence with comrades at the Front and dispatch of packages. I distribute my bread amongst poor, including children. From Rear Echelon Command 203 here in Kowel I am given use of the synagogue in Preussenstrasse for services over the entire festival period, for troops and the Jewish civilian population.

28 August. After about nine hours journey, arrived at the Front 11.30 p.m. Continuous travel along the Front. Very nice service, over 300 participants. Exceptionally kind reception at the division. After dinner with the Commander, he puts me in a car to Sokal, so that I am back in Kowel by 9.00 p.m. On the way back a small railway bridge is breached; no-one is injured. Paul is still not there.

29 August. Paul meets me in Kowel during the afternoon. We spend some happy hours together and then travel on together.

30 August: Trip to the first squadron of Ulan Regiment 20, where Paul is posted in the machine-gun section. Fritz also comes, happy reunion.

1 September. I must travel to Berlin tomorrow morning early in my official capacity, because of preparations for the holidays. I am travelling to the Front at Tverdyn, on the basis of telegraphic information, for burial of a brave comrade Erich Fuchs, Infantry Regiment 122, who only recently wrote to me and is in my card index. He spoke with me at the service in Osiekrov and was killed this evening. I am travelling there on request of his regiment. May God watch over us.

2 September. Burial of Private First Class Eric Fuchs, grave number eighty-two, military cemetery. Letter to the father. In Berestova Paul embarks and travels with me until Makovicze. From there he walks to Fritz's position. Paul is very dissatisfied – on the way back I travel via Osiekrov and speak with the division adjutant on Paul's behalf. I have just spoken by telephone to Paul about it.

3 September. Departure on a 48-hour official trip to Berlin: an unsuccessful struggle, because the Benevolent Society has no money

for the poor Jews, and the Verband der deutschen Juden has nothing left for the soldiers. The Verband makes thirty *Machzorim* available for 1,800 men.

7 September. Back to Kowel – A great deal of mail has arrived – nothing from home!! Concerns and work for the festival days!

8 September. Trip to Vladimir-Volynsk to prepare for a meal for a hundred men on the second day of Rosh Hashanah.

13 September. Permission from Division Staff of Seventh Württemberg Reserve Division that Jewish soldiers be given leave on the first day of Rosh Hashanah to travel to Kowel, and on the second day to Vladimir-Volynsk. Visit to Excellency von Bernhardi who receives me in a very kindly way and requests a list of poor Jews, for the distribution of 1,000 marks. Daily bulk dispatches (of gifts) to the Front; field hospital visits. The distribution of 2,000 marks occurs according to the list approved earlier.

16 September. Rosh Hashanah eve in Brest[-Litovsk], about 400 participants. Rosh Hashanah first day on September 17 in Kowel, about 800 participants.

18 September. Second day of Rosh Hashanah in Vladimir Volynsk. Paul and Fritz are there. About 800 participants. Lunch for 143 soldiers, price 596 Marks. Yom Kippur evening in Brest-Litovsk, about 200 participants; Yom Kippur day in Kowel, wonderful.

26 September. Paul is here; about 800 participants. I pray *Ne'ilah* passionately, with a very good sermon. Evening dinner for 248 men.

30 September. Telegraphic cancellation of service in the command barracks because I am ill.

2 October. Although still ill, I travel to Osiekrov, and hold a nice service there. Paul and Fritz are present. I pray on Hindenburg's seventieth birthday.

7 October. Departure for the Front – Icy night trip in light railway to Radzyn, 108 Infantry Division.[67]

8 October. Service in Radzyn: well attended. Clinic for curing horse mange.

10 October. Following telegraphic notification I perform the burial of Georg Nussbaum, military cemetery 10, Infantry Regiment 377. Letter to the parents. Huge amount of daily work, as always.

26 October. Yesterday night called by telephone to a burial at the 107th Infantry Division. Travelled there today – I buried a Hungarian soldier, Isak Klein, Austro-Hungarian Heavy Artillery Regiment 53, from Siebenbürgen. Letter to his widow.

1 November. Service for the First Reserve and Ninety-first Infantry Divisions. Weak participation.[68] I get monthly tickets printed.

5 November. Service in Mielnica for Twenty-second Reserve Division – in the line of fire – very well attended. Horrible trip by train, light train and wagon. Terrible weather.

8 November. Enough work to make one crazy. Telegraphic summons to Biala for 9 November for a burial.

9 November. Biala. Burial of train driver Jakob Meier, 46 years old, Rear Echelon Principal Driver. Very well attended. Music etc.; letter to widow.

12 November. Service in Osiekrov for Seventh Reserve-Division and Eighty-sixth Infantry Division. Well attended despite bad weather. Paul and Fritz are there. In the evening the 300 recruits from Württemberg in Kowel. Night march prevented.

17–22 November. Chaplains' Conference in Vilna [see Chapter 10] – Fritzi is with me – Reports by Baeck and Hermann Struck.[69] Very fruitful. Masses of daily work of every kind.

29 November. Division Adjutant of the Seventh Reserve Division informs me without me having to ask that Paul has received an 'especially good report' for his machine-gun course.

1 December. *An historical moment*! Just now, at 1.40 p.m., eight Russian officers – strapping men – in two cars, each with a German officer, have driven past us to Commandant General Bernhardi to negotiate a truce. May God be praised.[70] At 10.00 p.m. start of the ceasefire on the Army Group Linsingen Front. Evacuation of a hundred Jewish families is ordered in Kowel. *The evacuation does not take place*. The ceasefire only began formally on the afternoon of 7 December at 12.00 noon. Transports away from all parts of the Front. My lending library for the Front with 121 volumes functions splendidly.

9 December. Very well attended Chanukah service in Kowel. I preach about Chanukah morality for peacetime: religious fortitude. Distribution of cigarettes.

10 December. Very large distribution of books from the lending library.

12 December. Service in Brest-Litovsk at 9.30 a.m. Good participation. Service in Biala at 3.00 p.m. Salzberger has sent my memorandum to AOK without first informing me.[71]

16 December. At 4.30 p.m., service in Vladimir-Volynsk, about 300 soldiers participate despite bad weather. Paul was also there, thank

God he looks very well and hopes for promotion at Christmas time. I distribute 700 cigarettes. At 10.00 p.m. return to Kowel, where sad news of the death of one of my previous batmen arrives: he died in October, trampled to death by his horse – terrible. Tomorrow Fritz is also taking a machine-gun course. Paul received the best report for his.

19 December. I arrange with AOK the transfer to Berlin, as quickly as possible, of Lieutenant Herz from Heilbronn, who is lying ill with an incurable brain tumour in a Kowel field hospital. He will be taken by hospital train to Berlin. May God watch over him further.

25 December. Comprehensive field hospital visit; 132 patients suffering from skin and venereal disease in Kowel: nine Jews.[72] Work of all kinds. As befits the time, I see out the end of the year 1917 simply, with a letter to Bertha.

4 January [1918]. In response to my query, the director of Reserve Hospital One in Liegnitz informs me telegraphically that Lieutenant Herz has died. So everything was for nought. Terrible! I immediately send condolences to his father.

12 January. Well attended service in Kowel. Seventy to eighty mail shipments every day; on 15 January more than 120 mail shipments: books, smoking material, etc. to the Front. Wonderful weather: -30°C – I will surely freeze on this trip. Fritz writes that he has caught a cold.

26 January. Paul becomes Private First Class.

27 January. *Example of my work hours*:[73] Rise at 3.30 a.m. and departure to Turysk 5.00 a.m. Departure from Turysk to Kupiczew (Vladimir-Volynsk region) on the light railway at 7.15 a.m. Arrive at Tuleczov at 8.30 a.m., then two-hour car drive to Kupiczew: a well-attended service there. Departure by car at 11.30 a.m., arrival in Makovicze at 1.20 p.m. Paul and Fritz are there – great joy. Service at 2.00 p.m. After that car trip to Osiekrov: meeting there with Division Adjutant von Molo – 9.15 p.m.: light railway departure to Turysk – arrival 12.15 a.m. No question of sleep in the unheated room at the soldiers' home, so I play chess with two officers until 4.00 a.m. Then return to Kowel, standing because the train is overcrowded. Arrival in Kowel 5.00 a.m., then a half-hour walk to my lodgings. – Afterwards I write about these times in case I forget them. And tomorrow the schedule will be even heavier, though this does not happen because I am bedridden for three days with a swollen face and bad pains.

30 January. My forty-seventh birthday. Worked hard the entire day, the best way to celebrate a birthday! I carry on working despite my various physical symptoms.

8 February. Departure for Riga, for Friday Conference of Jewish Chaplains in the East. Saturday in Warsaw. I hear Sirota at the Tlomackie synagogue, though he is unfortunately partially *ausgesungen* [sung out].[74] I am called up to the Torah – a ubiquitous anti-German spirit. Sunday night in Vilna. Monday travel to Riga with (Chaplains) Sali Levi [pp.281–2] and Baeck. Arrive in Riga at 10.00 p.m.

12–13 February. Conference. How small many of the 'greatest men' are when looked at in the cold hard light of day! Theologians should only be viewed and appreciated from one specific perspective.[75] I deliver a well-received talk on the permanent foundation of a Conference Society, give a presentation about my memorandum on the organization of military spiritual care, and receive official thanks. A further presentation about provision of reading material is well received. Sonderling [see Chapter 9 pp.291–2] feeds us in princely fashion for 25 marks. We visit the beautiful city of Riga.

16 February. Return at night to Kowel where a giant bag of mail awaits me. News about the supposed peace with Russia. Declaration from Trotsky on 10 February.[76] On 17 February I am informed that the campaign in the Ukraine will be conducted by the Seventh Infantry Division, Forty-fifth Reserve Division, Second Cavalry Division and the Ninety-first Infantry Division. So Paul and Fritz will also be there. May God protect them. Kowel is swarming with Ukrainians in their fantastic blue uniforms.[77]

20 February. Service in Biala. Large distribution of gifts.

22–23 February. I return to Brest-Litovsk ill, lie in bed with a high fever until the 28th. A huge amount of mail. Preparations for the trip to Rovno-Zhitomir and Kiev and to my dear young sons. Continuing work of sending packages to the troops at the Front. Visits to field hospitals, correspondence, etc. No possibility of services for the moment because of wide dispersion of our troops in Ukraine. Great worry about Pesach! Huge numbers of Germans and Austro-Hungarians from Russian prison camps are marching through. Ukrainians in their blue uniforms. Paul and Fritz are in Berditschev. A Hamburger, Frau Alice Stein, collected 730 marks for me, in other words for the soldiers. May God reward her!

19 March. Departure at 7.00 a.m. from Kowel by truck; 9 hour journey to Lutsk where I arrive almost worn out. Despite written authorization, no single automobile to Rovno can be scraped up at the technical service centre or the gasoline station. I will therefore stay overnight in Lutsk and travel to the German Rear Echelon

Command from the other end of the town where someone says that quarters are assigned. I pass six hotels, but it is said that they are all occupied. No one wants German officers. So I return to the railway station to travel to Rovno at 11.00 p.m. at night. I have to pay 10 roubles (= 20 marks) for a 45-minute trip in a miserable hackney. Arrive at the station at 6.00 a.m.; that means a wait of 5 hours. But where? The entire miserable wooden station is overflowing with Bolshevik and Russian soldiers, lying on top of one another like herrings on the floor: no waiting room. A little room with the address 'For First and Second Class' is, in the same way, packed full, with an unparalleled stink. So, I walk around outside, despite the frost, with my batman. Then I collapse and find shelter in the German collecting location for sick and wounded, which shortly before held Russian latrines. At 10.00 a.m. at the station, where a crazy fight develops for places on the train passing through. I find a little space in a first class compartment that I carve out next to Russian officers. My batman's rifle works wonders. The seat consists of iron springs without cushion or cover, no window panes, a crazy journey. Arrive in Rovno at 3.00 a.m. at night. The same situation as in Lutsk because of massive numbers of Bolsheviks and other Russian military streaming back home. In pitch darkness we grope around in the town for the information office, where I find out exactly where Fritzi and Paul are located. I am finally allocated a room in a hotel with a bed which is no more than a mattress on which I rest for 2 hours. The filth in Rovno is indescribable, hatred of Germans overt, prices unspeakably high for every trifle. A postcard for example costs 80 pfennig. In these parts one really learns to appreciate the German compulsion for orderliness, such as in occupied areas. The Jews, all Zionists, represent the intelligentsia but hate the Germans (or do so out of fear of the Ukrainians). The journey from railway station to German Kommandatur, where I registered, costs 15 roubles, and there is no sleeping or resting accommodation. We Germans have no right of precedence, and eventually I am given one of the AOK rooms in the Grand Hotel – small, ugly, filthy and cold, without a heater! May God watch over me! Although dead tired, I visit Oberrabbiner Dr Gurewicz at 5.00 p.m., to advise him of the soldiers' Pesach services and Seder evenings, and to request his assistance. He wants to give me a decision in 2–3 days time. I find a reasonably friendly, older man who speaks Ukrainian to me, is indeed a Kronrabbiner, but mocks Zionists and does not behave in a collegial manner. And yet Herzl's picture hangs in his office.[78] Everything, everything about him is Russian.

Prices here are incredible. One order of tea without bread and butter costs 2.5 roubles, one salt herring or smoked herring costs 3 roubles (6 marks), etc. I got a shave and my beard trimmed in one of the stores today: the cost was 3 roubles (= 6 marks). Today, 22 March, I survived on bread, one apple and some tea. My resources do not allow a visit to an inn, not at these prices. The over-patriotic Ukrainian Rabbi Dr Gurewicz has not contacted me. I have bought a Russian grammar book and am working (unsuccessfully) on my writing and speech. My room has no heater. So starving, freezing, not sure of my life, having to pay enormous amounts of money for every trifle – these are my war experiences in Kiev. Paul and Fritz are on the way with their divisions to Yekaterinoslav, on the way to the Volga, very, very far from here, and therefore beyond my reach. As the single meal of the day I eat a bowl of potato soup in a less than elegant restaurant, for which they still charge me 2.9 roubles, with one slice of white bread at 5.8 marks. I go to bed at 6.30 p.m. and read until midnight. At 7.00 a.m. three well known officers from AOK inform me that tomorrow Excellency von Linsingen, with almost his entire staff, is moving to the Grand Hotel in Kiev, for which purpose almost all the rooms there are required. I must also vacate my own room. *Nitschewo*! [no matter]

24 March. Command allocates me, with great difficulty, a dark and dirty room in the Hotel Sofiowka; we eke life out. The Information Officer at Command will make enquiries about news of Fritz by telegraph. In the afternoon I visit Dr Gurewicz who gives me an address and good hope that both services and Seders will easily be able to be held together with the Ukrainian-Jewish soldiers. My 'hotel room' is deplorable. Right and left, Russian soldiers with *Weiber* [low women], the entire house echoes with political shouting, Bolshewiki, Germanski, Ukrainski, etc. I wish I was in Kowel again, hale and healthy.

25 March. Visit to Herr Rubinschik, a pious and most kindly man who lives in royally appointed rooms, receives me very well and will arrange services and Seder evenings free of charge. If only the Württembergers and my own dearest sons could participate. I go at once to General Command of the First Artillery Company and arrange a decree for assembly of soldiers in front of the Brodsky synagogue[79] at 5.30 p.m. on 27 March, as well as evening leave guaranteed until

10.00 p.m. I will be given a decision tomorrow on whether there is any objection to German and Ukrainian Jewish soldiers being mixed together. I receive the news of the so far triumphant course of the offensive and am overjoyed about it.[80] If only the mood here were not so inimical to Germans!

Notice: Members of the Jewish faith should assemble to celebrate Pesach on 27 March at 5.30 p.m.; on 28 March at 8.30 a.m. and at 5.30 p.m.; on 29 March at 8.30 a.m., in front of the Brodsky synagogue. For both festival evenings they have to get official leave until 10.00 p.m.

I go in the afternoon to visit and clean out the soup kitchen next to the Brodsky synagogue. A leader of the institution receives me there, and tells me without cause that he wishes the Germans would go to the devil, they are not our friends, have taken our bread away and cut Russia into pieces, etc. I made no excuses to the rascal. There was also one young Jewish woman and several young people who asserted that they understood only *Russian*. I gave the rabble my opinion. Bad night's rest.

I am told that the chief quartermaster does not want to have German soldiers together with Ukrainians at the Pesach services. I object to this, and he will give me the decision in the afternoon. Still no telegraphic answer from Fritz. In the afternoon the answer is that both services, together with the Ukrainian soldiers, and evening leave for the troops until 10.00 p.m. have been approved. Herr Jochemsohn takes me to Rabbi Aronsohn who will do what is necessary to look after the soldiers during Pesach. Eventually three rooms are made available to me, in case I transfer to Kiev after the holidays.

26 March. Two telegrams come to me from Kowel. They had got lost in the tremendous disorder at Command and at AOK. AOK has decreed that I serve at the First Artillery Command, but nobody has heard about it yet. Command here, command there, nobody cares. We are learning much about the Russians: we are preparing everything for Pesach services and Seders with untold effort and much cost, but I fear that the soldiers will not come. Gloomy general mood. The new Chief of German Command also wants to create some order in the matter of the Pesach. However, he emphasizes to me that today or tomorrow, on the anniversary of the Russian Revolution, a Putsch by the Ukrainians is planned. We Germans are prepared for this, but an increased troop alert has been ordered and service and Seders are forbidden for this evening. This can be called Pesach with impediments: money is

available, Seder, food, everything is prepared beforehand and yet it is impossible to celebrate. Baeck and Sali Levi telegraph me that they are making 1,000 marks available to me from the Rabbinerverband. Perhaps I can hold a Seder tomorrow.

28 March. In the morning from 9.00–11.15 a.m., a very nice service in the large soup kitchen hall: about 120 German, Austrian, Ukrainian and Russian soldiers participate, also many civilians including Rabbi Dr Gurewicz. I lead the service, preach and everything is very dignified. Then luncheon, all together. I make mention in my concluding talk of the blessing that our great victory in the West will make everybody atone for the frequent rebuffs to our hand of friendship.[81] Dr Gurewicz, who does not understand German well, compares this with the Russians, and complains about it during the meal. I clarify the misunderstandings immediately, to everyone's satisfaction. I distribute many hundreds of cigars and cigarettes, books and newspapers. In the evening a truly wonderful Seder evening from 6.00–9.30 p.m. – about 200 soldiers and many genteel civilians. Everyone is highly enthusiastic. Dr Herzfeld delivered a thank-you speech for me – it was wonderfully moving.

29 March. I foward to the Board of the Jewish soup kitchen 200 roubles for the kitchen itself and 100 marks for the personnel. Afternoon departure back to Kowel.

30 March. Return from Kiev. Concerning trip to Kiev and experiences. At 12.15 p.m. departure to Brest-Litovsk and Biala to hold services.

2 April. Beautiful service in Brest-Litovsk with about 400 participants. Afternoon in Biala. Nice service, well attended. The Kiev Jews have sent money (200 roubles and 100 marks) for food for the troops. I send Sali Levi a postal order for 300 marks for the prayer books.

8 April. Magnificent service in Kowel, over 500 participants, also sixty-four prisoners of war. In the evening a lovely dinner in the soldiers' home at my expense.

21 April. Surprise visit from Paul who arrives from Yekaterinoslav to take care of service-related matters in Kowel. He looks well, thank God.

21 May. I return from a vacation in Göppingen which, this time, went off well. However, most painfully and seriously, Paul has been severely wounded on 12 May at the battle for the bridgehead at Rostov-on-Don. I arrive back in Kiev on the 24th at 5.00 p.m. and

am quartered in the Hotel Nationale. Paul has been put in for an Iron Cross. My hotel room is horribly filthy. On 25th report to AOK, lengthy discussion with the chief quartermaster who requests my intervention regarding teaching the Jews about good aspects of the German character: he approves my requests: I take this verbally and in writing to the Headquarters Commandant, who will carry them out. I buy cigarettes and divide them between two field hospitals, pay for four meals for Jewish soldiers, and distribute 18 marks among the poor.[82]

25–26 May. From 8.23 a.m. on the 25th to 1.30 p.m. on the 26th. Reasonably good trip to Kharkov. A very large, beautiful, populous city, a horse tramway at the railway station, electric trams in the city. From 7.00–10.00 p.m. I wait in the first class station restaurant for the train to Taganrog, which departs at 12.30 a.m. Together with four other officers, we commandeer a special vehicle second class to Taganrog. Good journey, 22 hours, in a tattered, dirty coupé. The Ukrainian locomotive drivers are on strike and refusing to drive German military trains.

As soon as we arrive in Taganrog, I see, on 27 May late at night, a fight between German soldiers and a drunk, a giant Bolshevik wretch, who is being led away in a bloody, beaten-up state. Because no overnight provision has been made before the 6.30 a.m. departing train to Rostov, I assemble seven German comrades and obtain approval to sleep overnight in a second class coach. There is no question of sleep because embarkation starts at 2.00 a.m., although the carriage stands far away outside the station. At 7.00 p.m. we hear that the train is not going.

28 May. The area of track lies under Bolshevik fire. Eventually only carriages occupied by civilians are held back and our carriage departs. We travel for 3 hours until we reach one of the bridges blown up by the Bolsheviks, cross this in about 20 minutes by foot, and then travel in a cattle car to a small station 15 kilometres from Rostov where the Ukrainian drivers refuse to drive further. I hear from a comrade that he saw Paul in Taganrog field hospital thirty-three. I immediately travel in a cattle car with one of the trains of returning German prisoners of war which is ready to depart, back to Taganrog where I arrive at 6.00 p.m. I look up Paul that very evening. Sadly, he looks emaciated and conceals his pains from me. He has a bad penetrating wound from an infantry missile, and lay for eight hours until he was picked up: he shot at the enemy even while already wounded. A wonderful, brave young man. He was operated on under

anaesthesia and the bone splinters removed. I buy, for him and many other wounded soldiers, wine, white bread, butter and cigarettes, sausage, etc. for about 85 roubles. The soldiers, all Württembergers, are very grateful.

30 May. Spent the day with Paul. The dear young man feels tolerably well. The doctor tells me that the wounded shoulder will heal completely: let us hope so. I again distribute bread, eggs and cigarettes in the field hospital.

31 May. Many hours with Paul in the field hospital. Again, extensive distribution of all kinds of gifts, and 15 roubles cash to Private Tobias, Reserve Infantry Regiment One.

3 June. I am put in touch with Kronrabbiner Dr Goldenberg, to ask whether I will be able to use one of the beautiful synagogues for my service on 4 June at 10.00–11.00 a.m. He will make a decision at 7.30 p.m. and I am also invited for tea. In the evening he says that they are afraid to offer German soldiers anything because the Cossacks would accuse the Jews of doing something bad. I should therefore obtain a written order from Regional Command.

4 June. I receive the decision that the community refuses out of fear to open the synagogue to the German-Jewish soldiers. What a rabble! And at the same time here, as everywhere, German soldiers have been the saviours of Jewish lives – I take a hall in an empty grammar school for the service.

5 June. Extensive purchases in the market and on the street for field hospital 258, for distribution after tomorrow's field service in Rostov. Also large distribution in all rooms of the field hospitals. Again I spent a long time with Fritz – he is travelling tomorrow with the hospital train to Taganrog, where Paul too is embarking for Kiev. In the evening I hear that Paul has been awarded the Iron Cross Second Class.

6 June. Service in grammar school, Pushinskaya. Low attendance. Cigarette distribution eighty per man. Fritz has still not been put up for the Iron Cross. In the orderly room of the First Batallion 122 I receive Paul's Iron Cross Second Class and certificate. I hope to deliver this to him today in Taganrog still, if the field hospital is still there. Afternoon trip to Taganrog where I hear by telephone that Paul and Fritz have already departed earlier in the morning by hospital train. I therefore travel at 6.30 via Yekaterinoslav to Kiev. At 1.00 a.m. I have to get off at Charzisk and wait for six hours. A crazy business with refugees who are returning home at the station. I hear that a train is travelling in the direction of Kharkov, stopping at Nikitowka

at 1.30 a.m., and decide to use it. Upon disembarking at Nikitowka I ask a soldier standing there whether he knows anything about the hospital train. What an excellent coincidence! Less than 10 metres in front, he shows it to me; the carriages are almost all open, without any guards. At 3.00 a.m. I find Paul and Fritz together in two lower beds. The joy of seeing each other again is great. I hand over to Paul his Iron Cross Second Class.

7 June. In the morning at 7.00 a.m. I request the head of the hospital train, senior physician Dr Schneider, for permission to travel further in the hospital train with both of my wounded sons. This is granted because one car is occupied by only five men. I provide my own food.

8 June. During the journey, I record immediate fresh impressions of what I see:

a) The men's rations are dismal: miserable watery soup with meat fibres is all they get for lunch. Only a very few 'enjoy' this; almost all buy provisions at the stations. I make do with bread and tea.

b) The doctor hardly bothers with the men; once a day he walks rapidly through some, but not all, of the carriages, asks who needs to be bandaged and gives the accompanying nursing sister instructions for bandaging. Care is unbelievably negligent and everyone curses. Today my Paul was freshly bandaged: at 3.00 p.m.; he has a fever of 38°C. A medical orderly passing by chance through the car orders that the senior physician be informed, but Paul is not seen. In the evening Paul's fever is 40°C. At once I send for the doctor but a medical orderly comes accompanied by a Russian sister, with whom no-one can talk. I ask why the doctor did not come and am told by the orderly that the Herr *Oberarzt* is sleeping and resting (from doing nothing all day). I react energetically, and then the doctor finally appears and gives Paul two pyramidone tablets, explains that the fever is caused by the wound,[83] and disappears. I nurse Paul as best I can.

c) The train has only two or three German personnel, apart from them only Russian louts and an army of *Weiber* [low women] who live the noisy life of prostitutes with many of the sick.

d) The train travels at snail's pace, stops at even the smallest station, and will take a good four and a half days to travel from

Rostov to Kiev. Today it has travelled 75 kilometres in thirteen hours; at many stations the train stops for 5–8 hours, and the most fantastic detours are made because, unfortunately, the train is travelling through Austro-Hungarian territory. This all causes the wounded to suffer greatly; many already have fever. Paul still has a high fever. May God continue to watch over him.

9 June. Paul's twenty-first birthday. Thank God he is doing better and his fever is disappearing. By contrast I have developed diarrhoea even though I have been living off bread and tea for the last four days. The physician gives me opium;[84] by evening I have a fever of almost 40°C. A terrible night: I become unconscious. Paul and my batman nurse me and my batman carries me in his arms. Then terrible diarrhoea.

10 June. I notice blood in my stool and request the visit of a physician from the nearby field hospital 91, who wants to arrange my immediate transfer to field hospital 504. May God watch over me! The bacteriological examination has revealed dysentery[85] but I am feeling significantly better. Nursing and food are very good and I am being treated well by a physician and physician's assistant. Meanwhile my batman brings some mail from AOK. Today he is in Kowel, and will bring mail to me from there. Paul and Fritz write to me from Kowel that they are on their way to Brest-Litovsk. In eight days I hope to be in Kowel.

19 June. Paul and Fritz are both in a field hospital in Brest-Litovsk. Daily distribution of cigarettes and reading matter in field hospital. I receive six registered letters that evening, amongst these Fritz's Iron Cross Second Class, which I at once send on to Brest-Litovsk.

25 June. I am gradually recuperating but will have to look for a convalescent home because I am weak. This afternoon I travel to AOK and tomorrow hope to travel to Kowel.

6 July. Service scheduled for Kowel could not be held because only two soldiers, one physician, and four prisoners of war were there. There are only a few troops remaining in Kowel and its environs. The synagogue gallery serves as troop quarters.

9 July. Well-attended service in Brest-Litovsk – happy hours with Fritz. I am very weak, and on 17 July shall go to Jablon to the officers' convalescent home.

14 July. I receive the Hamburg Hanseatic Cross.

17 July. Arrival in officers' convalescent home in Jablon near Parczev. I sent home a box with all sorts of valuable things including a large broom and 10lb flour (58 marks).

21 July. From Jablon I send home two boxes with 34 German pounds of flour (68 marks) and 50 marks in cash; later two more boxes in the same way.

26 August. Because of festival days, I depart today and interrupt my treatment early, against the advice of the chief physician.

30 August. Arrival in Kiev after a good fifteen hours of travel. Car to AOK is waiting for me at the station.

31 August. Visit to the Brodsky synagogue where I am called up to the Torah and read the portion in the traditional manner: this creates a sensation. After this, conference meeting with Captain Lange in the German Regional Command Center regarding the location of Rosh Hashanah services. The situation in Kiev is horrible, rising prices too crazy to mention. This cannot end well. I have scheduled my current trip: Kiev – Kharkov – Rostov on Don – Yekaterinoslav – Simferopol – Sevastopol – Yevpatoria – Odessa – Kiev – Kowel.[86] After the trip ends in October, I want to go on leave. Only after that will I transfer to Kiev, although I have been assured that the war will certainly end this year. Much walking to and fro every day in preparation for Rosh Hashanah. In order to provide the Jewish soldiers with a communal luncheon on both days, I look up the superintendent of the Jewish soup kitchen in Mala Vasilovka, where I had previously catered for comrades. There I hear that she is in Odessa, but that I must look up her husband, the multi-millionaire Alexander Brodski, in the bank on Alexandrovskaya 43. Despite heat and tiredness I go there accompanied by my batman. It is a banking house like any other, with a large waiting room on the first floor teeming with *schnorrers* of every kind mixed in with refined gentlemen. Just like at a king's. After few minutes His Majesty the *Judenkönig* [King of the Jews] Brodski comes out of his holy-of-holies, immediately notices me in my uniform, and asks me: 'What do you want?' I answer: 'I want to discuss a small matter with you.' He: 'I have no time!', turns around and walks with his thickly padded bull neck like an original and authentic vulgarian back down into a corridor. At first I am speechless; then I inform all those present that they can tell the famous man of honour on my behalf that he acted very rudely. With proper contempt I turn my back on the man and his bank. In the future I will have something to say about this matter. I must look elsewhere for provisions. The fact that the man had no

idea of who and what I am is an example of the Jews' hatred of the Germans. And yet it was precisely the Germans who saved Brodski and his ilk from the Bolsheviks.

3 September. Prices in Kiev: One pear costs 2 roubles 20 kopeks; one small plum costs 5 kopeks. And we want to civilize this miserable nation of murderers, robbers and thieves, if we do not wish the Ukraine to become a German Gallipoli![87] Hatred of the Germans is overt and increases every day, especially amongst the Jews. I am begged at every step for every kind of assistance; but if I ever need something for the Jewish soldiers, then I am the hated German. Indescribably disgusting people and disgusting conditions!

5 September. Gradually things are beginning to resolve themselves. After having walked my feet raw, I have obtained a middle-sized school room below the Brodsky synagogue. The *Shamas* Schopiro will install whatever is necessary. He tells me about the many Jews in Kiev, who even on the High Holidays do not attend synagogue. Empty seats are rented out, and each person must bring a ticket along, otherwise they are not admitted. One of the most impertinent people I have met on this occasion is the administrator of the soup kitchen, Grusenberg: a miserable person. I visit Krenfis at 8.30 p.m. in pouring rain: a pious, learned Jew well-known for his good deeds. He gives me twenty prayer books, and ten packages for the soldiers. Before my departure he asks me about feeding the soldiers. I tell him that I have received a telegram this evening from colleague Arthur Levy [p.321], in which he states that the money from the Rabbinerverband has not yet arrived. On hearing this he gives me 600 roubles for three meals, in the first instance as a loan. I decline, because I do not know if I will receive money or how much, and also have to save for meals in Kharkov. On hearing this he tells me that he would then give me the money as a gift.

First day Rosh Hashanah (Saturday 7 September). Beautiful service, about 120 German and thirty Austro-Hungarian soldiers: 9.00–11.30 a.m. Everything goes very well and I receive congratulations from all sides. My heart feels quite Zionistically inclined. I make a similar speech at table – massive applause – ninety-two excellent luncheon meals. In the evening: wine cake, grapes, and two hours of conversation with the comrades in the soup kitchen. Krenfis says we will donate meals for the soldiers before and after Yom Kippur.

Second day Rosh Hashanah (8 September). Very nice service. I collect 102 marks for seventeen olive trees in Krenfis's name as a sign of our thanks.[88] *Excellent barley broth*.[89] I collect a tip of about 30 marks for the staff. Today at 8.00 p.m. I travel by fast train to Kharkov. Evening departure, AOK sends a car, the night is very comfortable in first class, despite numerous insect bites.

9 September. Arrival in Karkhov after a four-hour delay. A car from the Commandant General is waiting at the station. Although AOK has already commissioned lodging for me by telegram on 7 September, my arrival has not yet been prepared for. Kharkov is terribly overcrowded. All officers, etc. live in one small hotel. The community directs me to a nice, empty room in the Great Synagogue, Pushkinskaya that they want to prepare for me;[90] however, I decline because I fear that in the future the synagogue rooms will be taken up by the military. I am given a very modest room in a small Jewish guesthouse which I can equip at a basic level. The synagogue sexton Schmulewitsch, a good man, is the facilitator. Everything works out very well. With Schmulewitsch – who speaks fluent Hebrew – I visit Gurewicz, a very modern merchant, who promises to arrange everything very well, including the question of provisions. Then I visit General Command of the First Artillery Company, whom I inform about the good German-friendly conduct of the Kharkov Jews. I am received very well and can in a half-hour presentation document the fact that the Jews are well-disposed towards the Germans. My talk makes a visibly profound impression.

11 September. I get sick from drinking spoiled milk given to me in my inn. Despite this, afternoon tea visit with the excellent family Gurewicz and Aronsohn, modern, highly educated people whom I liked very much.

12 September. I go to the synagogue, as I do every day. My condition has improved. In the afternoon I am invited for tea with the multi-millionaire Moldawsky, the 'Brodsky' of Kharkov, but much more genteel. Everyone speaks fluent German: It was very enjoyable. In the evening at 6.30 p.m. I receive a telegram that Paul will be arriving here from Kiev tomorrow morning at 9.00 a.m.

13 September. I meet Paul this afternoon at 1.00 p.m. with his comrade Hausmann and we spend some happy hours together. At 7.05 p.m. they journey on to Rostov.

14 September. I visit the Choral Synagogue and am called up to the Torah.

15 September. I work with my batman the entire morning until my soldiers' synagogue is ready. The soup kitchen is also ready. May God assist us in our endeavour.

16 September. Yom Kippur went flawlessly. I preached twice and also led the *Shacharit*, *Mussaph* and *Ne'ilah* services. Also the food, two meals, was excellent. Tomorrow morning I travel by military train to Rostov on the Don. May God protect me: I am very tired.

17 September. 7.15 a.m. departure for Rostov. Arrive on 18 September at 1.00 p.m. I am instructed to quarter with the Chassidic Rabbi of Ljubavetscho, a famous *Gaon* and *Yeshivah* founder, and his only son. Their name is Schnersohn: they appear to be rich people, and have lived for three years in Rostov as refugees. I have much to do this afternoon, for tomorrow I want to travel to Paul's machine gun company in Nachitschevan. Fritz has his study leave of four weeks in conjunction with three weeks of recreational leave which started on 8 September.

19 September. I visit Paul in K. His battalion has been evacuated, but I luckily still meet with him and we spend two hours together. The Rabbi from Ljubavetsch. While I write these lines, overloud singing, shouting and sporadic clamouring echoes from the courtyard. The Rabbi's pupils are rejoicing because a wedding is taking place. They dance in a star-shaped circle, a kind of Polonaise danced in rows of four with a fluent, sung melody. This reminds me greatly of a Polish or Russian farm consecration. It is a lovely, genuine Chassidic activity. The Ljubavetsch *Gaon*, Sholom DovBer Schnersohn, is 58 years old, makes a highly dignified, awe-inspiring impression and enjoys boundless veneration. He not only teaches Talmud in his large *Yeshiva*h, but also (and chiefly) teaches a kind of philosophical explanation of Chassidism. He wears modern clothing and ranks as a great gentleman. I will visit with him tomorrow. This evening I saw how, in the greatest holiness and modesty, he married one of his pupils, a soon-to-be rabbi – poor and without position – to a poor orphan girl. The Chassidim are very friendly. I gave them a hundred German cigarettes. The rebbe is the fifth in the line of Rabbi Schneur Zalman,[91] the second successor of the Baal Shem Tov; hence the name Schnersohn. I donate 1,400 roubles for the *Yeshivah*. I am the rebbe's guest and eat with him in the Sukkah. They live very well there. There are many guests from out of town, admirers of the rebbe. He gives presentations on the philosophical approaches to Chassidic problems. Speaks terribly rapidly. The shaking of the audience who understand nothing. The lice! His own songs, melodies without words, known to all of his adherents. His own *Kavannah* in praying. The marvelous *Selbstbewußtsein* [self-confidence] of the Chassidim. All are fearful that the Germans, as is rumoured, might

evacuate Rostov. Tomorrow I travel to Taganrog and from there to Yekaterinoslav and Simferopol.

26 September. Arrival in Simferopol at 11.00 a.m. Excellent journey by express train. Very friendly welcome in the soldiers' home where I stay and also am scheduled to hold the service. In the afternoon I suddenly develop a high fever and go to bed. At 5.00 p.m. I am asked to visit Excellency von Kosch who wishes to get to know me better. I go immediately to General Command, where I am received with an invitation for dinner with His Excellency. But when the Adjutant sees my high fever he immediately sends me back. The fever rises, and at 8.30 p.m. at His Excellency's order the corps physician comes to tend to me.

27 September. The fever rises to 39°C. I am transported unconscious to field hospital 149. Terrible heat day and night – I hardly sleep, and eat nothing. It is severe influenza with light pneumonia.[92]

3 October. Still in field hospital 149. A better room, but a waspy, malevolent fury of a sister who answers the call when she feels like it: but no-one calls her. The physician who is treating me is charming. Food very bad, only slowly improves on my request. Painful days and nights in unbelievable heat.

7 October. In the morning to the Simferopol train station. Terrible heat; four hour wait. Bad physical and psychological condition. Around 12.00 noon departure to Sevastopol. The fruit and tobacco. The stone buildings and beautiful entrance to Sevastopol. First rumour of peace.[93] Enchantingly situated town. Evening departure to Kharkov. Bad night; oil heating.

8 October. Eight hours in Kharkov. I have severe diarrhoea.

9 October. Arrival in Kiev. AOK has sent my mail to Kowel.

11 October. Arrival in Kowel – ill – diarrhoea. Sick in bed until 15 October.

15 October. Request to return to Jablon. My glorious Paul, who has been ordered to attend Officer's School, visits me.

19 October. Arrive in officers' convalescent home in Jablon. Excellent reception.

21 October. I cannot tolerate eating meat and am miserable and sick in Jablon. Around evening I develop a type of intestinal obstruction which causes me indescribable pain. The doctor gives me two large morphine injections which don't help at all. The doctor and nurses watch over me the entire night and give me continuous camphor injections and warm compresses. A truly terrible night. The doctor

telephones the surgeon at Army Hospital Three in Biala to request that I may be taken there by ambulance in the morning for surgery, and this happens. He also telephones Fritz – who is passing through and coincidentally staying overnight at my lodgings in Kowel – to tell him that I am seriously ill and that he should come to Biala to visit me.

22 October. Transportation at 9.00 a.m. in a car to Biala. I am almost unconscious, but the pains have abated. An examination reveals that surgery is not necessary, but nevertheless I must stay for two days of observation. My wonderful Fritz comes that evening, stays for two days and cares for me superbly. May God reward him. Fritz, magnificent young man, has also completed his *Abitur* [high school examinations] and I give him 100 marks in recognition.

24 October. With 1,000 difficulties, I return to Jablon. I am dismally weak and everything shakes in and around me.

The Departure

28 October. On the basis of medical opinion I request discharge from military service and also inform the Stuttgart Oberkirchenbehöde and the Verband der deutschen Juden of this. I am still ill and weak.

4 November. I send home one box of peas and beans, insured: 100 marks.

5 November. Today I send to Bertha from Jablon: three boxes of flour, one box of eggs, etc., also insured.[94] Life in Jablon is boring, cold and I am often in pain.

11 November. Yesterday the armistice conditions of the Entente were made known. Unbelievable excitement in the house. This evening workers' and soldiers' councils are being constituted from the less-seriously ill and orderly sections. This morning their chairman tells us that all officers are required to leave immediately. There is now no car, and they demand the regulation of tips, and improved food, etc. The chief physician negotiates with them. I travel at 12.45 p.m. in a truck with two physicians to the Parczew railway station, from there at 5.00 p.m. to Lukov, where we arrive at 6.30 p.m. When we ask when the train departs for Berlin or Brest, we are told that there is no rail traffic any more and that Poles have taken over all the stations, etc. And indeed a delegation of four officers and one man of the Polish Legion soon arrive; they depose and disarm all German railway officials and take over all railway operations. Soon thereafter the battalion stationed in Lukov is disarmed, the General Staff

together with the Governor are arrested but set free the following morning. We spend a sleepless night in great agitation in the officers' room, and are repeatedly threatened with being shot. There is no prospect of railway transport or assistance. Nothing to eat or drink and soaking wet, lousy weather. The garrison in Lukov along with the Governor of Poland has been disarmed without resistance during the night. There is still fighting in Warsaw, near Biala, etc.; also plundering of rear Echelon stores by German soldiers. The same is happening in Kowel.

12 November. In the morning a train consisting of cattle trucks arrives at Lukov station, which the Poles have approved for the transport of 250 German railway workers to Brest-Litovsk. The Lukov-Warsaw section is blocked because the bridge has been blown up. On my advice and command we all jump onto the train, despite the Poles' shouting, hide ourselves behind the baggage lockers, and arrive safely in Brest-Litovsk that evening.

13 November. Trip to Kowel. I pack everything quickly with my batman's help. Despite the turmoil, bags and chests are sent as registered luggage and, to everybody's great astonishment, arrive in Göppingen three weeks later. I receive notification by telegraph of unlimited home leave approved by High Command in Kiev, confirm this with the soldiers' council in Kowel, dissolve my household there, and travel on.

15 November. I stay overnight with Dr Jacobsohn in Brest-Litovsk, where I hear that the officers' convalescent home in Jablon has been closed down and that patients, sisters, etc. have been fleeing on foot for two days to Brest. I was lucky to leave in time.

16 November. Departure to Bialystok and from there to Prostken in the afternoon, always expecting a Polish attack that doesn't come. At midnight the insanely overfilled train departs via Insterburg and Thorn – to Berlin.

17 November. Evening arrival in Berlin. At 9.00 p.m. travel further to Hof, change here to Augsburg, and eventually arrive safely in Göppingen on 18 November at 5.00 a.m. At the railway station I meet Paul, who has come from Ulm on the same train and *has been completely demobilized*. Enormous work at home; I take my position over at once despite illness and weakness. Great anxiety about Fritz, whose unit under Mackensen was assigned to Romania and has been interned there. No news despite all attempts. Paul is studying hard in Tübingen.

27 December. Great rejoicing! During dinner my wonderful Fritz arrives suddenly: he has escaped from Klausenburg. Praise be to God's Mercy, we have all survived the war and are together and healthy again. God help us further in all good things. My demobilization has not yet arrived. [End of diary.]

Author's Summary

The memoirs and war diaries of Aron Tänzer are unique for a number of reasons. He describes in detail the difficulties encountered even when a rabbi wished to volunteer for services as a chaplain, and also the financial obstacles put in his way by initial lack of response from the Prussian Ministry of War. His sense of patriotism, as a Württemberger and a German, is deeply felt despite the fact that he was born and brought up in a part of the Austro-Hungarian Empire.

Once his post is approved, he moves with resolution and vigour. He brooks no obstacles with the cumbersome military apparatus, arrives in Poland, and immediately sets about creating work for himself: almost every spare moment is filled with pastoral activity: visiting sick and wounded, organizing parcels for soldiers at the Front, and arranging services. In everything that he does, he is guided by the strictest letter of the law: this includes care for prisoners of war and the Jewish civilian population, who suffered terribly between the Russian and Austro-German armies. Wherever he sees the need, soup kitchens spring up for the starving (see Plate 10), and funds are found to support them.

Rabbi Tänzer's honesty and integrity are absolute: large amounts of money pass through his hands, and every pfennig is noted and accounted for. When he feels that he has been paid for time not spent in the military, he says so. His area of responsibility involves conditions that are often primitive, transportation that is not always efficient or comfortable, quarters whose cleanliness often leaves a great deal to be desired and weather of the most extreme kind without regular heating in winter. Infectious diseases of all kinds are rife and no antibacterials are available to treat them. Given his age when he enters the army (43) and his energetic travelling to and fro, it is surprising that he remains in relatively good health for as long as he does. But eventually, he becomes ill – at the very least with pre-1918 influenza and pneumonia, bacterial tonsillitis, food-poisoning, bacterial dysentery, and ultimately with influenza A in 1918. He travels fearlessly, with apparently little regard for his own health (although he does comment on bad food and drink, primitive living conditions and uncomfortable transportation). Throughout the war, he makes a point of treating all soldiers the same, irrespective of their faith. His courage is beyond question. Throughout his diaries there are only a few mentions of anti-Semitism (pp. 203–4), and nothing of the Jewish Census of 11 October 1916.

His regard and respect for his superiors is evident and sometimes exaggerated, given the fact that not all titled officers in the German army were educated or intelligent. His descriptions of the surroundings in which he finds himself are detailed, as is his grasp of the historical events which surround him. There is also no lack of humour, as when he speaks Hungarian in front of a group of astonished Prussian soldiers. Criticism of his own people when they take financial advantage of his good will is biting, and the word *Schnorrer* is much in evidence.

Rabbi Tänzer has great regard for the Jews of Russia (except for those in Kiev, who he criticizes mercilessly), but very little for the Jews (and other inhabitants) of Poland, regarding them as generally beneath him. His description of Cantor Gershon Sirota, perhaps the greatest cantor in recorded history, as *ausgesungen* [sung out] must be seen in this light. His description of the Jews of Kiev is biting and he is not blind to the faults of his own people when they are in evidence. His encounter with a group of Chassidim and their spiritual leader is, even in its brief diary form, very moving.

He is a stickler for protocol and shows little sympathy for Rabbi Sänger when he does not fully comply with army rules regarding civilians, and is much put out (see Chapter 10) when Rabbi Salzberger sends his memorandum directly to the Prussian War Ministry without consulting him beforehand.

No description of the initial February Russian Revolution is given; by contrast, graphic notes describing the chaos following the Bolshevik revolution and after the Treaty of Brest-Litovsk are given, as are the confusing events of the German invasion of Ukraine during 1918. Also, no report is made on the entry of the United States into the war in 1917: perhaps the Eastern Front was too far away to take notice. During the last part of 1918, not surprisingly, his health breaks down and he is invalided home. It is perhaps remarkable that, given where and when he carried out his pastoral duties for four years, he survived at all, testament to his physical and spiritual resilience and his ironclad sense of duty.

NOTES

1. A. Tänzer, 'Kriegserinnerungen', Leo Baeck Institute, New York, ME 640. The first two chapters are published in R. Vogel, *Ein Stück von uns. Deutsche Juden in deutschen Armeen 1813–1976: eine Dokumentation* (Mainz: von Hase & Koehler Verlag, 1977), pp.108–20. The exact date of manuscript preparation is unknown.
2. Tänzer, 'Kriegserinnerungen', pp.1–7.
3. The *Burgfrieden* (party truce) declared by the Kaiser on 4 August 1914, proclaiming that he knew only Germans, irrespective of faith or party.
4. *Tisha Be'Av* was observed on 2 August, beginning at sundown on 1 August, because of the intervening Sabbath.
5. Tänzer, 'Kriegserinnerungen', pp.8–16.
6. The River Bug is a left tributary of the Narew River flowing from central Ukraine to the west, passing along the Ukraine-Polish and Polish-Belarusian border and into Poland. At the start of the First World War it formed part of the border between Russian-occupied Poland and Russia.
7. German Lutherans who refused to join the Prussian Union of churches in the 1830s and 1840s. The legacy of Old Lutherans survives in the Independent Evangelical Lutheran Church in modern Germany.
8. His second wife Bertha. His first wife Rose had died in 1912.
9. A region that presently straddles the border between Poland and Ukraine but which during the First World War was in the main ruled by Austro-Hungary.
10. Killed cholera and typhoid vaccines were both available by 1914. The German word '*Typhus*' used in the text must be translated as typhoid, as no typhus vaccine was yet available.
11. Auschwitz (German).
12. The 1915 Gorlice–Tarnów Offensive (mid-May–October) resulted in the total collapse of the Russian lines and their retreat far into Russia.
13. Tänzer, 'Kriegserinnerungen', pp.16–28 (pages not all in order in original manuscript).
14. Cholera and other gastrointestinal infections such as typhoid fever and dysentery are spread when an unsafe and infected sewage disposal system contaminates the water supply.
15. Even Jews with foreign passports were usually denied entry into Russia beyond the Pale of Settlement.
16. Horses are not susceptible to human cholera and could safely drink the water.
17. There were no Jewish chaplains in the Tsarist army (Y. Petrovsky-Shtern, personal communication).
18. Yiddish has a German base but with many Hebrew words and others borrowed from the specific area in which the Jews lived. Its pronunciation varies with location. By 1914 Yiddish had developed a rich literature of its own.
19. No details given. The primary treatment of cholera is prompt replacement with fluid and electrolytes.
20. In October 1915, Austro-Hungarian and German forces (the latter led by Field Marshall August von Mackensen: 1849–1945), with the Bulgarian army, attacked Serbia and forced the Serbian army and large numbers of civilians to flee across the Albanian mountains to the coast, where they were evacuated, mainly to Corfu and to Salonika.
21. Rabbi Tänzer was born in Hungarian-speaking Preßburg (modern-day Bratislava, capital of the Slovak Republic), which was at the time part of the Austro-Hungarian Empire.
22. Tänzer, 'Kriegserinnerungen', pp.28–30.
23. Tänzer, 'Kriegserinnerungen', pp.31–47.
24. Probably *Volga Deutsche* (ethnic Germans other than Jews invited by Catherine the Great in 1762–63 to settle around the Volga Basin).
25. Originally this was the largest nineteenth-century fortress of the Russian Empire. It is located at the confluence of the Mukhavets and Bug rivers. The final works were carried out in 1914, culminating in a fortified area 30 km in circumference.

26. Eastern European/Russian horse and cart capable of operating even in the worst road conditions.
27. Tänzer, 'Kriegserinnerungen', p.47 to end of typescript.
28. Russian railways had a wider gauge than German and Austro-Hungarian railways.
29. This had to be more serious than a cold, probably incompletely healed or viral pneumonia (possible influenza). Rabbi Tänzer's constant travel and exposure to bacterial and viral droplet infection from large numbers of soldiers and civilians in various locations made respiratory infections (both viral and bacterial) inevitable.
30. In August 1915 the German army 'liberated' Warsaw from Russian occupation.
31. The Great Synagogue at 4 Tlomackie Street was the most important synagogue in Warsaw designed for 2,400 seats, 1,800 on the ground floor.
32. Samuel Abraham Poznański (1864–1921), a Polish Reform rabbi and scholar; rabbi and preacher at the Great Synagogue in Warsaw.
33. Rabbi Tänzer seems to have had little sympathy with the Polish language or Polish nationalism.
34. The typescript ends here. All further entries are from Dr Tänzer's hand-written 'Kriegstagebuch' (digitized at www.cjh.org, under *Arnold Tänzer, Kriegs-Tagebuch*'), which differs from the typescript in having apparently been written on the spot and not as memoirs at a later time.
35. Rabbi Tänzer's scrupulous honesty in financial matters is evidenced throughout his memoirs and diary.
36. Rabbi Tänzer had previously founded the Göppingen public library.
37. Jewish civilians on the Eastern Front suffered from both opposing armies. Towns were often occupied and relinquished more than once. The exact number of killed and dispossessed Jews in Eastern Front areas is not known.
38. The Yiddish word '*Schnorrer*' is untranslatable. A *Schnorrer* does not steal large amounts, but cadges (free meals, small amounts of money). *Schnorrers* were common in Jewish communities all over Eastern Europe.
39. The prevalent German-Jewish attitude at the time: Russian Jews were respected, Polish Jews generally not, and Jews from Galicia were at the bottom of the socio-economic ladder.
40. *Klezmer* (Hebrew '*Klei zemer*', 'musical instruments'): A musical tradition of Ashkenazi Jews of Eastern Europe. Played by professional musicians called *klezmorim*, the genre originally consisted largely of dance tunes and instrumental display pieces for weddings and other celebrations but was also taken up by choirs.
41. Probably to partially deliver the Brest-Litovsk liturgical objects.
42. 27 January.
43. Chaplains' conferences were held in different cities throughout the war. Minutes from one such meeting are provided in chapter 10.
44. Elijah the son of Shlomo Zalman Kremer, the *Gaon* (saintly genius) of Vilna (1720–97), a Talmudist, halachist, kabbalist, and foremost leader of non-Chassidic Jewry of the past few centuries.
45. Between droplet-acquired respiratory tract infections, infections due to contaminated food and water, and infections carried by various insect vectors, there is an entire menu of infectious disease(s) that could have been involved.
46. A huge amount of money at the time, testament to Rabbi Tänzer's honesty.
47. The first remarks about overt anti-Semitism in Rabbi Tänzer's memoirs and diaries.
48. The so-called Brusilov offensive (named after the Russian commanding general Alexei Brusilov, 1853–1926) occurred between 4 June and late September 1916 and was Russia's greatest feat of arms of the First World War, forcing Germany to halt its attack on Verdun and the Somme, and transfer considerable forces to the East. It broke the back of the Austro-Hungarian Army which suffered over 750,000 casualties (includes c. 380,000 prisoners) and was never again able to mount a successful attack on its own.

49. Paul was Rabbi Tänzer's son from his first marriage.
50. Two sons from his first marriage (Fritz and Paul) served on the Eastern Front (see Plate 11).
51. A Jewish chaplain serving in the Balkans (see Chapter 9, pp.282–3).
52. Rabbi Tänzer did in fact take care of the civilian population, but only in addition to his military duties and after careful official approval had been obtained in every case; apparently Rabbi Sänger did not follow the letter of the law, even if he achieved the same goal. A typical example of German *Gehorsamheit* [obedience].
53. A sarcastic entry to the effect that an unidentified chaplain from another area is not prepared to come and assist. A *Zaddik* is a righteous man in Chassidic context.
54. It seems strange that Rabbi Tänzer would travel approximately 125 km from Brest-Litovsk to Kowel on Yom Kippur eve. However, even according to strict Orthodoxy, if he entered a scheduled train and no money changed hands, this would have been considered acceptable for a chaplain in war-time.
55. *Sukkot*.
56. Another reference to the toll that army service was taking on his health.
57. As with his previous mention of eggs, the effects of the British blockade on the food supply is obvious.
58. Emperor Franz Joseph died on 21 November 1916.
59. There is no evidence that this was applied to Jewish chaplains.
60. Probably for the Kaiser's upcoming birthday.
61. Probably group A streptococcal throat infection – spread by droplet infection – which, in the pre-antibiotic era, could be fatal if the infection spread.
62. Another effect of the blockade was to raise prices in cities such as Warsaw that had not been greatly affected by the war. Severe inflation followed and profiteering flourished.
63. The first time that morale is brought up together with relative scarcity of rations for festivals. From now on the issue of rations will gain paramount importance.
64. No details given.
65. Kerensky initiative (17 June 1917): the last Russian offensive of the war. Rabbi Tänzer does not mention the February revolution, subsequent abdication of Nicholas II on 15 March (Gregorian calendar), 2 March (Julian calendar) and formation of a Provisional Government headed by Alexander Kerensky (1881–1970).
66. The German Jewish community was splintered, both with regard to religion and with regard to attitudes towards Zionism.
67. Text reads Roczyn, but geography is incorrect.
68. This is the first report of poor participation at services. Troop morale had become low by this stage of the war.
69. Hermann Struck (1876–1944), a noted German-Jewish artist known for his etchings, including those of German soldiers on the Eastern Front and Jewish civilians in Eastern Europe. In 1917 he became the referent for Jewish affairs at the German Eastern Front High Command.
70. The Provisional Government, led by Kerensky (see Note 65) tried to prosecute the war but Bolsheviks and other socialist factions campaigned for abandonment of the war effort. In the October Revolution (November new style), the Bolshevik party, led by Vladimir Ilyich Lenin (1870–1924), and the workers' Soviets overthrew the Provisional Government. The Bolsheviks appointed themselves leaders of various government ministries, seized control of the countryside, and immediately sued for peace.
71. Rabbi Tänzer is upset that Rabbi Salzberger had sent his memorandum directly to the Prussian War Ministry without his permission. This forms the topic of an entire afternoon's discussion during a chaplain conference in Riga (see Chapter 10, pp.302–3).
72. Before the antibiotic era, skin and venereal diseases were both treated by dermatologists.
73. Locations of Turysk and Tuleczow could not be ascertained. All the towns are given to provide an idea of Rabbi Tänzer's travel schedule.

74. Gers(h)on Sirot(t)a (1874–1943), one of the leading cantors in Europe during the 'golden cantorial age'. In 1917 Sirota was at the height of his powers, so Rabbi Tänzer's remark about his voice seems to be coloured by feelings other than music.
75. This may refer to Rabbi Salzberger because of the affair with the memorandum (see Note 71).
76. Leon Trotsky (1879–1940), Russian Marxist revolutionary, founder and first leader of the Soviet Army; also the chief Russian negotiator at the Treaty of Brest-Litovsk.
77. Germany concluded a separate peace with Ukraine on 9 February 1918. To clear the Bolsheviks out, the Germans and Austrians dispatched an expeditionary force into Ukraine. Ukraine was to became a critical granary for the Central Powers, who faced severe food shortages due to the Allied blockade. They invaded Ukraine, passing up through the Baltic states and coming within 150 kilometres of Petrograd.
78. Theodor Herzl (1860–1904), Austro-Hungarian journalist and founder of modern Zionism.
79. The main synagogue in Kiev, built in 1897–98, still in use today.
80. The Central Powers entered Kiev on 1 March, and by May 1918 had occupied Ukraine to a line roughly Mogilev-East of Kharkov-Rostov, including the Crimea and its Black Sea ports.
81. The Michael Offensive, started on 21 March 1918, Germany's last major offensive in the West. After initial successes it petered out several weeks later.
82. The amounts of money available have decreased precipitously. At that stage of the war, 18 marks bought very little.
83. The wound was almost certainly infected. Pyramidone is an analgesic and antipyretic which treated the symptoms, but not the cause, of the fever.
84. All opiates have, as side-effect, inhibition of movement of tubular organs including the colon. The symptoms were thus treated, not the cause.
85. Bacterial dysentery, caused by members of the genus *Shigella*. A sign that food and drink were contaminated with infected sewage.
86. Rabbi Tänzer's area of responsibility during 1918 stretched far into Ukraine.
87. Site in the Turkish Dardanelles of the disastrous Allied campaign of 1916 to capture Constantinople (Istanbul).
88. Then, as now, the planting of trees in the Holy Land was traditional.
89. At war's end, the Central Powers were subsisting mainly on turnips and dried barley. Inclusion of this sentence, as well as its underlining in the original diary, underscores the situation.
90. The Great Choral Kharkov Synagogue in Pushkinskaya, still the largest synagogue in Ukraine.
91. Rabbi Shneur Zalman (1745–1812) was the second successor of the *Baal Shem Tov*, founder of Chassidism (see glossary). Schneer Sohn = the son of Schneer (or Schneur).
92. Almost certainly the 'Spanish' influenza A strain that caused the 1918 influenza outbreak. Rabbi Tänzer was lucky to recover from this as it had a very high mortality rate.
93. The general armistice of 11 November 1918.
94. Germany at that stage was near starvation.

CHAPTER SEVEN

Sabbathgedanken (Sabbath Thoughts)

A collection of 'Sabbath thoughts' was published in 1918 by several Jewish chaplains (see Appendix A), mostly from the Western Front.[1] Their value lies not only in their content but also in the varied voices and points of view expressed by different personalities. Translations of some follow:

Emunah by Emil Levy [See Plate 1][2]

Unless your faith is firm you shall not be firm. (Isaiah 7: 9)

You know, dear comrade, the Jewish word *emunah*, which is roughly translated as *Glaube* [faith]. But this is not a satisfactory translation. In Judaism we have no blind forced religion against which reason rebels. *Emunah* is much more than mere faith; it is a stirring call to everything good and noble in the human heart; to unswerving labour for the future, indestructible confidence in Providence; holding firm and perseverance despite all trials, even when no miracle occurs, even when we cannot be certain of success and fulfilment. That is the *emunah* which our religion demands of us. In this context we can say: Without *emunah* there is no future for the German nation; without *emunah* there is no progress for Israel, without *emunah* there is no happiness or individual peace.[3]

The true significance and the decisive role of *emunah* in this World War cannot be described. It belongs to the imponderables: things that cannot be weighed and measured but are nevertheless crucial when things are weighed in the balance. For example: When the riflemen from the Tirol[4] descended into the valleys at the start of the war, they sang their departure songs so movingly that tears streamed down the faces of those who heard them, and they rejoiced: 'Nothing can happen to us, because the Germans are joining us in battle!' That was no logical conclusion, but an enrapturing sentiment of *emunah*, carried straight from the soul; boundless confidence in the allegiance and military power of the German nation. And whenever we join in the singing of the powerful melody 'We step forward to pray before

God, the Righteous',[5] we feel ourselves permeated with holy *emunah*. It is not the heavy mortars, not the numberless machine guns, not the steel-armoured ocean monsters that are decisive in a war. The nation which has faith in its own mission of *Kultur* and which possesses the greatest capability of sacrifice will be victorious in this terrible fight. The nation which is the most honestly and lastingly permeated with the righteousness of its cause, will win. This war has already confirmed the downfall of the materialistic world view: belief that 1 x 1 rules over moral world order lies in ruins, and the old Jewish saying shines in eternal clarity: 'Not by might nor by power, but by My spirit, says the Lord of Hosts' (Zechariah 4: 6).

We have experienced this in full measure in our own Jewish history. It is given special meaning by a feeling of *emunah*. The song of victory which our forefathers sang after the destruction of the Egyptians in the Red Sea[6] bears the title *Vaya'aminu* [and they believed/had faith]. In this world-historical moment,[7] they ceased to doubt and ponder, and were permeated by the knowledge that Moses, God's messenger, would lead them to the Promised Land despite the mundane logic of thousands of objections. Learned men toil in vain to find the solution of the riddle: why did the Jewish race not disintegrate centuries ago because of the terrible catastrophes that befell it? I say: 'What cannot be seen by logic of reason can be felt by a simple child-like soul.' *Emunah* was the talisman of our forefathers, their indestructible faith in God and the living will for their own immortality.

Emunah also escorts our exiled Jewish brothers in the East in all the sites of their misery, and drapes even beggars in its kingly robe of heavenly blue and starry glow. They do not abandon their *emunah* and will therefore also not be abandoned. All our practical efforts to lift Jewry up by charity and social welfare, colonization and organization would be in vain if we did not carry within ourselves the joyful feeling of *emunah*, and the fact that Israel in its smallness and weakness is nevertheless an eternal people, comparable to Germany in its greatness and power.

'Who is like the Lord our God, the One who sits enthroned on high; who looks down onto the heavens and the earth? He raises the poor from the dust and lifts the needy from the ash heap.'[8] Also in our personal and individual existences, we must not think that God has abandoned us. We are experiencing a vast drama. Men fall in their thousands and hundreds of thousands, towns and cities go up in flames. We may ask: What is the value of individual human souls in the face of such a mass catastrophe? Is it not presumptuous to believe in a personal dispensation of destiny and to want to attach our transient existence to the throne of the Almighty? We are instructed by Israel's sages that, through the feeling of *emunah*, we may confidently allow ourselves to be carried up to God's throne. Because see, in what a weak, wooden tabernacle He reveals Himself – and He nevertheless remains the Eternal God, Whose glory fills the heavens and the heavens' heavens. It would be no honour but rather a diminution of His omnipotence were we to want to loosen our individual destinies from the work of His hands. We are not soulless dust particles and machine parts without a will of their own; in each human being slumbers a spark of God, which can by a feeling of *emunah* be ignited to become God's flame.

And so I wish for you all that you too will be able to cry out with the Psalmist: 'I trusted in God when I said: I am greatly afflicted':[9] even if I have often felt weak and miserable, my soul has never been sunk into squalor because *emunah* holds me upright. Each individual has his own trouble during this time of war, but only he who has no *emunah* can despair. We do not hang our heads in misery but rather, like our patriarch Abraham, see the stars of hope shining into the night of our times. We have faith that God will lead humanity from darkness into light, and that our Fatherland is too healthy in body and spirit to be defeated in this fateful hour. We are confident that the Almighty will not allow Israel to perish. And with the fervour of the Psalmist we raise the chalice: 'When health and happiness blossom I will praise the name of God, but I will invoke the name of God also when need and worry strike me.' So may the harp of *emunah* sing and sound in us also in the darkness of these days: then the darkness will be transformed into the light of Sabbath morning, announcing God's merciful love. '*Lehagid baboker chasdecha ve'emunat'cha baleilot.*'[10]

The Procession of Worshippers by Georg Wilde [See Plates 1, 3 and 4][11]

Psalms 113–118
A long time ago our forefathers in the Holy Land came from far afield to worship God. From cities and towns, houses and huts they came. In long columns they moved down roads and paths. Young and old, men and women. They sang songs together, but each sang of his individual

joy, of his pain, hopes and aspirations. Each one saw his own house behind him but they all went out towards the same Temple.

The poor man sees his lowly hut but now he is walking to the Temple. Strength from the pious songs flows into their souls. 'You raise the poor from the dust, and seat them among the princes of his people.'[12]

The rich man looks back more earnestly than the poor man. His house is great but suffering and pain course through it. He prays with chastened soul: 'I found trouble and sorrow. Lord, deliver my soul.'[13]

The old man walks slowly; thanks fills his heart that he can still walk, because the old cling more to life than do the young. With tremulous voice he sings: 'I will walk before the Lord in the lands of the living.[14]

Children hurry alongside the procession, their love of life makes them run twice as far as the adults. They think neither of past nor of future; they merely hail the sun like birds, like plants. 'From the rising of the sun to the place where it sets let us praise the Creator.'[15] Their parents, who stride robustly, see their homes again and pray: 'Lord, bless the children.'

A young woman walks quietly beside the others; she sees an empty house, a small grave in front of it. But the Temple shines from afar as a hope for the future. 'He settles the childless woman in her home, as a happy mother of children.'[16]

So each one prayed for their individual home and then all prayed for their common home; for their country, for its people. They sang of heroic doings: 'O Israel, trust in the Lord: He is your shield and your protection.'[17]

Each one carried their own individual cares to the Temple and placed them down onto holy ground so that hope, power, and peace could grow out of them.

So did our forefathers once proceed from home to Temple, so they prayed on days of the New Moon, on the Pilgrim Festivals.

And here in the field?

We have become pilgrims again. We go from cities and towns, huts and trenches, to religious services. We go alone or together. What leads men to services out here? No magnificent Temple on soaring mountain awaits, simply the room and the service themselves. Men do not come from their homes, but from dugouts, trenches, or billets. No father, mother, wife nor child walks beside them. But precisely because of this, many people come. When they come to services they are seeking their home; accompanied by father and mother walking invisibly by their side. The room becomes a living room in which we sat with father and mother; now the old prayers awaken the senses: we pray with them.

One man wants to experience a sacred hour with his wife and children. He sees in the services here a table covered in white, candles and wine; he sees the Sabbath, a festival, a solemn hour at home. He is together with wife and children, wherever we stand. In church or forest, in room or hall, he sees only his home. The service tunes hearts, so that they beat together over distances of hundreds of miles, and they give each other news.

The war has brought us out of old and accustomed circles to a new environment. Many come to services, in order to find there a piece of home.

Another man seeks a grave, so that he can pray there. The grave is at home, or somewhere in the field. When he recites *Kaddish* here, he stands at the grave and sees the house which has become empty.

The father prays: 'Bless the little ones' and sees the children besides him. The son prays: 'Make father and mother happy again' and sees the shadow of his fallen brother.

Another man looks for his synagogue at home. At home he always said, 'I can go at another time'. Now he knows that death can intervene tomorrow. Therefore he comes, often travelling for many hours, like no-one does at home, and finds his home here in the House of God.

Each man sees his particular home and all men pray for their communal home, for the Fatherland. It should be like a Temple for the future, towering in majesty and beauty, in which all of its sons can live and work in peace.

We only see images: our house, future home temple in the distance. Services in the field resemble pious altars for the pilgrim on his long road. Our holy images are our homes, which we see in them. There we pray: 'God has heard me.' And then we walk on through war. The temple of home shines on a high mountain. There we will one day bring offerings of thanks, we pilgrims from the field of battle!

Untitled by Arthur Levy [See Plate 2][18]

> Unless the Lord builds the house, the builders have toiled in vain.[19]

This is a well-recognized quotation from the Psalms and its meaning is clear and simple. In the home that is a human being, there is more than just four walls and a roof; life and happiness are built upon things other than tangible realities. It is the spirit of things that rules; the way we lead our lives, joy in an ideal, divinely ordained morality lends correct meaning to our existence.

We only need to think of our own parents' house. What gives this its enduring, shining beauty with which its memory is transfigured, the eternal value and holy meaning to which we look up in loving reverence? Not the transient bounty of our destiny, not because of 'the cedars of our home's beams and the cypresses of its tables', but rather because a higher and more glorious life filled it, our father's work and our mother's deeds; because the Lord's spirit prevailed in it and consecrated the house in holiness. This pious, quiet sense of justice, love and faithfulness, dedication to work and duty, all the living expressions of devout striving that builds the house with God and lets His will prevail everywhere – these all unite to give our memory an image whose colours do not fade, which accompanies us throughout our lives as the ideal of nobility and of happiness.

And when we lift our gaze beyond the limits of our own being and look into the lives of nations over in the East, into the far country where God's Providence has allowed us to penetrate victoriously, we see an immense building, a powerful framework of this Eastern empire, and no nation's house is able to match it in the scope of its possibilities. As if on gigantic stone blocks, it is built upon the elemental power of a multitudinous people: in the distant borders of its land, its chambers extend almost to eternity, and the richness of its soil holds a wealth of possibilities. This empire is a gigantic building, but it is not solid because God did not build it. The spirit of disorder, disintegration, lawlessness and immorality gnaws like a burrowing worm at the building's woodwork and lays the spirit of perdition and decay over all improvement. This is an unmistakable sign that in this country the builders have toiled in vain, because the Eternal has not built the house.

Our actions out here are also an act of building and construction, and as paradoxical as it sounds, with our own hands which tear down, with our weapons which destroy, we labour in a work of constructive creation. Like once long ago for Jeremiah: 'See, today I appoint you over nations and kingdoms to uproot and tear down, to destroy and overthrow, to build and to plant.'[20] We build and plant our own selves, prepare the ground of our souls, deepen our character and forge our world view. The days and their experiences pass by none of us who serve here without leaving traces; their signs burrow deep into our heart and their events cause our souls to vibrate, like trees when storm winds sweep through the forests.

Every day we practise obedience and fulfilment of our duty, and give our best in service of the big picture. Never has more been demanded of us, never have we achieved more weighty things. As our strength has increased, as our will has grown, our competence has become greater, richer, deeper. We have experienced how strong we are, what we are capable of doing when we have to, when duty commands will. We have been forced to frugality and simplicity, we do without so much that makes life beautiful and enjoyable. How beneficial this is for us and how useful for our world view! We return to the primeval dimensions of things, learn to appreciate them again and rejoice in simple things. Our world gains a new and natural content, and like we did once as children we think again that everything is a gift from God, a bounty for which we must thank our Creator. And the whole solemn spirit of the time which has descended gloomily over our souls makes us forget the vanities in which our souls were once prone to lose themselves; all pettinesses and superficialities disappear, shrink into insubstantiality in the face of the Great Question for which men fight and die.

There are many building blocks that we can amass from events of our times, from which we fashion our world view and the structure of our character. And yet, if the Eternal doesn't build the house, the builders have toiled in vain. Days pass, and new times bring new experiences. One day inner compulsion will break away, and duty's bonds fall. The glow which purifies our souls will die and the hammer which forges it daily will rest. And then it can very easily happen that the soul becomes soft and dull so that scum adulterates it. The noble values that we have created for ourselves during the constraints of this time, all that we have built, can fall apart in the freedom of the coming days and become rubble exactly where, before, the most auspicious building had been erected. Therefore we must found the building on Eternity, on God. He is now and forever, His will keeps duty's consciousness constantly alive in us. In His great countenance we always find the measure of things; when we believe in Him humility and modesty send forth their tendrils; His proximity protects us from wantonness and superficiality and ennobles our awareness of life through joyful seriousness. Therefore when we build our house with God, we have not toiled in vain.

A palace that should have become the pride of humanity and the refuge of cultures may be seen in The Hague.[21] It was named the Peace Palace and was built with great love and erected with devotion. And yet – as shown by this terrible war – its builders toiled in vain. Because God did not build the house! Because truth and honesty, the free desire to do good, and national rectitude did not cause nations to build it, but instead hidden motives of selfish politics and fear of one another. Because what in reality was hypocrisy and lies was claimed to be a virtuous and godly enterprise. So humanity toiled in vain in the construction of the Peace Palace, its actions were fruitless and will remain fruitless while it is built without God. So long as humanity does not bring these building blocks to the task, the building of the Palace will not succeed, and world peace will remain an unfulfilled dream. It is wrong and presumptuous to complain to God about the terrible events of our time and to doubt His eternal righteousness. Humanity bears the blame and the rebuke should really apply to us: we are the ones who with wrong ideas and wicked hands have lit the fire that is now horribly destroying the building of our hopes.

An old Midrash teaches us a beautiful proverb: Jerusalem, so it says, is not destroyed, the Temple is not burned down. The beams, stones and carvings lie stowed away safely in a protected place; and when the time has come, the Lord God will unite everything in an eternal victorious building.

The Temple of Peace has not been destroyed, the beams, stones and carvings lie stowed away safely in a protected place. Each of us carries a piece of them in our innermost being and every pious reverently disposed heart is a building block for the noble structure. And when the time has come, the Lord God will let us collect these stones so that we can erect, out of reformed feelings and a newly born understanding of humanity, a Temple of Peace for all humanity. All the world's storms will break against the walls of this new building, from which the light of truth and enlightenment emanates for all nations, and it will be said of it for all eternity: 'The Eternal has built this house, therefore the builders have not toiled in vain.'

Be Strong by Leopold Rosenak [See Plates 2, 13 and 14][22]

Each of the Five Books of Moses is completed during our services with a threefold cry of 'Be strong, be strong, and let us become strong together.'[23] Strength in faith in God, strength in confidence in our own strength, strength in our faithfulness to each other.

I
We have experienced strength through faith since the start of the war. And no lesser person than our Kaiser has gone before us as a glowing example in each phase of the war. Every call to his people resounds with faith in God, each word and each action is carried by and pervaded with living faith. Hail to the King, whom one can so praise! Happy the people who can call him their own. When war was declared, I was at sea: the impression of the Kaiser's closing words will remain unforgettable to me: 'Now go to the churches and pray to God.' We stood moved to our innermost core and dumbly shook each others' hands. We felt deeply connected with the millions of people praying in the Homeland, and knew in that moment that we would be victorious. We felt like that pious rabbi, who was reported to have said: 'Whenever prayer comes easily to my lips, I know that it has been accepted.'[24]

Great events release unsuspected forces. Religion, too, proves itself to be a strong impetus to action when we, as now, experience God with deep emotion. The soldier in the field who willingly bears denials and deprivations, families at home who give up their hopeful sons as sacrifices to the Fatherland: all these have found within themselves the holiest power to selflessly conquer suffering. We draw this great and holy power from the living source of eternal faith which, consciously or unconsciously, was in us earlier as a spark, but now is kindled into a bright blaze which fills our whole soul. We have found the inner willingness of our souls that we lacked earlier. God has stepped into our lives as a great, overpowering Reality: He fills our whole lives and we let ourselves be fulfilled. As the thirsty calyx opens itself to refreshing dewdrops, so do all men open the hidden depths of their souls: and thus, from innermost desolation, all will come to powerful fullness of life and be strengthened in their faith in God.

II
'I have set the LORD always before me. Because He is at my right hand, I will not fear.'[25] That is the second call. The trust in the eternal power of the soul. It is not the power nor the proficiency of weapons alone, but rather the power of a steady religious spirit that leads to

ultimate victory. 'When you go to war against your enemies and see an army greater than yours, do not be afraid of them, because the Lord your God is with you.'[26] Jewish soldiers were exhorted in this way before they marched into battle. And just before the battle the priest said: 'Hear, O Israel: Today you are on the verge of battle with your enemies; war is near. Do not let your heart be faint, do not be afraid, and do not tremble or be terrified before them; for the Lord goes with you to help you.'[27] And finally the commander said: 'Is any man afraid or fainthearted? Let him go home so that his brothers will not become disheartened, as he is.'[28] He who goes to war must arm himself with courage and endurance; he must have self-confidence and may not give himself over to weakness. The world belongs to the brave and God helps the strong.

In olden times it was the prerogative of the privileged classes to commit their lives to a great event and a great idea. In Israel, by contrast, each individual soldier was reminded that he had to fill a breach, that he must develop his strength to the uttermost if he wanted to attach victory to his banner. With such soldiers the size of the two warring parties is not the decisive factor. 'The Lord did not choose you, because you were greater in number than other people; for you were the fewest of all people.'[29] Everything depends on the iron, tough will of the individual soldier. More than ever, our time demands strong men who have confidence in themselves and are conscious of their own strong character. Each man must know his duty, and that eventual victory depends on his own achievement. That applies not only to soldiers in the field, but also to those at home, in the same way as our Patriarch Abraham fulfilled God's call: 'Take your son, your only son, whom you love, and offer him up as a sacrifice to me.'[30] They have all experienced what service in war means for people on earth, and know that the sacrifices have not been in vain. No matter how many hopes and plans are buried, how many hearts are filled with anxious worry, or how many wounds you have suffered – be strong and firm! Believe in your own life and have confidence in yourself!

III

Confidence in one's own strength fosters mutual loyalty, the highest asset during war. Because how can your brother have confidence in you if you don't have confidence in yourself? What is the individual able to do, no matter how strong he is, detached from the others? On your own you are only a fraction, but in the community of others you can become an indispensable part of the Whole: 'You stand together today before the Eternal. Each of you enters into the covenant.'[31] That is the wake-up call of our great time. Do not believe that anyone can be submerged in the great multitude and be overlooked: No, he belongs to the Whole and must serve it. To the saying of our wise men: 'The best that we can learn from history is the enthusiasm that it engenders',[32] I add: 'mutual trust'. To the question of the Egyptian king about which people should leave Egypt, the answer comes: 'With our young and our old, our sons and our daughters we will go, to celebrate the Eternal.'[33] Although we yearn for peace, there should be no despair, no timidity, but always strong hope, powerful actions, rock-solid unwavering confidence in our victorious Commander-in-Chief; we should always look up proudly at our brave army! A considerable war benefit lies in this loyalty. May this most glorious blossom never fade in our victory wreath; may it bloom forever as a blessing on our Fatherland and all its inhabitants. Amen.

Untitled by Georg Salzberger [See Plates 1, 3 and 4][34]

> Am I my brother's keeper? (Genesis 4: 9)

'Where are you?,'[35] God asked the first human because he had transgressed the first commandment given to him and hidden himself from the Omniscient. 'Where is your brother?' God calls to Adam's son who has killed his brother. And in the same way that Adam, in fear of punishment, passes the blame on to Eve, saying that she led him into sin, so Cain looks to escape from his reckoning through evasion: 'I do not know. Am I my brother's keeper?' The murderer utters the words in hollow bravado, behind which the turmoil of a guilty conscience is badly concealed. Meanwhile, he tries to hide the seriousness of the deed from himself by repudiating it as laughable impertinence to suggest that he were obliged to take care of his brother, to watch over him and protect him. In fact, religion puts this 'impertinence' in all seriousness to each one of us. Because the story of Adam and Eve[36] has no other purpose but to teach us that man is responsible not only for himself as an individual, but to God for all of his brothers in mankind.

'Am I my brother's keeper?' It is a weighty question that has applied to man through the millennia. It is obviously an age-old concept that it is a sin to take one's brother's life. But we only later became conscious that, more than this, we also have positive duties towards him, and not only him. Very gradually the circle of people to whom the duty of responsibility applies has been extended: from blood relatives, through all *Volksgenossen* [fellow-Germans][37] until ultimately everyone with a human face is included. At the same time, the content of responsibility is broadened even further: It is necessary not only to refrain from harming the life, property and honour of a fellow man, but also to be his 'guardian' and protector. Social conscience is awakened. We are no longer satisfied knowing that this or that person has committed this or that felony, but we also examine why he could do it. We seek to explain the deed from general and specific political, socio-economic conditions or grievances; not to acquit the guilty from blame, but knowing that we ourselves cannot be totally acquitted in this matter. It is easier and more comfortable when an injustice occurs to turn oneself away from it with indifference or arrogant feelings of one's own innocence. 'What can I do about it?' 'I wash my hands in innocence.' But a character's moral level can be measured precisely by how far one feels responsible for the fault of one's fellow-man. The more developed the social conscience, the clearer it may be seen that the sinner has sunk to this level through poverty and need, inherited predisposition and education, acquaintances and environment, ignorance or unbelief. If the community shoulders the blame, each individual is part of the community as much as the one who has sunk low, who should have been protected by others from falling.

Humanity also has a responsibility, preached emphatically by this war which is submerging the world in a sea of blood. At the end of the day the blame for this war is shared by all warring nations, indeed by all nations on earth. This is so even if our enemies bear proximate blame for start of the war, as an inextinguishable blemish before the bar of history. But the war has changed meanings. 'Brother' no longer means just one's fellow man, but the non-enemy, and first and foremost one's fellow countryman. Killing the enemy stops being called fratricide, indeed it can become an unavoidable command. Moral justification for this lies in the fact that every soldier is forced to fight for his 'brothers', his father and mother, his wife and children, for the entire nation, for his life and preservation of his holiest possessions.

But the level of a nation's moral education can also be measured by how, even in a year of long and bloody fighting, it remains mindful that the price of war in the end should benefit his fellow-men. The fact that, unlike our enemies, we Germans have not allowed ourselves to be carried away by blind hatred and insatiable, destructive fury imbues us with high satisfaction. What our Kaiser has often said about great moral responsibility, and what our Chancellor has said about a Europe working together in a peace that grows from the seed of blood and tears: these words are spoken from the spirit of every German soldier, out of the heart of the entire German *Volk*. This strengthens us in the confidence that a holy but very hard and prudent gravity governs our sword and that victory which will ultimately be ours will help guard and protect humanity.

At a time when an entire nation demonstrates, in its most difficult hour, so high a feeling of responsibility, we Jews should not forget that our Bible is the original source of this sentiment. A Jew should not have to be told that 'Love your neighbour as yourself'[38] is an Old Testament phrase. But this phrase is properly illustrated only when applied to the poor, widow, orphan, stranger, yes even the enemy, who hungers and thirsts, as well as their animals, who all sink under the weight of the burden. 'You must not turn your back on him' is repeated in this context. These noble words are the most fitting answer to the question 'Am I my brother's keeper?' Judaism also teaches that the community carries joint guilt for the transgression of each of its members. In the solemn Confession of Sin on our holiest day of Yom Kippur, an entire alphabet of sins, some of a very grievous nature, is recited. The deep significance of this lies in the command that the community confesses itself in repentance as one. We have transgressed: where lies, theft and violence occur in our midst, we carry a share of the blame.

Our enemies have taught us what religion inculcates in this regard: They make the entire Jewish community pay for every transgression committed by individual Jews. It is no more than a hundred years since the entire community had to pay a fine for every theft – real or imagined – that a Jew may possibly have perpetrated. Today, when this measure cannot be legally applied, moral fines are still imposed upon us. Not 'Jew X has transgressed', but rather 'the Jews have done it'. We Germans have known since the beginning of the war how unjust and bitterly mortifying this generalization is, from experiences with Germany's enemies. Have they not used individual examples, which they have found in life or books, to caricature what they take to be typically German? May the hate-filled fallacy that marks the exception as the rule soon be recognized as such by the world, for both Germans and Jews!

But we Jews must for the time being reckon with the old prevailing prejudices. We know that there are good and bad people in our community, just as in any other. But more than any other community we must strive to decrease the number of exceptions to a tiny fraction. Everyone should and can help with this and always hold before his eyes: you are not standing for yourself alone. You are your brother's keeper. If you, as a Jewish soldier, exhibit lack of discipline and insubordination, your Jewish brothers will pay the price. If you lack courage and bravery, a hundred of your brothers will not be able to make good your mistake. If you are not honest and just in word and deed, you desecrate the name 'Jew'. If we wish to help implement the spirit of responsibility which our religion teaches us and make it into a victory that disarms all our foes, at home and abroad, then let us make the following words into a reality: '*Kol Yisrael arevim ze bazeh*' 'All Jews stand surety the one for the other.'[39]

Untitled by Martin Salomonski [See Plates 3, 4 and 5][40]

Dear comrade! These Sabbath thoughts should take the place of one of our field services. We see each other on a monthly basis and always hope for a happy peace and quick return home. But both of the things for which we yearn are dragging their heels. When you cannot come to services, whether because of trench duty, the long distance from your quarters, or if you have been wounded, then read this small pamphlet!

We in the field all have, apart from our duty as soldiers, a right of our own. You are willing to sacrifice your life to protect your Homeland. But you must also be able to accept the years of battle which oppress every spirit and paralyse all hopes, so that contentment will be yours, and your confidence in a redeeming transformation does not disappear. And this is not achieved when one acts like a sick man, swallows the drink of indifference, regards one's life's reckoning as completed, and remains despondent.

Dear fellow Jews! We do not carry within us so much strength – no man ever has – to make everything that is bitter sweet. If you wish to come to terms with yourself and not be at odds with your fate, your salvation must come from another place.

You need a source of strength for night hours, when sleep flees from you, painful thoughts let you see your loved ones, yet logic speaks of the terrible impossibility of really doing so. 'What will happen at home without me?' asks your steel helmet-burdened head when you are standing there ready to attack before the onslaught! I have something for you which will help you at once so that everything will become better. Please pay attention!

You have so often walked along the roads for long hours burdened by your equipment. The sun has stung you, beaten down upon you mercilessly, and all the limbs of your body have been tormented and fatigued. Then the command comes: 'We will rest in the woods!' How the sight of the greening trees has refreshed you! The branches have seemed to call out to you and all the leaves to greet you: Welcome, you poor, tired soldier! Rest here! And then, when you have had to move on, you have looked back thankfully at the giver of shade and said: 'You good, friendly forest! Now I really know what such a forest means. It doesn't stand there just so that man can strike at its wood for profit, nor to blanch its moss, nor chase away everything that lives, sings, and plays in it.'

We have come this far! Now I will introduce you to One who placed the forest in its position and did even more. He has given you life and all its joys. He has always fed you and kept you in good health. He has given death no power over you; no, He has destined you for great deeds and noble achievements. Can He be the enemy? And would you not like one day to know Him, the One, who has accompanied you from your home town and watches over you in the field? Because He is not like man, who is sometimes friendly but mostly causes affliction.

He always has time for you and always knows how to give counsel. He brings you fresh greetings from your parents and your wife every day, and tells you that your children speak to Him so full of trust before they go to sleep: that He wishes, just because of this, to do everything for you.

Why do we hesitate and not speak His name? It can only be the One: Your Creator, your Protector, your Helper, your God! He is passing over even as we speak and if you have courage and will and have things to say to Him, then say a word softly or loudly, which He can hear: '*Eilecha nasati et einai hayoshvi bashamayim*' [I lift up my eyes to You, to You who sit in Heaven] (Psalm 123: 1). But it cannot be this only. Our Holy Writings relate that Moses summed all his yearning after God with the cry: '*Har'eini na et kevodecha*' [Oh let me see Your glory] (Exodus 33: 18). And if you find or know any other words which come from your heart, call to God and desire to see Him! You will recognize Him, He will become your own, and you will not lose Him. But it depends upon your own eyes!

The mechanisms of sight are known to us as a great wonder; but we also need to be clear that seeing is also an expression of our wills and the mirror to our souls. We see how and what we wish to see. There are people who gobble and bore and rage with their eyes, and others who wink and entice and seduce. Oh, what a pity for their eyes and their souls! Both must suffer because of this. They should look around modestly and recognize: it cannot all belong to me. I must not be greedy and envious, defiant and insolent, hateful and vicious. They should realize that this is known already and helps not at all before God's Throne! The minute we actively seek evil, He covers His heavens and we rob ourselves of His love. My friend, your eyes now see completely differently! – like the eyes of your mother, your children, in which lie innocence and gentleness, faith and true love. *'Eilecha nasati et einai hayoshvi bashamayim.'*

You have, as a soldier, trodden the path of duty and taken it upon yourself to suffer for salvation of others. You have refrained from robbery and seen a friend in your wounded enemy, you have carried him and fed him. You have led your deluded eyes out of narrowness and selfishness. You can now therefore see properly. Now raise your eyes, look upwards and look towards God, so that the apparent evil of the war becomes a blessing for you. Could you have found Him at home in the midst of pleasure, luxury and decadence? Keep your eyes open and strike down all attacks that try to reach your soul through them!

But something more is required of you! In the beautiful Hebrew language '*Nasati*' means not only 'I raise', but also 'I carry'. 'To you, O God, I carry my eyes.' Now, when you feel relief because He who is enthroned on High has guided you back to innocence and love here in the field, then in return you must maintain your common bond with Him in gratitude, and conclude a pact with your God. Carry your eyes, carry your soul towards Him: learn to pray and give Him daily thanks and praise, as well as your requests!

Then you will experience salvation, and that same peace-giving reassurance will come over you that our ancestor Jacob experienced, when he beheld God for the first time in the dark field, alone and abandoned, and carried his suffering but also his prayer towards the

Almighty. Need and fear of death will then desert you like unsubstantial shadows, and your justified pleas will be granted because you will vow: 'When I return to my father's house in peace; then shall the Lord be my God.'[41] Dear brother, you no longer have to flounder between the fortune and enmity of the hour, between premature hope and measureless misery: 'Why do you say, O Jacob, and speak, O Israel: My way is hidden from the Lord, and my cause is disregarded by my God?'[42]

'Do you not know, have you not heard? The Lord is the Everlasting God, Creator of the ends of the earth. He does not faint nor grow weary, His understanding is limitless. He gives power to the faint and fresh strength to the weak. Even if young boys shall become weak and weary, and young men fall exhausted, they who wait for the Lord will renew their strength, they shall mount up on eagles' wings, they shall run and not be weary.'[43]

Dear comrade, let these comforting words enter into your heart during the Sabbath hour, so that it becomes joyful and your eyes shine! Drink from the source of salvation which flows so richly, during the roar of battle, in the wilderness of foreign lands! Breathe in the nearness of God and pray with confidence: '*Eilecha nasati et einai hayoshvi bashamayi*m.' Amen.

Untitled by Reinhold Lewin [See Plates 1, 3 and 4][44]

The fool says in his heart: there is no God. (Psalm 14: 1)

It appeared to the singer of the Psalms to be inconceivable and preposterous to say that a man disavows God. Only one who lacks all understanding is capable of doubting the workings of God or of questioning His Existence. Only a fool says in his heart: there is no God.

If the Psalmist's perception is accurate, we are surrounded during these days by senselessness and foolishness. The uplift that religion promised at the onset of war has long since ebbed. The surge has faded away and dried up in the sand. The longer the campaign lasts, the more seriously it threatens personal religion and the more strongly it jolts faith's foundations. As it adds one month to the other, the reproach sounds louder and louder: Is there a God? Why did it come to this spilling of blood? Does a will of righteousness and love, morality and mercy, prevail on High? Why does He not intervene against the foolishness which is desolating the world and tearing nations into pieces? Are the outbreak and duration of this war not like a devilish mockery of all Divinity?

No-one is so steadfast but that a doubt does not creep hauntingly into his heart. What ails him? Can the Psalmist still say that only a fool can pronounce: There is no God?

An objection lies in the way. Suppose that the campaign had proceeded differently! That it would have developed as promised: that Germany would within a few weeks have sealed its triumph, casting down its enemies everywhere, leading to a shining future of economic boom and political salvation. Would anyone, at least within our borders, have said 'Because of the war I repudiate God?' Certainly the sacrifices that sank into the earth would be mourned. The blood which had been shed would be remembered with pain. But nobody would embrace today's presumptuous complaint that there is no God, if he had been spared from loss or could see the whole of society excused.

The misgiving which connects denial of the Deity with impulses of petty selfishness does not solve the Great Question. At most, it defers and postpones it. He who is serious about his faith owes himself the answer. For him, proof of the Psalmist's assertion that only a fool can deny God's existence still remains. What does the claim mean that God, if He exists, should have stamped out the conflagration at its inception? Does it mean anything else but that God should, three years ago, have broken and violated the free will in men's hearts? Because, irrespective of what we believe today, we must concede one thing: at the time we, in a certain sense, wanted the war. We sighed with relief when mobilization broke the unbearable tension that pressed down upon Germany with oppressive closeness. When war knocked on the door we considered it as we would consider an inescapable necessity. With this limitation, we greeted the outbreak of war as a release – it was not as if we had invoked or provoked it.

What therefore should have happened in order to prevent it? The free will which glowed in us, the independent resolve that blazed up in us, would have had to be stifled and killed. And is it not the consciousness of our character that otherwise fills us with pride? That our feelings are not subjugated, that our moral decisions are freely made? Are not decisions and choices that we freely make the assets that ennoble us on earth and distinguish us from animals?

What diminishes us presses us down to the level of beasts. We would otherwise become more or less like prisoners of war, painfully limited in waking and sleeping, walking and working, and we would sink into animal-like lethargy. If we had to live like that every day, would that still be a life worth living? He who makes the Deity responsible for unleashing war therefore ascribes to Him a theft of the crown which belongs on our heads. If, for its sake, he embraces a higher power, he confirms the Psalmist's words: 'Only a fool says in his heart: there is no God.'

It is possible that some might agree with us thus far but then continue: 'Yes, we wanted war and it was a decision freely made, which entangled us in its misery. We followed the decision blindly and shortsightedly, because we did not know the horrors. Now that we have seen them face to face, we want to escape from them. Why does the Deity not have mercy upon us and tear open the bonds in which we became ensnared?' This expectation as well, examined more closely, amounts to foolishness. It requires nothing less than a formal miracle, a supernatural intervention, which descends to break through nature's divine laws.

Once upon a time we rhapsodized over the profound laws that interweave everything, and derived supreme knowledge from them. We were proud of how our investigation of the universe penetrated the eternal order. The way in which a comprehensive unity incorporated everything on earth carried us away in rapt veneration. From the noble order itself, we inferred the bringer of that order concealed therein, and from its mighty laws we inferred the higher will, whose wisdom they contain. Now we demand of Him that He contradict Himself; that, for the sake of our blindness, He repeal the age-old validity that He bestowed on His creation in the first place. If nature's foundations have faltered, they must at the same time unsettle our own foundations that are so tightly connected to them and anchored indissolubly in them. If the wells around us dry up, they would soon dry up within us too, because they draw sustenance and life from them alone. We could not work or plan for the coming day, nor lead a life of organized efforts through the years of our life. Humanity would have to sadly relinquish progress and perfection. Every foundation on which the possibility of life is constructed would falter. It boils down to nothing less than demanding of God a cessation of war with its threat and rage. Does this not confirm once more the saying of the Psalmist: 'Only a fool says in his heart: there is no God?'

One difficulty remains to be faced. Someone could ask, in answer to what we have said: 'What use to me is a religion which is enthroned on high and does not descend to earth? Why do I need a God who lets things here on earth take their course as dictated by the iron force of nature and perhaps also man's will?' He who believes that divine Providence should descend from above to recast our reality with supernatural intervention misunderstands His purpose and turns it on its head. It is in fact the exact opposite. It depends on us and it is up to us to strive towards faith here on earth, and adopt its spirit together with its commandments into our existence. We thus help its realization, and it can then change and ennoble our lives. Religion is the goal toward which we climb. Religion is our guarantee that a yet higher will prevails over the senseless occurrences here on earth. Religion is our assurance that, even if humanity's path is crooked and winding, we slowly stride towards the goal which fulfils the hope of the Prophet: 'And they shall beat their swords into ploughshares and their spears into pruning hooks; nation shall not lift up sword against nation, neither shall they learn war anymore.' (Isaiah 2: 4)

What Is The Meaning Of Prayer? by Leo Baerwald [See Plates 1, 3 and 15][45]

A Talmudic prayer (*Berachot* 29) reads as follows: 'The needs of men are many, but their understanding is short. May it be Your will, O Lord our God, to give each man what he needs for his sustenance and preservation. But, may Your will be done.'

'The needs of men are many'– They wish for what they need, and therefore they ask and they pray. *To pray means to wish*. Is that not the short answer to the question: what is the meaning of prayer? Since the awakening of the human spirit, since man has felt himself to be dependent on a Higher Being, he has come to Him with his desires and pain. Often these supplications were child-like: when humanity stood on the level of childhood, their prayers were like those of children. So we start praying like children, bringing our smallest cares into our prayers. But how many of us stop there and do not get beyond this type of prayer; how many of us think that if we just pray correctly, our prayers will be heard and that the Divinity who possesses the power of fulfilment will not disappoint those who honour Him?

Only a little contemplation is necessary for us to recognize how much such prayers harm the Majesty of Him to whom they are directed. Can one ask God to grant exactly what we request? And with what wishes and dreams have men come to Him! How unworthy, both of God and of ourselves, are some; how foolish and short-sighted are others! Have we not often experienced that what we requested did not bring us the desired blessing, and how, on the other hand, much that we ignored became most meaningful to us? We only need to have gleaned a little experience to recognize: 'Man's understanding is short.'

Yes, we do not see far! Human imperfection closes our view, and our path through life is merely a wandering in a fog out of which new and undreamed-of things confront us at every step. Therefore we should also be careful with our wishes and consider, before we pronounce them, whether fulfilment will be salutary for us. If we pray in such a way, then we have ascended to a higher level: and here we can say: *Praying means introspection.* Can our wished-for success be achieved without weakening or harming our fellow-man? Do we have the firm intention of making use of the gift of health, for which we pray with justification, in a correct way? Have we prayed for the insight which first of all empowers us to appreciate correctly other commodities, and to give them the correct value, as did King Solomon, whose prayer for wisdom includes all other men? If our prayer is self-examination, then it will also become self-improvement and in this way an ennoblement of our wishes, which otherwise are all too human.

When we have examined ourselves and our wishes, when we measure our paltry Self against the life upon whose waves we float as on a swaying boat, then we know how little is really necessary for a human life: a healthy body, a roof over our heads, a piece of bread for us and our loved ones. When concern about one of the latter appears, then we want to and must enunciate what is disturbing us: 'May it be Your will, O Lord our God, to give each man what he needs for sustenance and preservation.'[46] To declare all these life-cares before God cannot be denied us, and this must be the purpose of our prayer. *Prayer means tranquility*, and *finding strength* in that tranquility. Yes: just pray, O beleaguered human heart! Pray, O mother, at the bed of your child, for the recovery of your beloved. Pray also, you who have been hardened by life's battles: 'Inscribe us into the book of life and sustenance.'[47] Pray, when your life declines to its end, with the Psalmist's words: 'Do not cast me away when I am old, do not forsake me when my strength fails' (Psalm 71: 9). Yes, pray! Because in prayer you will find tranquillity!

Do not wait until you are overpowered and overwhelmed, until care and worry overwhelm you and press you to do unaccustomed things; do not let the cortex around your heart become so hard that a fire is needed to melt it. Open the book of Psalms and see how Israel's singer [David] prayed, so that your thoughts learn the path to tranquility. Then say your quick prayer quietly in times of stress and danger! Certainly it will not stop a bullet that is meant for you; but it will strengthen you inwardly and give you the spiritual equilibrium to lighten your heavy load.

Israel's prayer book can teach us to pray. Certainly there are also prayers in it for health, sustenance and earthly blessings; but these wishes pertaining to our life sound muted and restrained, because they are classified as praise of God, as if to tell us: Even if He does not grant what we desire, our mouth will still not stop praising Him, because He knows better than we what benefits us.

To express our cares and free ourselves from them in prayer: this is a heart's need. But when we have done this, we must follow the advice of our sages: It doesn't do men good to think about their prayer and to ruminate. That means, do not worry whether your prayer is heard, let that be God's concern because He knows better whether you will benefit by His answering it. Be happy that you have poured out your heart and have been able to liberate yourself from the pressure of your cares. In such a way we gain courage to face life and strength to act. We must of course include this strength in our prayer and profit from it; they who think their duty is done when they have expressed their good intentions remain stagnant. They may not leave God to do what behoves them, and may not escape to a higher world when there are so many tasks in this one to be done. Those who have prayed properly do not know the inner weakness that shifts responsibility from themselves to God, but have found strength to seek it within themselves. When they pray, they do not forget their duties but instead get to know them. We can judge the value of our prayers directly from whether we feel invigorated and strengthened by them, like Hannah, who prayed and raised herself from her distress to new strength and confidence.[48]

But such a confidence is a submission to God, without which at the end of the day every prayer remains only a patchwork: 'Let it be according to Your will.' With that, the highest level that the human spirit can reach in prayer is attained. *Prayer means humble submission.* If a man has first prayed: 'Fulfil my wishes', then he should reflect and say: 'Do only according to Your will, because You know better.' No longer should he say 'let my will be done, my will should become God's will', but rather 'God's will should become my will'. We wish to submit ourselves to Him: 'Take the Divinity up into your will, and it rises from its earthly throne.'[49] When we raise ourselves up to God, He allows Himself to come down to us. When prayer is thus performed it rises to the highest level: it becomes the humility that makes us small before God and allows us to experience the blissful certainty of becoming great through His mercy. We feel it to be His will that directs and leads everything; with this recognition the world and its occurrences take on another complexion. We feel that earthly life is governed by Divine laws, even if we don't understand them, and that harm may befall us but cannot conquer us. We attain the highest maturity when we submit to the Eternal will, experience religion in the highest sense, when we allow our own Self to be transfigured and ennobled in this humility and submission; when we know in the depths of our souls what the wisdom of our sages summarized in the few words: 'Whatever God does is done properly'.[50]

Chanukah and Purim by Max Wiener [See Plate 4][51]

Even those of our festivals which are preserved in memory of individual historical events show more than just what happened in ancient days; they are, all together, expression of a single and eternal Jewish destiny. It cannot be otherwise. Because there is something in our fate that must always recur[52] and as long as we exist, for so long will we be what we are. This nucleus of our Being, out of which life's destiny and natural character grow for us like branches from a tree trunk, rests in the fact that we always and everywhere have been interspersed as a special kind of minority in powerful majorities of differing character.

During the past generation, Jewish life has mostly been moved by argument over the character of our community. Religion or nation, that is the question. Certainly the emergence and strength of Jewish national thought owe their significance mainly to the prevailing world mood, which has urged the inner maturity and outward completion of a solid existence that is *völkisch* [based on national identity].[53] The World War, and the myriad political and economic entanglements which have led to it, is just the discharge of the tension caused by those ideas. But the door of Judaism was found so wide open only because there was rooted within it an unclear, but instinctively certain feeling of individual Essence and a particular Selfhood; also because this sense of self has been sustained through the most powerful currents in its surroundings, protecting it from laxity and sleep. It shines like a scarlet thread through the ribbon of our destiny from ancient days when the Jewish race met with foreign peoples, until the present time when, rebounding from the walls and boundaries that separated us from others, our feeling of individual personality has surged up, in pain or joy, mourned or welcomed, not always clear to us but always giving us self-confidence and self-assurance.

We have two festivals similar in their religious role, which, from two different sides, both demonstrate the destined character of our community in celebration of historical remembrances: Chanukah and Purim. Both festivals celebrate deliverance. The festival of the Maccabees [Chanukah] celebrates the memory of salvation from bad conscience and religious persecution; Purim celebrates the memory of a miraculous act of providence which mercifully deflected the consequences of an enemy intending to do evil and treachery away from the heads of our forefathers. Both bring to light the ever-resonant feeling that we, by the mere fact of our Jewish existence, always camp out on a threatened border, that we may never dare to enjoy the pleasure of our individual existences but are rather condemned to an eternal position of defence. And just as, seen from the borderline, there is an outside and an inside, in the same way both festivals together mould our eyes' orientation points towards the two basic directions in which the Jewish experience becomes conscious of itself.

Chanukah symbolizes the positive. From the clash between Jewish and foreign entities with the Hellenic spirit, the Jewish spirit receives clear conception of itself. Certainly during the days of the Maccabees this self-recognition is not made difficult. Because a possession was at stake, a possession that was seen as the grandest, the classic achievement of our people, that had long since been proclaimed as the soul of Jewish existence: the religion of our ancestors, faith in one God Who is not to be depicted and the purity of the moral insights arising from His revelation. This was not a blind, dumb, dull feeling of being different and being seen as different that collided with a consciousness which was just as unclear of its internal content, simply regarding itself as foreign. On the contrary, the call to battle echoed loudly and was heard clearly! Here is the One Eternal God – and here is Zeus! Here is the Greek, here the Jewish nature. The bright glow of an ideal shone through into the soul of our people. It felt most strongly that it was different, but only because what it was and what it intrinsically possessed was sensed with clarity and certainty. It was a struggle for the survival of self-assertion. But how powerfully and conscious of Self did this Self grow, as it was fiercely contested and finally saved. This nation lived its true life in mortal danger; its mind and soul was understood in the deepest sense. If we must experience not peace but war, fortunate are those who know for which objectives they bleed, and that these objectives are their own. Chanukah remains for us the eternal symbol of the hopeful battle of a minority for a holy ideal that signifies its clearly desired responsibility and its very being. And the entire glory of brave defence of one's own being, perceived as great and noble, forever crowns the figure of Judah Maccabee.

But that is merely one side of our destiny and our nature. The reverse side is called Purim. The Book of Esther tells the tale of the fickle despot Ahasverus, his haughty and vengeful vizier Haman, the beautiful and clever Esther, and her perceptive uncle Mordechai. But this book has been criticized for being the only book of the Bible which does not mention the name of God – even when not mentioning it must appear as contrived constraint. In truth: the idea for the sake of which Israel exists and remains, and wishes to remain, separate from other nations, appears to have escaped into the farthest background of the Book of Esther. It is not the usual battle for life, because this same life is dedicated to the noblest ideals. Nor is it a battle for sacred possessions because existence of these is threatened from the outside. It is rather salvation of the bare essence from evil and hate. Here enmity turns itself against the Jews not to impose a foreign faith and reasoning, nor to subject them to another spiritual world and make them happy against their will. No, the aim of this enmity is to blot them out root and branch, because they are felt to be 'different' by the population around them.

In the Maccabean battle idea stands against idea, spirit against spirit. And the swords which they have forged and wield against each other are, little as they match in the natures of their inner strength and outer violence, nevertheless both dedicated by a larger and sanctifying purpose. But their battle is waged in the field, out in the open. What arms the Jew-hater Haman against Israel is petty hate, malice and arrogance: one of the Jewish population has denied him his claim to idolatrous veneration. The weapons for his battle are slander, court intrigue and lies: and what eventually lays him low, insofar as conscious human will guides resistance to him, is clever exploitation of the weakness that the courtier shows before the despot. In the Maccabean destiny there is a heroic spiritual battle with the implements of honest battle, but in the story of Esther one encounters resistance to a planned Jewish pogrom on the slippery terrain of a corrupt court, where the ground for all artifices and cabals had been well prepared.

Despite having happened long ago, the symbols of these two festivals are eternal. Our entire history since the destruction of the Second Temple has been nothing but a history of relations between us and people of other faiths. Our consciousness of ourselves is always a feeling of limitation, never the calm and security of a firmly settled existence, but with tireless peering and listening over the barrier. The phrase repeated a thousand times must be recognized as a bitter truth: 'Our existence is a continuous battle.' We are not to blame for this: it is the destiny that we must bear because God has laid it upon us. But we are burdened with the heaviest blame, which is at the same time a burning pain, when we only see the No and not also the Yes, when we feel nothing else about ourselves except that, from the other side of the boundary, we are hated and envied, avoided and not looked on as full equals. Chanukah and Purim: both are part of Jewish tradition. The one is full of inner strength, of life and conviction, that believes clearly and truly in something for which it suffers and fights, for which it wishes to persevere and endure, for which the essence of its spirit is its God and honour, whose eternal fight for existence is only the external form of survival in this imperfect world. The other hears more clearly from its attackers than from the voice of its own nature that it really possesses life, soul, heart and existence, that occupies itself so unceasingly with its own defence and in the end forgets what it is really defending.

Our comparison may be a little exaggerated. But is it true or false that, in far too many of us, the essence of the Jewish spirit is nothing but resistance to anti-Semitism? This is necessary and must never find us tired and discouraged. But one important thing remains: that our existence must always achieve an inner focus that fends off all in our soul that is crooked and distorted, unhealthy and flippant, pretentious and downcast, dependent and immoderate. We celebrate Purim in joyful thanks that God did not leave us alone with our hardships; we celebrate Chanukah with the proud feeling that we possess a spiritual heritage for which we live and – if God wills – we are prepared to suffer.

Heroism by Georg Salzberger [See Plates 1, 3 and 4][54]

'Who is mighty? He who subdues his passions', for it is written (Proverbs 16: 32): 'He who is slow to anger is better than the hero, and he who rules his spirit than he who takes a city.'[55] What Ben Zoma preached in these sentences is nothing new: it is repeated in the proverbial wisdom of many peoples.[56] But it seems to us significant for no people more than for the Children of Israel.

All peoples who follow their history back into hoary prehistory proudly trace their pedigree, if not from gods and demigods, then from heroes and giants. Whether they fight with humans or vanquish lions and dragons, they reveal daring courage and unheard-of strength. We find nothing of that sort in Israel's history. Its Biblical patriarchs were modest shepherds. Certainly Abraham grasps the sword manfully when it is necessary to free defenceless prisoners from the enemy's hand. But neither he nor the other patriarchs seek to prove themselves by warlike deeds. And yet, is it not a powerful hero who silently strides to the top of Mount Moriah, next to him his beloved son, whom he is determined to offer to God because God wills it so?[57]

Ever and again the Bible presents the silent heroism that conquers the dragon in man's own breast and thus wins the prize of one who bravely struggles through life: the crown of a good name.[58] Thus did Jacob, surrounded by sly people (such as Laban), prevail and come to be called Israel, the contender with God.[59] Thus did Joseph learn to bend the arrogance of his youthful dreams into humility so that others bowed down before him.[60] Thus did Moses, whose tendency to hot temper[61] is broken by the loneliness of exile, become his people's leader. And even Samson, whose adventures most remind us of a heathen warrior, is depicted not merely as a man with strong muscles. His strength exists because he is dedicated to God, and it drains away when he, succumbing to a woman's seduction, reveals his divine secret.[62]

Certainly, there has been no lack of battles fought with courage and strength in Israel's history. From Joshua, past judges and kings through the priestly Maccabean family, commanders extend the victor's laurel from one to the other in bloody combat from army to army. But most significant is the fact that all the great victors – Saul, David, Solomon, Ahab – become small when set against the prophets' word of God, which always accuses them of inner, of moral, weakness. David's weakness because of Bathsheba silences him when Nathan hurls the words at him: 'You are the man!'[63] At the end of the day are not these prophets, who do not dread the king's anger or the crowd's hatred, greater heroes in the true sense of their ancestors? It was the prophetic spirit that, even surviving the demise of the Jewish state, lived on in the masses of the people. Because Jews have demonstrated an unparalleled heroism throughout the following centuries in practically all countries of the world. We do not even need to think of the martyrs, who by their thousands suffered most agonizing deaths because they refused to abandon their faith. The life of the community was often worse than death. But how few weakened and yielded to the superior power! Strength lay in the bloodlessly pale ghetto figures who withstood the most furious blind hatred and corroding contempt of an entire world.

Our forefathers drew this strength from their religion: 'Who is mighty? He who subdues his passions.' That is the spirit of the Jewish religion, that is the Jewish religion of the spirit. 'Not by might nor by violence but by my spirit says the Lord of Hosts':[64] this pulsates as a keynote through our Holy Writings. As God Himself is not quick to anger but forbearing, so does He require forbearance and compassion, love and confidence from us. God does not delight in the horse's power or man's strong limbs, but rather in one who reveres Him and awaits His mercy. 'Avoid evil and do good'[65] is the quintessence of God's commandments. This appears little, yet it is a great deal. Because it is often easier to subdue a lion than it is to control one's inner urges. This is the reason for the many positive and negative commandments, for Jewish rituals that encroach deeply into daily life. The Jew must be educated to submit himself to the Law, in order to become strong, free and master of himself.

In this war, deeds are performed on land and sea, deep under the water and high in the air, against which ancient heroism pales. Names of men who in defiance of death threw themselves at the enemy are inscribed in the book of history. But greater still is the nameless, quiet heroism of the uncounted, who for months and years and far from home, have borne with tenacious courage all the natural rigours, dangers and terrors of modern static warfare. Not to succumb to fear or despair under these conditions constitutes a strength of will bordering on the superhuman. 'The nation with the strongest nerves will be victorious' are the prophetic words of Germany's greatest military leader.[66] He certainly meant these words not only in the physical sense, but also in the spirit of our Prophets. Just as he himself, in the midst of all storms, has preserved the certitude of a controlling iron will and calm of a humble faith in God, so too the German people who stand behind him. And therefore we will win. In the end it will be the victory of spirit against violence.

'Who is mighty? He who subdues his passions.' With deep awe we see Jews verifying ancient Jewish wisdom in the heroism of our day. And if one thing reconciles us to the dreadful sacrifices which are still demanded daily, it is recognition that this heroism is not limited to war nor to the men who wage it, but also that it blossoms in better days, in man and woman, young and old. May we, if God grants our return home, delve even deeper into the history of our ancestors, and live out our religion more actively. Then we will feel their obligations not as fetters, but as 'bonds of love', that lead us to the heroism of Israel (Jacob), he who contended with God.

NOTES

1. Feldrabbiner des Westheeres (eds), *Sabbathgedanken für jüdische Soldaten* (Leipzig: Verlag von M.W. Kaufmann, 1918), pp.1–48.
2. Feldrabbiner des Westheeres (eds), *Sabbathgedanken*, pp.6–9.
3. The Hebrew word *emunah* is derived from the same root as *leha'amin* (to believe), from which is derived *Amen*, the Judaeo-Christian 'I believe'.
4. A mountainous region in western Austria.
5. *Wir treten zum Beten/vor Gott den Gerechten (Herren)*. The German translation of this prayer by Adrianus Valerius (c.1575–1625) became a potent symbol of the Throne- and Altar-alliance of German civil religion until 1918.
6. Exodus 14: 31.
7. According to Georg Wilhelm Friedrich Hegel (1770–1831), a creator of German idealism.
8. Psalm 113: 5–7.
9. Psalm 116: 10.
10. 'To declare Your righteousness in the morning and Your faithfulness every night': Psalm 92: 2.
11. Feldrabbiner des Westheeres (eds), *Sabbathgedanken*, pp.9–12.
12. Psalm 113: 7–8.
13. Psalm 116: 3–4.
14. Psalm 116: 9.
15. Psalm 113: 3.
16. Psalm 113: 9.
17. Psalm 115: 9.
18. Feldrabbiner des Westheeres (eds), *Sabbathgedanken*, pp.16–20. Arthur Levy is the only Eastern Front chaplain included in this sermon anthology.
19. Psalm 127: 1.
20. Jeremiah 1: 10.
21. The Peace Palace, inaugurated on 28 August 1913. Site during the First World War of the Permanent Court of Arbitration and the Peace Palace Library of International Law.
22. Feldrabbiner des Westheeres (eds), *Sabbathgedanken*, pp.20–3. Also published as a 'Commemorative leaflet for the concluding celebration of the year 5677 (1916) for comrades in the field.'

23. *Chazak, chazak, ve'nitchazek* (Hebrew).
24. R. Chaninah ben Dosa, B. Berakhot 34b.
25. Psalm 16: 8.
26. Deuteronomy 20: 1.
27. Deuteronomy 20: 3–4.
28. Deuteronomy 20: 8.
29. Deuteronomy 7: 7.
30. Genesis 22: 2.
31. Deuteronomy 29: 9–11 (modified).
32. 'Das Beste, was wir von der Geschichte haben, ist der Enthusiasmus, den sie erregt': Johann Wolfgang von Goethe (1749–1832), *Maximen und Reflexionen*, p.495.
33. Exodus 10: 9
34. See Chapter 2. Feldrabbiner des Westheeres (eds), *Sabbathgedanken*, pp.23–7.
35. Genesis 3: 9.
36. According to Jewish tradition Adam and Eve are allegorical figures.
37. A terrible irony: this was the word with which Adolf Hitler addressed the German people in many of his pre-war speeches (male *Volksgenossen*, female *Volksgenossinnen*): Jews were excluded from the *Volk*.
38. Leviticus 19: 18.
39. *Talmud Bavli* (*Shavu'oth*), 39a. The Mishnaic reference states *eilu la'eilu* (plural) instead of *ze bazeh* (singular) but the meaning is the same.
40. See Chapter 3. Feldrabbiner des Westheeres (eds), *Sabbathgedanken*, pp.30–4.
41. Genesis 28: 21.
42. Isaiah 40: 27.
43. Isaiah 40: 28–31.
44. See Chapter 8. Feldrabbiner des Westheeres (eds), *Sabbathgedanken*, pp.34–7.
45. Ibid., pp.38–40.
46. B. Berakhot 29b.
47. Part of the High Holiday liturgy.
48. 1 Samuel 2: 1–10.
49. *Nehmt die Gottheit auf in euren Willen/Und sie steigt von ihrem Weltenthron*. From Friederich von Schiller, *Das Ideal und das Leben* (1759–1805).
50. '*Was Gott tut, das ist wohlgetan.*' From Cantata BWV 100 by Johann Sebastian Bach (1685–1750); lyrics by Samuel Rodigast (1649–1708).
51. Feldrabbiner des Westheeres (eds), *Sabbatgedanken*, pp.41–5. This sermon was also published in *Jüdisches Gemeindeblatt für die Mitglieder der Synagogegemeinde Stettin* 2, no.1 (February 1918), pp.1–4.
52. 'Oh, how could I not be ardent for Eternity and the marriage – ring of rings – the ring of the return (recurrence)?' From *Also Sprach Zarathustra* by Friederich Nietzsche (1844–1900).
53. This adjective lay at the core of the exclusionary nature of National Socialism. Jews and certain other groups were not *völkisch* (see Note 37).
54. Feldrabbiner des Westheeres (eds), *Sabbatgedanken*, pp.46–8.
55. Ethics of the Fathers 4: 1.
56. 'Man is something to be overcome', Friederich Nietzsche, *Also Sprach Zarathustra*.
57. Genesis 22: 2–15.
58. Ethics of the Fathers 4: 13: 'Rabbi Shimon used to say: There are three crowns – the crown of the Torah, the crown of the priesthood, and the crown of kingship, but the crown of a good name surpasses them all.'
59. Genesis 32: 28.
60. Genesis 43: 17–30.
61. Numbers 16: 15.
62. Judges 13–16.

63. 2 Samuel 12: 7.
64. Zechariah 4: 6.
65. Psalm 34: 14.
66. Paul von Hindenburg (1847–1934).

CHAPTER EIGHT

Reinhold Lewin: The War as a Jewish Experience[1]

One sermon by Rabbi Lewin has already been included under '*Sabbathgedanken*' (Chapter 7). The essay below, which the author feels is important to reproduce separately, follows in translation:

The war as an experience – who dares discuss such a subject? How the war is perceived depends on whether one draws the circle of witnesses widely or narrowly. If one only thinks of trenches and hand-to-hand fighting, only a few would have something to say. The gunner with his heavy cannon is excluded, because he does not see with his own eyes the target to which he dispatches his shells. And the few soldiers who remain to tell the tale do not yield much constructive information. Who has not been disappointed by taciturnity of soldiers on leave who, even when asked, have left unfulfilled their friends' lascivious desire for tales of exciting adventures? The silence of the soldier from the Front, as has been consistently observed, is no coincidence. It corresponds to results of scientific psychological research. Nature reigned with such violence during the harrowing events that ragingly assailed the individual, that it blunted and killed his perception of distance. His soul's receptiveness withered. It is the same as when the pupil of the eye contracts in order not to be blinded by a bright ray or darting light. Shutting out the unbearable and keeping it below the threshold of consciousness saves spiritual life from collapse. Thanks to this the soldier does not fall victim to insanity – although, surrounded by a mass of men that force him forwards, led by orders that show him direction, he does not cease to act. But at the same time a reticence grows that dislikes chatter and bluster – a wonderful kind of quiet, active doing of one's duty, in contrast to that of the bogus, hyperbole-seeking war correspondent. And it is therefore recommended that, to objectively investigate experiences in the field, one should rather turn to someone who has been in the thick of things, and although he has a duty to stand above them, is closely linked to them, is moved and touched by them despite his being duty-bound to observe everything at a disengaged distance. Free from hyperbole, conscious of limits and provisos, I believe that I have these qualifications. For four full years I served as chaplain: I lived in the battle area and travelled regularly throughout an entire army area including the rear echelon. In so doing I got close to comrades through services and celebrations, spoke to them through all the rigours of battle, on their sick beds and torn apart by mortal wounds. How many of them came voluntarily to me, saw the signboard at my dwelling, confided and poured out their hearts to me! With the respect due them, and humility which is my duty, I wish to attempt to summarize my experiences. How did this violent war affect the hearts of German Jews who followed their country's call and their army's flag?

Firstly, the question must be posed: Did the average Jewish soldier comprehend the exact nature of war, i.e. combat, in the same way as comrades of other faiths? One cannot flatly dispute their difference or deny its possibility. How long did the constraint and isolation of the ghetto withdraw our arms from use of weapons! Jewish nature has been inoculated with certain habits over the centuries and is not suited to physical violence, nor by an appeal to naked power for arbitration. Our experience, schooled in suffering, has become refined: we have an instinctive abhorrence of everything bloody. This is something of which no culture need be ashamed. Because criminal statistics do not feature Jewish murderers and killers, it is presumed that the art of war does not appeal to Jews. Nevertheless it would be a crass defamation to advance the theory that enthusiasm is lacking, or that they will fail at the fateful moment. It is simply thus: a Jew never shoots merely for the sake of shooting. He doesn't stab or strike someone down because he enjoys it. I cannot imagine that a Jewish soldier anywhere would finish off a helpless wounded enemy who entreats him for mercy. Although he generally had to overcome greater inhibitions before he levelled his gun and fired for the first time, he performed his cruel duty just like the others. Certainly many were deeply troubled afterwards at a quieter time by recognition of how inhuman and unnatural was the duty enjoined on them for the sake of self-defence. But on the other hand I must confirm that I encountered sufficient men for whom demands of the campaign were not anything strange, outrageous or contradictory.

Belonging to the younger generation, they were enveloped in the breath of a *frisch-fröhlicher* [fresh and joyful] war. They did not originate from the assimilated social strata. As paradoxical as it sounds, they were often young Zionists, alert and enthusiastic nationalistic Jews, in whom German bravado sparkled. One might speak of breakthrough of Maccabean blood, its arousal in the youngest generation. For them no bombardment was too heavy, no patrol too reckless, and to the last week of the war they thrust themselves forward. In general the assertion may be made: Just as a gathering of Jewish soldiers hardly differs from other gatherings, just as it is very difficult to distinguish Jewish types melted into the monotonous mass of field grey, there is no discernible gap in experience and perception between the two groups. The diversity in character that forms the personality, both here and there, is preserved. An undiluted share in the renown of the German Front belongs to the Jewish soldiers right up to the Armistice: they held on to their positions, preventing flight, defending against the Homeland's enemies.

Less contested is examination of the second thing with which this war burdened hundreds of thousands of men: separation from home, disengagement of profession, distance from wife and child, father and mother. We know that nothing, at the Front or in the rear, resounded more deeply, cast a more familiar spell, than the name of the Homeland. It was felt and heard with longing, imagined and wept for with yearning. And nowhere was there a phrase that cropped up more in conversation, that resounded more in field post cards: it took shape most deeply, purely and tenderly in the souls of the Jewish soldiers, because time's vicissitudes have not spared our families either. Despite evil developments, the legacy of the past has not yet been obliterated. Without belittling everyone else, or detracting from our own reputation, it can be said that Jewish comrades were affected more deeply and suffered greater pain than Christians when the image of their own people rose up before them. I saw this in the field hospitals whenever I sat at their bedsides.

I tried to evade the older reservist when I could, because he started to talk of home, unfailingly fishing out photographs of his wife and children from his pocket book, and weeping bitter tears. I noticed it also at religious services: the room in which we gathered (a barn, temporarily erected barracks, or else the saints of a church looking down upon us) contrasted with the image of the synagogue at home; evoked the beloved and honoured figures that once populated it; created from the fount of memories solemn moments such as entrance of the Sabbath, which was greeted with similar sounds. Is it necessary to analyse the mood that came over us? I saw it most clearly when a festival neared. Accustomed to greeting such days in familiar circles, to allow its deep and exhilarating holiness to blossom and sparkle under a protective roof at the festive table, now the Jewish soldier was exiled and estranged, an unsettled, defenceless wanderer. How must such a contrast have penetrated their sensibility and torn them apart! Christians felt this, when at all, at Christmas, when they tried to seek forgetfulness in inebriation. But what could benumb the Jewish soldier? What could tear him out of *Heimweh* [longing for home] in whose depth he inexorably plunged, where the Shofar rang out, or *Kol Nidrei* echoed in his ear, the Menorah shone in front of him, or the Seder invited him to eat the bread of affliction, or simply the glow of the Sabbath candle? During the Pesach week, a soldier came to my quarters and I offered him matzoth; before he consumed the first piece, he began to sob, pitifully and unrestrainedly. Such innocence, imprinted unforgettably on the memory, is more convincing than long-winded gusts of words. We are reminded of the heroism of the Jewish fighter that puts him ahead of others: no enthusiastic cry of Hurrah roared around his struggle and his triumph, which was rewarded with no recognition or military awards adorning the chest that had received wounds and been marked with scars.

The reverse obtained: the attitude of those around contributed palpably to sharpening the conflict. Ringing songs have been sung about comradeship in the German army. The drum of publicity has been beaten and bombastic noise made upon patient calfskin, repelling the sensitized ear. But one thing is clear and cannot be doubted: whenever it was judged necessary during fire to run to the aid of a comrade in danger, assistance was given everywhere without batting an eyelid, request for reward or decoration. But it was sadly difficult to find anything that went beyond this most natural of reactions. To whom did it occur to transfer the physical sacrifice, almost mechanically made and accepted, to the spiritual domain, to spiritual consideration? Without the sentimental exuberance which imputes immature passions and insincerity to our soldiers in field grey, each one remained alone. Just as they usually kept their abundant gifts from home for themselves, and protected their property carefully and suspiciously, no one shared their troubles and joy. Their lot was spiritual isolation, something that the war spared no-one. The nearer one lived together physically, ate and drank together, lay awake and slept, the further one distanced oneself spiritually. The mutual getting-to-know-one-another with its tremendously intimate involvement, seldom taught human affinity: it uncovered diversity. It led to alienation, seldom to rapprochement; it built no bridges but instead hollowed out chasms. It sometimes led to a reaction that became more explosive the more closely people were forced together.

The situation complicated life for the Jewish soldier in a unique way. During my chaplaincy I met no-one who, if he made the association, withheld the information that only now did he realize in what a ghetto he had lived before: walls, trenches and ramparts that separated us from the world fell with our entitlement to citizenship. According to governmental decree, a *Judengasse*, twisty and winding, no longer exists.[2] But aside from governmental, commercial and cultural fusion, can we say – hand on heart – that synthesis with other citizens has been achieved? Did we not favour Jewish co-students in the school class, prefer to mix with Jews of the same profession, locate our home in streets inhabited by Jews? Do we not almost exclusively socialize with Jews – with the exception of the odd Christian acquaintance (I am tempted to adopt anti-Semitic jargon) as a type of foreign body? This situation is so natural and taken for granted that it doesn't penetrate our consciousness. We complain bitterly about how others misunderstand us. But how little do we know of them, their type and manner, behaviour and spiritual characteristics? Most of us do not open that door. We felt an unparalleled amazement when we encountered these in the field. It was as if scales fell from the eyes of Jewish comrades; it was as though they had discovered an unknown world. Heretofore we had mocked one another in fantastic caricatures. I will give one example. A high-ranking, educated officer greatly desired to accompany me to services but was apprehensive: after all, Jewish rite prescribes the cursing of Christ and his followers. It is true that a significant number of people have been cured of the delusion nourished uncritically by stories of ritual murders, that we have sinister, criminal characters, and that there are bloodthirsty werewolves amongst us; that the average Jew is, at the least, a worthless, crawling, wheeling-and-dealing huckster.[3]

But this type of enlightenment, accompanied as it is by a certain amount of good will, must not be overestimated. This lesson is balanced by the opposing view, which involves something delicate that a person experiences without speaking it out loud. Words do not describe it unequivocally, no hard and fast definition can be formulated; moreover the attempt to define it must avoid hurting others unjustly. However when I remember the drinking bouts in the officers' mess (wine does not invent anything but merely babbles), I see that I did not understand the coarseness that, when the curtain falls, degenerates into crudeness. I have a hard time understanding the lack of delicacy, of refinement, with which, quipping about matters of a sexual nature, a man can deliver his marriage to the guffawing of a drunken mob. The holiest of things, which strikes a positive note with Jews, found no echo.

How many were shut out who wanted to enter, by a thoughtless jest, an inconsiderate phrase, and poison-swollen insults! What malice and malevolence did anti-Semitism scatter, so that the seed may grow into corn: here a person was baited, there someone passed over for promotion and decoration, yet another driven to the edge of suicide by his superior's cruelty! It is yet to be determined whether the Front of itself tended toward such excesses, favoured their emergence, provoked their existence. Uncountable objections and complaints, streamed in to me. Officers and physicians assured me that in their mess good form was categorically preserved. They were joined by simple people who gave the most favourable and satisfied testimonials about their troops. But be that as it may, those at home worried that *Judenhaß* was still being nourished. Regardless of whether the opponent's political tendency found fertile ground in the field, or whether the bad behaviour of a lamentable number of Jews supported rumours of profiteering and shirking – anti-Semitism would have been brought back to life even if it had died there. It widened the crack that already gaped, although at first perhaps unconsciously and slightly. In many places it was torn open so widely that the Jewish comrade, if he did not close his eyes to deceive himself, thought himself isolated and alone. As the crown of these anti-Semitic activities, the War Ministry decree that Jewish soldiers had to be counted and their military dispositions ascertained by questionnaires[4] (the indelible, most shameful insult that has desecrated our community since we were allowed citizenship[5]) – is it necessary to describe in writing its impact on anyone who was even only slightly consciousness of his Judaism or had a spark of a sense of honour?

From the ferment arose something that, still colourless and indeterminate, may be called the Will to Judaism. What does the expression mean and into which sphere does it extend? Does the concept that connects habitual thought and speech with the name 'Jew' cover it? Or does it transcend the scope of purely religious, reaching beyond? It would be tempting to examine its cause, and insert something about connection between war and religion. I fear that this would be to go too far, which is why the boost that mobilization gave to church and synagogue collapsed after a short interval. The fiercer the initial urge, the more violent and powerful the setback that followed. If I had tried to hide a similar event in the field, it would have been like throwing sand into the eyes of others. The rush to attend field services waned significantly after the nimbus of The Extraordinary was stripped from them, after they became more frequent during more peaceful periods of fighting and when astonishment at the appearance of Jewish chaplains subsided. The special mood which surrounded them weakened. But enough remained behind to demonstrate clearly that while the flame which rose up in the Homeland flared briefly, crackling and smoking, the fire in the army camp was dampened – because it did not rise so high – into a quiet glow.

Almost all regular services, announced through division or corps order of the day, had their regulars. Their attendance at the pre-planned services became something anticipated, something familiar. And each time they were overpowered anew by the contrast between the room that united those who prayed – meadow and ruined sites, barn, church or billet – and what they were used to and loved at home. Time and again they were seized by the brevity of the service, neither artificially prepared beforehand nor polished, no more than about 30 minutes long, anchored in a variety of Hebrew pieces, framed by German prayers, culminating in a brief sermon. No paid choir had rehearsed – the community sang (they learned gradually to do so). A cantor, trained in singing, was seldom present – he who stood in *talit* in front of the others did what he could. No organ sound drowned out budding devotion – it sprouted and blossomed, sown in the heart and harvested in shy murmuring. A stamp of unity was imprinted on everything and everybody, because practically all functions were combined in me. And it may be said, on my honour, that not one of the innumerable services during my four-year chaplaincy left me – after the echo of the final priestly blessing had died away[6] – without the impression that our prayers were modest, pious and attentive! What men had accomplished in the field benefited Jewish field services. Without connection to home, a soldier was responsible for his own destiny. Trumpery and randomness left him, he withdrew into his innermost self and learned to distinguish sharply between things and soberly discern their nature. He could feel why he came to services, what they demanded from him and offered him. He was required to pray with an ardent heart, a wounded soul, to hold silent dialogue with the Highest, and not participate in the chattering and vanity which, unfortunately, blemish our synagogues. One could speak of a War Devotion, rebirth of religion in the field, revival of Judaism in the area that belonged to our race from olden times.

And there is something else that cannot be ignored or underestimated: something else present at services which gave them foundation and rootedness, colour and character, because it found in them its true exponent. It transcended the narrower area of godliness and broadened Judaism to a limitless and comprehensive entity. I refer to the negatives, which repelled the Jewish soldier threefold: The thick of battle wounded his humanity more deeply, his soul was linked more strongly with the loved ones back home, his particular characteristics withered spiritually amidst the others, insofar as they were not hated and avoided. Where could he find understanding and sympathy? Where could he go without fearing offence, without encountering scorn and insults? Where could he profess his Judaism by communication, prove that he was not, as alleged, hiding it shamefacedly or in a cowardly way? How paltry it would be to turn this into a cliché and neatly paste the label of Jewish nationalism on it! And it would be no less petty to insist that it must end politically in the aspirations and demands of Zionism, even though the movement attracted the broad mass of those participating in the war!

I mention a friend whose name is known in the Jewish newspaper world. At the beginning of the war he was excited about the fact that international relations with Jews in enemy lands should, once and for all, be severed and separated. As the campaign progressed during the second winter, he sent for a text-book and learned Hebrew. It was not because of formulas or hollow phrases that pleas for unity and calls for party unity rang out in army circles. He did not demand absolute egalitarianism. In him Jewish Composite Feeling triumphed. His flame burned consumingly and cathartically, maintained by prayer. When hundreds streamed together to celebrate, it was kindled and blazed and rose towards heaven. The swell of the chorus when the Torah was taken out, the Hagadah melodies at the meagre Seder, the roaring of *Maoz Tsur* in the flicker of the lights – anyone who threw himself into the stream of joy, to submerge himself in it and bathe his soul, would not be ashamed to tell of it with a pitiful stammer and moist eyes.

My personal opinions are based upon objective observations, on confessions and confirmation from those around me and confirmed by others. And if someone who was also in the field were to appear shaking his head and saying that he had experienced nothing of what I have attributed to him, he would not affect the general validity of my investigation. As dismissive and presumptuous as it sounds, I feel compassion for him. Because I do not abandon my belief that the nameless terror of this World War serves a higher design. Future generations will one day praise what it has given to humanity. We hope to see what it has brought to Germany once it is over, when the confusion has ended and ruins cleared. But for our Judaism I rely on the sublime vision of the Prophet: the house of Israel is seen as a pile of human bones, scattered over the surface of a valley, decayed and dried up. And yet God's command puts sinews on the skeleton, clothes it around with flesh, covers it with skin, breathes into it the eternal spirit which gives it life and puts it on its feet. The graves open and a resurrected nation rises out of the tomb.[7] May the storm of war, despite wounds and sacrifice, help us blossom anew! May we experience that there will be thousands who finally return home and, as soon as they settle down and put down roots, bring forth a renewal in our community – full of strength and courage and desire for activity, sure of a fruitful future!

Author's Note

This essay, published in 1919, is remarkable for facing head-on, more than that of any other Jewish chaplain, problems of alienation and anti-Semitism felt, to a greater or lesser extent, by all Jewish soldiers serving in the German army. Not only is it not glossed over but it is described in detail, emphasizing the fact that even at the beginning of the war, at the time of the *Burgfrieden*, fissures between Jew and non-Jew already existed and widened as war progressed and it became obvious that the German cause was lost. The relative social isolation of German Jewry before the war began is emphasized and must be borne in mind when considering the sudden appearance of tens of thousands of Jews in the mostly Christian German army in 1914.

No excuses for Jewish shirking and war-profiteering are given: these occurred undeniably amongst Jews, but only in the same measure as amongst non-Jews. The *Judenzählung* is recognized for what it was – an inexcusable insult to German-Jewish pride and honour, perhaps the worst since they were granted citizenship and a measure of liberty in 1812. The tenor of this essay is that the gulf between German Jew and non-Jew was and remained wide and perhaps unbridgeable.

However, he is hopeful that, as so often occurs in Jewish history, the tree would experience a rebirth and renewal. Jewish optimism is and remains indestructible. Tragically, Rabbi Lewin was murdered in the Holocaust.

NOTES

1. R. Lewin, 'Der Krieg als jüdisches Erlebnis', in *Monatschrift für Geschichte und Wissenschaft des Judentums* (Breslau: Schatzky, 1919), pp.1–14. Leo Baeck Institute, New York D 639 J4 L49 K7.
2. Medieval German towns and cities all had a *Judengasse* [Jew alley] where the Jewish population was forced to live under conditions of greater or lesser stringency.
3. The German *mauscheln*, a word created in the nineteenth century from '*Mauscheh*' (Moses or *Mosheh*, old pronounciation), is illustrative of all the Jews' purportedly low characteristics, including mispronunciation of classical German.
4. The *Judenzählung* [Jewish Census] decreed on 11 October 1916 by the Prussian War Ministry, ostensibly to confirm that Jews were not slacking front-line duty as was asserted by a minority of anti-Semitic extremists. The census gave rise to alarm and despair amongst Jewish troops. Questionnaires were completed and returned, but the census was discontinued in early 1917 and results never published.
5. King Frederick William III granted the Jews of Prussia citizenship on 11 March 1812.
6. Numbers 6: 23–7.
7. Ezekiel 37: 1–14.

CHAPTER NINE

A Greeting from the Field Chaplains for the 1915 Autumn Holiday Season; Miscellaneous Memoirs

In 1915 the *Verband der deutschen Juden* issued a booklet of chaplains' sermons for High Holiday and Succot festivals.[1] Translations of some of these are given here, together with various other chaplains' writings and memoirs.

The Grave on the Road (Sali Levi) [See Plate 2][2]

> 'Thus says the Lord: A voice is heard in Ramah, mourning and great weeping, Rachel weeping for her children and refusing to be comforted, because her children are no more.' (Jeremiah 31: 15)

Rachel weeps for her children. Rachel, Jacob's wife, died between Bet-El and Efrat while giving birth to her son Benoni-Benjamin.[3] 'And Jacob erected a pillar on her grave, which marks Rachel's tomb to this day' (Genesis 35: 30). She was buried on the way to Efrat: a grave on the road.

Today I also saw a grave on the road. Not the grave of a mother or a child. There it lies at the edge of a forest, on the road bordering a meadow: a young, blossoming man died while advancing into Russia. His name is engraved on a wooden stake bearing a helmet, with grass and weeds growing around. The youth is bedded down in the cold ground far from his loved ones. 'His grave would be so different at home: made of ore and stone, protected and tended, so near to the eyes who weep over the sleeping man.' Thus does the mother weep for her child, and the father reflects quietly with her: 'Out there, so simple and solitary, a grave in the road on the way to Russia – not on the way to the Promised Land!'

But a heroic voice speaks from the grave: 'At the place where I fought and suffered, stood and fell, there is where I wish to rest: even in death I wish to bear witness that the German soldier does not falter or yield! I advanced fighting victoriously with my comrades as far as here. The place where I fell, where blood of my mother and father ran from my wounds and soaked into enemy soil, is sacred: I have conquered this place. As far as this I was victorious on the road to our goal. Do you now want to tear from me this place, the place that I won while I was still alive and which cost me my life? Now that I am defenceless? "Rachel weeps for her children for they are no more." Rachel wept because her children had deviated from their path, their goal: I did not and will not yield, I wish to lie in a grave on the road to the Promised Land! Because once people pass by this road, they will remain standing at the grave on the road, they will reflect and realize: The grave on the road shows the way, the simple hills, half weathered and blown away: they will lead you to the heights in a future of freedom and joyful peace, in the Promised Land.

'Thus says the Lord: "Restrain your voice from weeping and your eyes from tears, for your work will be rewarded", declares the Lord, and they will return from the enemy's land.' (Jeremiah 31:16)

Religiosity in the Field (Jacob Sänger)[4]

'Another request, Herr Rabbiner', a severely wounded soldier whom I had visited in a field hospital said to me, 'could you give me a prayer book? I prayed in my childhood but have not done so yet as an adult. But now I wish to pray and thank my Creator in Heaven, as long as he keeps me alive.' These words, from the mouth of a man who has looked death fearlessly in the eye, held captive in the camp by excruciating pain, remained stuck in my mind. I was convinced that I saw before me one of the many thousands for whom religion symbolized something outmoded, who smiled in a superior yet sympathetic way when any form of religion approached him. I often expressed the concern that real religious feeling seemed to be rapidly disappearing. Many experiences in my professional life justified these fears. However, this request – and many others – for a prayer book made my misgivings disappear. There was a handshake of a wounded fellow-Jew, a handshake that I will never forget: a handshake that I did not at first understand until I read something in the eloquent, expressive eyes of the sick man: The poor man wanted to tell me, the representative of his religion, that he had found his God again in the field, in the thunder of battle, and that he had opened his heart wide to all the exhilarating and blissful expressions of religion.

And when I come upon a simple Jewish soldier on the wayside, deep in reading that little black-bound field prayer book that the Verband der deutschen Juden has handed to each soldier, that tells me that religiosity in the field is the heavenly gift that gives our heroes courage and strength, comfort and support, in war's countless dangers. Because this feeling has not been conveyed to the soldier from the outside, but rather expressed itself from the depths of his heart. And later, when the sun of peace has driven away the Angel of Death, religiosity found in difficult hours will never disappear from the hearts in which it has matured; it will be transplanted into coming generations as one of the greatest gifts that was nearly lost, but which this momentous time, despite its horror, has granted us anew. Religiosity in the field will be preserved and retained as religiosity at home and in the family. 'Behold: the protector of Israel neither slumbers nor sleeps!'[5]

The Eyes of War. For Yom Kippur Day (Georg Wilde)[6]

We prayed: 'Come in peace, O Sabbath', the voice of the prayer-leader sounded softly.[7] It was otherwise quiet in the dust-covered church; faces and clothes of supplicants were also dusty grey. They sat before a small table on which Sabbath lights burned. Outside, cannons sounded with fading thunder. Opposite me over the entrance I saw two holes that enemy bullets had torn into the wall: they stood in line like two eyes, staring at us with an empty, eerie look. The walls right and left looked like a giant head, the side walls like the body of a monster. Empty eyes stared down at those who prayed, like a monster looking at his victim. War looked at us and its eye sockets appeared to say: 'I am War. Destroyed towns and trampled countryside are my empire, men outside murdering each other my servants. Men who prayed with you four weeks ago are missing: I have swallowed them up. You sat with a severely wounded man today: I have chosen him for myself. I will never give back the man whom you buried yesterday. You speak to men of home, of mother and father, of wife and child: many will find their eternal home in my arms. Why do you pray: "Come in peace, O Sabbath?" Why do small Sabbath lights shine there? With the breath of my mouth I have extinguished Sabbath lights in almost the entire world. Now there is no peace, no Sabbath, now it is I: War!' The eyes of War looked down upon us, large and empty.

Clouds that had covered the heavens dispersed, the sun's rays broke through and suddenly shone through the two cracks. War looked through great eyes of sunshine at the crowd of men praying, and faces did not look dusty grey any more but bright; eyes didn't look tired but were now clear and courageous, and men were not victims any more, but heroes. The Sabbath song resounded joyfully, and the now sunny eyes of War said: 'I am the master, you are my servants. You stride through enemy territory, protect your homeland so that its towns and cities are not destroyed and your country is not invaded. If the house burns in which your mother and father, your wife and children are living, do you not jump into flames to save them? Your enemies have surrounded your entire land with a ring of fire. They want to burn everything and you rush outside to prevent this. But I am also the purifying fire. Although I may burn houses and bodies, I also burn pettiness and evil and bring goodness and strength to life. Let your Sabbath lights burn and your Sabbath songs sound! Did you not see my companions today at the dying man's bed? The man who, not realizing that he was dying, asked you to write to his parents so that they would not worry, who asked them to thank the two comrades who carried him from the fire, smiled at you in gratitude before he closed his eyes for the last time with peace in his heart. Did you see my companions there: the love of a child, the loyalty of a comrade, and human kindness? They grow so large and beautiful only because of me: War. Do young men otherwise think of their parents with such longing? Do people otherwise carry comrades in their arms away from misery and danger? Yesterday you stood at a graveside in which a fellow-Jew lay, but to his right and his left lay two others, one Protestant and one Catholic: three sons of the same Fatherland. You said *Kaddish* for your fellow-Jew according to ancient rite, and for the two others the Lord's Prayer according to their tradition. Did you see my companions – Faith, Unity, Tolerance – standing next to one another? During peace they are seldom found together. Here you speak to the men of their homeland, of quiet hours at home: one sees his parents' house, another sees wife and child, a third the house that he wants to build one day. – Are these hearts not more deeply filled with yearning for love, peace, devotion, happiness, than in peacetime, when these are everybody's property? Do you not see my companions: a yearning for home, a peaceful heart, devotion and belief in the future?'

Burn quietly, Sabbath lights! Sound softly, Sabbath melodies! The eyes of War shone like two suns, like child's love, a comrade's loyalty, and human love. They shone like the eyes of the God of the Universe,

Father of all Humanity; they gleamed like Sabbath lights, telling of a peaceful heart and domestic tranquillity. They shone like the eyes of a hero who goes out to save his Fatherland from evil. They gleamed like the eyes of a returning hero whose land – large and blossoming – has been liberated, whose people only now find life beautiful and worth living. A stream of strength will flow from the healthy, a stream of human love will flow over the wounded, and a stream of holy compassion over the fallen.

So I raised the cup and blessed the Sabbath and the wine, I raised my hands in blessing over the congregation, with the eyes of War shining down upon me. The Sabbath of Sabbaths, Yom Kippur, approaches! Through the eyes of War it looks down on those praying in the field as well as at home: not with empty dull eyes, covering our hearts with grey cobwebs, but glowing and atoning. Remember in thankful love those who have fallen; place your hope in abiding love for your loved ones; love and believe in your Fatherland and your own future! Let War's good companions into your hearts! Welcome love of home and humanity, brotherly loyalty and a devout mind, vitality and belief in the future – and you will participate in the spirit of Yom Kippur!

Come, bring peace to our hearts, O Sabbath of Sabbaths!

Yom Kippur 1914 (Heimann Chone) [See Plate 3][8]

The holy Rosh Hashanah days were for us a time of strengthened perceptions. I still can see so many solemn faces, tears in their eyes: Sons who missed the home and blessing of their parents especially dearly at this time; men who fervently prayed for their wife and children and a happy return to them – oh, so many of them who have gone the way of heroism are now covered by Mother Earth!

And now Yom Kippur approached, the Day of Atonement in the middle of this terrible war. Where will I spend it, where will I find a community around me? A few days before I was in Thiaucourt, coincidentally quartered with one of the two Jewish families living there. After a few words, the woman of the house learned that I was a *prêtre israélite* [Jewish pastor]. I will never forget the delight and astonishment on the face of the initially worried-looking French Jewish woman, and how she asked me: '*Ah, vous êtes un Raw?*' [Oh, so you are a rabbi?]. I found out from her that there was an old synagogue in this small Lorraine town, which had not been used for many years, because the community did not exist anymore. A chief vicar from

Baden, quartered beneath me in the same house had, by means of a notice on the synagogue door, ensured that the rooms would not be used to quarter soldiers. He led me there and enthusiastically enquired about individual inscriptions, some of which he had already deciphered. On Yom Kippur eve I went there and with the help of a soldier made sure that rooms were clean, and covered the four Torah scrolls with the available white wrapping. The white *Parochet* was returned to its original honourable use, and white curtains were located on the windows and as drapes in front of the woman's section. And so the synagogue was prepared for Yom Kippur.

Kol Nidrei alone, and yet not alone. Soon the room filled with white forms, shadows, dream images from the past and present. The glorious prayers with wonderful melodies enveloped me, sang in me and moved me, as though they were coming now as they had once come from my father standing at the prayer leader's lectern (Oh, it is three months since he left the land of the living!). How the tears flowed when out of the depths of my heart the words arose: '*Ya'ale tachanunenu me'erev*', and all the silent supplicants sang together at the end: 'You, O my refuge, my banner, my chalice, my portion, to You do I cry. Into Your hand I commit myself, when I sleep and wake, and with my soul entrust my body to You. I fear not. God is with me.'[9]

Early next morning I walked up the narrow stairway to the small, cosy *shul*. Oh, sweet memories of youth! Was it not the old synagogue in my home town with the white sand-scattered vestibule, the old-fashioned brass chandeliers hanging from the ceiling, with the *luach* on the rear wall, the beautifully inscribed verse from the Psalms 'I have set the Lord always before me',[10] in front of the prayer leader's lectern, with the white-painted benches on which old prayer books lay, and the Holy Ark crowned with both tablets of the Ten Commandments. The table was covered by a beautiful *Parochet*, donated seventy-three years ago 'for the honour of God and the Torah' by women of the then-flourishing community.

I stand in awe before you, O well-known table: 'Oh true God! King of Kings! Accept my entreaty mercifully! May the words of my mouth and the meditations of my heart be acceptable to You, my Rock and my Redeemer!'[11] And in the late afternoon we prayed: 'The day wanes. The sun is setting, we approach your heavenly gate.'[12] Sleep well comrades, sleep the eternal sleep, sheltered by God's mercy. You, for whom this fervent *Ne'ilah* prayer has since, in another sense, become true!

But you, O loved ones who experience this Yom Kippur day, pray the words, drenched with ancient tears but now calling you to new hope, and may God fulfil the wishes of your hearts: 'Be merciful to us, O Lord, be merciful! Hear us, O Eternal, hear us! Stand by us, God of our salvation! We rely upon You!'

You Have Chosen Us (Emil Levy)[13]

'You have chosen us from all other peoples.'[14] On every festival, we praise Israel's mission, and thank God by this statement whenever we are called to the Torah. But no concept was and is more misunderstood by the outside world than the fact of our having been chosen. 'Look at those smug, cocky Jews, who consider themselves better than other peoples!'

We counter these accusations as follows: Far from looking with disdain upon all humanity, we calmly continue calling Israel a Chosen People. That we have been chosen from the nations of the world for special world-historical tasks[15] is a historical fact that cannot be refuted. In contrast to the shameful religious superstitions of hopelessly confused civilizations of antiquity, we proclaimed the doctrine of one God, Creator of heaven and earth. We separated the *moral imperative* from all that was of secondary importance and placed it as a queen on the throne. The fact that we Jews were and are 'chosen' is not a reward but a task: constant moral endeavour, categorical imperative,[16] permanent admonition to purity and morality. 'You have chosen us and have sanctified us with Your commandments and chosen us by giving us His Torah.'[17]

Cultivation of a special community to special perfection must be as beneficial to the world around it as is an overflowing chalice of riches. Through its being chosen, Israel has become *humanity's teacher*, the world's conscience. The prophetic vision of Moses recognized this right at the beginning, when Israel became a people: just as an individual priest teaches and instructs his congregation: you will be a nation of God's priests[18] and do the same for the nations of the earth. In such a way 'chosenness' of the Jewish people becomes the national identity of all-embracing love of humanity.

Today's great cultured nations lay claim to 'chosenness' no less than Israel did in ancient times. The English nation especially lives in belief that their island is favoured by destiny, and they have therefore been compared a great deal with Israel. But one must point out clearly that England does not comprehend the concept of chosenness in the pure sense of Jewish ethics. For British, to be chosen means in the first place 'Rule Britannia', to behave as masters of the sea and of worldwide commerce, to be richer and more powerful than any competitor. The *messianic consciousness* of Israel is based on ideals, compared to the materialistic nature of English national arrogance.

This national arrogance, which does not serve the world well but rather wishes to rule it, is the reason for our German battle. We will not fall into the trap of proclaiming the German nation as chosen above all others; because every nation is, in a certain sense, 'chosen', with special faculties and skills that it translates into creativity for the world's benefit. Order, cleanliness, thoroughness, organizational talent are all characteristics in which we Germans are truly 'chosen' and in which we represent a 'nation of priests' for the entire world; this is noticed in enemy countries, whose culture carries in so many regards traces of neglect and backwardness. And what appears as organizational talent to outsiders is the collective concept of the noblest concealed virtues: the sense of duty, subordination, obedience, sacrifice. When our enemies dismiss these characteristics with the catchphrase 'militarism', we hope that this 'militarism' will remain preserved for a long time, for the well-being of the Fatherland. The German nation is too healthy and virtuous to peal the death knell; it will remain 'chosen' not to found an Empire but to continue to shower the world with the richness of its genius.

The fact that we Germans today have hardly a friend in the world, that an ocean of hatred and slander surges around us, must be considered not as refutation, but as confirmation of our chosenness. To be chosen is a gift from God full of bitterness: to be chosen is to be met with hostility. To be chosen means *to walk the streets of derision and mockery, of lies and slander, spitting and clenched fists*, without breaking down, always rising up again and remaining erect, supported by consciousness of one's mission. It calls for comparison with the Prophets of Israel, especially the tragic greatness of Jeremiah and fate of the Jewish people throughout the ages. Together with the most uplifting joy, the people of Israel also know the deepest pain of their calling; 'God's favourite' has had to sample an endless menu of joy and sorrow. But time and again, as emphasized in the Psalms, the lament turns into a song of joy: *there is justice*. And it is the spirit of the Hebrew Psalms that pervades German hearts at this time, filling them with melancholy but also unshakable confidence. We are 'chosen', both as *Jews* and as *Germans*, to continue to perform divine tasks for the world. As German Jews the two-fold sound of the Heavenly Voice, which once called to Jeremiah, calls to us: 'Today I have turned you into an iron pillar and a bronze wall to stand against the whole land. Even if they fight against you they will not conquer you, for I am with you and will save you.'[19]

[*Emil Levy also describes the two 1915 Pesach Seders in St Quentin which he organized, as follows. The menus of the two Seders can be seen in Plate 28.*]

In particular my efforts to obtain a large amount of matzoth were not in vain and proved essential ... It was thus possible for me to provide the present indigenous Jewish population of about twenty families, who had been cut off from the usual communications, with essentials. The Seder celebrations after services in the temple lasted from 8.00–11.00 p.m.; men were given leave until midnight. The conduct of the Seder including the meal was in traditional festive form and I may also remark that all the meat (50 kilograms) was slaughtered in accordance with tradition and ritually prepared. All Jewish troops were, where possible, given leave for both Seder evenings. Four services took place on the Front during the Festival week, which imparted some of the Pesach mood to the troops ... Unfortunately during that week I had to officiate at two burials.[20]

From the War's Sunny Side (Arthur Levy) [See Plate 2][21]

He who walks with open eyes through our time, bleeding from a thousand wounds, will not only see its pain-distorted visage but also signs of moving greatness and divine grandeur. I think of the stirring image that I often saw here in the field during the spring months and that imprinted itself unforgettably in my senses. Next to destroyed houses and huts devoured by fire I saw proudly blooming trees bordering the piles of rubble with their abundance of blossoms, their rich beauty, making a shocking contrast to the misery of the wrecked site. Right next to this terror beauty raised its head, with verdant hope and re-birth alongside decay and destruction.

Similarly, this entire period is a juxtaposition of fear and beauty, a multicoloured fabric of high and low. Deeds of human greatness and moral strength shine out from the shadow of its events; they arise comfortingly and full of encouragement from the churned-up soil of our time like drops of water springing from the depths.

Likewise, all of us who participate with hand and heart in achievements and creativity here in the field have seen much that is grave and devastating, but also much that is noble and sublime. We have experienced the truth of the sages' word: 'God has created the bitter herb as well as the honey to sweeten it.'

I was once called to the grave of a Jewish solder to pay him my last respects. He was a young volunteer who had given his life's riches joyfully and sealed his love of Fatherland with his early death. His mother and sister had hurried from the homeland and stood at the grave numb with grief in stony calm. And when we lowered the coffin into the grave the captain approached the grave and called two words out to his dead soldier which moved us all deeply and penetrated our hearts like a heroic song: 'honest and loyal!' Mother and daughter left more erect than they had arrived; melancholy pride dissolved the rigidity of their expressions and they took these last words back home like a crown with which they would from now on adorn the memory of their loved one. Whenever I visit the grave that carries the hero's name inside a modest *Magen David*, the words 'honest and loyal' sound out to me like a holy song.

At the start of the war men of one of the replacement battalions was mustered: they had to march out to the Front to fill in gaps left by fallen heroes. Amongst those chosen was a man from the territorial army who was leaving a wife and child at home knowing that they were worrying about him and trembling for his life. Calmly and quietly he took his place, ready for battle and doomed. Then a younger Jewish soldier volunteered and asked to be sent in his place, saying that he didn't have a wife or child and, footloose and fancy-free, was already prepared to die for the Fatherland. Deeply stirred, the captain shook the Jew's hand, moved by the spirit of true comradeship that manifested itself so upliftingly.

In October I got to know a soldier from the Rhineland; we met in a Polish village and spent a few useful hours together. Then I lost track of him and he moved further with his troops towards Warsaw. In February I met him again in Lodz. I did not recognize him again: the strong young soldier had become grey and old, and his furrowed features told of harsh experience. When he poured out his heart out to me and told me of the hardship and terror through which he had travelled, he said: 'I am eternally thankful to my father that he taught me our Jewish prayers, because earlier I did not want to know anything of these things.' When he said that, he wore his heart on his sleeve and I felt the deep warmth of his newfound faith.

A wounded soldier from Alsace lay dying in a Petrikau field hospital. He had been shot through the chest and all hope of life had gone. With a tired voice he relayed his last greetings for his loved ones to the nurse who was looking after him: his wan gaze rested earnestly on the photograph of his wife and child that he held in his shaking hands. Then the physician came, encouraged him, and promised him new strength if he would eat some pork. But he declined with a smile, saying, 'I have never done this in my life and will not do it when I am dying. There is only one thing that can help me', and he pointed to his pillow under which his Psalm book – his true companion from the very beginning – lay.

In November a fierce battle raged near the village of Dombie. Starting on Friday, shells howled over the battlefield and overwhelmed the inhabitants with chaotic terror. Necessities were hurriedly bundled together and people fled their homes in frantic haste. Only one person remained behind, sitting desolately in the solitude of the setting sun: the *Shochet* of Dombie. His child had died, and lay on the bier cold and pale. His father was holding the death watch. To leave the corpse did not come into consideration, but the holiness of the Sabbath forbade its interment.[22] He waited in fear and anxiety. Shells howled and menaced mercilessly, and here and there set houses on fire. The danger increased and got ever nearer: already his neighbour's house was in flames, and the father sat and waited, until eventually a missile hit his own house and drove him away. As he crossed the threshold, the walls collapsed and the corpse found an unexpected grave under the rubble of the house. But the father had held faith with his child and his God.

At Succot (Dr Jacob Sonderling) [See Plates 2 and 16][23]

'You shall dwell in booths for seven days ... so that your generations may know that I had the sons of Israel live in booths when I brought them out.'[24]

How well does the content of the Rosh Hashanah and Yom Kippur festivals match our mood in the field. When have we previously contemplated our past and future more earnestly than during this great and difficult time? When have we examined everything we do more thoroughly than now? But the meaning of Succot does not seem to fit everything that we are experiencing. 'Rejoice before the Lord!' Is this exhortation to rejoice not a gruesome irony when applied to soldiers who have been looking death in the face for months?

And yet it seems to me that we need nothing more than joy amidst the terrible handiwork of the war. I do not mean a *frisch-fröhlicher* [fresh and joyful] war;[25] that belongs today in the realm of fables more than ever before. I mean something else. Our forefathers celebrated the harvest festival in booths. When they had gathered the fruits of the field and the vine, joy entered into their booths.

Comrades! We have sown precious seed for more than a year. Countless young lives lie buried deep in the earth's bosom of the battlefields of Europe and sleep the eternal sleep. Harvest time is coming! Has the bloody seed not sprouted gloriously? Has the goal of our terrible sacrifice not been reached already? The homeland, threatened by hate and avarice, is now free of the enemy. No-one, as far as we know at the moment, can and will break through the living wall that protects the Fatherland. Should we not rejoice? Certainly it is a solemn joy that fills us. Joy mixed with melancholy, because it is the harvest of a heavy year that we gather.

We Jews in the field fulfil the festive command of Succot. We have left our secure homes and dwell in huts. Shell-fire has helped us see the starry sky from our camp, in accordance with religious commandment. But! The deeper sense of this meaningful custom has grown within us. Faith in the protection of our mighty God who is with us, as He was with our ancestors in the desert. Faith! Many have found it again in the dug-out, in the pillbox, and they rejoice their newfound belief.

So do we wish to celebrate this festival in the field as well as a harvest festival full of humble thanks to the All-bountiful. We must sow, let us also reap!

[Paul Lazarus (Plate 20) has left us a description of Pesach 1917 in Üsküb, Macedonia. His signed invitation to attend is presented in Plate 21.]

Four large chests of matzoth arrived from the Freie Vereinigung on my order about three weeks before the festival. *Hagadot* had already been partially provided by the Allgemeine Rabbinerverband, and partially bought in a Berlin book store. For those comrades who, also here in the field, keep the dietary laws, I ordered some bottles of kosher wine from Germany. The consciousness of having provided proper festival days for hundreds of Jewish comrades on the Macedonian Front will remain forever in their memory, and may be the best reward for all those from the Rhineland and Westphalia who assisted. About 300–400 men, from all parts of Germany, participated in the Seder evenings. Apart from them, many Austrians and Hungarians as well as Jewish prisoners-of-war were present. We took our places at a long white table, where possible decorated with flowers. The mood was joyful; each one was happy to be able to be a Jew amongst Jews again ...

Just as harmoniously as both Seder evenings, the field service of 7 April also went beautifully. It took place at 10.00 a.m. in the main synagogue in Üsküb. The spacious synagogue was filled up to the last place: German comrades sat beside Austrians, Hungarians beside Bulgarians. Some Christian officers were also present until the end of the service. Everyone returned to his post satisfied and with thankful heart. In all of us the wish arose: May all who have participated in these Seder evenings in far-away Macedonia be able to return home in the not-too-distant future, sound in body and spirit. May God soon give us the long-desired peace. God bless and protect our ardently loved Fatherland.[26]

The War Memoirs of David Alexander Winter

[As soon as war broke out Rabbi Winter volunteered but his appointment as chaplain came through only in 1916. He started service during the war with the Twelfth Army in Grodno, which he chose over St Quentin on the Western Front out of a desire to get to know the world of the Ostjuden. Upon arrival he noticed that relations between the Jews in his area were more cordial to the German than to the Russian army, so often associated with pogroms. He continues:]

My area lay between Vilna to the north, Baranowitz to the east, and Brest-Litovsk to the south, with logistical centres in Grodno, Lida and Bialystok. Jewish soldiers came from all parts of the Reich, united in a feeling of duty to the Fatherland. Jewish chaplains had to tend for Jewish soldiers entrusted to their care, but also, when possible, assist Polish Jews in their relationship to the German authorities. I arranged field services every second week, with rear echelon services in between.

I brought prayer books with me when I could, gave a sermon after services, and stayed awhile with the men, usually bringing along tea or beer, reading material, cigarettes, etc. I advised them, so far away from home, on family matters. The soldiers got to know each other and developed a close relationship with me. On one tragic occasion I gave a Jewish foot-soldier a lift to services in my car. A week later I heard the sad news of his death. I ensured that his grave was marked with a wooden Star of David, photographed it, and informed his next of kin where the site was located. I also helped arrange regular chaplains meetings [see Chapter 10] and synagogue services in the larger cities.

I remember one Chanukah in Bialystok how deeply the traditional melody of *Maoz Tsur* moved the non-Jewish guests who had not heard it before. We tried, wherever possible, to observe Jewish ritual. On Pesach I tried to supply all the soldiers with matzoth and kosher food, and to arrange beautiful Seders. All this greatly impressed the local Jewish population. Details of services were published in army orders and Jewish soldiers, where possible, were given leave to attend. Hundreds of soldiers attended services on Pesach and High Holidays, filling the local synagogue and providing soldiers with hours of peace and edification. Meals were organized in the local kosher hotel and a kosher field kitchen was made available, even with a *Shochet*. For Pesach I organized baking in Grodno of 800 packages of matzoth to send to the troops and Seders were attended by over 800 men. One bottle of wine was supplied for each two men. Men from all over the Reich sang the Seder songs and nobody wanted either evening to end. For Rosh Hashanah and Yom Kippur the atmosphere was more solemn. It was a pleasure to hear the *chazan* from Lida assisted by two boys singing the festival tunes.

My relations with military authorities, at the Front and elsewhere, were good and I was surprised at the friendliness with which I was received each time I visited the Front: officers always invited me to breakfast and lunch and each time I tried to explain that I could not dine because the food was not kosher. Once I was offered a large bowl full of shellfish, a delicacy, and everyone was surprised that I couldn't eat this either; also that sometimes I did not eat but just drank tea. On one occasion I was invited for a meal during Pesach and had to tell my hosts that I couldn't even drink a glass of water with them during this period. Once I visited a field hospital at the Front and was photographed with two Christian chaplains: a Protestant, Professor Kaverau, and a Catholic, Dr Schürmann: myself in the middle with a *Magen David* and the two of them, with crosses, on the sides.[27] Once, after a field service, I got stuck in a heavy snowstorm and took refuge in the nearest German position. I was invited into the officers' mess and offered a plate of roast meat which I again refused: none of the officers could understand how I sometimes managed with only tea and bread. Another time, my commanding general invited me for dinner. He understood about our dietary laws because he had already hosted a Turkish general,[28] gave me bread and tea, and awarded me the Iron Cross Second Class.

In 1917 the war with Russia ended. Meanwhile the Russian Revolution had broken out, the Tsar abdicated and a Provisional Government under Kerensky was formed. The Bolsheviks took over a few months later and the peace treaty of Brest-Litovsk, with very harsh conditions for Russia, including loss of a great deal of land, was signed.[29] Despite this a large part of the German army remained in Russia, and my services and hospital visits carried on as usual although there was no war. Despite cessation of hostilities, infectious disease outbreaks such as typhus sometimes occurred and one of the doctors fell victim to it while looking after his infected patients with no regard for himself. Relations between the Jews of Grodno and the German military authorities was good and Jewish soldiers and civilians got on well together. I still remember[30] celebration of Simchat Torah in the Grodno synagogue. Young and old gathered with the youth in the great synagogue to participate in the *Hakafoth* and women young and old came down from the balconies to watch. This was a true celebration which made all every day cares disappear. I was thus permitted to see the Jewish people in the true ardour of their celebration. I tried as much as possible to support the local *Yeshivoth* in Grodno and Lithuania with contributions from Germany. In Grodno, when the Germans approached, one of the rabbis offered himself to God as a sacrifice as long as the remaining citizens were spared. The city was occupied by the Germans almost without a fight; however, this rabbi died the same day that the Germans entered the town.

In 1918, because of the transfer of Rabbi Rosenak from Bialystok to Kovno as well as transfer of High Command, I was moved to the Tenth Army in Bialystok. There I met many notable people, including Reb Chaim Soloveitchik [Plate 18].[31] Bialystok had a thriving Jewish community with a rich cultural life, where richer merchants assisted the poor, and an orphanage (for which I received contributions from Germany). While we were feeling more and more at home in

Bialystok, war news from the West became increasingly serious and we got the feeling that the war would end badly for us. On 9 November a revolution broke out in Germany and led to the end of combat.

My relations with the soldiers were generally cordial, as I wanted them to be, and I was their friend and advisor. Jewish soldiers fulfilled their duty in the field, and about 12,000 were killed in the war. The standing and merit of Jewish soldiers was often damaged, and the burden of military service made heavier, by their faith. My own relations with Christian officers and men, which were good at the start, slowly changed especially after the *Judenzählung*.

[During 1918 Rabbi Winter travelled extensively, visiting Jewish communities large and small and yeshivas in today's Belarus, Poland and Lithuania and meeting with several famous rabbis and cantors, thereby giving us a moving glimpse of a vanished Jewish world. He writes:]

Something happened during a Sabbath service in Bialystok that I had not seen in Germany. In the middle of the Torah portion reading, twenty to twenty-five men and women broke into the service crying loudly and interrupting the reading. The people wanted to lodge a complaint that German troops had expropriated all their livestock, their only means of support. I promised to look into this after the end of the service and was eventually able to get this order rescinded, although I could not ascertain who had given it. Another time the Jewish civilians of a town were ordered to pave the road on Rosh Hashanah. After getting no satisfaction from the officer who gave the order, I went straight to High Command who agreed with me that Jews should not be required to work on their Holy Day, called the officer, and ordered him to cancel the order.

[Rabbi Winter goes on to describe how he interceded with the Polish authorities a few weeks before they were to occupy Bialystok at war's end, to protect its Jews from pogroms and persecution and also succeeded in transferring Jewish prisoners of war accused of Bolshevik activities to Grodno, so as to prevent them from being killed by the occupying Poles. He concludes:]

When the time came to say farewell to Bialystok I felt depressed to part from friends with whom I had shared sorrows and anxieties, and whom I had sometimes been able to assist during hard times. On my departure day, the end of February 1919, the orphans and their supervisors gave me a small album of songs, signed on each page by each child in Yiddish: I had never before received such a beautiful parting gift. I had been a chaplain in the East for three years and in the process got to know a special Jewish way of life with its own customs and people, spiritual life, literature, history of suffering, great schools and *Yeshivoth*, also hospitals, orphanages, old age homes and other institutions.[32]

NOTES

1. Verband der deutschen Juden (eds), *Ein Gruß der Feldrabbiner an die jüdischen Kameraden im deutschen Heere zu den Herbstfesttagen 1915* (Berlin: Verband der deutschen Juden, 1915).
2. Verband der deutschen Juden (eds), *Gruß der Feldrabbiner*, pp.6–7. The texts from Jeremiah are taken from the *Haftarah* of the second day of Rosh Hashanah.
3. 'Benoni' in Hebrew means 'son of suffering'.
4. Verband der deutschen Juden (eds), *Gruß der Feldrabbiner*, pp.9–10.
5. Psalm 121: 4.
6. Verband der deutschen Juden (eds), *Gruß der Feldrabbiner*, pp.12–15.
7. The fact that *Lecha Dodi* and Kiddush were recited over wine were recited means that this was a Friday Evening service, probably the Sabbath before Yom Kippur.
8. Verband der deutschen Juden (eds), *Gruß der Feldrabbiner*, pp.18–20; M. Berger, *Eisernes Kreuz, Doppeladler, Davidstern. Juden in deutschen und österreichisch-ungarischen Armeen. Der Militärdienst jüdischer Soldaten durch zwei Jahrhunderte* (Berlin: Trafoverlag, 2010), pp.57–8; M. Berger and G. Römer-Hillebrecht (eds), *Juden und Militär in Deutschland. Zwischen Integration, Assimilation, Ausgrenzung und Vernichtung* (Baden Baden: Nomos Verlaggesellschaft, 2009), pp.93–4.
9. Concluding lines of *Adon Olam*. God is referred to in the third person in the original Hebrew.
10. Psalm 16: 8. Hebrew: *Shiviti Adonai le'negdi tamid*.
11. Psalm 19: 14
12. Part of the *Ne'ilah* service.
13. Verband der deutschen Juden (eds), *Gruß der Feldrabbiner*, pp.22–5.
14. Part of the *Shmoneh Esreh* recited on the High Holidays.
15. German *Weltgeschichtlich*: A word much used by Georg Wilhelm Friederich Hegel (1770–1831), noted German philosopher.
16. One of Immanuel Kant's (1724–1804) most famous and central statements: 'Act only according to that maxim whereby you can, at the same time, will that it should become a universal law.'
17. Continuation of the High Holidays *Shmoneh Esreh*.
18. See Exodus 19: 6.
19. Jeremiah 1: 18–19.
20. S. Hank, H. Simon and U. Hank, *Feldrabbiner in den deutschen Streitkräften des Ersten Weltkrieges* (Berlin: Hentrich and Hentrich, 2013), pp. 338–9.
21. Verband der deutschen Juden (eds), *Gruß der Feldrabbiner*, pp.25 8.
22. Judaism requires that someone of the same sex remains with the corpse from moment of death until the body is washed and interred. Interment should where possible occur within twenty-four hours unless Sabbath intervenes.
23. Verband der deutschen Juden (eds), *Gruß der Feldrabbiner*, pp.28–30.

24. Leviticus 23: 42–3.
25. Term used at the beginning of the war by those who thought that the war would be 'over by Christmas'.
26. Hank, Simon and Hank, *Feldrabbiner in den deutschen Streitkräften*, pp.298–300.
27. See Plate 17. The Protestant Kaverau (left) has a plain, unadorned cross while the cross of the Catholic Schürmann (right) carries a crucifix with Christ's body. See also B. Goldberg, *Abseits der Metropolen. Die jüdische Minderheit in Schlwesig-Holstein* (Neumünster: Wachholtz Verlag, 2009), p.254.
28. Jewish and Muslim dietary laws are similar in some respects but there are differences.
29. On 15 March 1915 (new style) Tsar Nicholas II abdicated and a provisional government headed by Alexander Kerensky (1881–1970) took over. However, nine months later they were overthrown by the Bolsheviks under Vladimir Ilyich Lenin (1870–1924) in the revolution of 7–8 November (new style). The Bolsheviks sued for peace; a treaty was signed in Brest-Litovsk on 3 March 1918.
30. These memoirs were written between 1950 and 1951.
31. Also known as Reb Chaim Brisker (1853–1918), rabbi and Talmudic scholar.
32. A. Winter, 'Memoirs', chapters 5 and 6. Naftali Winter: personal collection.

CHAPTER TEN

Chaplain Conferences

During the war several chaplains' conferences were held in the East and West. A combined meeting of both groups was planned, but did not occur. This chapter presents translations of the minutes of one meeting in the West, and one in the East.

Minutes of the Jewish Chaplain Conference (West) on 5 December 1916 in Brussels, Hotel des Boulevards[1]

Present: Leo Baerwald, Heimann Chone, Bruno Italiener, Siegfried Klein, Reinhold Lewin, Martin Salomonski, Georg Salzberger, Georg Wilde

Beginning: 10.00 a.m.

Juden-Zählung
A thorough debate on the War Ministry Jewish Census decree occurred, reflecting dismay in Jews of Germany. It was unanimously determined that both the decree and its implementation have had a humiliating effect on comrades entrusted to our spiritual care and has had deplorable repercussions.

Combined Conference of the Jewish Chaplains in West and East
The combined conference of all Jewish chaplains in Berlin that was planned for early January 1917 will not take place, in deference to the concern which the *Referent* [advisor] on spiritual care to the War Ministry has expressed to the Chairman of the Western Jewish chaplain conference.

Allgemeiner Rabbiner Verband
It was decided to express the gratitude of Jewish chaplains of the West to the Allgemeiner Rabbiner Verband for generously providing support of Jewish comrades for celebrations in the field during the autumn festival period. The Verband should be requested to send Jewish literature with both instructive and entertaining content.

Verband der deutschen Juden
Because of repeated complaints, the Verband der deutschen Juden should be asked to repeat their request to the War Ministry for appointment of a Jewish chaplain for Army Divisions A and B.[2] For the upcoming Chanukah celebration, the Verband should be asked to send, as before, 300 copies of the Chanukah hymn[3] to each Jewish chaplain.

The Question of Associate Chaplains
It should be suggested that the Verband der deutschen Juden grant associate chaplains a one-time equipment expense allowance of 300 marks.

The group is informed that Colleague Chone, who up till now was attached to the Sixth Army, has by order of the War Ministry been transferred the First Army. Colleague Baneth [p.318], until now associate chaplain of the Second Army, has been transferred as associate chaplain of the Sixth Army.

Jewish War Graves
A thorough discussion was held about the pamphlet 'Jewish Tombstones in the Field'. The publisher's services are unanimously recognized with thanks. A few suggestions for changes should be discussed by Dr Salzberger with the publisher.

Wilde moves that the Jewish chaplains of East and West prepare and publish a collection of photographs of Jewish war graves.

Instructions
Lewin is requested to give the talk entitled 'Instructions for Jewish Chaplains' proposed for the general meeting in Berlin,[4] at the next meeting of Jewish chaplains of the West.

Russian Prisoners of War
Lewin reports about arrangements made by his Army High Command for spiritual care of Jewish Russian prisoners of war. The same should be attempted for services with Russian prisoners of war in other armies.[5]

Military Railways Division
The need for punctual notification of the few Jewish soldiers assigned to Military Railways Division of the upcoming Chanukah festival is again pointed out.

Ordering of Matzoth
It is decided to order 100 lb of matzoth for each Jewish chaplain from the newly founded Zentral für Ritualangelegenheiten in Frankfurt-am-Main.

Miscellaneous
A discussion on the spread of venereal disease was again held. Lewin reports that an article by him warning about this will appear shortly in the *Neue jüdische Monatshefte*.

A discussion was again held about visits to the trenches, with consideration of their wide area of spiritual care and increasing travel difficulties. Regarding the attitude of Jewish chaplains to comrades' complaints about anti-Semitism, reference is made to a point raised at the Conference of 16 May 1916.

Conclusion: 7.30 p.m.
Italiener.

Minutes of Conference of Jewish Chaplains of the East, Riga, 12–13 February 1918[6]

Present: Leo Baeck, Siegmund Hanover, Sali Levi, Arthur Levy, Leopold Rosenak, Jakob Sonderling, Aron Tänzer [See Plate 2]

Excused: Carlebach, Winter

Colleague A. Lazarus, after having been successfully active in the East for over a year, has been transferred to another theatre of operations.

Baeck: Reports about input of the past three months which gave rise to no further discussion.

A. Levy: Refers to the planned announcement of Colleague Baerwald concerning care of Jewish war graves before all collected material is available; supported by S. Levi.

The meeting decides:

To request Colleague Baerwald to limit his planned announcement to his area only; to request Eastern High Command – to whom all grave officers are referred – to mount the Jewish emblem on graves.

Colleague S. Levi should get in touch with the graves officer of the Tenth Army regarding Jewish emblems.

With a view to the possibility of demobilization,[7] the conference chairman should petition Eastern High Command that, in this event, colleagues are badly needed at home. Apart from a shortage of rabbis, some colleagues have been granted six months leave: the latter declare themselves ready to return to their old service area for a few days of spiritual care (in the field) each month. The chair will request to present this proposal verbally.

For upcoming Pesach celebrations [Plate 25], upon instruction of A. Levy it is decided to request Central Command for exemption of Jewish soldiers for three days because Sabbath follows the first two days of the festival. Additionally, allocation of flour for manufacture of the necessary matzoth is requested from Command for the main celebration

The Rabbinerberband will be requested to indicate the amount of money collected for festival celebrations, after deduction of 1/10 of the total amount, 1/3 of which is designated for colleagues in the Balkans.

According to the request by Tänzer, the conference decides: The Jewish chaplains active on the Eastern Front constitute a *Konferenzgemeinschaft* [conference community] for continuation of work begun during the war. Baeck is elected as Chairman of this Conference Community, with A. Levy as substitute. The chairman has everything necessary to achieve dissemination of the *Gemeinschaft* [community] proceedings. Colleagues from the Western Front will advise on their own joining of this conference community.

Tänzer's Memorandum Concerning Organization of Jewish Military Spiritual Care[8]
Colleague Tänzer presents two letters from Colleague Salzberger in the West at Army High Command, of 3 and 24 December 1917.

It is apparent that colleague Salzberger has handed the draft of my memorandum to the Senior Quartermaster of Command after inclusion of several suggested small changes – which he considered insignificant – for onward submission to the War Ministry. My name as the editor has been deleted. Neither I nor my colleagues on the Eastern Front were informed of this process in any way. I was first informed of this on 3 December 1917 after the memorandum had already been handed in, and immediately circularized all colleagues on the Eastern Front about this in writing, requesting their reactions. It was generally felt that Salzberger had found himself in a dilemma and, in the matter's best interests, could not have acted differently. However several rabbis made Salzberger responsible for a somewhat unsuccessful venture. Upon my request, Salzberger has sent me a copy of the version which he handed in. Comparison shows that the copy of my memorandum which he handed in is in form and detail fundamentally unaltered. The two altered points are:

1) Inclusion of an example for the unresolved official position;
2) A drastic change in point no. 3 of the organizational draft.

While all colleagues have agreed that my memorandum foresees appointment of military rabbis in peacetime only in a subsidiary capacity, with no official appointment of a military Oberrabbiner, the memorandum handed in by Salzberger suggests appointment of military rabbis without emphasizing the subsidiary office and appointment of a military Oberrabbiner. This suggestion, which concerns the entire rabbinate, should not have been made without agreement by all Jewish chaplains. There is also the correct fear that the planned military Oberrabbinat would constitute a subject of contention between different religious parties and Jewish movements. Perhaps the entire sought-for goal of the memorandum would be called into question.

Lengthy discussion of this matter was concluded with the following suggestion by Baeck: The Conference of the East expresses the expectation that in the future issues which affect the entire Jewish chaplaincy must be concluded only after advice and decisions by both Conferences (East and West). In urgent cases the Chairmen of both Conferences will make personal contact. The Conference thanks Tänzer again for his memorandum, and again stresses the service that he has rendered to all.

S. Levi reports regarding printing of the soldier's prayer book. He has submitted two-thirds of the prayer book (approximately a hundred pages) in sample printed sheets. It was decided to publish the book, with Jewish chaplains of the West contributing to costs. Baeck is tasked with contacting the Gemeindebund, the Centralverein deutscher Staatsbürger jüdischen Glaubens, and the Konferenzgemeinschaft of the large communities and large lodges with requests for financial support. The prayer book will be printed without title page and Lieutenant Hermann Struck[9] is especially thanked for his drawing. The eventual printing should be postponed for three weeks to ensure that money available is sufficient for the number of printed copies. In his presentation about the portion of the service that is sung, Sonderling emphasizes the value of musical moments and requests that the rabbis themselves should lead the singing, with general participation of all soldiers present. He also requests some German songs such as 'We Gather Together'[10] etc. He recommends that, in collaboration with professionals in the field, a simple musical appendix should be produced together with the prayer book. A. Levi does not agree with the musical supplement and asks the rabbis for a Cantor, because not every rabbi is gifted musically.

S. Levi requests development of a memorandum on this issue from Sonderling. Tänzer moves for a memorandum about the entire issue of the liturgy together with an Appendix on singing from Sonderling.

Baeck stresses the culture of religious services, their order and behaviour; also the value of the Hebrew language and the significance of singing.

Hanover, in his presentation of spiritual care of prisoners of war, requests holding of services in prisoner of war camps where possible, because of the difficulty of holding a common dialogue between German soldiers and Russian prisoners, and need for raising the prisoners' morale, showing them that their needs are being considered. He further requests proper provision with books as well as general care for the well-being of prisoners.

Sonderling speaks of the community spirit engendered by a common service for prisoners and soldiers. S. Levi and Baeck agree with Hanover's opinion and suggest that services must be together during festivals.

Tänzer informs about provision of Jewish soldiers with reading matter. A long debate results in the following resolution:

1) Provision of reading matter to Jewish soldiers is one of the tasks of Jewish chaplains, and should serve as a supplement to spiritual care and religious influence, and protection against spiritual degeneration.
2) In the interests of religious influence, writings that are disseminated should mostly be appropriate for knowledge of Jewish study, history and contemporary life.
3) Rapid formation of a central location with sufficient means to solve this issue rapidly and actively is essential.

During the course of the debate it was also decided that Baeck should draw up a new list of useful Jewish books, assisted in this task by all his colleagues. Baeck reported on current religious trends. After a very quiet period, new religious life has arisen. Rationalism, as it has ruled during the past few decades, has been replaced by experience and intuition of the depth and private nature of the religious world of thought. Rabbis too must consider this. All great spiritual revolutions have sprung from Judaism. We are experiencing a similar period today – a time of faith and hope. Perhaps the Jewish people and the Jewish religion are entering the world anew. It is for us to acknowledge that only through Judaism can the present wounded world be healed.[11] In conclusion, at the wish of some colleagues for whom this conference is perhaps the last one in the field, Baeck gives an overview on previously held conferences in the field, and ends with best wishes for fruitful common labours during peacetime. After this he was given a vote of thanks for his good and successful guidance.

Hanover: for the minutes S. Levi: for correctness of the copy.

NOTES

1. Centrum Judaicum Berlin. CJA, 75 C Ra 1, Nr. 7, #12517, Bl. 349-349RS.
2. Heinrich Cohn (see p.319) was appointed to serve with Army Groups A and B from 1917 to 1918.
3. *Ma'oz Tsur*.
4. The meeting did not occur.
5. No Jewish chaplains were appointed for spiritual care of the approximately 300,000 Jewish soldiers serving in the Tsar's army (Yochanan Petrovsky-Shtern, personal communication).
6. Centrum Judaicum Berlin. CJA, 75 D Ta 1, Nr. 4, #13367, Bl 4-32RS.
7. The Treaty of Brest-Litovsk, ending the war between Russia and the Central Powers, was signed on 3 March 1918. A separate peace had already been concluded with Ukraine on 9 February 1918.

8. See p.215, entry of 12 December 1917. This affair, which obviously caused Rabbi Tänzer distress and some anger, reflects his punctilious nature, following all rules and regulations to the letter. It obviously took a while, and the mediation of Leo Baeck, the peacemaker, to calm him down.
9. Hermann Struck (1876–1944), a noted German-Jewish artist known for his etchings, including those of German soldiers on the Eastern Front and Jewish civilians in Eastern Europe. In 1917 he became the advisor for Jewish affairs at the German Eastern Front High Command.
10. The German translation of this prayer (*Wir treten zum Beten*: Adrianus Valerius, c.1575–1625) became a potent symbol of the Throne- and Altar-alliance of German civil religion until 1918.
11. More of Leo Baeck's neo-Kantian musings.

CHAPTER ELEVEN

Epilogue – Betrayal

Chaplains came from all parts of the *Reich*, cities large and small, families rich and poor. Some came from rabbinical families (Baeck, Baerwald, Carlebach, Cohn, Hanover, Arnold Lazarus, Emil Levy, Salzberger, Sänger), others from the merchant class (Chone, Klein, Kronheim, Sali Levi, Rosenak, Salomonski, Sonderling, Steinthal).[1] They were not necessarily wealthy or even comfortably off: Emil Kronheim helped support himself by teaching stipendia, and Aron Tänzer, whose father died when he was young, existed 'on herring tails' during his studies. Most studied at the Jewish Theological Seminaries of Berlin and Breslau, at the time centres of German-Jewish liberal thought. Berlin, where Jews comprised approximately 5 per cent of the population, boasted more than five chaplains. Ages varied from 20s to 40s and no thoughts are evidenced in their writings about hardships or dangers. They left family and congregation (often against the wishes of both), and enlisted. Nor could there have been any pecuniary reason: in the beginning no uniform or any type of allowance was granted by the Prussian War Ministry. Only later was a uniform allowance and monthly stipend approved, but these were never sufficient (nor equal to sums approved for Christian chaplains), and had to be supplemented by personal funds and support from local congregations. Later in the war, when food shortages became acute, food (as much as possible) was sent in the opposite direction, from the fighting to the home front.

Cooperation of High Command in allowing and encouraging these spiritual activities is striking: nothing could have been achieved without their assistance. This is emphasized many times by different chaplains. Orders of the day were issued; leave and help with transportation given. Rabbi Tänzer reports provision of wood for one of his soup kitchens on the Eastern Front. When rabbis complained in 1916 that an additional chaplain was required for Army Groups A and B, Rabbi Heinrich Cohn was appointed. Christian soldiers and officers sometimes attended and appreciated Jewish services. Rabbi Salzberger reports that General Hermann von François, a hero of Tannenberg, attended services after his son had done so. Jewish chaplains were permitted, on both Fronts, to minister to the needs of Russian Jewish prisoners of war. Russo-Jewish soldiers had no chaplains of their own faith in their own army.[2] Numerous anecdotes attest to their satisfaction with German captivity. Leo Baeck describes services with prisoners of war most probably from England and/or the dominions.

Did Jewish soldiers and chaplains encounter anti-Semitism in the German army? If so, how serious and pervasive was the problem? Generalizations are problematic, and no one-size-fits-all conclusion is possible. Certainly anti-Jewish prejudice did exist in some units, promotions were in some cases delayed, and this worsened as the war progressed, no clear victory was foreseen, and a search for scapegoats ensued. The 1916 *Judenzählung* made matters worse and contributed substantially to post-war German anti-Semitism. However, reports of anti-Semitism in the chaplains' diaries are irregular. Rabbi Salzberger deals with this at the end of his memoirs; he also mentions an encounter with an anti-Semitic Protestant chaplain who 'could not tolerate Jews'. Rabbi Italiener states that reports of anti-Semitism must be confirmed, and Rabbis Salomonski and Baeck either do not mention it or do so obliquely. Rabbi Tänzer, in his long memoirs and diaries, mentions it only a few times and does not refer to the *Judenzählung* at all, although this was definitely carried out on the Eastern as well as Western Front. No mention of anti-Semitism is made in any of the *Sabbathgedanken* sermons or those for the holiday season of autumn 1915. By contrast, Rabbi Winter clearly states that anti-Semitism was present, and gradually worsened, especially after 1916, and Rabbi Lewin worries about it in his post-war pamphlet but states (as does Rabbi Salzberger) that it had the advantage of bringing Jews closer to their faith than they were before. Rabbi Wiener also worries about its effects in a post-war Germany. In view of the above and without citation of a wider spectrum of reports, David Fine's inference that Jewish chaplains were not especially troubled by anti-Semitism, and that the *Judenzählung* did not lead to increased discrimination,[3] seems untenable.

Three diaries and reports extend to November 1918: Rabbi Tänzer does not allude to the fact that Germany was about to lose the war, perhaps because he was too preoccupied with day-to day matters such as food, looking after soldiers entrusted to his care, the fate of his sons, and his own broken health. Rabbi Winter mentions an outcome only right at the end when the Western Front broke and revolution occurred in Germany. In a report dated 14 September 1917 Leo Baeck hints at deteriorating conditions but ends optimistically: 'When no new path leads into the distance, at least hope needs to be renewed ... but the present acts as a bridge to security and protection.'[4] As reported by Rabbi Salzberger, as the war progressed with no clear victory in sight, initial enthusiasm was replaced by a sense of duty, which lasted to the end of the war. None of the rabbis speak about atrocities that may have been committed, or that the German cause is anything but fair and patriotic and a German victory is correct and necessary.

Chaplains of all faiths were, in most cases, treated with equal courtesy by officers. Jewish chaplains repeatedly emphasize equal treatment for soldiers of all faiths. There is no reason to question the reciprocity of this feeling in most cases, and it can be imagined that in some cases the last face seen by a dying Christian soldier was that of a Jewish chaplain and vice versa.[5] Rabbi Winter describes a gradual deterioration of relations with officers and men, especially after the Jewish census, and this is also intimated by Rabbi Salzberger's mention of an overtly anti-Semitic Protestant chaplain.

Were there differences in attitudes and reports of Jewish chaplains which depended upon age, place of birth, education and religious community? I have alluded to deep belief in their Germanness, in the German Cause, and the superiority of German *Kultur*. Disparaging comments by Rabbis Salomonski and Salzberger about the French must be tempered by Rabbi Salomonski's appreciation of the good in French tradition, and the citation by Emile Zola that ends his book. Indeed, his comments about the 'maid of Orleans' and '*Madame l'Econome*' could have come straight out of a Zola novel. The Franco-Prussian war had left deep divisions between French and Germans, as well as a feeling of Prussian superiority. Of interest is the section in Rabbi Salzberger's diary dealing with the Dreyfus affair. His horror that such a thing occurred disguises the fact that it could never have happened in Prussia because Jews were not allowed to serve as officers in the Prussian army, let alone the General Staff. Rabbis Salzberger and Salomonski, to a greater or lesser degree, present the French in an unfavourable light compared to Germans: neither appears to appreciate justifiable French rancour at occupation, nor the loss of Alsace-Lorraine and the annual German celebration of Sedan Day. Emile Levy echoes the prevailing German sentiment that the British are interested only in power, commerce and money. There is appreciation of the value of Russian soldiers, their bravery and patriotism, despite pogroms and persecutions. By contrast – with the exception of Rabbi Winter – criticism of the Polish population, is unrelenting, especially by Rabbi Tänzer, who loses no opportunity to point out Polish ingratitude for having been 'liberated' by the German army from Russian domination.[6] Rabbi Tänzer spares no criticism for the Jews of Kiev, and does not understand why rabbis in Ukraine speak Russian and do not understand German. He refers to Jews from many locations as *Schnorrers* and feels that he is being taken advantage of, but this does not stop his charitable activities.

The conflict on the Eastern Front is an important but little-studied aspect of the First World War.[7] Apart from battle casualties, deaths from water- (typhoid, cholera, dysentery) and insect-borne diseases (particularly louse-borne typhus) were high. Jewish civilians living in these areas suffered greatly, and generally looked upon the German and Austro-Hungarian armies as liberators from Tsarist oppression. Memoirs of Rabbis Winter and Tänzer provide descriptions of this battlefront. Rabbi Tänzer also describes the invasion of Ukraine by the German army in early February 1918.

Difference in age between some chaplains seems to come into play only in the affair of the memorandum, where Rabbi Tänzer (then in his mid-40s) appears to feel slighted by Rabbi Salzberger (one decade younger). Most rabbis are down-to-earth and their comments apply to everyday life around them. Rabbi Tänzer's diary gives a fascinating look into the lost world of Eastern European Jewry (including a visit to the Rabbi from Lubavitch) and the chaos of the 1918 German invasion of Ukraine followed by their final defeat. He describes (sometimes from personal experience) various infectious diseases which claimed so many civilian and military lives on the Eastern Front. Rabbi Salzberger's tone is that of a gentle kind man but that of Rabbi Salomonski is Zolaesque, sometimes sarcastic, and incisive. However, the section at the end of 'On vacation' (p.105) is beautiful and evocative, and he was also the only one to publish poetry. Rabbi Baeck's reports are full of neo-Kantian musings and Rabbi Italiener's sermon on David and Jonathan represents an almost unbearable 'what if'. Reinhold Lewin, from the small amount of war literature which he left behind, was a deep thinker and clearly saw the potential danger for Jews in post-war Germany, although he hoped that it might prove otherwise. The photograph of a somewhat bemused-looking Rabbi Winter with Reb Chaim Soloveichik (Plate 18) depicts emancipated versus traditional European Judaism more clearly than words. Most chaplains were conservative-to-liberal and observance of dietary laws does not seem to have been punctilious. However, the Orthodox Rabbi Winter was careful in his observance, including of the dietary laws, passing up meat and shellfish and dinner invitations in preference for bread and tea, to the surprise of his hosts. His is the only memoir in which such dietary observance is detailed. Rabbi Rosenak and the Carlebachs were surely also orthodox, but this was facilitated by their being based in towns with large Jewish populations and kosher eating establishments.

The level of learning of these men, both secular and non-secular, was remarkable. Most had obtained doctorates after years of study at prestigious German universities and dissertations on the most diverse subjects (Plants in Mishnaic Times; Thomas Campanella; the Council of Basel; Luther and the Jews, etc.). Their writings are full of quotations from Hebrew Scriptures as well as those from German literature, and knowledge of English literature is also apparent. Rabbi Winter shows his knowledge of Jewish law by expounding on a section permitting interruption of the Sabbath Torah reading by a group of civilians complaining about the requisitioning of their cattle by German military authorities.

Most chaplains did not wait to be drafted but volunteered early in the war. Rabbi Tänzer, 43 years old and having lost his first wife and remarried between 1912 and 1914, volunteered immediately and pestered authorities until, a year later in 1915, approval was finally forthcoming and he was given perhaps the most difficult region in which to serve. The physical courage of these men is evident. Rabbi Siegfried Klein was wounded in action twice. Visits to trenches put the chaplains under fire, as did travelling on dangerous roads in all kinds of weather. Exposure to faecal-oral, respiratory and insect-borne infectious diseases was a constant danger, and no antibacterials were available. The 1918 influenza pandemic went on to claim twenty to fifty million lives worldwide. Rabbi Tänzer in particular was lucky to end the war alive.

The same spirit of patriotism was shown by the Jews on both sides of the conflict. Prisoners of war were, when possible, included in services and celebrations; the 1917 Pesach celebration in Skopje, Macedonia must have been a true meeting of nations: Jews from Germany, Austria-Hungary, Bulgaria, Macedonia, other parts of southern Slavic countries, Russian prisoners of war – all together under one roof reciting the same prayers.

Epilogue

After war's end, all of the Jewish chaplains returned to their home congregations, no doubt hopeful that the post-war period would herald a new era in German-Jewish relations. Diaries and memoirs available attest to this hope, but there is also a fear (voiced most clearly by Georg Salzberger and Reinhard Lewin) that the increased level of anti-Semitism which occurred when it was obvious that Germany would lose the war and a convenient scapegoat was sought, might not lead to this desired new era.

The thought that, after Jewish fellow-Germans had fought, bled and died together with their Christian comrades, a spirit of kinship would result similar to that found in every nation after a war was natural. However, although the Weimar Republic offered, for the first time in their history, real equal opportunities for Germany's Jews, it was based upon shaky politico-economic grounds.

It is not the purpose of this epilogue to describe the demise of the Weimar Republic and the rise of National Socialism, nor to report in detail on the specific post-war activities of all Jewish chaplains. The author would merely like to point out that all of them were subjected, after January 1933, to various degrees of persecution. There were four groups: i) Those who died before the war or before they could emigrate; ii) Those who escaped and continued their lives in other countries; iii) Those who were incarcerated but survived the war, and iv) Those who were deported and killed in concentration camps or other locations.

Aron Tänzer (he changed his name to Arnold after the war) returned to his Göppingen community. With the advent of National Socialism, he became increasingly disillusioned: his last published work was entitled '*Des Vaterlands Dank*' [The Fatherland's Thanks]. A year before he passed away in 1937 Rabbi Tänzer described his wishes for his future burial in his will. He wished to be buried by a work colleague. No type of memorial or anything of the like was to be held, also no kind of German prayer. His gravestone reads: Dr Phil Aron Tänzer, Rabbi in Hohenems, Meran, Göppingen, chaplain in the World War from 1915–1918, chevalier of high decoration, author of scholarly texts, born 30 January 1871, died 26 February 1937.[8]

Sali Levi was on the point of emigrating to the United States in 1941, when he died in Berlin. Emmanuel Carlebach died in Cologne in 1927, Arnold Lazarus in Frankfurt in 1932, and Jacob Sänger in

Breslau in 1938. Gravestones of Sali Levi and Arnold Tänzer are shown in Plates 32 and 12, respectively.

Leopold Rosenak died in 1923 on board a ship travelling to Germany from the United States, where he helped organize aid to Ukrainian orphans. Rosenak, who was closely associated with Paul von Hindenburg and called him friend, became increasingly disturbed by the growing anti-Semitism of the early 1920s and wrote to Hindenburg (whose influence on German life after the war was great), requesting help. He also wrote to Erich Ludendorff, who responded briefly (on 15 February 1921) that he would get to it but that he didn't have time at the moment. He received the following non-committal reply from Hindenburg a week later:[9]

> Many thanks for your friendly letter. I obviously remember most vividly our common activity during the Great War. I do not express myself on political matters in principle, and therefore feel detrimental actions of bad Jewish elements doubly strongly, because they occur mainly in commercial and political areas and are supported mainly by the rich. See to it that your upstanding fellow-Jews renounce their bad co-religionists, who should rather concern themselves with their own betterment. Then the entire race will stop being made responsible for the errors of the (unfortunately) not so few.

The majority of other rabbis fled Germany between 1933 and 1939: to Israel (Arthur Levy, Emil Levy, Siegmund Hanover, Paul Lazarus, Heymann Chone, David Carlebach); Great Britain (Georg Salzberger, Bruno Italiener, Alexander Winter, Georg Wilde, Ludwig Baneth, Heinrich Cohn); the United States (Jacob Sonderling, Max Wiener, Leo Baerwald, Albert Wolf); Canada (Felix Aber); Argentina (Fritz-Leopold Steinthal); Bolivia and Uruguay (Moritz Winter); and Sweden (Emil Kronheim). Some, but not all, rabbis who emigrated led congregations again in the country to which they fled. Georg Salzberger emigrated only after his synagogue in Frankfurt had been damaged during *Kristallnacht* and a brief imprisonment period in Dachau. Leo Baerwald's Munich Hauptsynagoge was burned to the ground on Hitler's express orders in 1938, and he was allowed to emigrate in 1940, also after a brief imprisonment in Dachau.[10]

Leo Baeck represents a special case. In 1933, after the National Socialists came to power, Baeck worked to defend the Jewish community as president of the Reichsvertretung der deutschen Juden, an umbrella organization that united German Jewry from 1933 to 1938. After the Reichsvertretung was disbanded during the November 1938 pogrom known as *Kristallnacht*, the Nazis reassembled the council's members under the government-controlled newly named Reichsvereinigung. Leo Baeck headed this organization as its president until his deportation to Theresienstadt in January 1943. He did not play a decisive role in Jewish administration of the ghetto until its last days. Yet he never ceased to be a symbol to, and a leader of, the Jews imprisoned in Theresienstadt. In Berlin, he had been a leader of the German Jews; in Theresienstadt he became a spiritual leader and symbol, leader to thousands of Jews from all parts of Nazi-occupied Europe. Until his deportation, numerous American institutions offered to help him escape the war and immigrate to the United States, but he refused to abandon his flock in the camps and declined the offers. He survived the Holocaust and died in London in 1956.[11]

Four chaplains and at least one assistant chaplain were murdered during the Holocaust. Hugo Gradenwitz fled to Holland with his family but was deported and killed in Auschwitz in November 1943. Siegfried Klein, who refused to abandon his congregation in Düsseldorf, was deported with his wife in late 1941 to the Ghetto in Lodz. His wife died of exhaustion in 1942, and he himself was murdered in Auschwitz August 1944.[12] Reinhold Lewin and his wife were deported in 1943 and both disappeared. Josef Carlebach remained with his congregation in Hamburg until 4 December 1941, when the remnants of the community were deported to the east. The Gestapo offered him the option of remaining behind but he refused, preferring to remain with his congregation. In March 1942 Carlebach, his wife and three youngest daughters were shot in a forest outside of Riga, Latvia. Siegfried Alexander became second rabbi in Düsseldorf after the war. A photograph of him officiating at a 1936 memorial service in Berlin Weißensee cemetery for Jews killed during the war (Plate 33) shows in his eyes the bleak future of Jews in Germany. Siegfried Alexander and his wife disappeared into *Nacht und Nebel* in Auschwitz in 1944. Martin Salomonski, a man whose heart glowed with the ardour of German nationalism, was deported to Theresienstadt and murdered in Auschwitz in October 1944.[13]

Veterans who served their country should be honoured and respected, not persecuted, driven out, imprisoned and killed. The remarkable thing is that, despite what happened during 1933–45, rabbis such as Leo Baeck and Georg Salzberger worked unceasingly until their death for German-Jewish rapprochement.

'Earth, do not cover my blood and let my cries find no resting-place!' (Job 16: 18)

NOTES

1. Unless stated otherwise, information is from M. Brocke and J. Carlebach, *Biographisches Handbuch der Rabbiner. Teil 2. Die Rabbiner im Deutschen Reich 1871–1945* (Munich: K.G. Sauer/Berlin: Walter de Gruyter, 2009). Additional information on rabbis who perished in the Holocaust is from http://db.yadvashem.org/names/search.html?language=en. Reinhold Lewin is not included in the latter, probably because his children and other family members perished in the Holocaust with him, and there was no written documentation of his death.
2. Yochanan Petrovsky-Shtern, personal communication.
3. D.J. Fine, *Jewish Integration in the German Army in the First World War* (Berlin: de Gruyter, 2012), pp.14–36.
4. Editorial, 'Die Woche', *Allgemeine Zeitung des Judentums*, vol.81 (14 December 1917), p.592.
5. M. Schian, 'Die Arbeit der evangelischer Kirche im Felde', vol.1, in *Die deutsche evangelische Kirche im Weltkriege* (edited at the behest of the Deutscher evangelischer Ausschuβ) (Berlin: Verlag von E.S. Mittler & Sohn, 1921), pp.256, 353.
6. It seems not to occur to him that the Poles would much rather govern themselves than become a proxy state for Germany and part of the new Germany's *Ostpolitik*.
7. J. Winter, *Remembering War. The Great War between Memory and History in the Twentieth Century* (New Haven, CT and London: Yale University Press, 2006), pp.80–1.
8. http://www.edjewnet.de/taenzer/taenzer.htm; Uri Tänzer, personal communications.
9. Leopold and Bella Rosenak Collection. Leo Baeck Institute, New York, Archives, AR 1071.
10. Jane Vogel-Kohai, personal communication.
11. G. Heuberger and F. Backhaus (eds), *Leo Baeck 1873–1956. Aus dem Stamme von Rabbinern* (Frankfurt am Main: Jüdischer Verlag im Suhrkamp Verlag, 2001), pp.77–146.
12. B. Fleerman and H. Jakobs, 'Fallbeispiel Westfront – Düsseldorf – Ghetto Łódź. Lebensstationen des Frontsoldaten und Feldrabbiners Dr. Siegfried Klein', in *Jüdische Soldaten – Jüdischer Widerstand: In Deutschland und Frankreich*, ed. M. Berger and G. Römer-Hillebrecht (Paderborn: Ferdinand Schöningh, 2012), pp.173–9.
13. Buchergruppe (eds), *Feldrabbiner: Joseph Carlebach, Leo Baeck, Walter Jacob, Martin Salomonski, Adolf Altmann, Max Friediger, Siegfried Klein, Leopold Rosenak* (Books LLC, German series, 2010), pp.11–12, 28–9; http://de.wikipedia.org/wiki/Kategorie:Feldrabbiner. The fates of Rabbis Hugo Gradenwitz and Siegfried Klein are reported on the web pages, not in the booklet.

APPENDIX A

Biographical Table of Rabbis

Name	Birth details	Education	Work History	War Service History
Leo Baeck	b. 1873 in Lissa (Posen) to Rabbi Samuel and Eva Baeck née Placzeck	Breslau and Berlin Theological Seminaries, University of Breslau, and Frederick William University, Berlin, PhD 1895	Rabbi in Oppeln, Düsseldorf and Berlin; lecturer Hochschule für die Wissenschaft des Judentums, Berlin	One of the first six Jewish chaplains appointed September 1914. Served first in Second Army (Western Front) and then First Army Command (Eastern Front)[1]
Leo Baerwald	b. 1883 in Saaz to Rabbi Aron and Fanny Baerwald née Lazarus	Jewish Theological Seminary Breslau and University of Breslau	Assistant Rabbi in Munich	Served as soldier and later chaplain in the Bavarian Army at Rear Echelon Inspectorate of Sixth Army (Western Front) August 1914 – October 1917. Awarded Iron Cross Second Class and Bavarian Military Service Order Fourth Class[2]
Ludwig (Leon Arjè) Baneth	b. 1891 in Krotoschin to Eduard and Dinka Baneth née Friedmann	Jewish Theological and Rabbinical Seminary Berlin	Graduated c. 1916	From 1916 served as gunner and associate chaplain in Second and Sixth Armies, assigned to Rabbi Salomonski (see below). Full chaplain in 1918[3]

Name	Birth details	Education	Work History	War Service History
Emmanuel Carlebach	b. 1874 in Lübeck to Rabbi Salomon and Esther Carlebach née Adler.	University of Berlin, Berlin Theological Seminary, University of Würzbürg, and Frankfurt Yeshivah	Rabbi in Cologne	During 1916–18 adviser to German military authorities in Warsaw on Jewish education matters and also served as chaplain[4]
Josef Zvi Carlebach	b. 1883 in Lübeck. Brother of Emmanuel Carlebach	University of Berlin (mathematics, natural sciences), Jewish Theological Seminary Berlin, University of Heidelberg. Obtained teaching certificate 1905, PhD around 1908. Ordained 1914	Taught at Jerusalem Teacher's Seminary (1905–07); senior teacher of mathematics, physics, chemistry, minerology Mommsen Gymnasium Berlin (1908–14)	1915–18 served in Lithuania advising the army on Jewish education; chaplain to Warsaw Gouvernement in 1918[5]
Hermann (Heimann) Chone	b. 1874 Punitz (Posen) to Isidor and Auguste Chone née Felbel	University of Berlin and Berlin Jewish Theological Seminary	Second rabbi in Nürnberg 1907, then from 1909 first rabbi in Konstanz	Served as chaplain on the Western Front: 1914–16 Sixth Army; 1916–17 First Army[6]
Heinrich Cohn	b. 1889 Basel, son of Rabbi Arthur Cohn	Preßburg Yeshivah, Universities of Lausanne, Basel, Straßburg, Jewish Theological Seminary Berlin. Passed teachers examination in English and French 1912, ordained 1915	Taught in Hirsch Realschule 1915–16; rabbinical assistant in Ansbach 1915–16	Served as chaplain on the Western Front (Army Divisions A and B) 1917–18[7]

BIOGRAPHICAL TABLE OF RABBIS

Name	Birth details	Education	Work History	War Service History
Hugo (Hirsch) Zvi Gradenvitz	b. 1876 in Rawitsch (Posen) son of Joseph and Johanna Gradenvitz née Jaffe	Berlin Rabbinical Seminary	Rabbi in Tarnowitz	Chaplain for Ninth Army in the Balkans 1917–18[8]
Siegmund Simon Adolf Hanover	b. 1880 Wandsbeck bei Hamburg, to Rabbi David and Rosa Hanover, née Hirsch	Berlin Rabbinical Seminary	Second Rabbi of Cologne, Chairman of Rhineland Rabbis Association	Rear Echelon Rabbi in Kowno, 1917–18[9]
Bruno Italiener	b. 1881 Burgdorf bei Hanover to Josef and Marianne Italiener née Adler	University of Breslau (philosophy, oriental philology) and Jewish Theological Seminary Breslau; one year military service 1902–03; PhD 1903, ordained 1907	Rabbi at Darmstadt Liberal Jewish Community	Served as chaplain 1914–18 on Western Front, Seventh Army[10]
Siegfried Klein	b. 1882 in Rheydt/Rhein to Julius and Jenny Klein née Grunwald	Universities of Berlin and Freiburg im Breisgau; Military training 1906–07, graduated PhD in Freiburg 1909	1904–14: teacher of religion at Berlin Community High Schools	Joined the army in 1914 and served sixteen months as a soldier, also serving as rabbinical assistant to Rabbi Salzberger (see below). Ordained 1915 during leave of absence and served as chaplain on the Western Front (Army Divisions von Strantz and A, B and C) between 1916 and 1918. Twice wounded and decorated with the Wound Badge in Black and the Iron Cross[11]

Name	Birth details	Education	Work History	War Service History
Emil Kronheim	b. 1890 in Guttstadt, East Prussia to Moses and Sara Kronheim née Lewinsohn	University of Berlin (?) and Jewish Theological Seminary	Studies and private tutor	1915–17: Served as a medical orderly and soldier in the Seventeenth Army in Russia, Italy and France. After obtaining rabbinical diploma at the Berlin Theological Seminary in 1917, served as chaplain in Belgium and France in the newly formed Eighteenth Army[12]
Arnold Lazarus	b. 1887 in Breslau, son of Rabbi Leiser Lazarus	Jewish Theological Seminary and University of Breslau. Obtained rabbinical diploma in 1905	Second rabbi in Frankfurt am Main Synagogue under Cäsar Seligmann, whom he succeeded in 1914	Served as chaplain 1916–18 in the Southern and Eastern Armies[13]
Paul Pinchas Lazarus	b. 1888 in Duisburg to Raphael and Betty Lazarus née Leseritz	Universities of Marburg, Breslau and Erlangen; 1911 graduated PhD in Erlangen (history). Jewish Theological Seminary in Breslau: obtained rabbinical diploma 1915	Second rabbi in Essen	After first serving as an ordinary soldier, served as chaplain with the Eleventh Army in Macedonia 1916–18: coordinated work with other chaplains in the region[14]
Sali(y)/ Salomon Levi	b. 1883 in Walldorf, Baden, son of William Levi	Jewish Theological Seminary and University of Breslau	Second liberal rabbi of Breslau	Served as chaplain for the Tenth Army in Vilna 1915–18[15]
Arthur Shimon Levy	b. 1881 in Hochfelden, lower Alsace	Rabbinical Seminary and Ecole Rabbinique in Colmar. Graduated in Straßburg 1908	Rabbi in Berlin-Schönefeld (Münchenerstraße) as well as the synagogue in Leipzigerstraße	Served as chaplain from 1914–18 for the Ninth Army on the Eastern Front[16]

BIOGRAPHICAL TABLE OF RABBIS

Name	Birth details	Education	Work History	War Service History
Emil Nathan Levy	b. 1879 in Dambach, lower Alsace, son of Rabbi Markus Levy	Berlin Orthodox Rabbinical Seminary (Ezriel Hildesheimer), University of Berlin (Egyptology, old Semitic languages); PhD in 1905	Rabbi in Berlin Religionsverein Westen; leader of Berlin community religious schools	Chaplain for Second Army (Western Front) 1914–16[17]
Reinhold Lewin	b. 1888 in Magdeburg	Jewish Theological Seminary and University of Breslau; graduated 1911, ordained rabbi in 1913	Second rabbi in Leipzig	Served as chaplain 1915–18 (Third Army, Western Front). Awarded Iron Cross Second Class and Knight's Cross of the Albrecht Order First Class with Swords[18]
Leopold Rosenak	b. 1868 in Nádasd (Hungary), to Samuel and Deborah Rosenak née Spitzer	Preßburg Yeshivah, Rabbinical Seminary and University of Berlin, PhD from University of Bern. Married Bella Carlebach, sister of Emmanuel and Josef (see above)	Orthodox rabbi in Bremen	March 1915 – October 1918 served in East, first in German South Army in Galicia, later with Army Division von Gallwitz in Twelfth Army and in Kovno, in the Tenth Army of General Ludendorff. Active from 1916 in committee for mobile libraries, and advisor to Military Administration in Jewish religion and culture. Played a leading part in the establishment of a Jewish soup kitchen in Kovno and re-opening of Slobodka Yeshiva. In 1917 was entrusted with a visit to Netherlands to obtain corn and potatoes for the German military (Plate 14). A programme for a Chanukah celebration organized by him is presented in Plate 22. Decorated with Iron Cross, Hanseatic Cross, and Turkish Iron Crescent[19]

Name	Birth details	Education	Work History	War Service History
Martin Salomonski	b. 1881 in Berlin, to Adolph and Bertha Salomonki née Koppenheim	Frederick William University (oriental philology) and Jewish Theological Seminary, Berlin: ordained 1908. PhD from University of Tübingen, 1910	Rabbi in Frankfurt an der Oder	Served as chaplain 1916–18 First and Second Armies, Western Front. Awarded Iron Cross Second Class[20]
Georg Salzberger	b. 1882 in Culm, West Prussia to Rabbi Moritz and Ann Salzberger née Freyhan	Jewish Theological Seminary Berlin (history, literature, homiletics) under Ismar Ellenbogen, and Frederick William University Berlin (semitic languages including Arabic), PhD University of Heidelberg 1907	Rabbi West End Synagogue Frankfurt am Main	Served in the Fifth Army throughout the war (one of the first six) and was personally awarded the Iron Cross Second Class by the Crown Prince[21]
Jacob Hirsch Sänger	b. 1878 in Bingen to Rabbi Hirsch and Babette Sänger née Kahn/Katz	University of Würzburg, Jewish Theological Seminary and University of Berlin. Ordained 1909, PhD University of Würzburg 1911	Rabbi and teacher Israelitisches Religionverein Ahawas Achim Berlin; also served as teacher in other Berlin religious schools	1915–18: chaplain in Eleventh Army in Romania, awarded the Iron Cross in 1916[22]

Name	Birth details	Education	Work History	War Service History
Jakob Sonderling	b. 1878 in Lipine, Upper Silesia to Wilhelm and Johanna Sonderling née Lebowitsch	Jewish Theological Seminary Vienna, Jewish Theological Seminary and University of Breslau, University of Tübingen (PhD 1904)	Rabbi in Göttingen and Hamburg	Chaplain on the Eastern Front with Niemen Army (1915) and Eighth Army (1917–18)[23]
Fritz-Leopold Steinthal	b. 1889 in Berlin to Heinrich and Clara Steinthal née Wiesenthal	Jewish Theological Seminary and University of Berlin, PhD 1911, ordained 1914	Assistant Rabbi in Berlin	Joined up first as a soldier, and then after becoming rabbi as a chaplain from 1914–17 on the Western Front, at the staff of the X. Ersatz-Division [Replacement Division]. Awarded the Iron Cross Second Class[24]
Aron (Arnold) Tänzer	b. 1871 in Hungarian Preßburg, to Heinrich and Marie Tänzer née Schlesinger	Preßburg rabbinical college; Universities of Berlin and Bern – PhD 1895.	Rabbi of Hohenems; rabbi in Meran; rabbi of Göppingen; founder of Göppingen public library	Bug Army, 1915–18. Awarded Iron Cross Second Class (1916), the Friederich Order First Class with Swords (1917), and Franz Joseph Order of the Emperor of Austria (1917)[25]
Max Wiener	b. 1882 in Oppeln, Upper Silesia to Isidor and Amelie Wiener née Marcus	Jewish Theological Seminary and University of Breslau (PhD 1906)	Rabbinical assistant Düsseldorf. Rabbi in Stettin	From 1917 served as chaplain for the First Army on the Western Front as successor of Heimann Chone[26]

Name	Birth details	Education	Work History	War Service History
Georg Wilde	b 1877 in Meseritz (Posen)	Jewish Theological Seminary and University of Breslau; University of Erlangen (PhD 1901)	Rabbi in Magdeburg	Served as chaplain with the Fourth Army (Western Front) throughout the war and received numerous decorations; played a large part in the publication of the *Feldbibel* [field bible][27]
David Alexander Winter	b. 1878 in Mönchengladbach to Josef and Sarah Winter née Rosenbaum	Jewish Theological Seminary and University of Berlin (ordained 1904); teaching degree in history and German (1910)	Rabbi in Myslowitz (Upper Silesia) and Bad Homburg	Served as chaplain 1916–18 on the Eastern Front, first with the Twelfth Army (Grodno) and latterly with the Tenth Army (Bialystok)[28]
Moritz Winter	b. 1886 in Magdeburg son of Salomon and Hulda Winter née Abraham	Universities of Berlin and Heidelberg (Semitic philology, Roman history); PhD 1908. Jewish Theological Seminary Berlin, ordained 1913	Rabbi in Königsberg	Chaplain for First Army (Western Front) 1917–18[29]

NOTES

1. G. Heuberger and F. Backhaus (eds), *Leo Baeck 1873–1956. Aus dem Stamme von Rabbinern* (Frankfurt am Main: Jüdischer Verlag im Suhrkamp Verlag, 2001), pp.15–43; M. Brocke and J. Carlebach, *Biographisches Handbuch der Rabbiner. Teil 2. Die Rabbiner im Deutschen Reich 1871–1945* (Munich: K.G. Saur/Berlin: Walter de Gruyter, 2009), pp.29–30.
2. Brocke and Carlebach, *Biographisches Handbuch der Rabbiner*, p.47.
3. Ibid., p.60.
4. Ibid., pp.112–13.
5. Ibid., pp.115–16.
6. Ibid., p.129.
7. Ibid., p.141.
8. Ibid., p.241.
9. Ibid., p.271.
10. Ibid., p.301.
11. Ibid., pp.334–5; B. Fleerman, and H. Jakobs, 'Fallbeispiel Westfront – Düsseldorf – Ghetto Łódź. Lebensstationen des Frontsoldaten und Feldrabbiners Dr. Siegfried Klein'. in *Jüdische Soldaten – Jüdischer Widerstand in Deutschland und Frankreich*, ed. M. Berger and G. Römer-Hillebrecht (Paderborn: Ferdinand Schöningh, 2012), pp.164–8.
12. Brocke and Carlebach, *Biographisches Handbuch der Rabbiner*, pp.356–7.
13. Ibid., p.367.
14. Ibid., p.369.
15. Ibid., p.379.
16. Ibid., p.381.
17. Ibid., pp.381–2.
18. Ibid., pp.394–5.
19. Ibid., p.506; Leopold and Bella Rosenak Collection. Leo Baeck Institute, New York, Archives, AR 1071.
20. Brocke and Carlebach, *Biographisches Handbuch der Rabbiner*, pp.529–30 (service given as in the Second army); M. Berger, *Eisernes Kreuz und Davidstern. Die Geschichte jüdischer Soldaten in deutschen Armeen* (Berlin: Trafoverlag, 2006), p.147 (service given as in the First Army).
21. Brocke and Carlebach, *Biographisches Handbuch der Rabbiner*, p.532.
22. Ibid., p.541.
23. Ibid., p.577.
24. Ibid., p.589.
25. Ibid., p.606.
26. Ibid., p.651. Writing from the Front for the newsletter of his congregation in Stettin, Wiener was not at all sanguine about the future of German Jews. The war, he recognized, had fuelled the fires of nationalism and, in spite of the much-lauded Jewish participation in it, he sensed that this heightened German nationalism did not bode well for the full participation of Jews in other spheres of national life once the war was past [R.S. Schine, *Jewish Thought Adrift. Max Wiener (1882–1950)* (Atlanta, GA: Scholars Press, 1992), pp.118–19].
27. Brocke and Carlebach, *Biographisches Handbuch der Rabbiner*, p.656.
28. Ibid., p.659
29. Ibid., p.661.

APPENDIX B

Biographical Table of Rabbinical Assistants and Rabbis Serving as Soldiers[1]

Name	Birth Details	Education	Work History	War Service History
Felix Aber	b. 1895 in Breslau, son-in-law of Leopold and Bella Rosenak (husband of Hanna née Rosenak)	University of Breslau	Student	Interrupted studies to volunteer; served 1914–18 as infantryman and later rabbinical assistant with the Seventeenth Army[2]
Siegfried Alexander	b. 1886 in Lobsens (Posen) to Wilhelm and Tina Alexander née Cohn	Universities of Berlin and Würzburg (philology, philosophy, paedagogics) and Jewish Theological Seminary in Berlin. Graduated 1915 in Würzburg, and obtained rabbinical diploma August 1918	Student	Volunteered (but not accepted) as chaplain, August 1914. Medical orderly on Western Front, promoted to non-commissioned officer in 1917. November 1917 – December 1918 worked as chaplain's assistant to Rabbi Georg Wilde in the Fourth Army High Command on the Western Front; awarded the Iron Cross Second Class in 1918[3]

David Carlebach	b. 1899 in Memel. Son of Emmanuel Carlebach	School	Student	After completing school, served at Front from September 1917 to end of war. Worked intermittently as chaplain's assistant and was at 19 years of age the youngest chaplain's assistant in the German army[4]
Albert Wolf	b. 1890 in Bichen	No details	Assistant rabbi in Offenburg	Volunteered November 1914 and became chaplain's assistant in 1917, serving in this capacity through the end of the war[5]

BIOGRAPHICAL TABLE OF RABBINICAL ASSISTANTS

NOTES

1. An unknown number of Jews served as rabbinical assistants: mention is made in Chapter 3 of chaplains assistants who were killed without providing details. Four examples of these assistants, who only obtained their rabbinical diplomas after the war, are provided. When rabbis were not available, services were held where possible under the supervision of non-commissioned officers or other soldiers educated in the holding of religious services (Plates 23–5); see also P. Pulzer, 'Der erste Weltkrieg', in *Deutsch-jüdische Geschichte in der Neuzeit; Band 3 1871–1918*, ed. S.M. Lowenstein, P. Mendes-Flohr, P. Pulzer and M. Richarz (Munich: C.H. Beck, 2000), p.358.
2. M. Brocke and J. Carlebach, *Biographisches Handbuch der Rabbiner. Teil 2. Die Rabbiner im Deutschen Reich 1871–1945* (Munich: K.G. Saur/Berlin: Walter de Gruyter, 2009), p.1.
3. Ibid., p.4. See Plate 19.
4. Ibid., p.112. The Carlebach family from Lübeck are remarkable in that out of twelve children (eight sons, four daughters), two sons (Josef and Emmanuel) served as chaplains. A daughter, Bella, married Leopold Rosenak, also a chaplain whose son-in-law Felix Aber served as chaplain's assistant. Emmanuel's son David Carlebach also served as chaplain's assistant. See also A. Schreiber, *'Gedenke der vorigen Zeiten'. Illustrierte Chronik der Juden in Moisling und Lübeck* (Lübeck: Edition Nord, 2009), pp.26–9.
5. Brocke and Carlebach, *Handbuch der Rabbiner*, p.664.

APPENDIX C

German First World War Military Ranks

Fähnrich	Ensign Cadet
Felddiakon	Field Deacon
Feldprop(b)st	Highest ecclesiastical rank in the Prussian army
Feldwebel	Sergeant Major
Feldwebel Leutnant	Sergeant Major Lieutenant (warrant officer)
Flieger	Private (flyer in army air service)
Gefreiter	Private first class
General der Artillerie	General (artillery)
General der Infanterie	General (infantry)
General der Kavallerie	General (cavalry)
Generalfeldmarshall	Field Marshall/General (army)
Generalleutnant	Lieutenant General
Generalmajor	Major General
Generaloberarzt	Surgeon General
Generaloberst	General
Hauptmann	Captain
Kadett	Cadet
Leutnant	Second Lieutenant
Major	Major
Oberarzt	Senior Physician
Obergefreiter	Corporal (artillery only)
Oberjäger	Acting Corporal
Oberleutnant	First Lieutenant
Oberpfarrer	Senior Pastor
Oberst	Colonel
Oberstabsarzt	Surgeon Major
Oberstleutnant	Lieutenant-colonel
Oberveterinär	Senior Veterinarian
Offizierstellvertreter	Acting or Deputy Officer
Pionier	Pioneer in Bavarian flying corps
Rittmeister	Captain (cavalry or airforce)
Sanitätsgefreiter	Medical Orderly (private first class)
Sanitätsunteroffizier	Medical Orderly non-commissioned officer
Sergeant	Sergeant
Stabsarzt	Surgeon Captain
Unteroffizier	Corporal[1]
Vizefeldwebel	Sergeant First Class (vice sergeant major)
Wachtmeister	Sergeant Major (cavalry, artillery)

NOTE

1. Could also be interpreted as non-commissioned officer in general, but is often used to denote corporal as it ranks below *Feldwebel* in published lists of First World War ranks. In today's *Bundeswehr*, *Unteroffizier* denotes sergeant, and a corporal is a *Haupgefreiter/Stabsgefreiter* (Israel Schwierz, personal communication). German non-commissioned officer ranks are complex, and have changed in modern times.

APPENDIX D

Hebrew and Jewish Religious Terms

Hebrew transliteration is given in the modern Sephardic pronunciation.

Adon Olam [Hebrew 'Eternal Lord' or 'Lord of the Universe']: A metrical hymn which has been a regular part of the daily and Sabbath liturgy since the fifteenth century.
Aleinu [It is our duty (to praise the Lord of all things)]: Concluding prayer recited three times a day on weekdays, Sabbaths and Festivals.
Aron Kodesh: The Holy Ark in which the Torah scrolls are stored.
Ashamnu; *Al Chet*: Confession of Sins. A list of sins read together by the community several times during Yom Kippur.
Avinu Malkeinu [Our Father our King]: Prayer recited on the High Holidays except on the Sabbath.
Avodah [Lit. work]: Service. The sacrificial offerings made on Yom Kippur by the High Priest. Recited during the Additional Service.
Bar Mitzvah: Jewish coming of age ceremony, at which a 13-year-old boy will be called to the reading of the Torah in the synagogue for the first time.
Beit-(ha)knesset [Lit. place of assembly]: Synagogue.
Beit-Hamidrash [Lit. house of learning]: Place for study of Jewish texts such as the Talmud; usually adjacent to the synagogue.
Birkat Cohanim: Priestly Blessing or Benediction (Numbers 6: 24–6).
Birkat Hamazon: A series of blessings recited after a meal.
Bitter herbs: Consumed during the Seder (to represent the bitterness of slavery).
Chanukah: The winter festival commemorating the rededication of the Temple following the victory of the Jews, led by Judah the Maccabee, against the Seleucid King Antiochus III in 167–165 BCE. Candles are lit on each of the eight festival nights.
charoset: A mixture of fruits and nuts (to represent brick-laying mud) consumed during the Seder ceremony.
Chassid (pl. *Chassidim*): Adherents to a branch of Orthodox Judaism that promotes spirituality and joy through the popularisation and internalisation of Jewish mysticism as the fundamental aspects of the Jewish faith. It was founded in eighteenth-century Eastern Europe by Rabbi Israel ben Eliezer (the *Baal Shem Tov* [master of a good name] (1698–1760).
Chazan: Cantor.
cheder [Lit. room]: A traditional elementary school in Eastern Europe teaching the basics of Judaism and the Hebrew language.
Days of Awe: The period of Rosh Hashanah through Yom Kippur including both holidays; also known as 'Ten Days of Repentance'.
Gaon: Title for heads of Babylonian Talmudic academies in early Middle Ages; later used for outstanding scholars of Talmudic literature.

Gemara: Record of rabbinic discussions of the Mishnah and other legal sources during the third to fifth centuries in Israel and Babylonia.

Haftarah: Additional reading from the Prophets following the Torah reading on Sabbath and holidays.

Hagadah (pl. *Hagadot*): Book from which the Exodus from Egypt and other hymns and prayers are recited during the two Pesach Seders.

Hakafot ['circuits']: On Simchat Torah all the synagogue's Torah scrolls are removed from the ark and carried around the sanctuary in a series of seven *hakafot*.

Kaddish: An Aramaic prayer praising God incorporated in various forms at transition points of the liturgy. Most familiar is the 'Mourner's Kaddish' said by mourners for close to a year following the death of a close relative and then on the anniversary of the death.

kasher (used as a verb): To prepare utensils for kosher food.

kavannah: Direction of the heart, concentration and proper intention while saying prayers.

Kiddush [Sanctification]: Blessing over wine and bread on Sabbath and holidays.

kittel: A white outer robe worn by men on solemn occasions such as Yom Kippur.

Kol Nidrei: The introductory prayer sung (in Aramaic) on Yom Kippur eve, the holiest night in the Jewish year, releasing Jews from their vows to God (but not from vows made to human beings).

kosher: Food prepared according to the Jewish dietary laws.

Lecha Dodi [Come my Beloved]: Song recited prior to the *Ma'ariv* service, welcoming the Sabbath as a bride.

luach: Hebrew calendar or bulletin.

Ma'ariv: Evening service, recited daily.

Machzor (plural *Machzorim*): High Holy Day prayer book.

Magen David: Star of David.

Mah Nishtanah: Four questions recited by the youngest member present at the start of the Seder service.

Ma'oz Tsur: 'Rock of Ages', Chanukah hymn.

matzoth: Unleavened bread, commemorating the haste with which the Children of Israel had to leave Egypt before the yeast had risen. Consumed during the entire Pesach period, during which no leaven may be eaten.

menorah: Seven-sided Jewish candelabrum. For Chanukah a nine-branched candelabrum is used.

meshugge (noun *meschuggene*) (Yiddish): crazy.

Midrash: A homiletic method of biblical exegesis. The term also refers to specific works of rabbinic interpretations of the Bible.

Minchah: Afternoon service, recited daily.

minyan: Quorum of ten adult (post Bar Mitzvah) males necessary for full recitation of services.

Mishnah: The main written redaction of Jewish oral traditions, mainly legal in content, compiled in the early third century.

Misrachtisch: Table facing east.

Mussaph: Additional service, recited on Sabbaths and Festivals after the morning service.

Ne'ilah: Concluding service on Yom Kippur.

Ner Tamid: Eternal light.
Omer: The counting of the *Omer* is a verbal counting of the forty-nine days between Pesach (beginning on the second day) and Shavuot.
parochet: The curtain on the front of the *Aron Kodesh*.
Pesach; Passover: Spring festival celebrating the Exodus from Egypt.
Pesach plate: A Seder plate on which bitter herbs, *charoseth*, and other symbolic foods are arranged.
Pirkei Avoth: Ethics of the Fathers. A Tractate in the Mishnah.
Rosh Hashanah: The Jewish New Year.
Schechita: Jewish ritual animal slaughter.
Seder [Lit. 'order']: The ritual meal that marks the beginning of Pesach celebrated on the first two nights.
Sefirah: Counting (of the Omer).
Shacharit: Morning service, recited daily.
Shamas: Sexton.
Shavuot; Pentecost: Festival of Weeks, seven weeks after Passover, celebrates the giving of the Torah to the Jewish people.
She'hecheyanu: 'Blessed are You O Lord King of the Universe, who has kept us alive (*she'hecheyanu*) and sustained us and permitted us to reach this day.' Blessing recited on festivals and at other special occasions.
Shema Yisrael: Ancient Hebrew profession of faith: 'Hear O Israel, The Lord our God the Lord is one' (Deuteronomy 6:4).
Shmoneh Esreh [Lit. 'eighteen']: The benedictions recited in traditional Jewish worship every morning, afternoon and evening on weekdays and in modified form on the Sabbath and festivals.
shochet: Ritual slaughterer of animals and birds for food according to Jewish dietary laws.
shul [school]: Yiddish word for a synagogue. Literally the place where one learns.
Simchat Torah: ('Rejoicing with/of the Torah') is a celebration marking the conclusion of the annual cycle of public Torah readings, and the beginning of a new cycle.
Succot: Festival of Tabernacles or Booths in the autumn, during which meals are eaten in specially constructed booths.
talit: Prayer-shawl.
Talmud: Combination of the Mishnah and Gemara.
Tefilah: Prayer or services.
tefillin: Phylacteries, placed on the head and arm during morning prayers in accordance with Deuteronomy 6:8.
Ten Days of Repentance: see 'Days of Awe'.
Tisha Be'Av: The ninth day of the Hebrew month of Av; the most important Jewish day of mourning, associated especially with destruction of the First and Second Temples in Jerusalem.
Torah: The five books of Moses, kept as scrolls in the Holy Ark of the synagogue.
tzizit: The fringes on the *talit* and on a small under prayer-shawl worn by orthodox male Jews, in accordance with Numbers 15: 37–41.
Vayehi Bachatzi Halailah [And it was at midnight]: One of the last hymns sung during the second part of the Seder, recited after the meal.
Ya'ale tachanunenu me'erev [May our entreaties rise up in the evening]: One of the prayers recited on *Kol Nidrei* eve.

Yahrzeit: The anniversary of the death of a relative, observed with mourning and the recitation of the *Kaddish*.

Yeshivah (plural *Yeshivoth*) [Lit. 'place of sitting']: An institution of higher Jewish education focusing on study of Jewish religious texts, primarily Talmud.

Yigdal: 'Magnify (O Living God)', a Jewish hymn which in various rituals shares a place of honour at the opening of the morning and the close of the evening service. It is based on the Thirteen Articles of Faith formulated by Maimonides (1135–1204).

Yizkor [Lit. 'May He remember']: Memorial prayers for the dead.

Yom Kippur: The Day of Atonement, on the 10th of Tishrei, a week after the conclusion of Rosh Hashanah.

zaddik: Holy or righteous man, mainly used by *Chassidim*.

Zochreinu: 'Remember us to life, O King, who delights in life.' Prayer recited on the High Holy Days.

APPENDIX E

Place Names Then and Now[1]

Antopol: Antopal (Belarus).
Baranowit(c)z: Baranavichy (Belarus).
Belzec: Bełżec (Poland).
Berditschew: Berdychiv (Ukraine).
Berestowa: Russian Federation.
Biala: Biała Podlaska (Poland).
Bialystok: Białystok (Poland).
Breslau: Wrocław (Poland), capital of Silesia.
Brest-Litovsk: This town has changed hands and names several times but is now Brest (Belarus).
Charzisk (Ukraine).
Chelm: Chełm (Poland). Often misspelled as Cholm.
C(K)ulm: Chełmno (Poland).
C(K)racow: Kraków (Poland).
Danzig: Gdańsk (Poland).
Diedenhofen: Thionville (France).
Domaczow: Domachevo (Belarus).
Dunaburg: Daugavpils (Latvia).
Gorochow: probably Horokhiv (Ukraine).
Grodno (Belarus).
Guttstadt: Dobre Miasto (Poland).
Insterburg: Chernyakhovsk (Russia, Kaliningrad Oblast).
Iw(v)anow(v)o: Poland.
Jablon: Jabłonna (Poland).
Kattowitz: Katowice (Poland).
Kharkov: Kharkiv (Ukraine).
Kiev: Kyiv (Ukraine).
Klausenberg: Cluj-Napoca (Romania).
Klodowa: Kłodawa (Poland).
Kobryn: Kobry(i)n (Belarus).
Königsberg: Kaliningrad (Russia, Kaliningrad Oblast).
Kowel: Kovel (Ukraine).
Kowno: Kaunas (Lithuania).
Krasznostav: Krasnystaw (Poland).
Krotoschin (Poland).
Kupiczew: Kupiczow (Ukraine).
Lemberg: Lviv (Ukraine). Capital of Galicia under the Austro-Hungarian monarchy.
Lida (Belarus).
Liegnitz: Legnica (Poland).
Lipine: Świętochłowice-Lipiny (Poland).
Lissa: Leszno (Poland).

Ljubawetscho: Ljubavitchi (Smolensk Oblast, Russia).
Lobsens: Łobżenica (Poland).
Lodz: Łódź (Poland).
Lu(c)kow: Łuków (Poland).
Lutsk: Luts'k (Ukraine).
Lüttich: Liège (Belgium).
Makowicze: Makovichi (Ukraine).
Memel: Klaipeda (Lithuania).
Meran: Merano (Italy).
Meseritz: Międzyrzecz (Poland).
Mielnica (Ukraine).
Minsk (Belarus).
Mogilev (Belarus).
Myslowétz/Myslowitz: Mysłowice (Poland).
Nachitschevan: Naxçıvan (Azerbaijan).
Nikitowka: Nikitovka (Russia).
Novo Alexandrovsk: Zarasai (Lithuania).
Oppeln: Opole (Poland).
Osiekrow: Osiekrów/Osekriv (Ukraine).
Oswiecim/Oświęcim: Auschwitz (Poland).
Parczew (Poland).
Petrikau: Piotrków Trybunalski (Poland).
Pinsk (Belarus).
Posen: Poznań (Poland).
Preβburg: Bratislava (Slovak Republic).
Prostken: Prostki (Poland).
Punitz: Ponieck (Poland).
Radzyn: Radzyń Podlaski (Poland).
Rawitsch: Rawicz (Poland).
Rogozno: Rogoźno (Poland).
Rostov (on Don) (Russia).
Rova-Ruska: Rava-Ruska (Ukraine).
Rovno: Rivne (Ukraine).
Saaz: Žatec (Czech Republic).
Schrimm: Śrem (Poland)
Siebenbürgen: Erdély (Romanian Transylvania).
Simferopol: Capital of Crimea (Ukraine).
Slavatvocz: Slawatycze (Poland).
Sokal (Ukraine).
Stettin: Szczecin (Poland).
Stradecz (Belarus).
Suwalk(i): Suwałki (Poland).
Taganrog (Russia).
Tarnow: Tarnów (Poland).
Tarnowitz: Tarnowskie Góry (Poland).
Thorn: Toruń (Poland).
Tilsit: Sovetsk (Russia, Kaliningrad Oblast).

PLACE NAMES THEN AND NOW 339

Tomaszow: Tomaszów (Poland).
Tverdyn: Twerdyn (Ukraine).
Uhnow: Uhniv (Ukraine).
Üsküb: Skopje (Macedonia).
Vilna: Vilnius (Lithuania).
Vinkovce (Croatia).
Vladimir-Volynsk: Volodymyr-Volinskyi (Ukraine).
Volhynia: Volynia, or Volyn is a historic region in western Ukraine located between the rivers Prypiat and Southern Bug, to the north of Galicia and Podolia.
Weichsel: River Vistula.
Yekaterinoslav: Dnipropetrovsk (Ukraine).
Yevpatoria: Eupatoria (Ukraine).
Zabern: Saverne (Alsace, France).
Zamosce: Zamość (Poland).
Zhitomir: Zhytomyr (Ukraine).

NOTE

1. Towns still in modern-day Poland or Russia and spelled the same way are not included. If the town has the same name but is now located in a different country this is indicated. Where names are illegible or cannot be located on the map, the first letter is given.

APPENDIX F

German-Jewish Associations[1]

(Allgemeiner) Rabbinerverband: (General) rabbinical association (of Germany).
Centralverein deutscher Staatsbürger jüdischen Glaubens: Central association for German citizens of Jewish faith: Formed in 1893 to combat anti-Semitism and protect the rights of Germany's Jews (with emphasis on German nationality first and Jewish religion second).
Freie Vereinigung: Free society.
Gemeindebund: Community association.
Gemeinderabbiner: Community rabbi.
Israelitische Oberkirchenbehörde: Jewish senior (upper) synagogue council.
Israelitische Zentralkirchenkasse: Central synagogue fund.
Kartell-Covent (der Verbindungen deutschen Studenten jüdischen Glaubens): An umbrella organization of German Jewish student fraternities, founded in 1896.
Kirchenvorsteheramt: Local synagogue council office.
Konferenzgemeinschaft: Conference communities.
Kreisrabbiner: District rabbi.
Kronrabbiner: Crown rabbi: existed in Russia (starting in the early nineteenth century). They were non-traditional and not widely accepted by the communities because the government appointed them.
Oberrabbiner (Großrabbiner): Chief rabbi.
Reichsbund jüdischer Frontsoldaten: German Jewish veteran (front/combat soldiers) association.
Reichsvertretung (from 1938 Reichsvereinigung) der deutschen Juden: An association that attempted to protect German Jewish rights during the National Socialist period.
Verband der deutschen Juden: Association of German Jews. Founded in 1904 on the initiative of the Centralverein as an umbrella organization for all other existing groups to represent Germany's Jews in dealings with state authorities.
Vereinigung für die Interessen des orthodoxen Judentums: Society for the interests of orthodox Judaism.
Vice-Ober-Landesrabbiner: (Vice) Senior Regional Rabbi.
Zentral für Ritualangelegenheiten: Central office for ritual affairs.

NOTE

1. 'Israelite' or 'Mosaic' was used instead of 'Jewish', and synagogues were referred to in official documents as 'Israelite churches'.

Bibliography

Archival References
Archives of the Alte Synagoge, Essen: Archiv, AR.4004.
Central Archives for the History of the Jewish People, Jerusalem: *Bericht über die Jüdischen Herbstfeste 1917 bei einer Armee im Westen in Form von Feldbriefen.* Druck der Armee-Druckerei. P 24/10, pp.1–8.
Centrum Judaicum Berlin. CJA, 75 C Ra 1, Nr. 7, #12517, Bl. 349-349RS; CJA, 75 D Ta 1, Nr. 4, #13367, Bl 4-32RS; CJA 1, 75 , Ve 1, Nr. 397, #13020, Bl. 221; CJA 1, 75, C Ve 1, Nr. 380, Bl. 127.
Deutsche National Bibliothek, Berlin: *Gemeindeblatt der Jüdischen Gemeinde zu Berlin*, 1911–1937.
Italiener, B. *Berichte des Herrn Dr. Italiener aus dem Felde an den Vorstand der israelitischen Religionsgemeinde Darmstadt* (London: Leo Baeck College, 1915), ITL/BER: 1. and 2.
Leopold and Bella Rosenak Collection. Archives of Leo Baeck Instutute, New York: AR 1071.
Tänzer, A. 'Kriegserinnerungen'. Archives of the Leo Baeck Institute, New York: ME 640 (typescript).
Tänzer, A. 'Kriegstagebuch' (hand-written) (digitized at www.cjh.org, under '*Arnold Tänzer, Kriegs-Tagebuch*'), Archives of the Center for Jewish History, New York.

Publications
Barish, L. (ed.), *Rabbis in Uniform: The Story of the American Jewish Military Chaplain* (New York: Jonathan David, 1962).
Berger, M., *Eisernes Kreuz und Davidstern: Die Geschichte jüdischer Soldaten in deutschen Armeen* [Iron Cross and *Magen David*. History of Jewish Soldiers in the German Armies] (Berlin: Trafoverlag, 2006).
Berger, M., *Eisernes Kreuz, Doppeladler, Davidstern. Juden in deutschen und österreichisch-ungarischen Armeen. Der Militärdienst jüdischer Soldaten durch zwei Jahrhunderte* [Iron Cross, Double Eagle and *Magen David*. Jews in the German and Austro-Hungarian Armies. Military Service of Jewish Soldiers over Two Centuries] (Berlin: Trafoverlag, 2010).
Berger, M. and G. Römer-Hillebrecht (eds), *Juden und Militär in Deutschland. Zwischen Integration, Assimilation, Ausgrenzung und Vernichtung* [Jews and the German Military: Between Integration, Assimilation, Exclusion, and Destruction] (Baden Baden: Nomos Verlaggesellschaft, 2009).
Berger, M. and G. Römer-Hillebrecht (eds), *Jüdische Soldaten – Jüdischer Widerstand: In Deutschland und Frankreich* [Jewish Soldiers – Jewish Resistance in Germany and France] (Paderborn: Ferdinand Schöningh, 2012).
Brocke, M. and J. Carlebach, *Biographisches Handbuch der Rabbiner. Teil 2. Die Rabbiner im Deutschen Reich 1871–1945* [Biographical Rabbinical Handbook. Part 2. Rabbis in the German Reich 1871–1945] (Munich: K.G. Sauer/Berlin: Walter de Gruyter, 2009).
Buchergruppe (eds), *Feldrabbiner: Joseph Carlebach, Leo Baeck, Walter Jacob, Martin Salomonski, Adolf Altmann, Max Friediger, Siegfried Klein, Leopold Rosenak* (Books LLC, German series, 2010).
Elon, A., *The Pity of it All: A Portrait of the German-Jewish Epoch 1743–1933* (New York: Henry Holt and Company, 2002).
Feldrabbiner des Westheeres (eds), *Sabbathgedanken für jüdische Soldaten* [Jewish Chaplains of the Western Army: Sabbath Thoughts for Jewish Soldiers] (Leipzig: Verlag von M.W. Kaufmann, 1918).
Fine, D.J., *Jewish Integration in the German Army in the First World War* (Berlin and Boston, MA: de Gruyter, 2012).

Goldberg, B., *Abseits der Metropolen. Die jüdische Minderheit in Schleswig-Holstein* [Outside the Metropolis: The Jewish Minority in Schleswig-Holstein] (Neumünster: Wachholtz Verlag, 2009).
Grady, T., *The German-Jewish Soldiers of the First World War in History and Memory* (Liverpool: Liverpool University press, 2011).
Hank, S. and H. Simon, *Feldpostbriefe jüdischer Soldaten, 1914–1918* vols 1 and 2 [Military Letters of Jewish Soldiers] (Teetz: Hentrich & Hentrich, 2002).
Hank, S., H. Simon and U. Hank, *Feldrabbiner in den deutschen Streitkräften des ersten Weltkrieges* [Jewish Chaplains in the German Armies of the First World War] (Berlin: Hentrich und Hentrich, 2013).
Heuberger, G. and F. Backhaus (eds), *Leo Baeck 1873–1956. Aus dem Stamme von Rabbinern* [From the Tribe of Rabbis] (Frankfurt am Main: Jüdischer Verlag im Suhrkamp Verlag, 2001).
Italiener, B., *Von Heimat und Glauben. Kriegsbegtrachtungen* [Of Homeland and Faith. War Observations] (Darmstadt: H.L. Schlapp Buchhandlung, 1916).
Kestenberg-Gladstein, R., *Neuere Geschichte der Juden in den böhmischen Ländern. Erster Teil: Das Zeitalter der Aufklärung, 1780–1830* [More Recent History of Jews in Bohemian Territories. First Part. The Period of the Enlightenment, 1780–1830] (Tübingen: Mohr, 1969).
Lewin, R., 'Der Krieg als jüdisches Erlebnis' [The War as Jewish Experience], in *Monatschrift für Geschichte und Wissenschaft des Judentums* (Breslau: Schatzky, 1919).
Lindner, E., *Patriotismus deutscher Juden von der napoleonischen Ära bis zum Kaiserreich* [Patriotism of German Jews from the Napoleonic Era to the Period of Imperial Germany] (Frankfurt am Main: Peter Lang GmbH, 1997).
Lowenstein, S.M., P. Mendes-Flohr, P. Pulzer and M. Richarz (eds), *Deutsch-jüdische Geschichte in der Neuzeit. Band III. Umstrittene Integration 1871–1918* [German-Jewish History in Modern Times, volume 3, Integration in Dispute, 1871–1918] (Munich: C.H. Beck, 2000).
Meyer, M.A., *The Origins of the Modern Jew: Jewish Identity and European Culture in Germany, 1749–1824* (Detroit, MI: Wayne State University Press, 1967).
Meyer, M.A. (ed.), *Leo Baeck Werke*. Vol. 6: Briefe, Reden, Aufsätze (Gütersloh: Gütersloher Verlagshaus, 2003).
Reichsbund Jüdischer Frontsoldaten (ed.), *Kriegsbriefe gefallener Deutscher Juden* [War letters of Fallen German Jews] (Berlin: Vortrupp Verlag, 1935). Reissued with an Introduction by Franz Josef Strauß (Stuttgart: Degerloch, 1961).
Rosenthal, J., *Die Ehre des jüdischen Soldaten. Die Judenzählung im ersten Weltkrieg und ihre Folge* [The Honour of Jewish Soldiers: The Jewish Census in the First World War and its Consequences] (Frankfurt am Main: Campus Verlag, 2007). Also published in Hebrew as *Episodah shel 'rish'ut'? 'Sefirat ha-yehudim' bemilhemet ha-olam ha-rishonah* (Jerusalem: Hakibbutz Hame'uhad and Leo Baeck Institute, 2005).
Salomonski, M., *Ein Jahr an der Somme* [A Year on the Somme] (Frankfurt an der Oder: Verlag der königlichen Hofbuchdruckerei Trowitzsch & Sohn, 1917).
Salomonski, M., *Jüdische Seelsorge an der Westfront* [Jewish Spiritual Care on the Western Front] (Berlin: Verlag von Louis Lamm. Ueberreicht vom Centralverein deutscher Staatsbürger jüdischen Glaubens, 1918).
Salzberger, G., *Aus meinem Kriegstagebuch. Von dem Feldgeistlichen bei der 5 Armee* [From My War Diary: From the Chaplain of the Fifth Army] (Frankfurt am Main: Sonderabdruck aus der Monatschrift *Liberales Judentum*, 1916).
Saperstein, M., *Jewish Preaching in Times of War, 1800–2001* (Oxford: The Littman Library of Jewish Civilization, 2008).
Schian, M., 'Die Arbeit der evangelischer Kirche im Felde', vol.1, in *Die deutsche evangelische Kirche im Weltkriege* ['The Work of the Evangelical (Protestant) Church in the Field' vol.1, in The German Evangelical Church in the World War] (edited at the behest of the Deutscher evangelischer Kirchenausschuß) (Berlin: Verlag von E.S. Mittler & Sohn, 1921).

Schine, R.S., *Jewish Thought Adrift. Max Wiener (1882–1950)* (Atlanta, GA: Scholars Press, 1992).
Schorsch, I., *Jewish Reactions to German Anti-Semitism, 1870–1914* (New York: Columbia University Press, 1972).
Schreiber, A., '*Gedenke der vorigen Zeiten'. Illustrierte Chronik der Juden in Moisling und Lübeck* ['Thoughts of Times Gone By' – Illustrated Chronicle of the Jews in Moisling and Lübeck] (Lübeck: Edition Nord, 2009).
Sieg, U., *Jüdische Intellektuelle im Ersten Weltkrieg. Kriegserfahrungen, weltanschauliche Debatten und kulturelle Neueuntwürfe* [Jewish Intellectuals in the First World War: War Experiences, Ideological Debates and New Cultural Concepts] (Berlin: Akademie Verlag, 2001).
Slomovitz, A.I., *The Fighting Rabbis: Jewish Military Chaplains and Military History* (New York: New York University Press, 1999).
Stern, M., *Aus der Zeit der deutschen Befreiungskriegen 1813–1815* [From the Time of the German Wars of Liberation 1813–1815] (Berlin: Verlag Hausfreund, 1918).
Tama, D. (ed.), *Transactions of the Parisian Sanhedrim* [sic] *or, Acts of the Assembly of Israelitish Deputies of France and Italy, Convoked at Paris by an Imperial and Royal Decree Dated May 30, 1806*, trans. F.D. Kirwan (London, 1807).
Tannenbaum, E. (ed.), *Kriegsbriefe deutscher und österreichischer Juden* (Berlin: Neuer Verlag, 1915).
Verband der deutschen Juden (eds), *Ein Gruß der Feldrabbiner an die jüdischen Kameraden im deutschen Heere zu den Herbstfesttagen* [A Greeting from the Jewish Chaplains to Jewish Comrades in the German Army] (Berlin: Verband der deutschen Juden, 1915).
Vogel, R., *Ein Stück von uns. Deutsche Juden in deutschen Armeen 1813–1976: eine Dokumentation* [A Part of Us: German Jews in the German Armies 1813–1976: A Documentation] (Mainz: von Hase & Koehler Verlag, 1977).
Vogt, A., *Religion im Militär. Seelsorge zwischen Kriegsverherrlichung und Humanität. Eine militärgeschichtliche Studie* [Religion in the Military. Spiritual Care: Between Glorification and Humanity. A Military-Historical Study] (Frankfurt am Main: Peter Lang, 1984).
Winter, J., *Remembering War. The Great War between Memory and History in the Twentieth Century* (New Haven, CT and London: Yale University Press, 2006).

Index

Please note that page numbers relating to Notes will have the letter 'n' following the page number.

Aber, Felix, 313, 327
Abraham (Biblical patriarch), xx, xxi, 241, 248, 265
abscesses, 79n
Adam and Eve, 249, 268n
adaptability of young soldiers, 39–40
Adon Olam hymn, 297n, 333
Ahasverus (Purim), 263
Akeda (binding of Isaac), 26, 79n
alcohol consumption, 107
Aleinu prayer, 19, 32, 333
Alexander, Siegfried, 314, 327
All Quiet on the Western Front (Erich Maria Remarque), xix
Allgemeine Rabbinerverband, 292, 299
Allgemeine Zeitung des Judentums, 17, 21–2
Alsace/Alsace-Lorraine, 87, 161, 172n, 291, 309
American Jewish Welfare Board, 3
amputation, 40, 79n
Amstbrüder (brother ministers), 55
Andacht (devotion), 92
animals, distinguished from humans, 256–7
antibiotics, lack of, 78, 79n
anti-Semitism, xviii, xxii, 12, 13n, 74, 264, 275, 276, 301; in France, xxiii, 42; in Germany/German army, 4, 7, 22, 115, 171, 308, 313; memoirs of G. Salzberger, 30, 42; *see also Judenhaß* (hatred of Jews)
AOK (Army High Command), 184, 185, 186, 191, 194, 196, 206, 225
appointment of Jewish military chaplains, historical, 2–3
Arbeitsdienst (work service for Germany army), 8
Argonnes, France, 53
Ark *see* Holy Ark
armbands, 6
army service, historical recruitment of Jewish men, 1
Arndt, Ernst Moritz, 131, 143n

Aron Kodesh (Holy Ark), 8, 32, 68, 113, 192, 286, 333
Ashamnu (Confession of Sins), 27, 79n, 251, 333
Ashkenazi Jews, 118n
associations, German-Jewish, 341
Audignicourt, France, 149, 152
Auschwitz, xx, 235n, 314
Austria/Austro-Hungary, 2, 5; Army, 236n; war declared on by Romania (1916), 99, 118n
Austro-Prussian War (1866), 17
Avinu Malkeinu prayer, 26, 27, 53, 146, 333
Avodah service, 28, 333

Baal Shem Tov, 229
bacterial pneumonia, 78, 79n
Baeck, Rabbi Leo, xxiv, 9, 10, 12, 23, 209, 215, 301, 317; activities post-war, 313–14, 315; as best-known German-Jewish chaplain of First World War, 145; as chosen leader, 6, 11; conferences of Jewish chaplains, 56, 59, 170, 302, 304; Hearing and Hope sermon for upcoming New Year, 156–9; as philosopher, 169, 170; regard for, 171; war activities *see* Baeck, Rabbi Leo (reports on war activities)
Baeck, Rabbi Leo (reports on war activities), 142, 145–73, 306n, 307, 308–9, 310; of 27 September 1914, 145; of 15 October 1914, 145–6; of 30 October 1914, 147–8; of 4 January 1915, 148–9; of 17 January 1915, 149–50; of 2 February 1915, 150–1; of 20 February 1915, 151–2; of 2 March 1915, 153; of 15 March 1915, 153–4; of 18 May 1915, 154–5; of 6 June 1915, 155–6; of 18 June 1915, 156; of 7 August 1915, 159–60; of 20 August 1915, 160; of 21 October 1915, 160–1; of 5 March 1916, 161–2; of 6 July 1916, 162–3; of 6

August 1916, 163–4; of 22 August 1916, 164; of 20 September 1916, 164–5; of 21 October 1916, 165–6; of 19 August 1917, 166–7; of 20 December 1917, 167–8; of March 1918, 168–9; death and burial, memories of, 146, 152; field hospitals, 146, 148, 153, 167; Jewish Festivals, 165; religious services, 147, 151, 169–70; on Sabbath, 154, 159; summary of experiences, 169–71
Baerwald, Rabbi Leo, 307, 313; biography/family background, 317; conferences of Jewish chaplains, 56, 58, 299, 302; on prayer, 258–61
balloons, field, 88–9
Baneth, Ludwig (Leon), 300, 313, 317
Bapaume, France/Battle of Bapaume (1918), 90
barley broth, 228, 238n
Bathsheba, 265–6
Beethoven, Ludwig van, 129, 143n
Beit-(ha)knesset (house of assembly), 74, 333
Belgium, 83, 84; Brussels, 107
Benevolent Society, Jewish, 213–14
'Benoni' (son of suffering), 281, 297n
Berachot, 29, 258
Berger, Michael, 12n, 23n, 24n
Berlin Jewish community, 99, 307
Bernhardi, General, 215
Bezaponin, France, 150
Biala (Podlaska) (Rear Echelon Headquarters), 195–231
Bialystok, Poland, 294, 295, 296
Bible, Hebrew, 6
Bildung, xxii
Bildungbürgertum (educated middle-class), 23
biographical tables: rabbinical assistants/rabbis serving as soldiers, 328–9; rabbis, 318–25
Bismarck, Otto von, 117n
blame, 250
Bloch, Abraham, 4
Blumenstein, Isaac, 2–3, 18–21, 22, 24n
Bolsheviks, 222–3, 227, 237n, 238n, 295, 298n
Bonaparte, Napoleon, 1–2, 15
Book of Esther, 263, 264
Brandenburg, 93
bravery, 123–4, 234
Breslau, Silesia, 177, 178, 180; rabbinical seminary, 3

Brest-Litovsk, 183, 185, 186–94, 232; destruction of, 188; Military Railways Division, 205, 209, 210; Treaty (1918), 234, 295, 298n, 305n
Brisker, Reb Chaim, 298n
Brodski, Alexander, 226
Brodsky synagogue, Kiev (Ukraine), xx
Brusilov offensive (1916), 236n
Brussels, 107
brutality of war, 11; *see also* death and burial; wounded soldiers
Bug Army, 178, 185, 187, 206
Burg, Meno, 2
Burgfrieden (civil truce), 1914, 79n, 142n, 235n, 279
burial *see* death and burial

Cain and Abel, 249
Cambrai, France, 90
Carlebach, David, 313, 328
Carlebach, Emmanuel, 312, 318
Carlebach, Josef Zvi, 318
Carlepont, France, 147, 150
casualties of war, 11
Catholic Church, xviii, 48
cemeteries, military, 125, 152, 155, 211, 214; *see also* death and burial; graves, war
Census of 1916, xxi, xxii, xxiv, 11–12, 280n, 296, 299; memoirs of G. Salzberger, 74, 78–9, 81n
Central Powers, 78, 190, 238n
Chanukah, 33, 44; conferences of Jewish chaplains, 300, 301; *Maoz Tsur* (song), 51, 278, 294, 305n, 334; memoirs of G. Salzberger, 51, 333; memoirs of A. Tänzer, 199, 209, 215; and Purim, 261–4
Chassidism, 170, 207, 208, 229, 237n, 333
Chazan, 65, 66, 294, 333
Chelm, Poland, 179–86, 211
Children of Israel, 265
Chiry, France, 155
Chivres, France, 151
cholera, 8, 78, 97, 181; vaccines, 235n
Chone, Rabbi Heimann, 307, 313; biography/family background, 318; conferences of Jewish chaplains, 56, 299, 300; on Yom Kippur (1914), 285–7
Chosen People (Israel), 287–9
Christian chaplains, 6, 47, 56; memoirs of L. Baeck, 149, 153, 165

INDEX

churches: as field hospitals, 153; Jewish workshop conducted in, 5, 9, 48
clothing, military chaplains, 6
Cohen, Hermann, xxii–xxiii, xxv, 23, 169, 307
Cohn, Heinrich, 305n, 307, 313, 318
comrades/comradeship, 34, 45, 48, 50, 68, 131, 134
conferences of Jewish chaplains, 299–306; associate chaplains, question of, 300; Baeck, Rabbi Leo, 56, 59, 170; in Hirson (1915), 55–6; Hotel des Boulevards, Brussels (December 1916), 299–301; in Lille (1915), 7, 57–8, 59, 141; matzoth, ordering of, 301; memoirs of L. Baeck, 164–5; memoirs of G. Salzberger, 54–9; memoirs of A. Tänzer, 236n; Military Railways Division, 301; in Riga (1918), 217, 301–5; in Sedan (1915), 58, 59; in St Quentin (1915), 58, 59, 141; in Vilna (1916), 202, 206, 215; in Warsaw (1916), 204
Confession of Faith *see Shema Yisrael*
Confession of Sins, 27, 79n, 251, 333
Corps Commander, 68
Cossacks, 189
counselling sessions, 107
Cracow, Poland, 178

Daath (knowledge), 67
David and Jonathan (Biblical figures), 138, 139, 142, 310
Day of Atonement *see* Yom Kippur (Day of Atonement)
Day of Judgment (*Yom Hadin*), 26; *see also* Rosh Hashanah
Day of Remembrance (*Yom Hazikaron*) *see* Rosh Hashanah
Day of the Blowing of the Shofar (*Yom Tekiat Shofar*), 26; *see also* Rosh Hashanah
Days of Awe, 27, 52, 333
death and burial: agony of death, 41; whether death evil, 89; honouring of the dead, 46; Jewish rituals, 291, 297n; memoirs of L. Baeck, 146, 152; memoirs of M. Salomonski, 87–8, 89, 95, 96–7, 102–3; memoirs of G. Salzberger, 30 1, 34, 36, 40, 41, 45–6; memoirs of A. Tänzer, 197; three faiths united in, 30–1; *see also* graves, war; *Kaddish* prayer; *Yizkor*

Declaration of the Rights of Man and of the Citizen, 150, 172n
Deuteronomy, 79n, 141, 142n, 268n
Deutschland über alles, 69
devotion, 21, 92, 137
diarrhoea, 35, 225, 230
dietary laws, 293, 298n; *see also* kosher food
disfigurement by war, 39–40
Division Adjutants, 48, 68
Division Command, 25, 48, 68, 153
Division Pastor, 47
doubts about God, 11
Dreyfus affair (1894–1906), xxiii, 42, 43, 80n, 114, 119n, 309
Druckposten (cushy jobs), 97–8
dual identity, as German and Jewish, 31–2
dumdum bullets, 40
Dutch Prayer of Thanks, 81n, 107, 129
duty, 245, 254; *see also* responsibility
dysentery, 78, 79n, 97, 225, 235n, 238n

Eastern Front, 5, 8, 98, 160, 236n, 303, 310; memoirs of A. Tänzer, 178, 234
Ecclesiastes, 16
ecumenism, 8
education, French, 108
égalité, xxiii
Ehrlich, Paul, 80n
Eichhorn, Hermann von, 9
El hagadol ve'hanora/El rachum ve'chanun, 136
Elon, A., 23n
empathy/fellow feeling, xix, xx, 11
emunah (E. Levy), 239–41, 267n
Entente (1917), 117n, 118n
Epagny, France, 151
Eschenroeder, Pastor, 105
Esther, Book of, 263, 264
Ethics of the Fathers, 81n, 268n
Eucharist, 39
Euskirchen, Hermann Baer von, 212
Exodus, 81n, 119n, 297n; *see also* Passover
expenses, payment of, 5
Ezekiel, 280n

faith, 20, 39, 122–3, 157, 239; crisis of, 11–12
family, separation from, 91, 273; *see also* letters home
fatalities *see* death and burial
Fein, Rabbi Chaim, 204
female company, loss of, 91, 273

Festivals, Jewish *see* Jewish Festivals
Feuchtwanger, Dr, 204
Fichte, Johann Gottlieb, 131, 143n
field balloons, 88–9
field hospitals, xix; memoirs of L. Baeck, 146, 148, 153, 167; memoirs of B. Italiener, 124, 133–4, 141; memoirs of M. Salomonski, 88, 90; memoirs of G. Salzberger, 33–42, 45, 61, 77; memoirs of A. Tänzer, 180, 184, 190, 191, 194, 197, 212, 216, 230
Fine, David J., 13n, 308, 315n
First Army Corps, 18
First World War, 11; Battle of Somme *see* Somme, Battle of (1916); Brusilov offensive (1916), 236n; Eastern Front *see* Western Front; Entente (1917), 117n, 118n; entry of United States into (1917), 115; as an experience, 271–80; Gorlice–Tarnow Offensive (1915), 178, 185, 235n; Jewish contributions to, xxii; Marne, First Battle of (1914), 172n; Michael Offensive (1918), 238n; nature of, understanding, 272; positive side of, 88–9, 154–5, 289–91; Western Front *see* Western Front; Ypres, First Battle of (1914), 172n; *see also* Verdun, France/ Battle of Verdun, 1916)
Fischer, Felddiakon, 197
Five Books of Moses, 246–7; *see also* Deuteronomy; Exodus; Genesis; Leviticus; Numbers; *Torah*
Flemish peoples, 84
flies, 96, 190
Fort Douaumont, 80n
France: anti-Semitism, xxiii, 42; appointment of Jewish military chaplains, 3–4; country and people, 108–10; Dreyfus affair (1894–1906), xxiii, 42, 43, 80n, 309; French Jewry, 161, 172n; homes, French, 109; memoirs of G. Salzberger, 42–4; Northern, 9, 55; road infrastructure, 150–1; two-child policy/celibacy rates, 108; *see also* Metz, France; Verdun, France; *specific cities such St Quentin*
François, Hermann von, 77, 81n, 307
Franco-Prussian War (1870–71), 2, 17, 85, 117n, 131, 143n, 309
Frankfurt am Main, West End synagogue, 78
Franz Joseph, Emperor, 208, 237n

fraternité, xxiii
fratricide, 249, 250
Frederick the Great, 143n
Frederick William III, King, 280n
French Revolution, 150
frisch-fröhlicher (fresh and joyful) war, 272
Fuchs, Erich, 213
Funcke, Major, 198, 201

gas gangrene, 61, 79n
Gaspard II de Coligny, 118n
gastrointestinal infections *see* cholera; diarrhoea; dysentery
Genesis, 24n, 79n, 81n, 118n, 249, 268n, 281
Geneva Red Cross, 35, 176
German army, Jewish soldiers, 5, 7
German Rabbinical Association, 100
German-Jewish associations, xxii–xxiii, 142, 289, 341
Germany: anti-Semitism, 4, 7, 22, 115, 171, 308, 313; *Burgfrieden* (civil truce), 1914, 79n, 142n, 235n, 279; discipline, 127; German Jewry, 159, 172n, 279; history of Jewish military chaplains, 2–3; National Anthem, 81n, 142; Nazi Germany *see* Nazism/Nazi Germany; pastoral role, 7; Reichstag election (1912), 4; Weimer Republic, 81n, 312
Gestapo, 314
gezerah (evil decree), 1
gifts of love (*Liebesgaben*, November 1914), 7, 129–30
Glast, Herr, 65
Glaube see faith
Glossmann, Pejssa, 213
Goethe, Johann Wolfgang von, 81n, 164
Goldschmidt, Ludwig, 199
'Good Comrade, The', 143n
Gorlice–Tarnow Offensive (1915), 178, 185, 235n
Gradenv(w)itz, Hugo (Hirsch Zvi), 314, 319
Grady, Tim, 12n
Grand Ducal City Rabbinate, 21
Grandpré, France, 53
Grave on the Road, The (S. Levi), 281–2
graves, war, 41, 88, 155; Jewish, 46, 141, 290, 300; mass graves, 46, 103; memoirs of B. Italiener, 125–6; *see also* death and burial; wounded soldiers
Great Choral Kharkov Synagogue, Pushkinskaya (Ukraine), 238n

INDEX

Great Question, 245, 256
Great War *see* First World War
Grodno, Belarus, 293, 294, 295
Grünburg, David, 199
Gurewicz, Rabbi, 219

Haftarah, 20, 147, 334
Hagadah, 64, 65, 66, 140, 211, 278, 334
Hague, The (Peace Palace), 246, 267n
Haman (Purim), 263
Hamburg Hanseatic Cross, 6, 225
Hank, Sabine, 13n
Hanover, Siegmund Simon Adolf, 301, 307, 313, 319
hate, overcoming, 169
hauliers, 97
Hearing and Hope sermon (Leo Baeck), 156–9
Hebrew Bible, 6
Hebrew language, 32, 180, 254
Hebrew Union College (Reform seminary), 3
Hegel, Georg Wilhelm Friedrich, 267n
Heimweh (longing for home), 274
Herbesthal, Belgium, 83
heroism, 124, 125, 265–7
Herrnstadt, Walter, 171
Herzl, Theodor, 218, 238n
Heubes, Major, 204–5
High Command, xviii, 141, 155, 296, 307; memoirs of A. Tänzer, 183, 184, 185, 186, 191, 193, 194, 196, 206, 225
High Holidays *see* Jewish Festivals
Hindenburg, Paul von, 269n, 313
Hindenburg Line, 114, 118n
Hirschberg, Sergeant L., 21, 24n
Hirson, France, 55–6
Hitler, Adolf, 268n
Hoffmann, David Zvi, xxi, xxv
holiday season (1915), miscellaneous memoirs, 281–98; Grave on the Road (S. Levi), 281–2; Religiosity in the Field (Sänger), 282–3; Yom Kippur, 283–7
Holocaust, xx, 118n, 235n, 314
Holy Ark, 8, 32, 68, 113, 192, 286, 333
Holzmann, General von, 186
Hope and Confidence sermon (Weyl, 1813), 15
horses, 235n, 236n
hospitals *see* field hospitals
Hotel des Boulevards, Brussels (December 1916), 299–301

Houlihan, Patrick J., 13n
humanity, common, 168

idealism, 11
identity, Jewish, 170
incendiary bombs, 99
infectious diseases, 8, 235n, 236n; memoirs of M. Salomonski, 97; memoirs of G. Salzberger, 35, 61, 78, 79n, 80n; memoirs of A. Tänzer, 230; *see also specific diseases, such as cholera*
influenza, 230, 236n; 'Spanish' influenza (1918), 238n, 311
informality of services, religious, 10
insects, 96, 190
inter-faith relations, xviii, xxv, 25–6, 36, 77–8
inter-Jewish divisions, falling away of, 75
Iron Cross, 6, 19, 30, 38, 77, 102, 205, 223
Isaac (Biblical figure), xx, 26, 79n
Isaiah, 20, 79n, 80n, 117n
Israel, 287–9
Israelitische Zentralkirchenkasse, 177, 197
Italiener, Rabbi Bruno, 313; biography/family background, 319; conferences of Jewish chaplains, 56, 299; war reports *see* Italiener, Bruno (war reports)
Italiener, Rabbi Bruno (war reports), 121–44, 308, 310; of 19 April 1915, 140; of 2 November 1915, 140–1; field hospitals, 124, 133–4, 141; friendship (August 1915), 137–41; German song (October 1914), 123–5; gifts of love (*Liebesgaben*, November 1914), 129–30; graves, soldiers' (November 1914), 125–6; home (July 1915), 132–3; *Ich hatt einen kameraden*, 130–2; New Year (January 1915), 127–9; nurses, memories of (November 1914), 126–7; sermon of August 1914, 121–3, 141–2; strength through God (September 1915), 135–7; summary of experiences, 141–2

Jablon, Poland, 185, 196–7, 200, 225, 226, 230, 231
Jacob (Biblical figure), 254, 265, 281
Jeremiah, 19, 52, 79n, 117n, 244, 267n, 281, 297n
Jeumont, France border, 84
Jewish Festivals, 17–18, 21; holiday season (1915), miscellaneous memoirs, 281–98;

memoirs of L. Baeck, 165; memoirs of B. Italiener, 141; memoirs of G. Salzberger, 25–9, 51–2, 77; *see also* Chanukah; Passover; Purim; Rosh Hashanah; Simchat Torah; Succot; Yom Kippur (Day of Atonement)
Jewish military chaplains *see* military chaplains, Jewish
Jewish soldiers, 1, 5, 7; and nature of war, 272, 273; rabbinical assistants/rabbis serving as, 328–9
Joseph II of Austria, 1
Joshua (Biblical figure), 265
Judengasse (Jew alley), 275, 280n
Judenhaß (hatred of Jews), 30, 42, 54, 75, 276
Judenzählung (Jews' Census, 1916), xxi, xxii, xxiii, xxiv, 11–12, 280n, 296, 299, 308; memoirs of G. Salzberger, 74, 78–9, 81n

Kaddish prayer, 68, 94, 146, 147, 173n, 210, 243, 284, 334
Kaiser Wilhelm II, xviii, xxi, 5, 54, 74, 247; birthday celebrations, 44, 105–6, 200
Kant, Immanuel, 97, 118n, 170, 297n
Karfunkel, Aaron, 15
Kerensky, Alexander/Kerensky initiative (1917), 237n, 295, 298n
Kestenberg-Gladstein, R., 12n
Kharkov, Ukraine, 222, 223, 228
Kiddush, 173n, 297n, 334
Kiev, Ukraine, 226
Kirchengut (church property), 193
Kishinev pogrom (1903), 4
Klein, Isak, 214
Klein, Siegfried, 299, 307, 314, 319
Klezmer (musical instruments), 199, 236n
Knights Cross, 207, 208
Kobryn, Belarus, 199
Kol Nidrei, 27, 53, 274, 286, 334
Königsberg Synagogue, 16
kosher food, 63, 334
Kowel, Ukraine, 201, 206, 211, 212, 216, 217, 225; Main Synagogue, 207, 208
Krasznostav, Poland, 181
Kriegspsalm (war psalm), 10
Kremer, Elijah ben Shlomo Zalman, 236n
Kristallnacht, 313, 314
Kronheim, Emil, 307, 313, 320
Kultur, German, xxii, 170, 309

La Mourière, military cemetery, xvii
Lamentations, 52, 81n
Lamprecht, Ferdinand, 85
Landau, Ezekiel (rabbi of Prague), 1
Last Rites, 39
Lazarus, Arnold, 307, 312, 320
Lazarus, Paul Pinchas, 291, 301, 313, 320
Le Mesnil, France, 152
Lecha Dodi (song), 297n, 334
Lenin, Vladimir Ilyich, 237n, 298n
Leshanah Haba'ah Biyerushalayim ('Next Year in Jerusalem'), 66, 80n
letters home, 36, 41, 62, 88, 137
Leuthen, Battle of (1757), 143n
Levi, Naftali, 197
Levi, Sali(y) Salomon, 281–2, 307, 312, 313, 320; conferences of Jewish chaplains, 301, 302, 304
Leviticus, 24n, 79n, 298n
Levy, Arthur Shimon, 243–6, 289–91, 313, 320; conferences of Jewish chaplains, 301, 302
Levy, Rabbi Emil Nathan, 239–41, 287–9, 307, 309, 313, 321; conferences of Jewish chaplains, 56, 58
Lewandowski, Louis, 159, 172n
Lewin, Rabbi Adolf, 22
Lewin, Rabbi Reinhold, 10, 11, 308, 310, 314; biography/family background, 321; conferences of Jewish chaplains, 56, 58, 299, 300; on First World War as an experience, 271–80; on Sabbath, 255–8
Liberal Judaism, 9, 10
liberals, German Jewish, 4
Lille conference (1915), 7, 57–8, 59, 141
limbs, loss of, 40, 96; *see also* amputation; wounded soldiers
Lincoln, Abraham, 3
'Linsingen bridge', 187
Linsingen Front, 215
Lithuanian Jewry, 172n
Ljubavetscho, Rabbi of, 229
Loewe, Emmanuel, 17
Longwy, France, 51
Lord's Prayer, 31
Lorraine, France, 87
loyalty, 30, 78, 248
Ludendorff, Erich, 313
Lutherans, 177, 235n
Lützow, Ludwig Adolph Wilhelm von, 131, 143n

INDEX

Ma'ariv service, 65, 147, 334
Maccabees, 10, 33, 44, 51, 262, 263
Machzor prayer book, 52, 334
Mackensen, August von, 235n
Magen David, 6, 56, 65, 113, 141, 290, 295, 334
Mah Nishtanah (Four Questions, Seder night), 52, 334
Malachi, 80n
malaria, 97
Mannheim Jewish community, 2–3
Manteuffel, Edwin Freiheer von (General), 3, 18, 24n
Maoz Tsur (Chanukah song), 51, 278, 294, 305n, 334
Maria Theresa of Austrlia, 1
Marne, First Battle of (1914), 172n
Mars la Tour, Battle of (1870), 25, 79n, 143n
Marshall, Brest-Litovsk Gouvernement Provost, 206
matzoth, 200, 274, 294, 301, 334
medals: Hamburg Hanseatic Cross, 6, 225; Iron Cross, 6, 19, 30, 38, 77, 102, 205, 223; Knights Cross, 207, 208; Red Cross, 35, 97, 176
Medical Corps, 34, 42
Meier, Jakob, 215
memorials, grave, 103
Mendes-Flohr, P., 24n
Menorah, 51, 274, 334
mental illness, 96
Metz, France, 3, 17, 18, 43, 53, 87
Meyer, Michael A., 12n, 13n
Michael Offensive (1918), 238n
Midrash, 246, 334
militarism, 288
Military Administration, 176
military authorities, 7, 100, 294; *see also* Division Command; High Command; Regional Command
military chaplains, Jewish, 6, 7, 11, 47; age differences among those studied, 310–11; anti-Semitism encountered by, 308; associate chaplains, question of, 300; conferences *see* conferences of Jewish chaplains; in countries other than Germany, 2–4; differences in attitudes/reports among those studies, 309–10; education level, 311; and November 1918, 308–9; numbers involved in war, 85–6; patriotism, xvii, xxii, 7, 11, 15, 16–17, 30, 175, 311; payment, 5, 80n; prior to First World War, 1–4; relationship to German Army, 5–6; volunteering by, 311; *see also specific chaplains and memoirs*
military ranks, German, 331
military service, historical Jewish attitudes to, 1
Minchah service, 21, 69, 334
minyan, 80n, 334
Misrachtisch table, 18, 334
missing persons, enquiries as to, 46
mobile war, 47
money, forwarding to next of kin, 37
monotheism, 9
moral imperative, 287
Mordechai (Purim), 263
Moriah, Mount, 265
morphine, 41
mortality *see* death and burial
Moses, 28, 240, 253, 265, 287; *see also* Five Books of Moses; *Torah*
Moulin sous Touvent, France, 156, 172n
Mount Sinai, revelation of Torah on, 53
music, religious services, 106–7
Mussaph service, 20, 21, 28, 53, 66, 229, 334

Nachum of Gamzu, Rabbi, 118n
Napoleon III, capture of (1870), 80n
Napoleonic Wars (1803–15), 1–2, 15, 131
National Anthem, German, 81n
national identity, 23
National Socialists, 79n, 312
nationalism, Jewish, 278; *see also* Zionism
nations, concept, 169
Nazism/Nazi Germany, xvii, xviii, xxiv, 314; *see also* Holocaust
Ne'ilah prayers, 21, 28, 53, 146, 229, 286, 297n, 334
Ner Tamid, 69, 113, 335
Nesle, France, 88
news reports, 137
newspapers, Jewish, 50
Nicholas II, Tsar, 298n
Ninth of Av, 175
Nobel, Rabbi Nechemiah Anton, 63, 80n
Novo-Alexandrovsk, 163
Noyon, France, 147, 152
Numbers, 268n, 280n
nurses, memories of, 97, 126–7

Nussbaum, Georg, 214

obedience, 245
Oberkirchenbehörde, 176, 197, 205, 231
Oberrabbiner, military, 303
occupied territories, travelling through, 44–5
officers' mess, 275–6
Old Lutherans, 177, 235n
Old Testament, xviii, 251; *see also* Five Books of Moses
Omer, 65, 335
omnipotence of God, 241
opiates, 238n
Oppenheim, Berthold, 17
Ostjuden, 170, 293
Owen, Wilfred, xix, xx, xxi, xxv

Pale of Settlement, 235n
'Parable of the Old Man and the Young' (Owen), xx, xxv
Passover: conferences of Jewish chaplains, 302; *Hagadah*, 64, 65, 66, 140, 211, 278, 334; *Mah Nishtanah* (Four Questions, Seder night), 52, 334; matzoth, 200, 274, 294, 301, 334; memoirs of B. Italiener, 140; memoirs of M. Salomonski, 113, 115; memoirs of G. Salzberger, 51–2, 59–66, 78; memoirs of A. Tänzer, 203, 220; 'Next Year in Jerusalem' recital (*Leshanah Haba'ah Biyerushalayim*), 66, 80n; Seder service *see* Seder service; in Skopje (1917), 311; in St Quentin (1915), 289; at Verdun, 59–66, 78
patriotism, xvii, xxi, xxii, 7, 11; memoirs of G. Salzberger, 30; memoirs of A. Tänzer, 175; preached by rabbis, 15, 16–17
payment of Jewish military chaplains, 5, 80n
Peace Palace (The Hague), 246, 267n
periodicals, Jewish, 50
Pesach *see* Passover
Petrovsky-Shtern, Yochanan, 305n, 315n
pets, aiding of loneliness, 118n
philosophy of life, 73
Pilgrim Festivals, 242
Pinsk, Belarus, 181, 199, 205
pneumonia, 78, 79n, 230
poetry, xix, 91–2, 95–6, 111–12, 115, 117n
pogroms, 4
Polish Jewry, 182, 196, 199, 234
Polish language/nationalism, 236n

positional warfare, 35
poverty of Jewish population, in East, 8, 162, 164
Poznanski, Samuel Abraham, 195–6, 236n
prayer, meaning, 258–61
prayer books, 6, 21, 32, 100, 147, 184, 334
prisoners of war (PoW), 172n, 311; Jewish, 154, 163; Russian, 46–7, 80n, 141, 163, 180, 207, 213, 300
Prophets, 27, 53, 60, 90, 266
Protestant Church, xviii
Proverbs, 265
Prussian Jews, 2
Prussian Union of churches, 235n
Psalm books, 51
Psalms, 147, 241, 255, 257, 260, 288; Psalm 16, 297n; Psalm 19, 297n; Psalm 27, 10; Psalm 71, 259; Psalm 103, 144n; Psalm 113, 267n; Psalms 113–18, 241–3; Psalm 115, 267n; Psalm 116, 267n; Psalm 118, 144n; Psalm 121, 79n; Psalm 130, 94; Psalm 144, 79n; Psalm 145, 32
Purim, and Chanukah, 261–4
pyramidone, 238n

rabbinical families, 307
Rachel (Biblical figure), 26, 281
railways, Prussian, 118n; Prussian-Hessian express train, 83
Ramerupt, northern France, 55
Rashi (Rabbi Shlomo ben Yitzhak); note in Salzberger chapter (2)
rations, 190
Rear Echelon Command, 51, 56, 199, 210, 213, 217
Rear Echelon Headquarters, 195–231
Rear Echelon Inspectorate, 183, 197
recruitment of Jewish men, for army service, 1
Red Cross, 35, 97, 176
Red Sea, 240
Regimental Commanders, 48
Regional Command, 183, 193
Reichelsheimer, Hermann, 211
Reichstag election (1912), 4
Reichsvereinigung, 314
Reichsvertretung der Deutschen Juden, 314
religious separations, falling away of, 25–6, 36, 75
religious terminology, 333–6
Remarque, Erich Maria, xix

INDEX

remuneration issues, 5, 80n
respiratory tract infections, 78, 79n, 236n, 237n; 'Spanish' influenza (1918), 238n, 311
responsibility, 249, 250, 251; *see also* duty [*Pflicht*]
Rheims, northern France, 55
Riga conference (1918), 217, 301–5
Rippner, Rabbi Benjamin, 22
rituals, Jewish, 266, 291, 297n
River Bug, 178, 185, 187, 206, 235n
Romania, 99, 118n
Rosenak, Rabbi Leopold, 7, 8, 13n, 246–9, 295, 301, 307, 313, 321
Rosenberg, Isaac, xix
Rosenthal, Jacob, 12n
Rosh Hashanah, 18, 26, 51, 291, 294, 335; alternative names, 79n; memoirs of L. Baeck, 165, 166; memoirs of B. Italiener, 135, 141; memoirs of M. Salomonski, 101, 115; memoirs of G. Salzberger, 52, 56; memoirs of A. Tänzer, 192, 193, 194, 207, 214, 226, 227–8
Rossbach, Battle of (1757), 143n
Rothschild palace, Ferrières (outside Paris), 3
Rova-Ruska station, 179
Rubinschik, Herr, 219
Russian Jewry, 199, 234
Russian prisoners of war, 46–7, 80n, 141, 163, 180, 207, 213, 300
Russian Revolution (1917), 115, 172n, 234, 237n, 295
Russian roads, 179–80
Russo-Jewish soldiers, 308

Saalschütz, Rabbi Levin Joseph, 16
Sabbath/Sabbath sermons, xxi, 239–68, 284–5, 308; *emunah* (E. Levy), 239–41; memoirs of L. Baeck, 154, 159; memoirs of M. Salomonski, 110; memoirs of G. Salzberger, 27–8, 48, 49; procession of worshippers (Wilde), 241–3; Psalms 113–18, 241–3
sacrifice (Biblical), xx, 26, 79n
Saint Barbe (German army camp outside Metz), 3, 18
Salomonski, Martin, xxv, 307, 309; biography/family background, 322; booklets *see* Salomonski, Martin (booklets of 1917 and 1918); conferences of Jewish chaplains, 299;
murder in Auschwitz (1944), xx, 314; Sabbath/Sabbath sermons, 110, 252–5; writing style, 114, 310
Salomonski, Martin (booklets of 1917 and 1918), 83–119, 308; autumn celebrations, 99–101; camp background, 87–9; death and burial, 87–8, 89, 95, 96–7; field hospitals, 88, 90; France, country and people, 108–10; Kaiser's birthday (27 January 1917), 105–6; mourning and hopelessness, 101–4; poetry, 91–2, 95–6, 111–12, 115, 117n; quarters, 86; religious services, 90, 106–7; shootings, beginning, 89–93; Somme, Battle of, 85, 86, 94–8, 115, 117–18n; summary of experiences, 114–17; on vacation, 104–5, 310; Western Front, journey to, 83–5; winter, memories of, 106–8; women acquainted with in war, 86–7
salvarsan, for syphilis, 78, 80n
Salzberger, Natalie Charlotte (wife of Georg), xix
Salzberger, Rabbi Georg, xix, 9, 25–78, 237n, 238n, 307, 313; biography/family background, 322; character, 78; conferences of Jewish chaplains, 54–9, 299, 300, 303; as Division Chaplain, 45; on heroism, 265–7; inter-faith relations, xviii, xxv, 25–6, 36, 77–8; memoirs *see* Salzberger, Rabbi Georg (memoirs); Sabbath/Sabbath thoughts, 27–8, 48, 49, 249–52
Salzberger, Rabbi Georg (memoirs), 308; death of soldiers, 30–1, 34, 36, 40, 41, 45–6; Dreyfus affair (1894–1906), 309; in enemy territory, 42–4; field hospitals, 33–42, 45, 61, 77; Jewish holidays in the field, 25–9, 77; journey through army, 44–7; *Judenzählung* (Jews' Census, 1916), 74, 78–9, 81n; Passover, at Verdun, 59–66; on relearning, 66–78; religious services, 45, 47–54; spiritual care in the field, 25, 29–33; summary of experiences, 78–9; *Torah*, 26, 27, 28, 32, 49; war diaries, xvii, xix
Sandherr, Oscar, 206
Sänger, Jacob Hirsch, 282–3, 307, 312–13, 322
Sassoon, Siegfried, xix
Saul, King, 138

Schian, M., 315n
Schleswig-Holstein War (1864), 17
Schnersohn, Sholom DovBer, 229
Schnorrer (petty thief), 198, 226, 236n, 310
Schorsch, I., 24n
scrub typhus, 79n
seasons, 106–8, 162–3
Sedan, Battle of (1870), 80n
Sedan Conference (1915), 58, 59
Seder service, 10, 278, 335; *Mah Nishtanah* (Four Questions, Seder night), 52, 334; memoirs of E. Levy, 289; memoirs of G. Salzberger, 63, 64–6; memoirs of A. Tänzer, 203; Seder plate, 65, 140, 335; *see also* Passover
Sefirah, 66, 335
sermons, 9–10, 22–3; of Rabbi Baeck, 156–9; of Rabbi Blumenstein, 19; of Rabbi Italiener, 121–3, 141–2; of Rabbi Lewin, 255–8, 271; of Rabbi Saalschütz, 16; of Rabbi Salzberger, 29, 50; of Rabbi Weyl, 15; *see also* Sabbath/Sabbath sermons
services, religious: church, conducted in, 5, 9, 48; comfort provided by, 10–11; informality, 10; memoirs of L. Baeck, 147, 151, 169–70; memoirs of M. Salomonski, 90, 106–7; memoirs of G. Salzberger, 45, 47–54; music in, 106–7; *see also* synagogues (*shuls*)
sexuality, 7
Shacharit, 20, 32, 64, 66, 147, 152, 229, 335
Shamas, 227, 335
Shavuot, 51, 335
She'hecheyanu prayer, 53, 335
Shema Yisrael, 53, 146, 172n, 335
Shimon, Rabbi, 106
Shmoneh Esreh, 297n, 335
Shochet, 294, 335
Shofar, 274
shrapnel wounds, 40, 79n
Sieg, Ulrich, 13n, 24n
Simchat Torah, 8, 295, 335
Simon, Ernst, xxiii–xxiv, xxv
Simon, Hermann, 13n
sin, confession, 27, 79n, 251, 333
Sirota, Gershon, 234, 238n
Social Democrats, Germany, 4
social meetings, 107
Solomon, Biblical King, 16
Soloveitchik, Chaim, 295, 310

Somme, Battle of (1916), memoirs of M. Salomonski, 85, 86, 94–8, 115, 117–18n
Sonderling, Jacob, 11, 291–3, 307, 313, 323; conferences of Jewish chaplains, 301, 304
soup kitchens, 198, 199, 200, 201, 202, 204, 220, 221, 226, 228, 307
'Spanish' influenza (1918), 238n, 311
Spessart, General von, 203
spiritual care: memoirs of M. Salomonski, 92, 96, 101; memoirs of G. Salzberger, 25, 29–33, 55, 61; Tänzer's memorandum concerning organization of Jewish care, 302–5, 306n, 310
splinters, shrapnel, 40
St Léger, France, 153
St Quentin, France: cathedral, 85, 105; conferences of Jewish chaplains, 58, 59, 141; memoirs of M. Salomonski, 85, 90, 93, 94, 105, 110, 113, 117n; memoirs of G. Salzberger, 80n; Passover in, 289
Stahlhelm (steel helmet), 118n
Star of David, 6, 56, 65, 113, 141, 290, 295, 334
static war, 47, 51
Steinthal, Fritz-Leopold, 307, 313, 323
Stern, M., 23n
Stolzmann, Major General von, 201
Strasbourg (Straßburg), France, 87
strength of spirit, xx, 289–91
stretcher-bearers, 97
Struck, Hermann, 215, 237n, 306n
subordination of individual to the cause, 71–2
Succot (festival of tabernacles), 28, 29, 115, 291–3, 335
suicide, attempted, 96
superiority, German sense of, 114
synagogues (*shuls*), 5, 9, 16, 286, 293, 335; Frankfurt West End synagogue, 78; Great Choral Kharkov Synagogue, Pushkinskaya (Ukraine), Kiev, Brodsky synagogue, xx; 238n; Main Synagogue, Kowel, 207, 208; memoirs of L. Baeck, 159; memoirs of M. Salomonski, 90; memoirs of G. Salzberger, 27, 48–9, 68, 69; memoirs of A. Tänzer, 207; Warsaw, Great Synagogue Tlomackie Street, 195–6, 236n; *see also* services, religious
syphilis, 78, 80n

INDEX

Taganrog, Russia, 223
Takkanot (legislative enactments), 80n
talit, 27, 50, 277, 335
Talmud Bavli, 268n
Tam, Rabbeinu, 55
Tannenbaum, Eugen, 12n, 13n
Tänzer, Aron (Arnold), 6; biography/family background, 307, 323; character, 233–4; conferences of Jewish chaplains, 301, 302–5; death of, 312, 313; volunteering by, 311; war reports/diary *see* Tänzer, Aron (Arnold), war reports/war diary
Tänzer, Aron (Arnold), war reports/war diary, 175–238, 308, 310; at Armeeoberkommando, 186; Belzec-Chelm-Vlodava journey, 179–86; Biala (Rear Echelon Headquarters), 195–231; Brest-Litovsk, 183, 185, 186–94, 232; departure from military service, 231–3; enlistment and departure, 176–9; field hospitals, 180, 184, 190, 191, 194, 197, 212, 216, 230; first year of war, 175–6; soup kitchens, 198, 199, 200, 201, 202, 204, 220, 221, 226, 228, 307; summary of experiences, 233–4
Tänzer, Bertha (second wife of Aron), 197, 204, 208, 210, 235n
Tänzer, Fritz (son of Aron), 208, 211, 212, 213, 217, 219, 223, 224, 237n
Tänzer, Paul (son of Aron), 208, 211, 212, 213, 214, 215–16, 217, 219, 221, 223, 224, 225, 228, 229, 237n
Tänzer, Rose (first wife of Aron), 235n
Tefilah, 27, 335
tefillin, 21, 335
Teichmann, Major von, 204
Temple, 242, 264
Ten Commandments, 286
Ten Days of Repentance see Days of Awe
tetanus, 40, 79n
Theological Seminaries, Jewish, 307
Theresienstadt, xxiv, 314
throat infections, 237n
Thuringia, Germany, 150, 172n
Tilsit, Treaty of (1807), 23n
time difference, France and Germany, 117n
Tisha Be'Av, 52, 335
Tomaszow, Poland, 180
Torah, 20, 32, 66, 278, 335; memoirs of L. Baeck, 147; memoirs of G. Salzberger,

26, 27, 28, 32, 49, 53; memoirs of A. Tänzer, 192
Transylvania, 118n
trenches, 48, 61, 78, 88, 134
Trotsky, Leon, 217, 238n
Troyes, northern France, 55
Tsarist Russia, anti-Semitic, 4, 182
typhus/typhoid, 35, 78, 79n, 97, 118n; vaccines, 178, 235n
tzitzit, 21, 335

U-boats, 98
Uhland, Ludwig, 143n
Uhnow, Galician border, 178, 179
Ukraine, German invasion (1918), 310; *see also specific regions in Ukraine*
U'netaneh Tokef prayer, 117n
Union of churches, Prussian, 235n
United Kingdom (UK): appointment of Jewish military chaplains, 3; 'National Day of Fast and Humiliation' (2 January 1915), 143n
United States (US): appointment of Jewish military chaplains, 3; entry into First World War (1917), 115; missiles, 90; munitions, sale of, 115, 117n; pastoral role, 7
universalism, 9

vacation periods, 104–5; *see also* Jewish Festivals
Valerius, Adrianus, 81n, 143n, 267n
Valhalla, 34
Vaya'aminu, 240
Vayehi Bachatzi Halailah, 64, 335
venereal disease, 80n
Venislach, 27
Verband der deutschen Juden (association of German Jews, created 1904), 6, 22, 283, 297n, 298n; Baeck as leading figure in, 170; conferences of Jewish chaplains, 300; memoirs of M. Salomonski, 99–100; memoirs of G. Salzberger, 50–1, 52, 55, 56, 64, 76; memoirs of A. Tänzer, 184, 199, 214
Verdun, France/Battle of Verdun, 1916), xvii, 25, 43, 44, 49; Passover at, 59–66, 78
Vilna, Poland, 212; conferences of Jewish chaplains, 202, 206, 215
Vilna Gaon (Elijah), 202, 236n *see* Kremer, Elijah ben Shlomo Zalman

Vladimir-Volynsk, Ukraine, 211, 214, 215, 216
Vlodava, Poland, 184, 185, 187
Vogel, Rolf, 76, 81n
Vogt, Arnold, 13n, 23n, 24n
Volga Deutsche (ethnic Germans other than Jews), 235n
Volksgemeinschaft (people's community), 41–2, 79n
Volksgenossen (fellow Germans), 250
volunteering for military service, German Jews, 5

Walloon peoples, 84
war, art of, 272
War Distribution Department, France, 43
war graves *see* graves, war
War Ministry, 6, 21, 22, 55, 176, 177, 276; Jewish Census decree (1916), xxi, xxii, xxiv, 11–12, 74, 78–9, 280n, 296, 299
war poets, xix
Wars of Liberation (1813–14), 1–2, 15
Warsaw, Great Synagogue, 195–6, 236n
Warsaw Gouvernement, 195, 196
water pollution, 78
Waterloo, Battle of (1815), 2
weather conditions, 101–2, 150–1
Weimer Republic, 81n, 312
Weltanschauung (world outlook), 160
Western Front, xvii, xviii, 59, 83–5, 143n, 178
Weyl, Simon, 15, 23n
Wied, Prince von, 201
Wiener, Max, 308, 313; biography/family background, 323; on Chanukah and Purim, 261–4
Wilde, Rabbi Georg, 9, 313; biography/family background, 324; chaplain conference of December 1916, 299; on holiday season (1915), 283–5; on Sabbath, 241–3

Wilhelm II, Kaiser *see* Kaiser Wilhelm II
Will to Judaism, 276–7
Winter, David Alexander, 293–7, 298n, 308, 309, 310, 311, 313, 324
Winter, Moritz, 313, 324
Wolf, Albert, 313, 328
Women's Association of the Frankfurt Lodge, 63
World War I *see* First World War
Worms, Germany, 118n
wounded soldiers, 7; memoirs of B. Italiener, 124; memoirs of M. Salomonski, 88, 90, 96; memoirs of G. Salzberger, 35, 36, 77; memoirs of A. Tänzer, 205; *see also* amputation; disfigurement by war; limbs, loss of
Württemberg War Ministry, 176

Yeshivoth, 295, 297, 336
Yiddish language, 193, 196, 235n
Yitzhak, Rabbi Shlomo ben (Rashi), 55, 80n
Yizkor, 20, 101, 145, 146, 194, 336
Yom Kippur (Day of Atonement), 3, 20, 24n, 28, 251, 283–5, 291, 294, 336; of 1870, 17, 18; of 1914, 5, 10, 285–7; in 1917, 9; memoirs of L. Baeck, 145, 165, 166; memoirs of M. Salomonski, 100, 115; memoirs of G. Salzberger, 51, 52, 53; memoirs of A. Tänzer, 194, 229; *see also* Kol Nidrei; Yizkor
Ypres, First Battle of (1914), 172n

Zalman, Rabbi Shneur, 229, 238n
Zamosce, Poland, 180
Zechariah, 240, 269n
Zionism, xvii, xxiv, 4, 237n, 272, 278
Zlocisti, Theodor, 23n
Zochreinu prayer, 26, 336
Zola, Emile, 114, 119n, 309, 310
Zoma, Ben, 265

940.478 APP
Loyalty betrayed : Jew
chaplains in the Germa
 during the First
war

*"In memory of my cousin,
Captain Charles Worn, U.S. Army,
who played war games with me on large maps
when we were in our teens, and dedicated also
to his grandchildren and all children who need
to be saved from war in this dangerous age."*